World labour report *2*

Labour relations, international labour standards, training, conditions of work, women at work

International Labour Office   Geneva

ISBN 92-2-103848-3

First published 1985

Printed in Switzerland

Preface

This is the second volume of the first *World labour report*, to be followed by two more reports during this decade. The first volume, published at the beginning of last year, discussed employment and incomes; the second deals with labour relations, international labour standards, training, conditions of work and the position of women at work. Together, the two volumes give an overview of the main labour issues in the world. The next Report will concentrate on one particular theme – the question of pay.

The two volumes of the first *World labour report* show that the social and labour situation has deteriorated in many parts of the world since the mid-1970s. Unemployment and underemployment have reached high levels. Social security, training and conditions of work are given lower priority because they are thought to claim a disproportionate share of resources in a time of economic recession. The ILO is receiving an increasing number of complaints on Conventions covering basic human rights, such as freedom of association. A positive development, however, is that women are playing a more active role in the world of work and development – even though there is still a long way to go before an equal partnership can be achieved between the sexes. Moreover, educational opportunities have increased considerably, particularly in developing countries, resulting in a more skilled labour force.

It would be a grave mistake to think that – even in a time of economic stagnation – social and labour questions should take second place. Economic development is not an aim in itself, but a means to a social end: a better life for all and in particular for the disadvantaged.

Economic and social development cannot be conceived of as separate processes. Economic growth makes the expansion of social programmes possible. Likewise, a climate of security, the participation of the social partners in development, and proper training and working conditions are not only desirable in themselves but are a requisite for long-term economic growth. In some cases, excessively high social expenditure may jeopardise the long-term prospects for a higher standard of living, including those of the disadvantaged. But I firmly believe that if sacrifices have to be made in the name of economic development, they have to be negotiatied with all groups in society and borne by each according to its capacity.

I hope that this volume will contribute to a better knowledge and a well-informed discussion of economic, social and labour issues in the world.

Francis Blanchard

Contents

V

Contents

Annexes

List of tables and figures

Part 1

Labour relations

Introduction

Labour relations exist wherever people work together. They may be individual relations, i.e. relationships between single workers and employers (private and public), or collective relations, i.e. relationships between organisations of workers and employers and between these organisations and the authorities.

The most common individual labour relationship is the employment contract concluded between an individual employer and an individual worker, the type of contract by which the majority of workers in the world are covered. The three main phases of this relationship are hiring (including the explicit or implicit conclusion of an employment contract), fulfilment of contractual obligations, and termination. For certain types of workers, the individual labour relationship may not be an employment relationship and may include transactions involving not only labour but also production, credit or land. Tenants and share-croppers, for example, have a relationship with landowners which includes a transaction covering not only labour but also the use of land and/or credit. Such "interlocking" contracts also exist between members of producers' co-operatives, and include transactions on labour, production, the use of land and the distribution of profits. Family workers, on the other hand, are not bound by a contract, but usually accept family work as part of the cultural, social and economic obligations governing household and family life. Finally, in the case of self-employed workers, the question of an individual labour relationship does not apply.

In 1980, the world labour force consisted of about 1,800 million workers, with China, India and other Asian countries accounting for over half (see table). Most workers are in wage employment, i.e. almost all workers in industrialised socialist countries, more than three-quarters in developed market economies and between one-quarter and three-quarters in developing countries. Self-employed workers hardly exist in the socialist countries, but they constitute between 10 and 25 per cent of the labour force in the industrialised market economies and between 25 and 50 per cent in the developing market economies. More than half of the Chinese labour force is engaged in some form of collective farming, while the percentage of workers engaged in such farming in the industrialised socialist countries is low. The proportion of family workers is usually small in industrialised countries, but generally varies between 10 and 25 per cent in developing countries.

Labour force in the world, 1980

	Millions
Developed socialist countries	194
Developed market economies	341
Africa	170
Latin America and the Caribbean	117
China	422
Rest of Asia	551
Total	1 795

Source: ILO.

3

A vast number of workers, including roughly 150 million day-labourers and about 300 million self-employed and family workers in the agricultural and informal sectors of the developing market economies, have little protection, either through membership of a workers' organisation or by effective legislation. Day-labourers are completely dependent on what the market offers them in the way of employment and wages. Peasants and family workers, though they have the security of a small plot of land, are usually obliged to seek additional work as day-labourers or seasonal workers. Since they are not organised, day-labourers and seasonal workers are in a very insecure situation.

In the following three chapters we shall examine recent trends in collective labour relations, i.e. relationships between organisations of workers and employers and between these organisations and the authorities. Broadly speaking, collective labour relationships exist in almost all sectors of the industrialised socialist countries, in most sectors of the industrialised market economies and in the so-called modern sectors of the developing countries. Chapters 1 and 2 deal with workers' and employers' organisations, while Chapter 3 examines recent trends in labour-management relations, including collective bargaining, workers' participation and collective labour disputes.

Chapter **1**

Workers' organisations

The term "workers' organisation" covers a wide variety of associations such as trade unions, farmers' leagues, tenants' and share-croppers' associations, workers' co-operatives, public service employees' associations, professional associations and "benevolent" or "friendly" societies. In this chapter, however, we shall concentrate mainly on trade unions, because it is these associations that include most of the organised workers.

Historically speaking, trade unions were born in Europe and North America and gradually became part and parcel of Western, industrial, pluralistic societies. During this century they have also gradually spread to all industrialised and developing regions – as well as to all economic sectors.

This may be illustrated by a comparison of the Workers' delegations to the 1919 and 1983 Sessions of the International Labour Conference. There were 25 Workers' delegates in 1919; 130 (with 337 advisers) in 1983. In terms of geographical distribution, the Workers' delegates present in 1919 came predominantly from Western Europe and North America. The Workers' group of the 1983 International Labour Conference represented practically all the countries of the world.

Types of trade unions

There are four broad types of trade unions: craft unions, enterprise unions, industry unions, and general unions. A craft union is open to all persons with the same occupation, such as electricians or printers. Unions can also seek to recruit all persons employed in the same enterprise or industry. The fourth broad category is the general union, which is rather similar to a federation in that it covers workers from many industries and crafts.

Craft unions – the oldest type of trade union – were particularly important in the industrialised countries, though they are now also found in a number of developing countries (in the printing and construction industries, for example). Industrial unions are the predominant form of organisation in continental Europe. They are the result of a deep sense of solidarity among workers, regardless of training, trade and occupation. General unions are more typical of small, developing countries (e.g. certain English-speaking African and Caribbean countries), although some are also found in Australia, Ireland, New Zealand, the United Kingdom and the United States. Organisations of this kind have often been set up by craft or industrial unions that were willing to organise workers beyond their initial boundaries. Enterprise unions constitute the predominant type in developing countries where crafts are not deeply rooted and where the organisation of a whole industry could be too complicated. Socio-cultural considerations have also contributed to the appearance of enterprise unions in certain industrialised countries; in Japan, for instance, it is the traditional identification of workers with their enterprises that explains the Japanese preference for enterprise unions. The sheer size of large undertakings may also bring about the establishment of enterprise unions, even in countries where other kinds of workers' organisations tend to prevail.

The growth of the labour movement during the past few decades has highlighted the advantages and disadvantages of the above-mentioned types of unions. Enterprise unions constituted a basic form of work organisation from which other levels or variants could be developed; they also placed workers' organisations in the thick of labour-management relations and in close contact with the rank and file. Experience has shown, however, that this type of union may give rise to an excessive fragmentation of the labour movement and compel workers' organisations to spread thin their leadership and financial resources.

The proliferation of unions has tended in turn to affect the average membership of unions. To take some Latin American countries, for instance, it is as low as 74 in Ecuador, 128 (for enterprise unions) and 119 (for craft unions) in Chile, 207 in Costa Rica, 220 in Venezuela and 383 in Panama.[1] Similar figures are found in some Asian countries, such as India (around 300 in the Delhi area), Pakistan, where the average size of unions was estimated at 129 members in 1979,[2] and the Philippines (before the recent rationalisation). In India the average membership per union has been steadily declining almost since the inception of the labour movement.[3]

Craft unions were based on historical and well-entrenched forms of brotherhood with relatively well-defined boundaries in the manufacturing sector and building trades. Their main impact has probably been to place some key workers in a strong bargaining position. Others – not being organised – were somewhat left aside, and in some countries this development may have led to an erosion of solidarity between workers. However, the impact of new technologies has not been favourable to craft unions; some old trades such as typesetters and draughtsmen are being eliminated, transformed or simplified and a number of craft unions have been forced to merge or disappear (see

Volume 1, Chapter 7). In the United Kingdom, for instance, there were ten craft unions in the printing industries in 1948; today there are only five. Similar mergers have occurred in many other countries.

The trend nowadays is in the direction of industrial-type unions, and the reasons for this are clear. Industrial unions (as well as the principle of "one industry, one union", which has been widely applied in socialist countries and recently accepted in certain developing countries) seek to overcome the shortcomings of the proliferation of small enterprise unions and to avoid the divisions and, at times, hierarchical tendencies characteristic of other types of unions. Moreover, trade unions inevitably reflect the more complex political and economic environment in which they must operate. Workers' organisations that came into being spontaneously and developed unplanned during the early stages of industrialisation are now experiencing the need to adapt to a different milieu. Moreover, it became clear that with the increasing use of mass production and automation many unskilled and semi-skilled workers were often not covered by occupational organisations. Workers in major industrial sectors were also confronted with similar problems. By organising themselves along industrial lines, they could strengthen their bargaining power and speak with one voice in their dealings with employers and government. Even some governments (as in Ecuador) have actively promoted the setting up of industrial unions.

This trend towards industrial unions may have an impact on the traditional three levels of the labour movement: the enterprise or local level, the larger (industrial, occupational or territorial) second-degree level and the confederation. A two-tier structure now tends to exist in certain countries where workers' organisations at the enterprise level are mere branches of the industrial union. The latter is also replacing some older structures of unions based on geographical considerations. However, such structures still exist, for example in the construction industry in Canada and the

United States and in various European countries, including France, Italy, Spain and Sweden.

Where industrial or general unions do not constitute the prevailing types, federations consisting of occupational organisations are normally set up. Various federations can then establish national centres or confederations. In both cases legislation usually requires a minimum number of constituent units, or lays down other, and stricter, limitations. In Latin America, for instance, recent legislation in Chile and Uruguay has attempted to prohibit the establishment of full-fledged national confederations. In Brazil, national confederations can only be established at the sectoral level and the 1943 Labour Code does not officially permit a central confederation. Some sort of an umbrella workers' organisation was set up in 1983 but has not yet been recognised by the Government.

National centres or confederations may have only limited functions of co-ordination and orientation, as in the United States, or they may be vested with the authority to bargain (e.g. in the Scandinavian countries) or to fix the outer limits of bargaining (e.g. in Italy and Spain). As governments step up their involvement in economic and social affairs, and especially as they set out to apply incomes policies, the power of confederations has tended to grow. However, the level within the labour movement actually exercising the power (centralisation versus decentralisation) has usually been determined by a number of historical factors such as bargaining practices, the structure of employers' organisations and the importance of higher or lower levels of the labour movement, as well as of some typical features concerning the workers involved.

In many developing countries, workers' organisations have been greatly influenced by the law, which has played an important and sometimes decisive role in shaping the trade union movement. This is particularly true in some Latin American countries (Argentina and Brazil, for instance, and more recently Chile and Uruguay) and in a number of Asian and African countries. However, some English-speaking developing countries have followed the example of the United Kingdom, where there are no legal provisions governing the structure of trade unions; in these countries any group of workers (above the established minimum number of six or seven) can form their own union.

Fragmentation and rationalisation in the labour movement

In many developing countries the labour movement is fragmented because each union prefers to keep its own structure. While such pluralism is also found in some industrialised countries, the problem has become particularly acute in those developing countries where (1) the labour movement includes a substantial proportion of enterprise unions, (2) unions rely heavily on political action and (3) several political parties are competing for trade union support.

Trade unionists in many countries find that trade union pluralism provides the possibility of choice and stimulates competition and emulation among different organisations. However, excessive union fragmentation, particularly at the enterprise level, may have some unfavourable consequences for both management and unions. Management may be faced with different and sometimes conflicting demands, put forward by various unions. In the best of circumstances unions may waste time, energy and financial resources, while in the worst they may be played off against one another. Other negative consequences may be reduced productivity and a deteriorating climate of industrial relations.

At this point, it may be useful to make a distinction between pluralism due to ideological, religious or political rivalries and pluralism due to the coexistence of different types of unions. Ideological, religious and political pluralism exists in certain European countries (such as Belgium, France, Greece, Italy, Luxembourg and Spain) but it is more widespread in countries of the Third World. In the latter countries there is the additional problem that many unions have the same jurisdiction and operate at the same level. In some industrialised countries there are large numbers of unions that do not necessarily conflict or overlap with each other. In Japan, for instance, there were 73,694 trade unions in 1981[4] but there were few cases of pluralism within the same bargaining unit. Similarly, in the United States there were some 75,000 local unions at the end of the 1970s but the overwhelming majority were subdivisions of the existing 173 national unions; moreover, the principle of exclusive representation of the majority union rules out any possible overlapping.

In recent years the ideological rivalries between European unions and parties have declined. It is true that different currents of unionism still exist but efforts to overcome problems of pluralism have voluntarily taken place within the trade union movement of certain countries. This is the case in such European countries as Ireland and the Netherlands and in Japan, where all trade unions launch every year the so-called "spring offensive" and have established an All-Japan Council of Private Sector Unions (Zenmin Rokyo). Moreover, mergers and amalgamations of unions at the industry level have taken place in such industrialised countries as Canada, New Zealand, Norway, Sweden, the United Kingdom and the United States. In the United Kingdom there has been a steady decline in the number of trade unions, dropping from 543 in 1970 to 421 at the end of 1981.[5] In Sweden only 24 trade unions now constitute the Swedish Trade Union Confederation (LO). Union concentration has always been a feature of industrial relations in the Federal Republic of Germany, where only 17 trade unions constitute the central organisation (DGB). Indeed, the process has been so marked and far-reaching that some recent studies point to the appearance of

a new type of trade union, the multi-industrial or conglomerate union.

The situation is different in developing countries. Ideological rivalries cover a wider spectrum and include not only the Communists, Socialists, Social Democrats, Reformists and Christian Democrats, but also the populist and nationalist orientations. Personal animosities can sometimes further fragment and divide the labour movement. This is particularly the case of several Asian countries, such as Bangladesh, India, Pakistan, Sri Lanka and Thailand, and most Latin American countries. In the latter, however, it is the national centres that are fragmented; such fragmentation does not usually occur at the enterprise level. In the above Asian countries fragmentation tends to pervade all levels of the trade union movement. Extreme cases of fragmentation can be observed in some large undertakings of India, such as Bokaro Steel Mills (44 trade unions).

In several Latin American countries (Colombia, Mexico and Panama, for instance) the trade union movement itself has tried to unify or at least to co-ordinate its actions and organisations. In other countries, however, this initiative has come from outside the trade union movement. In many African countries, as well as in a few Asian ones (e.g. Indonesia, Malaysia and the Philippines), governments have sought to restructure and unify the trade union movement in order to rationalise its operations and to do away with jurisdictional disputes. Government measures of this kind have been taken particularly in Africa, where only a handful of countries (e.g. Burkina Faso, Cameroon, Madagascar, Mauritius, Morocco and Senegal) now have more than one trade union centre. The most striking examples are Ethiopia, where a reorganisation in 1975 reduced the number of unions to nine national unions, and Nigeria, which transformed in 1978 over 800 enterprise unions into 46 national industrial unions.[6] In such Asian countries as Indonesia, Malaysia and the Philippines, governments are also trying to rationalise the trade union movement, sometimes

Table 1.1
Trade union membership as a percentage of the economically active population in OECD countries in the early 1980s

Degree of unionisation (percentage)	Country
80–90	Finland, Sweden
70–80	Belgium, Denmark
60–70	Austria, Luxembourg, Norway
50–60	Australia, Ireland, Italy, United Kingdom
40–50	Federal Republic of Germany, New Zealand
30–40	Canada, Greece, Japan, Netherlands, Switzerland
15–30	France, Portugal, Spain, United States

in co-operation with the trade unions themselves. In the Philippines, government statistics show that the number of registered trade unions decreased from about 7,000 in 1975 to 1,660 in 1980.[7]

Trade union membership

Membership of trade unions varies from one country to another, ranging from nearly 100 per cent of the workforce in certain industrialised centrally planned economies to single percentage figures in some developing countries. Exact and comprehensive statistics are not always kept and the figures available are sometimes misleading. Some rough approximations can nevertheless be given. For the 22 member countries of the OECD, for instance, the approximate ranges of trade union membership as a percentage of the economically active population[8] are shown in table 1.1.

Over the past 20 years trade union membership has gone up and down with labour market fluctuations but also with recruitment drives, the union's overall performance, the stock of accumulated demands and grievances and the political attitude of governments. Total membership of trade unions in many countries has declined recently, chiefly as a result of the general recession

and the structural changes experienced in the manufacturing sector. In the United Kingdom, for example, union enrolment fell by 3.7 per cent in 1980 and 5.9 per cent in 1981;[9] in the Netherlands and Sweden, the declines were about 4 per cent; in the Federal Republic of Germany the drop was 2½ per cent during the same year.[10] In Spain, union membership decreased considerably during the period 1980-83, owing not only to high levels of unemployment but also to the relatively secondary role assigned to trade unions at the enterprise level.

However, membership has not declined everywhere. In Denmark and Norway, for instance, membership in the LO Confederations continued to rise in 1980, 1981 and 1982. Furthermore, the development of unionism during the present century shows that periods of decline or stagnation are followed by periods of growth. A 1980 analysis of total union density in selected industrialised countries indicates that there has been a long-run trend towards expansion.[11]

Demographic trends have also affected and will probably continue to affect both the number of union members and the role of trade unions in collective bargaining. In industrialised countries declining birth rates, combined with growing restrictions on the entry of foreign workers, might lead in the future to manpower shortages. While these shortages could increase the bargaining power of trade unions, they may not improve total membership figures. In developing countries, where birth rates continue to be high, unions will probably find themselves in the opposite situation, i.e. with more affiliates and less bargaining power.

Other factors affecting the growth of unions are numerous and varied: difficulties encountered in organising certain regions or sectors where anti-union sentiments or indifference towards organisation run high; the lingering opposition of certain employers; the prevalence of small and medium-sized enterprises in some countries where lasting organisations are difficult to set up; the inability of some workers to perceive the advantages of unionisation in countries where some other bodies are assuming trade union functions; and the increasing number of part-time migrant, transient and temporary employees, all of whom are difficult to organise. These factors may explain why union membership in the United States has remained at around 22 per cent of the labour force for about 12 years.[12] Union rivalries and priority concern for macro-sociopolitical objectives, at the expense of enterprise-level activities, may account for the relatively small degree of unionisation in other countries. However, the relatively low percentage of union affiliation in some countries should not obscure the fact that union membership tends to concentrate in certain key industries and the public service, which means that in some sectors unions actually exert more influence than the overall percentage might suggest.

The inclusion of union security clauses (an arrangement whereby union membership or some of its financial obligations become a condition of employment) in many collective agreements in a number of industrialised countries (Australia, Canada, New Zealand, United Kingdom, United States) has contributed in the past to the rapid growth of membership. While in some parts of the world (e.g. most of continental Europe, certain French-speaking African countries and Latin America) the closed shop and the union shop (in which only union members may be employed) and their modified versions continue to be prohibited or are regarded as superfluous, a number of developing countries (Ghana, Mauritius, Mexico, Philippines, Venezuela) now authorise the inclusion of such clauses in collective agreements or even make provisions for their application in the law. From being a purely Anglo-Saxon phenomenon, union security has thus spread to a number of other countries and new groups of workers (e.g. public employees and white-collar workers). In addition, the underlying purpose of union security arrangements seems to have changed. Nowadays they tend to reflect the socially recognised need to promote a strong and stable trade union movement rather than the original concern with mere survival.[13]

The growth of trade unions in developing countries

The above-mentioned difficulties regarding the reliability of union membership data are particularly acute in developing countries. In most of them trade unions do not keep accurate records because a considerable proportion of their members may live in remote areas or may be employed irregularly, as in the case of migrant and seasonal labour. Quite often unions tend to inflate the membership figures for the purpose of gaining influence or recognition. In a few cases, however, local unions prefer to deflate figures in order to pay lower fees to the national centre. All of this has led some experts to suggest that in developing countries the notion of "dues-paying members" should be replaced by that of "followers" or "sympathisers" and that the measure of the real power of a workers' organisation is better represented by, for instance, the number of workers who are willing to support the union in a strike or who usually attend union meetings.

Data on dues-paying members exist for a number of countries, but they are often not comparable between countries. This is so because different criteria are used to calculate the percentage of trade union membership. Sometimes this is given in respect of the total number of wage earners or even wage earners in the non-agricultural sector, and sometimes reference is made to the total labour force or the economically active population. In spite of these difficulties, and with all due reservations, table 1.2 gives some rough indications of union membership rates in relation to the total labour force in 40 countries.[14]

Rates of unionisation in developing countries have also been affected by the current economic

Table 1.2
Trade union membership as a percentage of the economically
active population in developing countries in the early 1980s

Degree of unionisation (percentage)	Country
40–50	Algeria, United Republic of Tanzania (including peasants)
30–40	Argentina, Barbados, Chile, Ethiopia, Fiji, Guyana, Singapore, Sri Lanka, Venezuela
20–30	Colombia, Egypt, Gabon, Jamaica, Mexico, Trinidad and Tobago
10–20	Botswana, Brazil, Costa Rica, Ecuador, Kenya, Malaysia, Nigeria, Panama, Peru, Philippines, Zambia
Below 10	Bangladesh, Dominican Republic, Haiti, India, Indonesia, Nepal, Pakistan, Papua New Guinea, Senegal, Sierra Leone, Thailand, Togo

recession and inflation, reduced production levels and falling commodity prices. In some Caribbean countries where unionisation rates have been rather high, the loss of union membership reached 20 per cent at the end of 1982.

There are various reasons why it is so difficult for trade unions to organise workers in developing countries. A first and important one is that in many countries freedom of association does not exist – an issue that is discussed later on in Chapter 4. Many societies find it difficult to reconcile effective government with full respect for human rights.

Another major difficulty relates to the potentially organisable labour force, which is usually found in the urban, modern sector and accounts for a small minority of the economically active population. In most developing countries there is a scarcity of large industrial and commercial undertakings where unionisation is easier and existing unions are well implanted. To organise the profusion of small and medium-sized undertakings involves enormous financial and human efforts. It is small wonder that in some developing countries (e.g. the Philippines) more than 60 per cent of organised labour is found in the main

metropolitan area. In Brazil it is in the industrial belt of São Paulo, the so-called ABC region, where the most dynamic trade unions are to be found.

A major challenge, too, is the organisation of the informal sector. How can trade unions organise the growing mass of self-employed people, family workers, casual and temporary workers, and employees in small or clandestine shops? Some efforts have already been made in Latin America, for example, to organise street vendors, bootblacks, newspaper boys and other workers included in the broad definition of *marginales*. In Africa the Organisation of African Trade Union Unity (OATUU) launched in 1979 a programme known as "trade unions and the labouring poor" aimed at bringing workers and peasants together in order to help the latter to organise themselves. In India there are several organisations (e.g. the All India National Rural Labour Federation and the All India Kisan Sabhas) catering to share-croppers and agricultural labourers and grouping around 3 million workers. Their membership, however, accounts for less than 5 per cent of the estimated number of poor peasants and agricultural workers.[15]

There are other obstacles to the growth of trade unions in developing countries that should be easier to overcome. One is the lack of trained, experienced and dedicated leaders. Another is the existence in some countries of rigid legal requirements concerning the minimum number or percentage of workers or registration formalities that unnecessarily hamper the formation of unions. The usual minimum membership is 20 or 25 workers, but some countries (e.g. Egypt, Panama, Iraq and Somalia) require 50 and others stipulate a minimum percentage of the total number of workers concerned; in Turkey this is 33 per cent and in El Salvador as much as 51 per cent (in the case of enterprise unions). These requirements differ sharply from the situation in a number of English-speaking countries where the old provision allowing any seven persons to form a union is still in force.

In addition to low memberhip rates, some recent reports and studies indicate that trade unions in some developing countries are still suffering from transient membership, reluctance to pay union dues and relatively poor involvement in internal union affairs.

Trade unions in centrally planned economies

Trade unions in centrally planned economies operate under a socio-political and economic system that is quite different from that in other countries. The Marxist-Leninist Party of the working class is considered to be the guiding force in a socialist country. It deals with issues of capital importance (including medium- and long-term planning), and it determines the country's major political choices. The government executes this policy and is responsible for the management of the State and of the state economy. The trade unions transmit the policy of the Party to the working classes and take part in its preparation and implementation. According to Lenin, trade unions should function as a "transmission belt" between the Party and the working people. This means that the unions help the State in raising productivity and disciplining workers but that the unions, being a social organisation, have different means of achieving this than the State. Union leaders persuade and educate workers, and thus the unions develop into "a school of administration, a school of economic management, a school of communism".

The Party, the State and the trade union organisation have a common objective which is to build a communist society and any opposition or any serious clashes between the trade unions and the authorities can only harm working class interests. As a result, trade unions have their specific role and place in socialist society.

In most industrialised socialist countries the large majority of workers are trade union mem-

bers. Typically, the rate of unionisation is between 94 and 98 per cent. However, in some categories, such as construction workers and co-operative employees, the percentage is substantially lower. Union members enjoy a number of social and cultural benefits not available to non-union workers, including various allowances, loans, cut-rate holiday facilities, convalescent homes, etc. Furthermore, enterprise home loans, housing built by the enterprise and accommodation in holiday facilities provided by it, etc., are allocated by decision, or on the recommendation, of the trade union bodies at the workplace.

Since the 1960s the role of trade union organisations has become more important. Over the past 20 years or so trade union confederations have come to play a growing part in all aspects of socialist society, particularly in the planning process of the national economy. In the preparation of the plan, the government and trade unions hold extensive discussions on wages and the distribution of the so-called social consumption fund. They have also the right of legislative initiative, a right that exists in all socialist countries.

At the enterprise level, trade unions have two distinct functions. The first is to ensure that socialist law, principles and morals are strictly observed; they exhort workers to increase their productivity and they condemn and endeavour to prevent any anti-social acts. The other is to defend the rights and the interests of union members against any bureaucratic excesses of management and to collaborate with management in three fundamental areas of action. First, there is a wide field of problems on which management asks advice from the trade unions, without being legally bound by their recommendations. Second, there are a number of questions on which management cannot take a decision without the prior consent of the trade union bodies. Such questions include issuing or amending the rules of employment; regulating working hours; ordering unavoidable overtime work; introducing wage and salary systems and works bonus rules; altering the forms of remuneration employed; fixing the detailed allocation of the wage funds; earmarking appropriations for the fund for cultural and social needs of workers and determining their purpose and use; engaging and dismissing workers; assigning workers to their posts or jobs, placing them in classes on the basis of their skill, fixing their remuneration, transferring them to another job; and allocating workers' housing. Third, in some countries trade union bodies also act as arbitrators in labour disputes between management and individual workers.

The trade unions also have extensive powers in the sphere of social security and of social and cultural services for workers. In all socialist countries the trade unions help the State in carrying out health care and social security (including pension) schemes. In a number of countries they even run health insurance schemes themselves. In other countries the entire state social insurance budget (including the pension schemes) is managed and administered by trade unions.

Changes in the composition of the trade union movement

While the traditional strongholds of the trade union movement – metalworking trades, construction industry, mining, transport and, in some countries, commerce – still constitute important segments of organised labour, their share in total union membership has no doubt decreased in recent years. New groups of workers are now entering the trade union movement such as white-collar and professional workers, including public servants and teachers, rural workers (particularly in developing countries) and women workers.

The changing composition of trade union membership naturally reflects the economic trends of the day. The "services" sector is the fastest-growing sector at present – and in some countries,

the only sector that is growing (see Volume 1, Chapter 2). Even in countries particularly hard hit by the recession and in sectors where blue-collar workers have tended to predominate, a growing number of white-collar workers have joined trade unions. In the United Kingdom, for instance, white-collar employees constituted about 40 per cent of total union membership in 1979, compared with 37 per cent in 1968 and 23 per cent in 1948.[16] By the end of the century white-collar workers will probably outnumber blue-collar workers. In Australia white-collar union membership between 1969 and 1981 increased from 30 to almost 40 per cent of the total number of organised workers.[17] In the Federal Republic of Germany the number of unionised clerical and technical white-collar workers in the construction industry increased by a little more than 15 per cent between 1975 and 1978.[18]

As the number of white-collar workers has grown, the dividing line between blue- and white-collar workers has tended to disappear. Modern white-collar workers no longer have a sense of belonging to a separate and somewhat superior category to which the expression "worker" does not apply. They have now come to occupy a very strong position in the trade union movement, in line with their increased membership. In many national trade union centres the strength of white-collar workers is equal to, or even greater than, that of the manual workers. This trend is not confined to clerks and shop assistants; new white-collar workers such as bank tellers, nurses, technicians, teachers and doctors have all joined trade unions or staff associations and make their presence felt in national and international workers' organisations. The magnitude of the trend should not be exaggerated, however: in some countries there are groups of technicians, high-level experts and white-collar employees, particularly in electronics and high technology, who are still reluctant to become trade union members.

The change has been particularly dramatic in the public service. A generation ago, in many countries, it was unthinkable that officials in the

13

service of the State or the local administration could become part of a national trade union movement. In some it is still not only unthinkable but also unlawful, although this does not in any way diminish the validity of the trend. Public servants for many years have demanded – and sometimes won – the right to organise, but it was not until 1978 that the International Labour Conference adopted the Labour Relations (Public Service) Convention (No. 151) which recognised that right and, with it, the right to participate in the determination of their terms and conditions of employment.

Today public service unions are among the fastest-growing organisations in many industrialised and developing countries. The American Federation of State, Council and Municipal Employees (AFSCME) and the Mexican Federation of Trade Unions of Government Employees (FSTSE), each with about 1 million members, have clearly demonstrated how fast public service unions can grow. Five of Japan's 20 largest unions, including the two heading the list, represent employees in public corporations or government enterprises. The three largest organisations in Canada are composed of public servants. In Italy unionisation rates in the public sector reached 59 per cent in the late 1970s. In the Federal Republic of Germany the organisation ratio of public employees ranges from about one-quarter for wage earners *(Arbeiter)* to three-quarters for civil servants proper *(Beamte)*. In some countries almost all post office employees are trade union members. Since the mid-1970s the same high organisation ratios were recorded for the British and Swedish national public administrations.[19] Members of the police, fire-fighters and prison guards have also set up unions in several countries.

Rural workers have always had the greatest difficulties in organising themselves. Not only are they handicapped by the fact that they tend to work in small groups and in different locations; they have also suffered from various forms of oppression and from serious organisational problems.

Table 1.3
Percentage of male and female workers in total trade union memberships in selected OECD countries in the early 1980s

Country	Male	Female
Australia	53	47
Canada	73	27
Denmark	57	43
Japan	71	29
United Kingdom	66	34
United States	73	27

Sources: G. Bain and R. Price: *Profiles of union growth* (Oxford, Basil Blackwell, 1980); International Federation of Commercial, Clerical, Professional and Technical Employees (FIET): Report of the ASIA-FIET Seminar on "Towards greater participation of women in trade unions in the 1980s", 15-16 May 1980, Singapore.

Plantation workers and other agricultural wage earners usually have their homes on land that belongs to their employers. Facilities for trade union meetings have to be found on that same land, which may expose organised workers to pressures by the employer. None the less, rural workers' organisations have persisted in their efforts, helped both by the adoption of the Rural Workers' Organisations Convention, 1975 (No. 141) (covering their role in economic and social development), and by the various ILO programmes designed specifically for their needs. The number of countries where it is forbidden by law to form a rural workers' trade union is declining. In two Latin American countries (Dominican Republic and Honduras), for instance, the major legal restriction on agricultural unions is that they must consist of more than ten workers per undertaking to qualify as an officially recognised union. Irrespective of legal or *de facto* barriers, plantation workers have, on the other hand, continued to develop strong organisations in South Asia, East and West Africa, Central America and the Caribbean. Alongside plantation workers' unions, there are other, more heterogeneous organisations catering to different types of workers. In Venezuela, for instance, the Peasants' Federation (FCV) includes agricultural unions, peasant leagues, associations of small and medium-sized agricultural producers and rural co-operatives. In 1982 the FCV enjoyed the support of some 700,000 rural workers.[20]

Over the past 20 years the position of women workers in society has changed dramatically. Particularly in the industrialised countries, more and more women have taken up a job. While their increasing participation in the labour force has not yet led to a proportional increase in union membership, there has been a clear rise in the number of female trade union members; in addition, women are beginning to occupy leading positions in the trade union hierarchy. This trend is particularly noticeable in European industrialised market economies (see table 1.3).

The share of women in total union membership is generally lower in developing countries, though it has increased in recent years. Some 1979 data concerning Asian affiliates of the International Federation of Commercial, Clerical, Professional and Technical Employees show increases ranging from 4.9 per cent in Malaysia to 19 per cent in India.[21]

A less positive kind of change has overtaken the skilled manual worker. Samuel Gompers, one of the founding fathers of the ILO, was a skilled cigar maker; most cigars are now made by machine, hand-made cigars are for the élite. There will, of course, always be a need for skills but the position of the skilled worker, especially in the industrialised countries, has steadily declined. Not only is there less demand for his services, and thus fewer skilled jobs, but his social position as the aristocrat of the working world has all but disappeared. Skilled workers once dominated congresses and conventions of national trade unions, but now they account for a relatively small minority.

Other categories of workers that have recently broadened the ranks of trade unionism include professional athletes, journalists, musicians, domestic workers and part-timers. Finally, managerial and supervisory staff are increasingly pressing for the right to organise and to bargain collectively. While in some countries they are only allowed to form separate organisations, in others they are entitled to join trade unions, provided they do not belong to the higher levels of the management hierarchy. However, where those levels start continues to be controversial in many industrialised and developing countries. Managerial and supervisory staff are, for example, included in the Central Organisation of Salaried Employees (TCO) in Sweden, which has 1 million members (70 per cent of the organisable salaried employees), and in the French Confederation of Executive Staffs (CFE), which is the largest of several centres catering in that country to technicians, supervisors, engineers and other professional employees. It may be noted that in France, Norway and several other European countries the traditional trade union centres have special sections for supervisory personnel, professionals and salaried employees.

Trade union activities

Most trade unions in market economies have traditionally pursued two major and related objectives: to defend the interests of their members and to promote changes in the society at large. To achieve these objectives, they have generally used collective bargaining and political action. Some organisations have placed the emphasis on the former, seeking immediate, tangible benefits; others have preferred to aim at longer-term, socio-political objectives through their own political activities or with the support of political parties. Although the relative importance of these objectives and means of action varies from one country to another, it can be said that most trade unions nowadays use both means of action to achieve their aims.

In industrialised market economies there are many different ways in which trade unions and political parties are linked to each other. There is first the British pattern of organic links between the trade union and the Labour Party – a pattern

15

that can also be found in Australia, Denmark and Sweden. Other less institutionalised arrangements include the more flexible forms of collaboration that are found in Norway, between LO and the Social Democratic Party, or in Belgium between the General Federation of Labour and the Socialist Party, or in Spain between the General Union of Workers (UGT) and the Workers' Socialist Party (PSOE). A similar alliance prevails in those European countries where denominational unions and parties are still in operation. In some countries the ties are even looser and depend only on the presence of trade union personalities in the party hierarchy or are limited to certain electoral arrangements. There is finally a group of countries where trade unions have avoided permanent links with political parties; they may share certain principles and aspirations with a party but keep their options open and attach higher priority to maintaining their independence. Trade unions in the United States consider collective bargaining to be their main task, although they do lobby to promote or prevent certain labour legislation.

However, no rigid demarcation line can be drawn between these groups, and one could even point to some shifting patterns and blurred areas. In Canada the major national federation officially launched the New Democratic Party and in the United States the AFL-CIO has a Committee for Political Education (COPE) which usually supports the Democratic Party. In Japan, where collective bargaining is the main function of trade unions, both SOHYO and DOMEI have nevertheless maintained some institutional connections with the Japanese Socialist Party and the Social Democratic Party. Recent developments such as recession, stagflation and unemployment have changed government policies and the above arrangements, and have led some unions to adopt a more independent attitude vis-à-vis governments and political parties.

In developing market economy countries trade unions have adopted different approaches, depending largely on the nature of the existing political systems. In some African countries with a one-party system, the party usually holds a commanding position and workers' organisations receive guidance and protection from it. In countries where a multi-party system exists, trade unions often seek the support of certain political parties and the latter normally request electoral and financial help from trade unions. Such connections cover a wide range of possibilities, from occasional contacts that do not affect the freedom of action of trade unions or political parties, to closer relationships apt to create mutual obligations. In some Caribbean countries where trade unions historically have been closely associated with major political parties, payment of dues to the political party gives workers automatic trade union membership. The opposite is true in Zambia where trade union members are automatically affiliated to the ruling UNIP party. In both one-party and multi-party systems there are also trade unions that have managed to maintain a position of independence. While it is frequently stated that the ability of a workers' organisation to maintain its own autonomous course depends mainly on its own strength, experience shows that it also depends on historical factors and the stability of the political system. In a number of countries trade unions have been able to engage in independent collective bargaining in spite of the fact that they are constituent parts of a political party. This is the case, for example, in Mexico, where the Confederation of Mexican Workers (CTM) is incorporated in the ruling Institutional Revolutionary Party (PRI).

In both industrialised and developing countries the most significant development since the Second World War has been the increasing participation of trade unions in government, semi-public or tripartite bodies at the industry and national levels. This phenomenon, which is due in part to the consistent promotion of tripartite co-operation by the ILO, also reflects a recognition of the place that trade unions have come to occupy in modern societies. Although some unions have reservations about certain forms of participation, most of them have come to realise that the social dialogue is also an integral part of trade union functions.

In addition to the bargaining, political and participatory activities, trade unions in many countries have tended to expand their traditional function of directly providing services to their members. In some countries these include a wide range of health, educational and recreational services. Unions have acted as agents of modernisation, helping rural workers to adapt to the industrial environment, filling gaps in the government provision of social services, supplementing social security benefits and catering to a variety of needs and aspirations of their members. It is, indeed, the wide range of non-bargaining services provided by Histadrut (Israel) that partly explains its ability to maintain its membership rate among the highest in the world (over 90 per cent of the labour force). In some industrialised and developing countries trade unions have also embarked on industrial, agricultural and commercial activities of their own. Suffice it to cite in this respect the examples of the banking and housing ventures of the German DGB, the co-operative services of the Singaporean SNTUC and the network of social services supplied by the Light and Power Union and other Argentinian unions until 1976.

Leadership, administration and finances

There are numerous types of trade union government and administration in market economy countries. No prevailing pattern of union leadership can be identified in contemporary industrial relations. However, certain basic features of union administration are almost everywhere determined by the same factors: the representative character of workers' organisations, the level and structure of the unions concerned, membership figures, the centralised or decentralised nature of the trade union movement,

financial possibilities, the types of functions performed by the union and in some countries certain statutory requirements that union constitutions must take into account. Enterprise or local unions generally choose their form of government and elect their officials directly from the rank and file in accordance with the relevant rules and regulations. For the higher levels of the structure or for large industrial unions, the usual procedure provides for the election of delegates who then proceed to elect the executive committee and officers, who in turn appoint the union's staff.

Beyond formal requirements, the authority and power within national centres and large unions are usually distributed between the elected leadership, the hierarchy of the union bureaucracy, the activists and the members. In a few countries the legislation provides for a system of checks on the central power, but in most unions this is achieved more effectively through their own internal democratic processes and the existence of other rival unions. However, in some countries charismatic and emotional leadership is so strong that internal democratic rules are not applied.

Trade unions in industrialised market economy countries have long produced their own leadership, usually risen from the rank and file. Developing countries are obviously facing more serious problems in this regard owing to lower levels of literacy, education and training. However, as the levels have tended to improve in recent years, unions in developing countries have been able to recruit more and more leaders and officials with a genuine worker's background. The fact remains that in some countries they still have to take on lawyers, teachers, former government officials or politicians to provide union leadership. The presence of these outsiders is particularly noticeable in some South Asian countries, such as Bangladesh, India, Indonesia, Nepal, Pakistan, the Philippines and Sri Lanka, though it is also found in a few African and Latin American countries.

Opinions are divided as to whether such outsiders play a positive or negative role. The legislation in India, Pakistan and Sri Lanka establishes restrictions on the number or percentage of outsiders allowed at different levels of the trade union movement. In Bangladesh all outsiders are prohibited from becoming union officials at the enterprise level. Nevertheless, a number of observers in these countries still feel that outsiders play a beneficial role in certain circumstances and consequently should not be excluded by law. They will eventually become superfluous as a result of gradual changes and evolution.

But the ability of a union to hold its own in the field of labour relations does not depend solely on the strength of its membership or the quality of its leadership. Financial constraints may also affect the union's capacity to engage full-time officials, to accumulate strike funds, to provide services to its members or to carry out research for collective bargaining. In some countries financial problems prevent trade unions from hiring adequate supporting staff. In 1981, for instance, only 53 of the 85 Irish trade unions had one or more full-time officials.[22] In most cases the lack of financial resources is due to the irregular collection of – often low – trade union dues.

To help overcome these problems, employers have increasingly agreed to deduct trade union dues automatically from the pay of their employees and to distribute the proceeds between the local union, the federation and the national centre. Voluntary forms of payment are increasingly included in collective agreements in market economy countries. Compulsory forms of payments applicable only to trade union members can be found today in Bolivia, Brazil, Greece, Ghana, Indonesia, Kenya and Nigeria (with respect to civil servants). Where the compulsory payments are extended to include non-union members as well, who after all benefit from the agreements concluded by trade unions, this system gives rise to a new form of union security called the agency shop. Agency shop arrangements are now provided for

in the legislation of Colombia, Ecuador, Honduras and Panama in Latin America and in that of a few other developing countries in Africa and Asia.

In some countries governments have strengthened the financial position of trade unions, even where membership rates are high, as happens in most European countries, although it is a rather exceptional approach. In a number of developing countries where unions are weak or incipient institutions, government subsidies are given to trade unions as a means of helping them to achieve certain objectives. This is the case in Iraq and the Syrian Arab Republic. In other developing countries, such as Algeria, Costa Rica, Lebanon, Nigeria and Panama, government economic aid is given for specific purposes, mostly for the development of workers' education programmes. In still other Third World countries, such as Burkina Faso, Gabon, Guinea, the Ivory Coast and Madagascar, the subsidies are granted in kind, e.g. premises and offices placed at the disposal of trade unions.

The international scene

It would be misleading to refer to "the world trade union movement" since there is no single movement of workers in one direction, let alone one united organisation. Nevertheless, members of the various international workers' organisations have much in common, as shown by the fact that most decisions taken by Workers' groups at ILO conferences and meetings are unanimous.

There are three "global" organisations that embrace trade unions in the broadest sense: the World Federation of Trade Unions (WFTU), which has affiliates in many parts of the world but whose main strength is in the centrally planned economies of Eastern Europe; the International Confederation of Free Trade Unions (ICFTU), with fewer members in all but with a broader international constituency; and the World Confederation of Labour (WCL), whose strength is concentrated in a relatively small number of countries. Membership of the three international confederations is difficult to estimate. Nevertheless, some indications concerning total membership, trends and regional distribution can be found in some recent studies, directories and encyclopaedias.[23]

All three international organisations have full consultative status with the ILO; they therefore play an important role at ILO conferences and meetings, and co-operate with ILO activities. Within their own ranks, they co-ordinate the policies of their members, provide advisory services and formulate submissions not only to the ILO but, increasingly in recent years, to the United Nations, including ECOSOC, and to other specialised agencies.

Another distinct trend in the activities of the so-called "Big Three" is the much wider interest being taken in broad economic questions, including world development and the North-South dialogue. They have developed considerable expertise and are able to render useful services to their affiliated organisations. They also deal increasingly with peace, disarmament and related questions, and with the growth of multinational enterprises, which they regard with varying degrees of distrust and apprehension, and endeavour to exert pressure through the United Nations, the ILO and other international bodies.

Alongside the "Big Three" stand organisations variously called international trade secretariats, trade union internationals or international federations, some of which are older than any of the "Big Three". These are founded on the principle of solidarity among workers in the same trade, occupation or profession. Together they cover almost the entire membership of the three international confederations and operate in close co-operation with one or another of them. Thus, for example, in most countries outside the socialist group – with the exception of countries where governments do not permit such affiliation – many

trade unions of iron and steel workers, engineering workers and others in associated trades are affiliated to the International Metalworkers' Federation (IMF). Each trade secretariat concerns itself with one particular economic sector, or with the problems of special categories of workers, such as metal or chemical workers, public servants or commercial, clerical and technical employees. These organisations are particularly active in the Industrial Committees of the ILO, and often do a great deal of preparatory work to enable Workers' delegates to profit fully from these meetings. International trade secretariats have also taken the initiative in setting up co-ordinating sectoral groups or councils to deal on a global basis with multinational corporations, to promote education and research and to explore prospects for consultation, negotiation and solidarity action at the multinational level.

Recent years have witnessed the growth of regional organisations of workers, either closely related to the "Big Three" or independent. Particularly important are the European Trade Union Confederation (which groups some 40 million members in Western Europe), the International Confederation of Arab Trade Unions, and the Organisation of African Trade Union Unity (OATUU), which has full consultative status with the ILO. The three regional organisations in the Americas (ORIT, CLAT and CPUSTAL) and their predecessors are of older vintage. Subregional organisations are also spawning, as shown in Europe with the Council of Nordic Trade Unions, in Asia with the ASEAN Council of Trade Unions and in the English-speaking Caribbean with the Caribbean Congress of Labour. This development is in part the natural consequence of the growth of regional intergovernmental organisations. The workers have demanded, with some success, that these regional organisations should follow the example of the ILO and adopt the principle of tripartism. This has nowhere been achieved in full, but certainly there is a noticeable growth in consultation and participation in discussions before decisions are taken.

[1] See: G. von Potobsky: "Trade unions", in E. Córdova (ed.): *Industrial relations in Latin America* (New York, Praeger, 1984), p. 38.

[2] B. A. Khan: *Trade unionism and industrial relations in Pakistan* (Karachi, Royal Book Company, 1980), p. 27.

[3] Government of India: *Report of the National Commission on Labour* (New Delhi, 1979), p. 27.

[4] See "The 1981 Basic Survey on Trade Unions", in *Japan Labor Bulletin* (Tokyo), Apr. 1982, p. 5.

[5] "Membership of trade unions in 1981", in *Employment Gazette* (London), Jan. 1983, p. 26.

[6] *Labour relations in Africa: English-speaking countries*, Proceedings of and documents submitted to a Symposium (Nairobi, 22-26 November 1982), Labour-Management Relations Series, 64 (Geneva, ILO, 1983), p. 35.

[7] See J. Schregle: *Negotiating development: Labour relations in southern Asia* (Geneva, ILO, 1982), p. 42.

[8] Based on C. A. Blyth: "The interaction between collective bargaining and government policies in selected member countries", in OECD: *Collective bargaining and government policies* (Paris, 1979), pp. 59-93; and the relevant monographs included in R. Blanpain (ed.): *International Encyclopaedia for Labour Law and Industrial Relations* (Deventer, the Netherlands, Kluwer, various dates).

[9] "Membership of trade unions in 1981", loc. cit.

[10] United Nations Department of International Economic and Social Affairs: *Report on the world social situation* (New York, 1982; doc. E/CN.5/1983/3), p. 122.

[11] G. S. Bain and R. Price: *Profiles of union growth*, A comparative statistical portrait of eight countries (Oxford, Basil Blackwell, 1980).

[12] See United States Department of Labor, Bureau of Labor Statistics: *Directory of Unions and Labor Organisations* (Washington, 1982).

[13] See E. Córdova and M. Ozaki: "Union security arrangements: An international overview", in *International Labour Review*, Jan.-Feb. 1980, p. 19.

[14] Based on studies, articles and reports available in the Office.

[15] See P. Kumar: "Unionisation and industrial relations in agricultural labour in India, in International Industrial Relations Association: *Sixth World Congress* (Kyoto, 1983), p. 173.

[16] R. Price and G. S. Bain: "Union growth in Britain: Retrospect and prospect", in *British Journal of Industrial Relations* (London), Mar. 1983, p. 50.

[17] G. Griffin: "White-collar unionism, 1969-81: Some determinants of growth", in *Journal of Industrial Relations* (Kensington, Australia), Mar. 1983, p. 28.

[18] H. Bayer, K. Schmahl and B. Süllow: *The construction industry in the Federal Republic of Germany*, Research Series, No. 71 (Geneva, International Institute for Labour Studies, 1982), p. 62.

[19] See Bain and Price, op. cit., pp. 78 and 146.

[20] D. F. Hodsdon: *The Federación Campesina de Venezuela* (Geneva, ILO, 1982), p. 5.

[21] FIET report cited in connection with the table on union density by sex, p. 6.

[22] M. Redmond: "Ireland", in Blanpain, op. cit., para. 377.

[23] See, for instance, J. Windmuller: "International trade union movement", in R. Blanpain: *Comparative labour law and industrial relations* (Deventer, the Netherlands, Kluwer, 1982), pp. 102, 105 and 106, and "International trade union movement", in Blanpain, *Encyclopaedia . . .*, op. cit., pp. 62, 90 and 110.

Chapter **2**

Employers' organisations

This chapter is primarily concerned with organisations that promote the interests of employers as participants, with the workers, in the industrial relations process. It is not so much concerned with organisations of a general professional nature characterising employers as producers, investors, taxpayers, competitors in export markets and economic agents generally. Admittedly, the latter so-called "economic" concerns are closely interconnected with the labour, or "social" aspects and both types of issues are commonly dealt with by the same organisational structure.

The chapter begins with a section on the functions performed by employers' organisations today, highlighting their relations with the public authorities, the trade unions and the community at large and the services they provide for their affiliates. Two sections are then devoted to the position of employers' organisations in centrally planned economies and in developing countries. Since the countries in each of these two groups have their own distinctive historical origins and societies, it is necessary to discuss their experiences separately. The organisational patterns of employer representation are the subject of the next section, which begins with a brief review of organisational arrangements for dealing with economic and social issues and goes on to a description of the organisational structure at three major levels — regional and sectoral, central, and international. The concluding remarks give a short summary of the main trends described in this chapter.

Membership and functions

Membership

Employers' organisations consist of enterprises, or groups of enterprises, rather than individuals; in this they differ from trade unions, with their rank-and-file constituency of natural persons. It is a legitimate question how far such a heterogeneous grouping — including enterprises varying in size, legal or ownership status (public/ private) and technical characteristics — can be, and should be, accommodated within the same organisational structure.

Size does not seem to be, generally speaking, a membership criterion. Most organisations accept large, medium-sized and small firms, and appear to appreciate this formula as one making for broader representativeness. Restrictions usually concern only very small firms, such as handicraft enterprises. The question of heterogeneity is not so important in industry federations. The fact of being engaged in similar industrial operations in itself guarantees some degree of homogeneity: it is scarcely conceivable that any one industry would cover the entire spectrum from corporate giants to handicraft workshops. None the less, the presence of small- and medium-sized enterprises alongside large or very large ones within the same organisation can be a source of difficulty: in wage negotiations, for instance, the smaller units, less secure financially, may be reluctant to adopt as generous a position towards the unions as the larger firms. Furthermore, their priorities may not be the same in drawing on the services which the employers' organisation can provide – and whose cost is likely to be borne mainly by the larger enterprises. The demand for services may, in any case, not be just a matter of size but involve other factors such as the degree of technological sophistication. Again, arrangements designed to give all affiliates a fair share in decision-making while taking due account of their relative size and importance can raise delicate problems. Tensions, therefore, can and do arise, but the policy of central organisations is, by and large, to seek the widest measure of representation of small enterprises, and there appears to be an awareness among employers both large and small of their common interest in being represented by the same organisation. Nevertheless, there are countries – France and the Netherlands, for instance – in which small and medium-sized enterprises have their own organisational structures separate from and parallel to the major central inter-occupational federations.

Another question concerns the affiliation of enterprises in the public sector. In Switzerland and the United States, for example, where there are very few public enterprises, employers' organisations do not admit them. In most countries, however, the public sector is large and growing, and in many cases is the biggest single employer. In such countries public sector enterprises have been given some degree of representation in employer organisations. This can vary from virtually unrestricted access to membership – e.g. in the United Kingdom and certain English-speaking African countries, where even public enterprises like the post office may join – to cases in which restrictions may be imposed on other grounds. An enterprise may be excluded, for instance, because it constitutes a state monopoly. Enterprises usually qualify as members, not because of their legal status or ownership, but because of the way they manage their business – i.e. in accordance with market economy principles. The issue, in other words, is not "private enterprise" but "free enterprise". In a very few cases public sector enterprises are excluded from membership in employers' organisations not by the organisations themselves but as a result of public policy decisions. In Italy, for instance, under an Act of 1956 companies in which the State has a direct or indirect interest may not join employers' federations.

Functions

Traditionally, employers' organisations had a defensive – or reactive – attitude reflected in ad hoc responses to government or trade union initiatives perceived as a threat to their interests. The more modern attitude – sometimes referred to as "proactive" – puts the stress on more systematic, continuous and often institutionalised forms of action aimed at promoting employer interests and viewpoints and, beyond that, wider social objectives. Elements of both are present in the relations between employers' organisations and the public authorities, the unions or the community at large, and in the services provided to their members.

Employers' organisations and the public authorities

In their traditional "defence" role employers' organisations tended, at least initially, to rely more on direct, and usually informal, approaches to those in authority than on direct contact with the unions. This was no doubt normal at a time when government policies, and more particularly the development of labour legislation, were perceived as a more direct threat to employer interests than the trade union movement. Of course, the growing strength of the unions soon altered that picture, and collective bargaining developed as the technique most suitable for dealing with a wide range of employment and working conditions; even so, efforts to influence the process of government directly have remained a privileged form of action.

These means do not include participation in political decision-making through direct representation in organs of government or parliamentary assemblies. Nor do they include formal alliances

22

with political parties: even if employers' organisations do have political preferences and express them through certain forms of political action, e.g. in election campaigns by supporting candidates favourable to business interests, they generally stay away from active partisan politics. In their representative functions vis-à-vis state authorities employers' organisations normally rely on techniques open to any organised pressure group.

Originally, the defence of employers' interests largely meant preservation of an existing social order. More recently, employers have also tried to promote change, and in particular to reverse unwelcome trends. Historically speaking, efforts to preserve the status quo have probably outweighed those meant to alter it; pressure by the Confederation of British Industry in favour of the adoption of the 1971 Industrial Relations Act has been cited as a successful example of the latter, and the lobbying campaign by American employers to block labour law reforms in the 1970s as one of the former.

The effectiveness of lobbying activities naturally depends on the credibility and representativeness of those engaged in them in the eyes of those at whom they are directed. In this respect, employers' organisations may enjoy some advantage over trade unions in that "employers are able to achieve a solid front in their position, or at least an appearance of one, more easily than trade unions whose decision-making procedures are frequently more open and more exposed to public scrutiny".[1]

The degree of influence which employers' organisations are able to exert depends largely on their willingness to use all means of action open to them, especially by approaching all government branches and agencies concerned with social and labour policy, including the administrative and judicial authorities. For example, the central employers' federation in the Federal Republic of Germany – the BDA – brought a lawsuit against the Government to have the "Co-determination

Act" of 1976 declared unconstitutional after its efforts to block passage of the law had failed.

It is, however, one thing for employers' organisations to exert pressure on governments in pursuit of their immediate interests; it is another for governments to seek their views and advice in social policy matters, including proposed legislation, and thus to associate them as partners in the national decision-making process. This has, in fact, developed as an important aspect of the increasingly positive role which employers' organisations have been assuming. It reflects official recognition both of the legitimacy of their interests and of the expertise they can contribute. It also constitutes, in the eyes of employers, a factor offsetting to some degree the growth of state intervention in economic and social matters. At present the principle of prior consultation of economic groupings is embodied in a number of legal or even constitutional texts – e.g. article 32 (3) of the Swiss Federal Constitution – and the practice is generally accepted by most governments.[2]

The representative function of employers' organisations is largely carried out through established bipartite or tripartite machinery, the origin of which dates back to the First World War. After the war, the application of the tripartite principle was extended to the international level, especially by the establishment in 1919 of the International Labour Organisation. It may be added that the ILO in turn has promoted the setting up of national tripartite machinery in many of its member countries.

Institutional arrangements for representing employers and other economic or social groupings are embodied in a variety of organs set up at different levels and in different sectors of the government structure. At the top level these are exemplified by bodies like the Economic and Social Council in France – as well as the councils in French-speaking African countries set up on the French model – and similar bodies in many other countries. These bodies, while integrated within

23

the political structure, have purely consultative rather than decision-making functions, as is true by and large of the many other government committees in which representatives of employers and other non-governmental groups participate. There is, however, a wide variety of other bodies, dealing at various levels with more specific or technical questions, in which employers' organisations are associated in administrative and management functions; these include, for instance, the running of national employment offices or social security schemes.

Role within the industrial relations system

A major function – if not the most important single function – of employers' organisations is to participate in negotiations with trade unions for the fixing of wages or other employment conditions. This negotiating function need not be considered as strictly limited to direct two-way "bargaining" or to discussion of working conditions in the narrow sense: an element of negotiation is present in the whole spectrum of activity in which the two sides of industry are jointly associated, including the arrangements for bipartite or tripartite consultation described in the preceding section.

As already mentioned, employers' organisations in the early days were less inclined to seek dialogue with the trade unions than to approach the public authorities direct: it was only later, with the growth of trade union power, that they found themselves engaged in a bargaining process with the unions. Even so, employer attitudes towards unions fluctuated for many years, ranging from cautious – if not grudging – acceptance to outright hostility. It is difficult to discern any consistent trend in the cross-currents of that period: certain organisations "that initially had been prepared to seek an accommodation with organisations of their employees later became militantly anti-union. The National Metal Trades Association in the United States would be an example. Others, recognising the improbability of success in eliminating their adversaries, . . . switched to a

more or less reluctant acceptance of a bargaining relationship".[3]

Nowadays, employers' organisations play a key role at all levels of the bargaining process, despite the variety of national systems and irrespective of whether they are direct parties to collective bargaining. The central confederations in particular, even where they do not, or may not, sit as full-fledged parties at the bargaining table, occupy a unique position and can exert a powerful influence through national bipartite and even tripartite "concertation" arrangements.

Direct assistance to affiliated enterprises engaged in bargaining is another form of involvement of employers' organisations. This function meets a need felt especially in developing countries, where enterprises may lack experienced staff to carry out the negotiations. Therefore, officers from an employers' organisation regularly assist the negotiators, sometimes even taking their place at the bargaining table. "The result can be considerable cohesion among the employers and an outcome comparable to that arrived at through negotiations conducted by an organisation."[4]

Employers' organisations may also be involved in industrial disputes. This is a natural extension of the bargaining function, in particular where a dispute arises from a breakdown of negotiations to which an employers' organisation is a party and is submitted to voluntary or compulsory arbitration; in that case, the organisation is represented in the same way – and often by the same individuals – in the settlement procedure as in the dispute.

Another way employers' organisations can be involved in labour disputes is through the organisation and administration of strike insurance or defence funds. The early development of this function in the face of growing trade union use of the strike weapon was, indeed, one of the more typical manifestations of the defensive reaction which initially induced employers to organise.

Strike defence funds, based either on the insurance or on the mutual aid principle, are now common in a number of countries – for example the Nordic countries and the Federal Republic of Germany – though not in all. In the United Kingdom, for instance, a comparatively recent effort by the Confederation of British Industry (CBI) to establish such a fund was unsuccessful. Schemes of this sort are not so useful in situations where strikes are generally of very short duration and this may explain, for example, why there are so few strike funds in a country like France.

Strike funds based on the insurance principle – i.e. based on contributions from all affiliated firms and payment of benefits to those afflicted by a strike – may be set up at various levels; they may, for instance, be administered by a central employers' confederation or an industry association; in the former case the beneficiary may be an entire industry, in the latter an industrial firm hit by a strike. Arrangements based on the mutual aid principle rely on the assumption that the losses caused by a strike in one firm are offset by the higher profits in others, which are accordingly called upon to make up the losses sustained by the less fortunate ones.

The lock-out may be used either as an offensive weapon – like the strike – or as a defensive one, the latter case being by far the more frequent. As a defensive device, it constitutes a form of joint employer action to counter union tactics aimed at dividing employers through successive plant- or enterprise-level strikes. It consists in meeting such union practices, commonly referred to as "whip-sawing", by locking out the entire industry or sector affected. Successful resort to the defensive lock-out requires a high level of discipline on the part of the employers' organisations, rarely found outside countries such as the Nordic countries or the Federal Republic of Germany, where "employers' associations have disciplinary power over affiliates to ensure that lock-out decisions are heeded".[5]

Employers' organisations and the community at large

There is nothing spectacular about the consultative and negotiating functions reviewed in the preceding sections, and the issues they deal with seldom make headline news, except perhaps in times of crisis. Some organisations are indeed content to function inconspicuously and anonymously, and hence – in their view – more effectively. Most, however, have felt a need to supplement the activities through which they seek to influence governments by others aimed at the public at large or at specific target groups like educators, churchmen or, indeed, employees of their own affiliated enterprises.

Such activities are now carried out in a highly systematic way, far removed from the purely reactive approach. They rely on the full range of modern communication methods, including publications – as well as other types of information material, like films or video tapes – issued by the organisations themselves, and on the various information techniques – statements for the press, interviews and so on – which give access to the mass media. All these activities have effectively focused public attention on employers' organisations and helped to establish their status as the authorised voice of a key sector of society. This is especially true of national central confederations with overall competence in both the economic and the social area, like the CBI in the United Kingdom and the CNPF in France, whose pronouncements on general issues of national policy are not likely to go unheeded.

Employers' organisations have not, as a rule, identified themselves too closely or been directly linked with any political party or movement. That is especially true today: about the only "ideology" to which they are committed is that of free and competitive enterprise, not excluding acceptance of a limited degree of state intervention as is now generally practised in market economy countries. They are careful not to exceed certain limits, aware that "an industrial organisation cannot turn itself into a political party or it will run the risk of compromising the interests of its members and creating confusion prejudicial to the workings of democracy".[6]

Employers can, however, react sharply when they feel that an attack is being mounted against a society reflecting their basic philosophy and ideals. An example is a demonstration organised by the Swedish Employers' Confederation on a recent occasion (see box 2.1).

Service to the membership

Although employers' organisations have many representative functions, they also provide various services to their members. As mentioned before, one such service may consist in helping an enterprise to conduct its collective bargaining; the employers' organisations provide the negotiating firm with expertise it lacks, such as economic, statistical or technical data, negotiating skill and experience. Similar demands are placed on employers' organisations in other fields – such as legal matters, personnel administration, management and productivity, or occupational safety and health. Such assistance usually takes the form of information, advice, education and training.

The legal problems confronting individual enterprises are often so complicated that outside advice is needed. Small and medium-sized firms, in particular, rely extensively on the advisory services of their employers' organisations in ascertaining their rights and obligations under statutory texts dealing with social or labour questions, taxes, protection of the environment and any other economic or social issues, as well as under contracts (including collective agreements) to which they may be a party. The expertise required, moreover, is often not limited to the purely legal aspects of problems: industrial safety and health regulations, for example, may be complex and intricate enough to call for the services of technical specialists in that area. These the employers' organisations must also be equipped to provide.

26

2.1

Employers' reaction to the Swedish "wage earners' fund"

A striking example of an employers' organisation being engaged in a political issue is the battle waged by the Swedish Employers' Confederation to block passage of a law establishing so-called "wage earners' funds" (also referred to as "employee investment funds"). The law has now been passed by the Swedish Parliament and entered into force on 1 January 1984. It provides for the setting up of five regional funds to be financed by a combination of profit-sharing and an additional payroll levy. Each fund, on whose governing body the employee representatives will have a majority, can buy a maximum of 8 per cent of the equity capital of individual Swedish enterprises, i.e. a total maximum of 40 per cent. In addition, a pension fund managed by government, employers and workers can buy up to a maximum of 10 per cent of this equity capital. According to present legislation the supply of new money to the funds is supposed to stop at the end of 1990, by which time they will have received 14,000 million kronor (about US$1,700 million), equivalent to about 7 per cent of the current total volume of Swedish public stock. The Swedish Employers' Confederation claims that in seven years the five funds, together with the General Pension Fund, could take over many large business concerns. This, according to the Swedish employers, threatens the market economy system and strikes at the very roots of the country's pluralistic society; in addition, it is likely to discourage investment, creation of new enterprises and employment expansion. Not only, therefore, did they mount an unprecedented public relations campaign through all available media against the funds, but they were also able, in the autumn of 1983, to arrange a protest march with more than 75,000 participants – a unique event in the history of employers' organisations.

Employers' organisations also provide education and training in management – not only the functions related directly to industrial relations such as personnel management or worker participation, but also the full range of managerial responsibility in such fields as productivity, work organisation and occupational safety and health. They may be called upon to provide information and advice on the introduction of new technology and its implications for safety, work organisation and productivity. Most of the larger organisations run full-fledged training centres, but even the smaller ones, particularly in the developing countries, attach enough importance to management training to include one or more training officers in their staff.

The interest of employers' organisations in training does not stop at management development. They also organise their own vocational training programmes, including the setting up or sponsoring, usually by industry federations, of apprenticeship centres or adult training schemes. In some cases employers' organisations participate in education or training programmes sponsored by other institutions, e.g. universities or government-related bodies. In others they have organised or sponsored vocational training or apprenticeship programmes jointly with trade unions, as in the Netherlands and Sweden. Small enterprise development, too, constitutes an increasingly important activity for many organisations.

To carry out all these activities employers' organisations need to have a large and competent specialised staff including lawyers, economists, trainers, technicians and public relations experts. Whether an organisation can provide a complete range of services in such a variety of fields naturally depends on its financial resources. These are in the best of cases limited, and priorities must be set. Areas to which employers attach special importance include occupational safety and health – even the less affluent organisations usually managing to employ one or more specialists in this field – along with management development and development of small-scale enterprises.

Employers' organisations and their activities are normally financed through contributions paid by affiliated firms and commensurate with each firm's capacity to pay, as measured by such criteria as the size of the workforce, the wage bill, sales volume or others. There is, of course, a direct relationship between the amount of contributions affiliates are ready to pay and the services they can expect from their organisation. Some firms may prefer to pay less and receive less elaborate service, resorting in case of need to fee-charging agencies,[7]

while others like to rely more fully on the organisations, even if this means somewhat higher dues. In the developing countries, where most enterprises are small and have limited means, this raises a painful dilemma: employers must look to their organisations for services which they cannot afford to finance directly, but the organisations themselves, whose means are also limited, cannot afford to provide them; yet it is precisely in the developing countries that the need for such services is most critical.

Centrally planned economies

In centrally planned economies the means of production are owned by the community, and as a result there is no scope for the existence of a separate employer interest group. In many of these countries even the term "employer" is rejected, because the economy is not in the hands of owner-operators guided by the profit motive but run, in the sole interest of the community, by a class of "managers" responsible to the community alone.

In spite of this basic difference in their role, managers in centrally planned economies find it useful to discuss common problems in institutions such as chambers of commerce or industry, which deal in addition with problems of commerce, trade and related economic matters. In some countries these chambers are increasingly consulted by the government on issues related, for example, to productivity, wages or long-term planning. At the international level they also play an important part by designating managers to participate in meetings convened by the ILO.

The councils of directors in the USSR provide an example of these chambers of commerce or industry. They were set up during the economic reforms of the late 1960s when state undertakings began to enjoy substantially greater freedom of

27

management than in the past; one of their tasks is to arrive at optimum decisions regarding the management of industrial personnel.[8] Today they perform their advisory functions at various levels of the national economy, depending on the organisational structure. In some cases, the councils of directors are composed of heads of undertakings belonging to large groups of undertakings in the same branch of activity (production associations); in other cases, they are composed of heads of undertakings which, although in different branches of activity, are located in the same town. Representatives of the ministries concerned may also take part in their work. The councils of directors set out to exploit to the full the potential of each labour collective in order to attain production goals. It is also the work of these councils to study the best methods of management and to exchange positive experiences, which are later passed on to all the undertakings concerned.[9]

In centrally planned economies basic wages are normally fixed by the authorities, in consultation with the trade unions. In the USSR, for instance, this function is performed by the State Committee for Labour and Social Affairs. At the same time, however, plant managers have important responsibilities in a number of fields such as production planning, personnel policy, work organisation, productivity, incentives, workers' welfare, and safety and health.[10]

The practices discussed so far relate to the socialised sector which, of course, covers the overwhelming majority if not the totality of employees in the countries concerned. In the USSR, for instance, the private sector is limited to one-person enterprises; thus there are in that sector neither employers nor employees, but only self-employed individuals. In some socialist countries, there is however a limited amount of experimentation with private enterprise.

Similarly, the management pattern in the predominant socialised sector is not necessarily

---

2.2

Associations of managers and small private employers in Hungary

The Hungarian economy has undergone a number of changes over the past two or three decades. In that process the year 1968 was a watershed, marked by the introduction of far-reaching changes in economic policy, including wider recognition of the economic role of market mechanisms. A major feature of these changes was the granting of increased autonomy to enterprises within the framework of a planned economy and, as a corollary, greater scope for managers to make their views heard through associations of their own.

At present, there is only one body of this type – the Hungarian Chamber of Commerce – but it would appear that there are no legal obstacles to the setting up of others; membership in the Chamber of Commerce is, moreover, voluntary. The Chamber performs functions similar to those of corresponding bodies in other centrally planned economies; these include labour matters, in which it is playing an increasingly important part. In this capacity it participates in the work of the Labour and Wages Council – a tripartite body – and is seeking to institutionalise contacts with the trade union movement.

Small private employers in Hungary are represented by two organisations – one grouping small handicraft enterprises and the other small businesses. Membership in the former is compulsory, although the possibility of making it voluntary is being discussed. In the latter, where it is already voluntary, about 98 per cent of the sector is affiliated. Both organisations represent the interests of small enterprises vis-à-vis the Government, which is required to consult them on matters affecting their interests, in particular proposed legislation. Enterprises in this sector do not conclude collective agreements; however, the ILO mission has reported that, according to officers of the trade union movement, the role of the movement in such a rapidly growing sector raises a problem which at some point will have to be considered.

---

one of rigid and unchangeable uniformity. In this area too attempts have been made to introduce a measure of flexibility and management autonomy. The likely effects of such developments in the industrial relations area, in particular on the management side, could be significant. A case in point is that of Hungary, where the system has evolved considerably in recent years. The industrial relations system in that country has recently been studied by an ILO mission appointed for the purpose by the ILO Governing Body (see box 2.2).[11]

Employers' organisations in developing countries

In many developing countries the creation and growth of employers' organisations had much the same origins as in the industrialised market economies. In the former as in the latter employers felt the need to meet pressures generated by a growing trade union movement. Thus the purpose originally served by the new organisations was essentially defensive. As in the industrialised market economies, moreover, enterprises formed associations in defence of their economic interests before the social aspects of their concerns were recognised as corresponding to a separate function. Initially, it was these economic associations, i.e. chambers of commerce or industry, or producers' associations, that assumed responsibility for labour matters. In some countries they have continued to do so, while in others labour questions are dealt with by separate organisations, i.e. employers' organisations properly so called. This is true, in particular, in the former United Kingdom territories of the Caribbean, where such organisations were set up at a comparatively recent date and have developed significantly since independence. By contrast the unitary formula has continued to prevail among their Latin American neighbours.

Many of these organisations, particularly in the newly independent countries of Africa, Asia and the Caribbean, were set up after the Second World War, although some – for example in India and Sri Lanka – date back to the period between the two World Wars. Many of them draw their inspiration from a common model, such as the organisations set up in former colonial territories, either before or after independence, by an expatriate employer community representing the industrial traditions of the former metropolitan power. Even so, given the historical, social, economic and political diversity typical of the developing countries, the situation varies widely from one to the other, just as it does among the industrialised market economies.

Nevertheless, there is a basic difference, because employers' organisations in most developing countries have grown so much faster than those in industrialised market economies. In the latter, employers' (as well as workers') organisations had essentially a grass-roots origin: they developed through a gradual process of centralisation, progressing from the local through the regional and sectoral levels to that of the national central confederation. This process extended over most of the second half of the nineteenth century and the first half of the twentieth. In most developing countries the corresponding process has had much less time in which to unfold, and it seems safe to say that in many cases the establishment of central organisations overtook, so to speak, the development of lower- and intermediate-level structures, instead of being the culmination of a process of gradual growth of such structures. This is because of a widely perceived need – perceived, in particular, by the governments of the countries concerned – for organisations able to represent the business community, and indeed social groups generally, at the level at which national development decisions are made. In a number of developing countries the governments themselves have actively encouraged the development, on both the employers' and the workers' side, of central bodies able to serve as focal points for official contacts. Of particular importance are participation in national planning activities and representation within tripartite consultation machinery, such as the economic and social councils set up on the French model in French-speaking African countries, as well as in international bodies, particularly the ILO and its various tripartite organs.

This role, however, whether viewed primarily as one of "defensive" representation of employer interests or of positive – or "pro-active" – participation in the nation-building process, requires that employers' organisations really do speak in the name of a broadly based constituency. How far can that condition be regarded as fulfilled in most developing countries? In many cases these

29

central structures have yet to be built up, with the active support of the whole employer constituency, whether actual or potential.

Moreover, there is little homogeneity in the enterprises they do (or could) represent. A distinction may be drawn here between three categories of enterprises: first, those wholly or partly owned by foreign interests; second, public sector enterprises; and, third, small businesses. As regards the first group – which includes multinationals – these enterprises usually identify themselves with the national development objectives to which national firms subscribe and are, with only a few exceptions, active members in the employers' organisations. As regards public sector enterprises – which in many developing countries account for an important part of the industrial, agricultural and commercial sector – the problems which their membership raises are the ones already discussed;[12] normally these enterprises also join the employers' organisations. As for small enterprises, they are often run on paternalistic lines with a small non-union workforce and may not feel any real need to join an organisation.[13]

The weaknesses to be overcome to enable employers' organisations to play their full development role were recently highlighted by an ILO seminar for Latin American employers' organisations.[14] Many Latin American employers' organisations mentioned the as yet "artificial" character of national tripartite consultation machinery, and the reluctance of the social partners and the government to make full use of it. Some even suggested that governments were interested in it only so far as they could use it to further their own purposes.

These examples illustrate a situation common to some developing countries, where conditions may not yet favour the emergence of a strong and representative network of employers' organisations, but where development imperatives have nevertheless thrust upon the employer sector an important role in the nation-building process.

This is not, however, to say that nothing has been or is being done. Employers' organisations have been playing a significant role in support of the development process, most notably, perhaps, in the area of training. They have organised a number of management development training projects; in some cases, for example in Africa, they plan to establish permanent centres. Their training courses cover key areas of industrial relations, for instance personnel management; they have also taken an active interest in vocational training and apprenticeship through participation in national advisory bodies and, in some cases, provide direct support to major training institutions such as the National Service for Industrial Apprenticeship (SENAI) or the National Service for Commercial Training (SENAC) in Brazil and the National Apprenticeship Service (SENA) in Colombia.

The gap between existing needs and the means available for meeting them remains, however, immense. Some multilateral aid is accordingly provided for developing countries in this field, especially through the ILO's programme of assistance to employers' organisations in those countries. The aim of the programme is to strengthen such organisations and equip them to play their part in meeting the challenges of development within a tripartite framework.

Organisational patterns

In discussing organisational patterns, we shall first consider arrangements for dealing with economic and social issues and go on from there to examine the organisational structure at three major levels – regional and sectoral, central or national, and international.

Economic and social issues

In the preceding description of employers' organisations a distinction has been made between "social" issues and "economic" ones. However, the distinction is not consistently reflected in an organisational pattern under which some organisations deal exclusively with the former and the others with the latter. In some countries a system of organisational dualism did develop, largely as a matter of convenience and in response to the growing challenge posed by organised labour and pro-labour government policies; a limited number of these countries – e.g. the Federal Republic of Germany and the Nordic countries – have retained it to this day. Others have kept to the unitary formula or have embraced it after having for many years followed the dualist pattern. This category includes, for example, the United Kingdom, where the Confederation of British Industry was formed in 1965 through the merger of the British Employers' Confederation, the Federation of British Industries (the central "economic" organisation which until then had represented the trading interests of the major manufacturing firms) and the National Association of British Manufacturers (which had represented smaller manufacturers). Similarly, in the Netherlands the Federation of Dutch Industries (VNO) came into being in 1968, when two previously existing central organisations responsible for social and labour problems and for commercial and economic affairs decided to merge.

The dualist approach has the advantage of facilitating united employer action in labour-management negotiations, on which employer views and interests are more likely to converge than on purely economic matters; and where these latter issues are concerned, members remain free to go their separate ways without being bound by organisation policies. It has also been observed, in defence of the dualist formula, that bargaining conducted by a single organisation with dual competence might tend to make economic policy a subject of negotiation or joint consultation. This argument, however, may have lost some of its force with the development of institutionalised bipartite and tripartite negotiation extending up to the highest levels of government and involving the social partners in discussions on a wide range of broad policy issues.

The fact is that economic and social issues tend increasingly to call for a combined approach. Even where the dualist system has been maintained, organisations specialised in social matters claim a direct interest in economic policy. Practically all industrial relations issues have an economic dimension, e.g. the price implications of wage policies, their effects on the monetary situation, their relationship with fiscal matters or incomes policy generally; besides, broader issues of economic policy, as in the trade or tax fields, may have at least a passing effect on industrial relations. On all such matters employers are anxious to present a united front vis-à-vis their partners in negotiation or discussion, and to avoid conflicts and overlaps such as have at times complicated relations between different organisations representing business interests. Thus even where the dualist pattern prevails the separate organisations strive to co-ordinate their activities closely by concluding agreements that define their respective spheres of competence, holding joint meetings and even being represented on each other's executive boards. Such co-ordination arrangements are normally not confined to the central level of organisation, but extend to the industry and regional levels.

Levels of representation

This section will deal successively with affiliation patterns at the intermediate level, i.e. the sectoral or territorial bodies to which individual firms are directly affiliated; the central level itself, i.e. the national inter-occupational and inter-regional organisations; and the international level.

Regional and sectoral organisations

At the intermediate level enterprises may affiliate with associations established either on a nation-wide basis by industry or regionally on an inter-occupational basis; often they join organisations of both types. The pre-eminent role of industry-level organisations in the industrial relations context, and in particular their responsibility

31

– sometimes exclusive – for representing employers at the bargaining table, has already been stressed in the preceding pages. Not much has been said, on the other hand, of the role of organisations set up on a geographical, i.e. regional basis.

Here again, the picture is complex. At the national level, sectoral and regional organisations constitute a pattern in which the "vertical" classification scheme (i.e. industry-level organisations) cuts across the "horizontal" (i.e. regional bodies). There are cases in which national industry federations, i.e. organisations of the vertical type, are made up not of individual enterprises, but of smaller organisations within the industry established on a territorial (i.e. horizontal) basis. Thus, in the Federal Republic of Germany enterprises commonly belong not directly to the national organisation catering for their industry, but to a regional industry association which, in turn, is affiliated both to the national industry federation and to the regional (usually *Land*) inter-occupational federation concerned.

Regional organisations generally play a less important part where major labour questions are concerned than those set up at the industry level, although there are exceptions. The regional structure tends to be stronger, for example, in federal States and, generally speaking, in countries composed of sharply differentiated territorial units; in Italy, for instance, the importance of some provincial associations exceeds that of the industry-level organisations. Even in countries where the role of the regional structures is less prominent there is a trend towards strengthening them, in recognition of the growing importance of the regional dimension in the overall consideration of national economic and social issues.

From a world perspective the picture is of course one of still greater variety and complexity, in view of the wide differences from country to country as regards the size, relative degree of development, role and importance of the various types of organisations.

Central organisations

As a rule, employers and their organisations at the various intermediate levels are represented at the national inter-occupational level by central confederal bodies. This is a feature – perhaps the only one – common to virtually all national organisational structures. The functions and activities of these central organisations, especially their negotiating role and their areas of competence, vary widely, and so does their formal structure.

In most countries there is a single central organisation, but in some there are several, each with its own network of affiliates, whose membership and/or competence may overlap. The membership of central organisations is normally made up of industry-level or regional organisations, or both. Sometimes individual firms are directly affiliated along with associations. This may happen, for instance, in a developing country where a particular industry is represented by too few firms to justify the existence of a separate industry organisation. An extreme case is, of course, that of the very small country with only one employers' organisation, where individual firms have to be directly affiliated with the central organisation.

In a number of countries the central confederation covers all economic sectors; in others the exceptions commonly include agriculture, mining and the tertiary sector, which in that case may have central organisations of their own. In some countries where industry-level bargaining is the rule, only sectoral organisations may become affiliated; in others, where bargaining takes place at the enterprise level and the regional structure is strong, affiliation may be restricted to regional organisations.

Where affiliation is open to both sectoral and regional organisations, individual firms affiliated to organisations of both types – a by no means infrequent occurrence – will, as a result, enjoy dual representation at the top level. In practice this raises no problem in view of the functional differentiation between intermediate-level organisations; bargaining in particular (where it does not take place at the enterprise level) is normally handled by either the sectoral or the regional organisation, but not by both. The existence in some countries of parallel organisations may result in further cases of multiple affiliation. A notable example is that of the coexistence in the Netherlands of a Christian organisation and a non-denominational organisation covering much the same economic sectors, with many firms affiliated to both; this is one of the few cases in which a central employers' organisation has been set up on a denominational basis.

International employers' organisations

The role of international employers' organisations, under present conditions at least, cannot be one of collective bargaining. This is precluded by the lack of homogeneity of national structures, and particularly the fact that many national-level central confederations are themselves not empowered to bargain. However, existing arrangements for joint or tripartite consultation at the world, regional or subregional level afford ample scope for activities closely akin to a form of bargaining.

The role which the International Organisation of Employers (IOE), with its present membership of 95 organisations covering 91 countries, plays in the activities of the International Labour Organisation constitutes perhaps the most striking example. It is true that in ILO tripartite meetings employers – like their worker counterparts – are represented not by their international federations but by delegates appointed by governments from the most representative national-level organisations. These delegates, however, are ad hoc appointees, designated for individual meetings, and it is the IOE that, through its regular attendance at such meetings, provides an element of continuity, comparable to that provided at the national level by standing arrangements for the representation of social partners in consultative bodies. Its guidance on such occasions helps to ensure that the positions taken by the employer

representatives at the meeting accurately reflect the policies of the world-wide IOE constituency. It may be added that, unlike meetings of national consultative bodies established at the top policy-making level, whose role is purely advisory, tripartite ILO meetings have a decision-making function in which employers and workers participate on the same footing as governments. Moreover, the process by which decisions are arrived at, particularly in the standard-setting work of the International Labour Conference, is essentially one of tripartite negotiation.

Such a pattern admittedly has no counterpart at the regional and subregional levels but, as mentioned earlier, a representation structure has been developing at these levels as well and can be expected to lead to increasingly active involvement of organised employers in policy matters of concern to them.

Conclusion

The foregoing pages have stressed the wide variations among countries as regards employer representation systems. These variations, reflecting differences in political, economic and social environment and in degree of development, are particularly striking in the area of industrial relations proper: for instance, where collective bargaining or settlement of disputes is concerned, arrangements differ vastly from one national situation to another according to the degree of cohesiveness, centralised control and rank-and-file discipline achieved by employers through their organisations.

These differences should not, however, obscure the important features employer representation schemes have in common. Most basic among these, perhaps, is the fact that they have invariably developed in a climate favourable to entrepreneurship, if not always in a pure market economy environment then at least in a mixed economy allowing for the operation of market economy

33

principles, even if it entails the existence of a large public enterprise sector. Not only are the existence and normal functioning of employers' organisations compatible with a mixed economy, but such organisations commonly admit public sector enterprises to membership, provided only that they are run on market economy principles, i.e. as "free" if not as "private" enterprises.

To carry the reasoning a step further, it is not inconceivable that, even in a centrally planned economy, some degree of recognition of the economic role of market mechanisms and of private entrepreneurship might lead ultimately to the emergence of employers' organisations performing representation functions comparable to those of their counterparts in market economy countries. The Hungarian example suggests at least such a possibility.

However that may be, the emphasis on entrepreneurial freedom remains a feature common to employers' organisations generally, and it figures as a central theme in the public information and

relations campaign in which they are increasingly engaged. It is clear, of course, that this does not amount to a concept of absolute and unqualified freedom in a spirit of rugged individualism more typical of an earlier age. The mere fact that employers have continued to form associations in defence of their common interests implies some surrendering of individual interests.

Moreover, they have assumed wider responsibilities in a whole range of activities, in particular training and education which they provide as a service to their membership and to society. Tripartite consultative arrangements at the various levels of government administration – particularly promoted by governments in developing countries – serve the same purpose by giving the social partners a voice in larger policy questions linked but not confined to industrial relations issues. This consultative role is a function which, so far as employers' organisations are concerned, can only be strengthened by the tendency to adopt an increasingly co-ordinated approach to economic and social issues.

---

[1] See A. Gladstone: "Employers' associations in comparative perspective: Functions and activities", in J. P. Windmuller and A. Gladstone (eds.): *Employers' associations and industrial relations*, A comparative study (Oxford, Clarendon Press, 1984), p. 26.

[2] See J. J. Oechslin: "Employers' organizations", in Blanpain, *Comparative labour law . . .*, op. cit., p. 193.

[3] J. P. Windmuller: "Employers' associations in comparative perspective: Organization, structure, administration", in Windmuller and Gladstone, op. cit., pp. 2-3.

[4] J. J. Oechslin: "Employers' organisations: current trends and social responsibilities", in *International Labour Review*, Sep.-Oct. 1982, p. 505.

[5] Gladstone, op. cit., p. 41.

[6] Oechslin, "Employers' organisations . . .", op. cit., pp. 507-508.

[7] In some cases, employers' organisations have provided consultancy services for a fee; by and large, however, they tend to refrain from this practice, which they regard as inconsistent with their status

as service organisations (cf. Windmuller and Gladstone, op. cit., p. 34).

[8] V. Poliakov and A. Silin: "Personnel management in Soviet undertakings under the economic reform", in *International Labour Review*, Dec. 1972, pp. 527-542.

[9] See the editorial in *Pravda* (Moscow), 15 Apr. 1982.

[10] See Poliakov and Silin, op. cit.

[11] ILO: *The trade union situation and industrial relations in Hungary*, Report of an ILO mission (Geneva, 1984), especially Chapter III ("Organisations of heads of enterprises").

[12] See above, p. 22.

[13] Schregle, op. cit., pp. 94-97.

[14] See ILO: *Papel de las organizaciones de empleadores en el desarrollo económico-social en América latina*, Informe de los trabajos y documentos presentados al Seminario regional para las organizaciones de empleadores de América latina (Buenos Aires, 21-25 de abril de 1981) (Geneva, 1983) (available in Spanish only).

Chapter 3

Labour-management relations

Employers' and workers' organisations exist to express, represent and defend the interests of their members; these interests will frequently diverge, and unless a compromise can be found that is satisfactory to both parties – and sometimes to the government as well – the result may be a labour dispute with all the disruption that this entails. Collective bargaining is a powerful instrument for arriving at such compromises, i.e. for accommodating and reconciling the interests of employers and workers. This usually takes the form of discussions between the two sides with a view to the conclusion of collective agreements, i.e. documents that, with few exceptions, are legally binding and fix the wages and conditions of employment of a certain group of workers. The scope of collective agreements depends on the level at which they are concluded, which may be that of the enterprise, that of the branch of activity (for example the textiles, chemical or metalworking industry) or that of the whole economy (sometimes known as the inter-occupational, central or national level). Collective agreements are generally concluded at the level of the enterprise in Canada, Japan and the United States, most centrally planned economies and the great majority of developing countries; in some developing countries, however, especially in French-speaking Africa, bargaining takes place at the branch level. In Western Europe the negotiation of collective agreements has generally taken place at the level of the branch, though central bargaining has long been important in the Scandinavian countries. Over the past few years, however, there has been some diversification in Western Europe, for,

although branch bargaining remains predominant, central bargaining and bargaining by enterprise are becoming more important in an increasing number of countries.

There are today many procedures for reaching a decision that, without meeting the definition just given of collective bargaining, basically perform the same function. These include all the negotiations between employers, workers and sometimes the government that result in agreements relating directly or indirectly to labour matters. Examples of such negotiations are the discussions between the government and the large confederations of employers' associations and trade unions that have mainly taken place in Western Europe and that aim at drawing up plans of action against inflation and unemployment. Other examples are the discussions that take place in the centrally planned economy countries – at the central and the branch levels, between the state bodies and the higher trade union organisations – and that aim at formulating and carrying out economic and social plans. Collective bargaining in the broad sense also includes the discussions within the enterprise as part of consultation or co-determination procedures, which are generally known as workers' participation in decisions. All these discussions and procedures are, in fact, basically similar to the negotiation of collective agreements, since in each of them all the parties concerned try to find an acceptable agreement on labour problems.

The first section of this chapter will examine recent trends in collective bargaining, including

---

3.1

Workers covered by collective agreements

For the industrialised market economy countries, there are few national figures (that is for the whole economy). The following estimates have been drawn from existing public and private sources and should be regarded as only approximate.

It is even more difficult to estimate such figures for the developing countries. Collective bargaining hardly exists in the informal sector, which generally accounts for over 50 per cent – and sometimes even over 90 per cent – of the labour force. The situation in the modern sector varies greatly from country to country. At one end of the scale there are countries like Argentina or Mexico. In Argentina, collective agreements in 1975, when collective bargaining was suspended, covered practically all non-agricultural wage earners. In Mexico, there are at present about 60,000 collective agreements (most of them concluded for the enterprise), which suggests that most medium-sized and almost all large enterprises have their own agreements. At the other end of the scale, there are some countries in Latin America, Africa, Asia and the Middle East where there are no more than a few dozen agreements signed in a year at the enterprise level. The great majority of developing countries come between these two extremes. In some of them, including India, Kenya, Malaysia, Singapore and Venezuela, the number of workers covered by collective agreements runs into hundreds of thousands and sometimes accounts for up to one-third – or even more – of the wage earners in the modern sector. In other countries collective bargaining is also spreading, though more slowly than in the countries just mentioned. Elsewhere, there has been less progress in collective

bargaining, since industrialisation is more recent and the trade unions are even less well established.

Percentage of workers covered by collective agreements in industrialised market economies (early 1980s)

Country	Percentage
Austria	Over 90
Belgium	Over 90
Sweden	Over 90
Federal Republic of Germany	90
Netherlands	80
Norway	75
United Kingdom	75
Switzerland	65
Finland	50
France	45
Canada	40
United States	30
Japan	25

Source : ILO.

---

discussions and negotiations that do not directly lead to collective agreements. Forms of workers' participation in decisions within enterprises, such as the representation of workers on works councils, boards of directors or supervisory boards, will be dealt with in the second section. The third section will discuss collective labour disputes.

Collective bargaining

The scope of collective bargaining

Collective bargaining has certainly gained ground over the past few decades, particularly in developing countries, but it could usefully be applied to many more labour problems.

Statistics, although they are not always very abundant or very recent, show that the number of

collective agreements and the number of workers covered by them have increased over the past 20 years. This is particularly true of developing countries, where the scope for expansion has obviously been greatest. Countries where the number of workers covered has greatly increased during the past 15 years include Colombia, India, the Ivory Coast, Kenya, Malaysia, Nigeria, Panama, the Philippines, Sri Lanka, Tunisia and Venezuela. Data for selected industrialised market economies and some estimates for developing countries are given in box 3.1.

The increased coverage (particularly in the industrialised market economies) is also due to the fact that collective agreements have been applied to new sectors of activity and new groups of workers. The use of collective agreements has spread considerably in the public service during the past two decades – for example in Canada and Belgium, following the adoption of new legislation in 1967 and 1974 respectively. Moreover, particularly in Canada, the United States and Western Europe, collective bargaining is more and more resorted to in fixing the salaries and conditions of employment of teachers and technical and supervisory staff. The question of collective bargaining coverage hardly arises in the centrally planned economies, where the negotiation of collective agreements is prescribed by law in practically all enterprises.

Another trend in collective bargaining is the increasing range of subjects it covers. At first it dealt, as a rule, with only a small number of issues, among which wages and daily and weekly hours of work were the most important. Since then collective bargaining has gradually broken out of these narrow limits, not only in the industrialised market economy countries but also in the developing countries, where, however, the process started later and has been less noticeable. Little by little, the parties to collective bargaining have thus come to deal with questions as varied as occupational safety and health, supplementary benefits under social security schemes, vocational rehabilitation or workers' housing. At the same time, employers' and workers' organisations in a growing number of countries have signed basic agreements or other agreements intended not to fix the wages and conditions of employment of individual workers but to establish institutions and procedures at every level enabling the organisations concerned to entertain correct and constructive relations (see box 3.2 overleaf).

In recent years this trend towards negotiation on more and more subjects has been developing rapidly, with the result that collective bargaining now covers practically every problem relating directly or indirectly to labour. Thus, in the industrialised market economies a number of agreements have recently been concluded with a view to combating inflation and unemployment. At the same time, many agreements have been concluded in both industrialised market economies and developing countries on other topical matters. In Sweden, for example, the central agreement of 15 April 1982, following the Co-determination at Work Act of 1976, provides for the participation of the workers in most of the decisions taken in the enterprise; in Italy during the 1970s, Fiat concluded several agreements on the investment policy of the enterprise. In various European countries a number of agreements have been signed on such problems as employment protection and the introduction of new technologies; the organisation of work in the workshop; or the protection of temporary workers supplied by agencies. In the developing countries several agreements have been concluded on subjects such as the elimination of illiteracy among workers or the promotion of family planning.

Some of the agreements that have just been reached are obviously intended to improve the "quality of life" at work, in particular through greater participation by the workers in decision-making in the enterprise and the workshop. It might well be that this trend would be more marked if the recession had not shifted attention to the problems of inflation and unemployment and their consequences.

Collective bargaining in the centrally planned economies, though it differs in many respects from the agreements concluded in the market economy countries, has also dealt with an ever growing number of questions in recent years. Discussions and negotiations are now taking place on matters such as the carrying out of the national plan, the development of socialist emulation, the strengthening of labour discipline, the participation of workers in the management of production, the application of scientific and technical progress and the promotion of cultural, educational and sporting activities for workers and their families.

Basic rates of pay in these countries are fixed nationally by the public authorities, which prescribe minimum and maximum rates after consul-

37

3.2

Basic agreements

Certain agreements do not aim at fixing specific terms and conditions of employment but rather at establishing basic principles and guide-lines governing the relations between employers and workers. In other words, these agreements stipulate "the rules of the game". They are usually concluded at the central level and deal with the whole range of issues that may affect the relations between the two sides. They are often referred to as "basic agreements", "industrial relations charters" or "industrial relations codes". There are also agreements concerned only with one specific problem of labour-management relations (such as trade union representation within the enterprise or the settlement of labour disputes). Although these agreements are usually not called "basic agreements", they will nevertheless be discussed here since they pursue the same fundamental objective.

All these agreements have one important feature in common: they all presuppose a basically constructive attitude of the parties towards each other. As a result, they have usually had a stabilising effect on industrial relations.

The first basic agreements – all bipartite – were concluded in the Scandinavian countries, because the central employers' and workers' organisations wanted to improve the functioning of industrial relations at a time when drastic government measures in this field were to be feared. All these agreements are still in force today, although they have been revised in the meantime.

The oldest example of a basic agreement is the so-called September Agreement concluded in Denmark in 1899. That agreement contained various provisions concerning the conduct of labour relations; it recognised the trade unions as well as management prerogatives and established rules for declaring strikes and lock-outs. The September Agreement marked a turning point in Danish labour relations that paved the way for the peaceful coexistence of unions and employers' organisations.

In Norway, the central organisations of employers and workers drew up in 1902 an agreement on the use of mediation and arbitration. In 1935, the organisations concerned concluded a full-fledged basic agreement, which exerted a further beneficial influence on the development of labour relations. In its most recent version, this agreement deals in great detail with various subjects, such as the right to organise, the right and duty to negotiate, the establishment and role of shop stewards and works councils and the settlement of labour disputes.

Another landmark was the Saltsjöbaden Agreement concluded in Sweden in 1938 between the central employers' and workers' organisations. This basic agreement included uniform procedures for negotiations, the handling of grievances and the settlement of disputes in essential services. It also led to the creation of the National Labour Market Board, a joint body responsible for administering the agreement which has played a significant role in Swedish labour relations.

At a later stage, a number of agreements dealing with particular aspects of labour-management relations were concluded not only in the Scandinavian countries but also in many other Western European countries. Examples are the agreement concerning peaceful industrial relations in the engineering and metalworking industries of Switzerland (concluded in 1937 and periodically renewed and amended since then), the Belgian central agreement concerning trade union representation within undertakings (concluded in 1947 and replaced in 1971), the recommendation on conciliation adopted in the Federal Republic of Germany (1954), the Danish agreement on co-operation and co-operation committees (concluded in 1947 and replaced in 1964 and 1970) and the Swedish agreement on efficiency and participation (1982).

In the meantime, a number of basic agreements have also been concluded in an increasing number of countries outside Western Europe. Some of them, such as the industrial relations codes of Cyprus (adopted in 1962 and replaced in 1977) and Fiji (1973), the industrial relations charter of Kenya (adopted in 1962 and replaced in 1980), the Malaysian code of conduct for industrial harmony (1975) and the code of practice for the promotion of labour relations adopted in Thailand (1981) are fairly detailed. Others, such as the Colombian agreement on labour relations (1981), the Indonesian joint statement on labour relations (1982) and the Mexican pact of national solidarity (1983) are much shorter and of a fairly general nature. Many of these agreements concluded in developing countries are tripartite. Quite often, governments have taken the most active part in their preparation, because they were very keen on promoting industrial peace in order to speed up the process of national development.

tation with the central trade union organisation concerned. On the other hand, the unions play a direct role in the distribution among manual and non-manual workers of numerous material benefits financed by the social consumption funds. These funds, which are administered at enterprise level, represent the resources earmarked by the State for various social purposes: the development of free general education and public health, scholarships, pensions, annual holidays, child care in pre-school establishments and other social allowances and benefits granted to citizens in addition to their wages. The social consumption funds, to which workers pay no direct contribution, are roughly equivalent in size to one-fifth of the workers' cash earnings.

In spite of its growing importance, the development of collective bargaining still runs up against difficulties. First, there continue to be countries where collective bargaining has been temporarily suspended as a result of political upheavals, or at least made subject to severe restrictions (see Chapter 4 for more details). Furthermore, collective bargaining is well established, generally speaking, only in industrial and commercial enterprises of a certain size. It is much less prevalent – and often even completely absent – in agricultural enterprises other than large plantations, in small industrial and commercial enterprises and in craftsmen's enterprises. The reasons are that in these enterprises the unions are often very weak, or do not exist at all, and that as a rule employers are not very open to the idea of collective bargaining. It must not be forgotten that these enterprises are particularly numerous in the developing countries, where they are part of the informal sector, which generally accounts for over 50 per cent – and sometimes even over 90 per cent – of all workers.

Collective bargaining in periods of economic difficulty

A major problem facing collective bargaining today is that it has to take place in a particularly difficult economic situation. In such circumstances the public authorities often fear that the free play of discussions between employers and workers may have harmful effects on the general economic situation of the country and they therefore try to exert unusually strong influence on collective bargaining. This, however, is by its nature a voluntary process and any attempt at external control is likely to undermine its essence.

The problem of government interference is not new in most countries of the Third World, which have almost always operated under severe economic constraints. In the industrialised market economy countries, on the other hand, it is more recent, since it is only since 1973 that they have encountered serious economic difficulties, marked principally by inflation and unemployment. The problem hardly arises, however, in the centrally planned economies. The main reason for this is that collective bargaining must in all circumstances take place within the limits laid down by the national plan and that it does not usually cover the total amount of wages (see box 3.3). To this may be added, as was pointed out in the Report of the Director-General to the Third European Regional Conference of the ILO (Geneva, 1979),[1] that the major problems affecting economic development are not the same in the countries of Western and Eastern Europe. As was already mentioned in Chapter 3 of Volume 1, the latter have to deal with a shortage of labour, which itself is closely related to the inadequate productivity both of labour and of capital.

When the developing countries became independent, they inherited systems of labour-management relations based on those of the colonial Powers and thus inevitably marked by Western conceptions. After a number of years, many observers claimed that these were unsuited to the requirements of rapid economic development in the countries of the Third World. In their view legislation that is too liberal in respect of labour-management relations will often lead to an excessive number of disputes or, at least, to a situation in which too many resources are devoted to consumption and too few to productive investment and employment creation. Furthermore, too liberal a system of labour-management relations, because limited almost wholly to the modern sector of the economy, will often lead to an even more unequal distribution of resources between this sector and the rural and urban informal sector. For these reasons, development policy should be the almost exclusive responsibility of the State, which, as guardian of the general interest, should supervise the trade unions, bring collective bargaining under its own control and prescribe a system of compulsory arbitration for labour disputes.

Many other observers, however, do not share these views, considering development to be a

3.3

Collective agreements and workers' participation in centrally planned economies

The system of centralised planning is perfectly compatible with the institution of collective bargaining, which is the key element in industrial relations in centrally planned economies. The outcome of collective bargaining has to reflect the possibilities offered by economic growth, and does not depend on the mere bargaining power of the parties involved. As a general rule, the trade union committee and management of the enterprise (or the production association) jointly prepare the draft agreement, taking into account the Plan's objectives, the funds earmarked to the enterprise and the requirements of social planning. There are usually three stages involved in the conclusion of a collective agreement: the drafting of the text; the discussion and approval of the draft by the general staff meeting (the standing production conference); the signing of the agreement by the head of the enterprise and the chairman of the trade union committee.

Each collective agreement lays down the workers' and management's reciprocal commitments to:

(1) implement the economic plan, making the fullest possible use of the know-how derived from scientific and technological progress;

(2) improve the organisation of work and output standards, and strengthen labour discipline;

(3) improve the system of workers' remuneration through judicious use of material incentives; raise the skills of manual and white-collar workers, engineers, technicians and managers.

Other clauses in the agreement cover such issues as workers' participation in production management, industrial safety, social amenities (accommodation and catering), cultural and sports services, social insurance and medical care.

Even though the text of collective agreements incorporates the remuneration rates and systems established by the government after consulting the central trade union organisation concerned, the existence of various material incentive funds ensures that the contracting parties have room to manoeuvre during collective bargaining. These funds are used for a wide range of bonuses, grants, benefits, social advantages or other wage supplements such as free accommodation in spas and convalescent establishments; opportunities to place children in day-care centres, kindergartens and pioneer camps; and cultural and sports activities. Any differences between the management and trade union committee concerning the content of the collective agreement are settled by economic bodies and trade unions at higher levels.

Although in most centrally planned economies collective agreements are signed every year at enterprise level, the central trade union organisations represent the interests of all workers (whether or not they belong to the union) in medium-term national planning (usually every five years); above all, they make sure that economic resources are distributed fairly between investments and consump-

tion, discuss the introduction of new pay systems and supervise the application of labour legislation. Indeed, the major decisions on production, investment and consumption are regarded as matters of general state policy. This is therefore the key level for collective bargaining in the centrally planned economies, especially when such policy takes the form of joint decisions by the Party, the State and the central trade union organisation.

The social ownership of the means of production and the system of centralised planning determine the character of workers' participation in the management of enterprises, which is carried out in various ways and at different levels. Alongside traditional forms of participation (by means of trade unions and collective bargaining), there are many institutions which guarantee this participation and give it a concrete form: joint meetings and committees, working groups, councils (for example, workers' councils, labour productivity councils), staff and union members' assemblies and conferences, workers' self-management bodies, standing production conferences, voluntary trade union committees, "creativity" organisations and people's supervisory bodies. Socialist emulation (continuous competition between enterprises, workshops, brigades and workers) is considered an important form of workers' direct participation in the management of the enterprise, alongside the mass movement of inventors and rationalisers.

Provisions concerning workers' direct participation in the management of production and social matters are contained in constitutions, labour codes and other legal texts. Participation in management is therefore a worker's right in the labour legislation of centrally planned economies; furthermore, it is binding on the management of enterprises, as well as on higher state and socio-economic bodies. Since the interests of trade unions, the State and the Party in centrally planned economies basically coincide, workers' participation does not involve the problems common to other countries in the world. However, in spite of the very high rate of union membership (more than 90 per cent of workers and employees), this participation is not yet total. It is both party and state policy to make constant efforts to perfect the system, and thereby ensure that the greatest possible number of workers participate in management. A new step in this direction was taken on 17 July 1983, when the Supreme Soviet of the USSR adopted the Act on workers' collectives and the extension of their role in the management of enterprises, establishments and organisations.

It is important to understand the dual role of trade unions in the process of participation in these countries: they both defend the workers' immediate interests and promote the wider interests of the State. All issues pertaining to labour and pay are dealt with jointly by the state bodies and the trade union representatives. The latter participate in the drawing up and the implementation of economic and social development plans. For example, in the USSR, the State has entrusted the trade unions with drawing up and administering that part of the national budget which is devoted to social security.

process in which all groups should participate. In their view, productive activities can only be ensured in a lasting way if the parties enter freely into the necessary commitments, for experience shows that the mere legal prohibition of disputes is often not very effective. They also consider that a true development policy is always a compromise between different interests; in other words, there is always a trade-off between the improvement of wages and conditions of work, an increase in productive capital and the transfer of income from the stronger to the weaker sectors of the economy. A development policy has little chance of success if it is not based on the general agreement of all who are to apply it. In these circumstances, collective bargaining can play a central part in the development policy, since its very purpose is to make compromise possible. Accordingly, if collective bargaining is to have its fullest effect, representative organisations of employers and workers need to be developed, the machinery to ensure orderly discussions between the parties must be set up and the necessary steps taken to ensure that any disputes arising during these discussions can, as far as possible, be settled amicably.

It is obviously not easy for the governments of developing countries to choose between the above alternatives. The temptation of the restrictive approach is certainly very strong, particularly in periods of acute economic difficulties, and many countries have taken this course in the past or still resort to it. Nevertheless, the idea seems to be gaining ground that greater freedom of movement for employers and workers and their organisations can contribute effectively to the success of a national development policy, because it allows this policy to be firmly based on the agreement of all. Many developing countries have therefore tried to establish procedures which, although they reserve for the State a considerably greater part in labour-management relations than in the industrialised market economies, do allow collective bargaining to function, through the conclusion of collective agreements (generally at the enterprise level), or through other forms of bipartite or tripartite

discussions. Most governments of South Asia thus consider at present that collective agreements are generally a suitable means of fixing wages and conditions of employment and should be encouraged. For example, there have been official campaigns to promote collective agreements in Indonesia and the Philippines, and they have long been an essential element in the labour relations systems of India and Sri Lanka. In Malaysia and Thailand, efforts to promote collective bargaining even led to the signature, in 1975 and 1981, of industrial relations codes of practice by the central employers' and workers' organisations and the Government. The purpose of these tripartite documents is to develop relations between the parties in a spirit of co-operation. In 1972 the Government of Singapore, also following the tripartite approach, set up a tripartite National Wages Council, which every year publishes directives (not binding but in fact very effective) intended to align the wage clauses of collective agreements on the general economic trends of the country. Furthermore, central tripartite consultation meetings are frequently held in certain Asian countries, including India and Pakistan, to discuss current major problems. The conclusion of collective agreements is also encouraged in many African countries, both English- and French-speaking, and industrial relations codes of practice, similar to those negotiated in Malaysia and Thailand, have been concluded in several African countries, including Kenya and Sierra Leone. At the same time a number of countries in Latin America have tried generally to free collective bargaining from the machinery for settling labour disputes. As a result of these efforts, the number of disputes settled exclusively by direct contacts between the parties (that is to say without resort to the official conciliation and arbitration machinery) and of negotiations undertaken without any open dispute between the parties concerned has considerably increased in many countries of this region.[2]

None the less, in the great majority of developing countries the public authorities still exert a

41

comparatively strong influence on labour-management relations, particularly as regards the structure and functioning of employers' and workers' organisations, the procedure of collective bargaining and the settlement of labour disputes. (The restrictions imposed by the authorities on freedom of association and the right to strike are considered elsewhere in this report (Chapter 4).) Moreover, recent measures very often provide that wage agreements are to remain within certain limits fixed by the authorities or that they must be approved by the authorities before they can come into force. The authorities have sometimes even removed certain subjects from the scope of negotiation, frozen wages for a certain period or themselves fixed the maximum amount of increases permissible during a specified period.

In the industrialised market economy countries, many governments, particularly in Western Europe, have – since the beginning of the economic crisis – also started to play a more active part in labour-management relations. Their action however has generally been much less vigorous than in the developing countries, for two reasons: first, it relates only to collective bargaining proper and is not intended to supervise or control the employers' and workers' organisations or to restrict the right to strike; secondly, the influence that the public authorities try to exert on collective bargaining is generally less coercive and more selective than in the Third World.

Indeed, a rapid survey of the past ten years clearly shows that the industrialised market economies are reluctant to take compulsory measures and have more faith in the virtues of persuasion, discussion and compromise. Canada and the United States continue as a rule to place their confidence in freely negotiated collective agreements. On the other hand, the governments of many Western European countries and Japan often try at central tripartite meetings to steer the conclusion of collective agreements towards the

solution of the major economic and social problems facing society as a whole. In many of these countries informal meetings of the kind take place almost continually on the various problems raised by inflation and unemployment. Very often, however, there are meetings of a more formal nature that follow a specified institutional and procedural pattern or result in the signing of actual agreements.

There are various examples of tripartite consultation that have worked successfully for long periods, such as the "concerted action" instituted in the Federal Republic of Germany in 1967[3] and the Government-employers-workers round table (Sanrokon) that has operated in Japan since 1975. Under both systems tripartite meetings are held periodically at a very high level to discuss the important economic and social problems of the moment and to contribute to their solution through joint action. A special characteristic of these meetings is that the autonomy of the employers' and workers' organisations is not at all restricted.

Another example is provided by Austria where the Joint Committee on Prices and Wages and its subcommittees have been playing a very important part in the fixing of wages since 1957. The Joint Committee, which is tripartite in composition, was set up by the Federal Government on the proposal of the trade unions. Its decisions are taken unanimously, but the Government representatives have waived their right to vote since 1966. The unions have undertaken to submit all their wage claims to the Joint Committee, which then has to consider not so much the extent of the claims as the choice of the moment for concluding a new collective agreement. If the Committee fails to reach an agreement – which has not happened for many years – negotiations on the claims in question can start after a period of 11 weeks.

Yet another method of tripartite wage fixing has been used in certain European countries, including Belgium, Ireland, Italy, the Netherlands, the Scandinavian countries and Spain. Since the beginning of the last recession, wages policy in these countries has often been determined in central framework agreements (that is to say agreements that lay down only general principles to which a more explicit form is given later in collective agreements concluded at lower levels). The governments have made a decisive contribution to the working out of these central agreements, although they have not always been parties officially. The signature of most of these agreements, indeed, has been possible only because the governments, along with the employers and workers, also accepted certain commitments aimed, for example, at creating employment or at reducing taxes on wages and the employers' contributions to social security. These commitments of the government then made it possible for the employers' and workers' organisations to accept the wage clauses of the agreements in question which were considered too generous by the former and too limited by the latter. This system of central framework agreements has introduced two innovations. The first is obviously that agreements that have hitherto been bipartite are now tripartite – if not always in law, at least in fact. The second is that wage bargaining, at least in respect of the fixing of general principles, has been raised to the central level, except, of course, in certain countries such as the Scandinavian countries, where central bargaining has existed for many years. It may even be said that in the European countries mentioned in this paragraph the process of tripartite consultation and that of the negotiation of central framework agreements have often been merged.

Although the governments of the industrialised market economy countries generally prefer the voluntarist approach, whether bipartite or tripartite, for solving the problems arising from the recession, they sometimes consider that all the possibilities of this approach have been exhausted without much success. As a result, many of them

have adopted provisions to restrict the autonomy of the employers' and workers' organisations. The nature and scope of these provisions, which are normally applied only for short periods, vary greatly: sometimes, they simply restrict or prohibit the adjustment of the highest wages to the cost-of-living index; sometimes, they place certain ceilings on wage increases; yet again, they may decree a more or less general freezing of prices and wages for a limited period. Even though actions of this kind are never taken light-heartedly, most governments of the industrialised market economy countries have instituted some coercive measures during the past ten years. To give a few examples, one could mention the case of Denmark where an austerity programme was imposed by law; this included a wage freeze, a temporary suspension of the automatic wage indexation system, an increase in social security contributions and cuts in social benefits. In Canada, legislation determined the maximum permissible wage increases in the Federal Civil Service under the Public Sector Compensation Restraint Act of 1982. Wage and price freezes lasting limited periods have also been in force in France. Restrictive measures of various kinds have similarly been taken in other countries such as Belgium and the Netherlands.

Our analysis shows that in periods of economic difficulty, collective bargaining in market economy countries has been characterised by three principal features. The first is that the balance between freedom and constraint in collective bargaining varies considerably between countries and over time. The second is that most industrialised market economies and also certain developing countries realise that the principal economic and social problems cannot, in the long run, be solved by coercive measures. Canada and the United States seem to prefer the unrestricted negotiation of collective agreements, whereas most of the countries of Western Europe, Japan and certain countries of the Third World seem to prefer some form of tripartite consultation as a means of influencing the negotiation of collective agreements. The third of the findings is that the decisions or guide-lines that arise out of tripartite consultation seem difficult, and often impossible, to put into practice if the collective agreements are negotiated in too decentralised a way. This is why, with the exception of, for example, Japan (where collective agreements are negotiated for the enterprise), the process of tripartite consultation has developed properly only in countries where branch bargaining is the rule and why it has often even led to the development of central bargaining. It has therefore been suggested that the developing countries should now negotiate agreements not only at the enterprise but also at the branch level in order to create a link between the summit and the base and so to permit the development of really effective central tripartite consultation.[4]

However, the possibilities of centralised collective bargaining are not unlimited. National practices in respect of the level of bargaining are so firmly rooted in tradition and so dependent on a number of other factors, such as the extent to which employers' and workers' organisations are centralised, that it would be difficult to change these practices in the short run. Furthermore, in certain countries, including Canada and the United States, the centralisation of collective bargaining and hence of the employers' and workers' organisations does not .even seem to be desired, because it would be considered incompatible with the free functioning of markets.

So far we have looked only at the consequences of the difficult economic situation for certain procedural aspects of collective bargaining. It is obvious, however, that the recession has also had a considerable impact on the content of bargaining. The major issues here are the protection of employment, the stagnation or even decrease of real wages and the whole question of wage indexation. These issues were discussed in detail in the chapter on wages and incomes in Volume 1 of this report.

Workers' participation in decisions within undertakings

The term "workers' participation in decisions within undertakings" at present covers four principal mechanisms: workers' self-management, the representation of workers on the managing bodies of the enterprises (often called "co-determination"), participation in works councils or similar bodies, and the special systems in force in most of the centrally planned economies of Eastern Europe.

From the conceptual point of view, self-management is the most advanced form of participation, since it implies the management of the enterprises by their own workers. It came into existence in Yugoslavia at the end of the Second World War and is now almost universal there. Forms of participation based on Yugoslav self-management also exist, though generally on a limited scale, in certain other countries, most of them in the developing world.

The presence of workers' representatives beside those of the shareholders on the managing bodies of enterprises – that is to say the boards of directors or supervisory boards and sometimes the bodies responsible for day-to-day administration – is found in many public enterprises in all parts of the world, generally on a minority basis. In private enterprises, this form of representation is extremely rare outside north-western Europe and systems attaining parity or coming close to parity have been introduced only in the Federal Republic of Germany.

Works councils or similar bodies – which are widespread in Western Europe, though also found in smaller numbers in certain African and Asian countries – are composed either of representatives of the workers and the management or of representatives of the workers alone. They are established as a rule by law but sometimes also by collective agreements, and they generally have the right to be kept informed on the economic and financial situation of the enterprise and its prospects, particularly in respect of employment. They also have the right to be consulted and – at least in Western Europe – certain powers of co-determination covering a number of social and staff questions (for example the beginning and end of the working day; methods of calculating and paying wages; the prevention of industrial accidents; general criteria for recruitment, promotion and dismissal and, in certain cases, individual decisions in these fields).

In the centrally planned economies of Eastern Europe – other than those where some form of self-management has been adopted – the participation of workers is based mainly on direct relations between the management and the trade union, which brings together in a single structure all the manual and non-manual workers of each enterprise and co-operates closely with the party in power. The union exercises its functions through several bodies, the most important of which is the enterprise trade union committee. The functions of the union, which frequently extend to co-determination, relate mainly to the management of production, social planning, conditions of employment, staff questions, labour inspection and the welfare and recreation of the workers (see also box 3.3).

What is the difference between participation and collective bargaining and how do they coexist? These questions arise mainly in market economy countries, which for this reason will be considered first. Collective bargaining and participation have basically the same purpose, namely to associate workers in the taking of the decisions that concern them. Collective bargaining is thus a form of participation in the broad sense, and vice versa. There are, however, differences between the two institutions.

The first difference concerns the partner on the workers' side. Traditionally, collective bargaining is considered to be an exclusive prerogative of the trade unions, which represent as a rule only the unionised workers, whereas the workers' representatives on the various participation bodies represent all the workers of the enterprise, whether they belong to a union or not. It is no doubt true that in many countries collective agreements negotiated by the trade unions apply – if not in law at least in fact – to all the workers, including non-unionists, and it is also true that the workers' representatives in the participation bodies are very often in practice active trade unionists. Although, then, this first distinction may to some extent be theoretical, it is no less important from either the conceptual or the practical point of view: one of its consequences is that the trade unions tend to be suspicious of participation when they have reason to believe that it will be so used as to encroach on their collective bargaining powers.

The second difference between collective bargaining and participation concerns the extent to which the workers' representatives can influence the decisions to be taken. Where there is participation, the workers can obstruct a decision only in a few cases (for example that of equal representation in a supervisory board or a board of directors or that of powers of co-determination on a works council), whereas they can always do so under collective bargaining, since no collective agreement can be concluded without the consent of the trade unions.

The third difference relates to the subjects dealt with. Broadly speaking, the purpose of collective bargaining is to deal with conflictual matters – mainly wages and basic conditions of work – whereas the machinery of participation is used to deal with questions on which employers' and workers' interests tend to converge, such as the economic and financial management of the enterprise. This criterion has had a strong influence on the legislation of the Federal Republic of Germany concerning works councils, which contains a section providing that "the employer and the works council shall work together in a spirit of mutual trust".[5] The legislation also provides that a dispute in the works council shall not give rise to a strike or lock-out – as it may in collective bargaining – but shall be submitted to arbitration. The distinction should not, however, be interpreted too narrowly: in Italy, for example, collective bargaining is practically the only channel of communication between employers and workers and is sometimes also used for dealing with subjects such as the investment policy of the enterprise; in the Federal Republic of Germany, too, the discussions in the works councils on the "social plan" to cope with possible redundancies sometimes have a strong resemblance to conflictual bargaining.

The most important difference between collective bargaining and participation is that, unlike a trade union signing a collective agreement, the workers' representatives who participate in the taking of decisions assume responsibility for the decision taken. It may even be said that in the long run greater participation leads to a closer integration of workers into the existing economic and social system.

The distinction between collective bargaining and participation is much less sharp in self-management systems, where collective bargaining plays only a very modest role. The question does not arise acutely in centrally planned economies either, where almost all workers are trade union members and where the distinctions between conflictual and non-conflictual matters and between responsibility and non-responsibility for the decisions taken are much more blurred than in the market economy countries.

Some trade unions in the latter countries regard participation negatively, or at least without enthusiasm. Such an attitude may be due to any one of the following three reasons. Firstly, there are trade unions that follow the Marxist ideology and reject any real form of participation because they will on no account have any part in the market economy system. Next, there are unions like the

AFL-CIO in the United States that do not wish to have anything to do with the management of the enterprises – which, they maintain, must remain a prerogative of the employers. They believe that all problems arising between employers and workers should be dealt with by means of collective bargaining. Lastly, there are unions that, without being opposed to participation in principle, are afraid that employers may use it to weaken the position of the unions in the enterprise and to hamper, or even prevent, the normal operation of collective bargaining. The coexistence of participation and collective bargaining gives rise to particularly acute problems in countries where collective bargaining takes place at the enterprise level and where the unions are not yet sufficiently established to insist on their rights. This is particularly true in a number of developing countries in Asia, Africa and Latin America where the unions are often indifferent, or indeed hostile, to works councils and other possible forms of participation. Recent experience seems to show that this hesitancy of the trade unions can be overcome only if they are fully associated in the process of participation, for example through the strong representation of unionised workers on the participation bodies.

The history of participation started in the Scandinavian countries where it is still most firmly established. In these countries there was a vacuum to fill, because unions were mainly active outside the enterprise and collective bargaining was traditionally carried out at the branch level. With the passage of years, participation has been regarded more and more as a method of taking decisions with its own merits that can usefully supplement collective bargaining rather than replace it. However, in countries where collective bargaining takes place at the enterprise level, the distinction between collective bargaining and participation is not always maintained very strictly and certain problems may be dealt with successively by bargaining bodies and by participation bodies. This is shown very clearly by surveys that are carried out periodically in Japan, where enterprise bargaining and bodies of the works council type are found together.

If participation is to be a success, it must on no account be used against the trade unions. Another extremely important condition – which is obvious but far from being observed universally – is that the workers' representatives should have received adequate training for their functions and that they should enjoy the necessary protection and facilities.

Another very important condition is that there should be no misunderstanding about the aims being pursued, which can – roughly speaking – be of an ethical, a politico-social or an economic nature. In the first case, participation is mainly intended to promote the personal development of the worker. In the second, its main purpose is to achieve industrial democracy, i.e. to give the workers more influence on economic decisions. In the third, its main purpose is to create an atmosphere of peace and co-operation conducive to greater productivity and efficiency in the enterprise.

It is obviously possible to pursue more than one of these aims at the same time. It can also happen that the social partners disagree on the aims to be pursued by the national system of participation. Recent experience also shows, however, that such a system may not work in a satisfactory way if each of the parties attaches a completely different priority to these aims. Normally, a situation of this sort should no longer arise in the industrialised market economies, where the principal aim of trade unions today invariably seems to be to increase their influence in the enterprise, and the employers – although they may not necessarily like it – are fully aware of this. In most developing countries, on the other hand, one often finds a sharper contrast between the aims of the employers and the government, whose main objective is increased productivity, and those of the unions, whose primary concern is to exert greater influence on economic decisions.

Systems of participation have recently encountered a new difficulty in the developing countries. Contrary to what happens in industrialised market economies, several governments of developing countries have taken the initiative of introducing systems of participation (generally to improve the economic performance of the enterprises), which the unions have never really called for. It need hardly be said that the unions seldom show much enthusiasm for putting such a system into practice.

So far we have looked at the various problems related at present with participation. These problems have not, however, prevented participation from developing greatly over the past 15 to 20 years. It is indeed no exaggeration to say that participation is a concept that has aroused marked interest in all parts of the world and that it is still under active discussion in many countries. To put the point neatly: "workers' participation is no longer a question of 'whether' but of 'how'".[6] In other words, while the principle of participation is established, the systems applied vary greatly between countries and over time. An influential factor was the development of the self-management system in Yugoslavia which – with some variations – has been introduced in certain enterprises in Algeria, Israel, Madagascar, Malta, the United Republic of Tanzania and elsewhere. On the other hand, experiments with self-management carried out in some countries of Latin America, including Peru, have been practically abandoned. Furthermore, trade union participation has greatly increased in Eastern Europe since the economic reform carried out at the end of the 1960s. That reform increased the autonomy of the enterprises and provided that when they reached or exceeded the planned objectives, they could use part of the profits for workers' wage or welfare funds. Many developing countries have attempted to increase participation, particularly through works councils and workers' representation on the boards of companies, the latter form of participation however being almost always confined to public enterprises. In Western Europe, the work-

47

3.4

Workers' participation in the Federal Republic of Germany

Under an Act of 21 May 1951 applicable to large companies in the mining and iron and steel industries, the workers appoint to the supervisory board the same number of members as appointed by the shareholders. An additional independent member is appointed jointly by the two sides. Two of the worker members – one wage earner and one salaried employee – come from within the company and are elected by its works council; the remaining worker members are appointed by the trade union concerned.

The supervisory board appoints the management board of the company, which it supervises and to which it provides general policy guidance. One of the (usually three) members of the management board responsible for current business matters, the "labour manager", may be appointed or removed only with the consent of the majority of the worker members of the supervisory board. This person, who is therefore in fact a workers' appointee, is in charge of all labour and personnel matters in the company; he also participates on an equal footing in all decisions coming within the competence of the management board as a whole.

Under an Act of 11 October 1952, applicable to companies employing between 500 and 2,000 workers in the other sectors of the economy, the workforce elects by direct and secret ballot one-third of the membership of the supervisory board. (Two of the workers' representatives must be employees from within the company, while the others may be trade union officials.)

Under an Act of 4 May 1976, the supervisory boards of companies employing more than 2,000 workers outside the mining and iron and steel industries have a quasi parity worker representation (the chairman who has a casting vote is in practice always a shareholder representative). Among the workers' representatives there must be a proportionate number of executives.

Works councils are regulated by the Act of 15 January 1972 and are compulsory in all undertakings employing five workers or more. The whole workforce of the undertaking elects the members of the works council by secret ballot, with proportional representation for wage earners and salaried employees. Each establishment of an undertaking has its own council, while a central works council is set up for the undertaking as a whole. In the case of a combine, there is provision for the possibility of having a works council for the combine.

The employer and the works council collaborate in good faith within the framework of the collective agreements (they may not have recourse to strikes or lock-outs in their relationships) and in co-operation with the trade unions and employers' organisations. They may conclude company and/or plant agreements, under certain conditions. The works council also deals with grievance settlement.

The works council receives prior information and is consulted on such matters as the construction and transformation of premises, installations and processes, recruitments, promotions, transfers, and individual and collective dismissals (in specified cases it is entitled to object to them on certain grounds). It has the right of co-determination on guide-lines on a number of matters, such as guide-lines on recruitment, transfers, regradings and dismissals; the commencement and termination of the daily working hours; disciplinary measures; determination of principles governing wages and payment by results; vocational training; and the organisation and management of welfare services. A "social plan" must be set up when major changes contemplated would lead to unfavourable repercussions for the personnel.

Each year, the employer or his representative must report to a general staff meeting on the situation of the undertaking and on personnel matters.

In establishments with more than 20 workers, safety representatives are appointed by the employer in consultation with the works council. In establishments employing at least five workers under the age of 18, young workers' representatives are elected by direct secret ballot for a term of two years. These representatives take part in the works council's discussions, and vote on matters directly concerning young workers. They are also allowed to make their own proposals to the council.

In undertakings employing over 100 workers the works council appoints an economic committee which may include senior executives and which receives information from the employer each month on production methods and plans and the financial situation of the undertaking. It must be informed of investment plans, structural changes and any project that could substantially affect the interests of the staff.

ers' representation on the boards of companies expanded greatly during the first half of the 1970s, a period when it was considerably strengthened in the Federal Republic of Germany (see box 3.4) and introduced in other countries including Denmark, the Netherlands, Norway and Sweden. Contrary to the expectations of some people, however, this movement has slowed down recently. This is illustrated by the fact that the draft text of the Fifth Directive of the Commission of the European Communities, which aims at extending this form of participation to all the countries of the Community, has still not been adopted at the present time. It had to be toned down several times because employers, certain governments and certain trade unions expressed strong reservations.

The most important development that has occurred during the past five or six years in Western Europe is probably the growing importance of the works councils: for one thing, they have been set up in new sectors of activity such as the public service, small- and medium-sized enterprises and the tertiary sector; and for another, they have much more say in questions of safety, health and vocational training, but also – and this is important in the present economic situation – in decisions about collective dismissals.[7]

Collective labour disputes

A growing number of countries divide labour disputes into two large groups: conflicts of law and conflicts of interest. Conflicts of law, or legal disputes, concern the interpretation or application of an existing legal rule, such as a law or a collective agreement. Conflicts of interest, or economic disputes, arise during collective bargaining on a new union claim, e.g. for higher wages or shorter hours of work. Another distinction, of French origin, is that between individual and collective disputes, which continues to be made in a number of countries, including Belgium, Spain, certain countries of Latin America and the French-speaking countries of Africa. This distinction is in fact a subdistinction within the group of legal disputes, for in practice conflicts of interest are always collective.

The distinction between legal disputes and conflicts of interest has become more important because it has been introduced over the past ten to 15 years in many developing countries. This happened for example in Malaysia and Sri Lanka, whose original legal system was strongly influenced by the British system, in which this distinction was completely ignored for many years and is still practically non-existent for a number of reasons that cannot be gone into here. The increasingly widespread adoption of this distinction has had considerable consequences in practice. The idea underlying it is that in a modern State only conflicts of interest can lead to strikes or other forms of direct action, whereas legal disputes must be submitted to the binding decision of a labour court or similar body.

Since a detailed discussion of the structure, competence and procedures of labour courts and other bodies responsible for settling legal disputes would probably be of too technical a nature, this section will deal only with conflicts of interest. Furthermore, it does not cover the centrally planned economies, where collective bargaining is defined not as a conflictual process but as a means of ensuring full co-operation between the managers of enterprises and the workers in carrying out economic and social plans. In these countries, the occurrence of interest disputes between the parties to collective bargaining is regarded as almost impossible, and in Yugoslavia as quite improbable.

Collective labour disputes – at least where they come to a trial of strength – are always spectacular events that the mass media are delighted to seize on and to which they tend to give exaggerated importance. The public is thus likely to lose sight of the fact that only a negligible number of negotiations end in open dispute. Care must therefore be taken not to exaggerate the numerical importance of labour disputes.

Nor is there good reason to conclude that labour disputes, particularly when they lead to direct action, no longer have any place in a modern State. First of all, in a pluralist society some disputes seem inevitable and are part of the dynamics of labour-management relations. Since collective bargaining is essentially a means of settling problems through agreements reached freely between all the parties concerned, it implies by its very definition the possibility of disagreement. In other words, whoever is in favour of collective bargaining must, by that very fact, accept the possibility of disputes.

Broadly speaking, there are two principal methods of settling labour disputes that appear to be deadlocked: conciliation and arbitration. Conciliation, which is in fact assisted negotiation, implies that an independent third party helps the parties to resume their discussion and reach agreement, on the understanding that if their efforts are unsuccessful, each of them will be free to resort to a trial of strength. Conciliation may be provided for by law or a collective agreement and, in either case, recourse to it may be compulsory or voluntary. Arbitration, which is brought into play as a rule only after the failure of conciliation, implies that the dispute shall be settled by the binding decision of an independent third party. Like conciliation, arbitration may be based on a law or a collective agreement. Similarly, the parties may be obliged or not, as the case may be, to place their dispute before an arbitrator. In practice, recourse to strikes or other forms of direct action is virtually out of the question under systems of compulsory arbitration.

Practically speaking, the industrialised market economies have only one legal method of settling labour disputes, namely conciliation in its various forms. It is true that voluntary procedures of arbitration have also been set up in most of these countries, but they are hardly ever used. Compulsory arbitration is laid down only for exceptional cases such as disputes in the essential services or, should the case arise, in the public service.

The general approach adopted by the industrialised market economies to the problem of labour disputes is based on the same philosophy as collective bargaining. Successful conciliation amounts in fact to agreement between the parties, in the same way as a collective agreement, and thus has the same advantages over any solution imposed from outside. The fact that this system has not undergone any fundamental change in many years must no doubt be explained by a very deeply rooted ideology underlying the political, economic and social organisation of industrialised market economies. It seems, indeed, that the only significant development in recent years has been a less frequent recourse to compulsory arbitration in

the public service in some of these countries, for example Canada.

In a good many of the countries of Africa, Asia and Latin America compulsory arbitration is much more important than in the industrialised market economies. In certain extreme cases any dispute that is not settled by conciliation is automatically submitted to arbitration. More often, such a dispute is placed before an arbitrator only if the government so decides. In a number of countries, the government can exercise this power only for certain categories of disputes considered to be particularly serious – because they affect an "essential service" or jeopardise the "national interest" – but very often these concepts are so broadly defined that the restriction on the powers of the government has little effect in practice.

The way in which the developing countries approach the problem of settling labour disputes can obviously be explained by the fear that leaving too much liberty to the social partners may have damaging effects on the economy, because strikes or other forms of direct action may lead to losses of production.

The legislation on the settlement of labour disputes in the developing countries has not changed fundamentally in recent years. However, in a number of developing countries it has recently undergone certain amendments. Not all these amendments have the same purpose, since some liberalise existing legislation, whereas others make it more restrictive. Even when these amendments are intended to liberalise existing texts, they may not necessarily reduce the importance of compulsory arbitration but rather introduce minor technical adjustments.

In practice compulsory arbitration in developing countries plays a much less prominent role than could be expected on the basis of existing legislation. The great majority of disputes are settled at the stage of conciliation and so never reach that of

50

arbitration. Experience also shows that governments do not necessarily submit to arbitration all the disputes that have not been settled during conciliation. Furthermore, it is certain that when an arbitrator is actually dealing with a dispute he will generally make a final attempt at conciliation before deciding to impose his own solution on the parties. Lastly, it may be added that legislation placing severe restrictions on the right to direct action is as a rule not particularly effective and very often fails to prevent disputes from coming to a trial of strength.

Most countries today recognise the right to strike and the right to declare a lock-out in enterprises of the private sector that are not considered essential. However, this recognition is to a large extent theoretical in countries where compulsory arbitration has an important place. The right to strike in the public service is explicitly recognised at present only in some 15 countries, including Canada, France, the Ivory Coast, Mexico, Norway, Portugal and Sweden. The right of public servants to strike is also tolerated to a varying degree in a number of other countries, including Israel, Italy and the United Kingdom. Practically all countries have provisions that prohibit strikes in essential services or, at least, restrict recourse to strikes in order to ensure that truly vital services can continue to operate. Legislation and the case law on lock-outs have sometimes tended to become narrower in recent years and to recognise only the defensive lock-out, that is to say the lock-out through which an employer tries to protect himself against a strike that has already started. This is the position, for example, in the Federal Republic of Germany.

Of greater practical interest are recent trends in the number of days of work lost as a result of strikes or lock-outs in the various countries. However, it is very difficult to collect reliable and comparable statistics on this subject. For example, the ILO *Year Book of Labour Statistics* gives only absolute figures (by country and by branch of activity) on the number of disputes, the number of workers involved and the number of working days lost. It gives no information on the percentage of days lost in total hours worked, because it is extremely difficult to measure the latter concept, particularly in countries where the informal sector is very important. In addition, as the *Year Book* states, absolute figures on days lost are difficult to compare because of the " variation between countries in definitions, sources, scope and statistical treatment of data at country level". None the less, information from the *Year Book*, supplemented by that from some other national and international sources, permits a few general observations.

The number of working days lost owing to strikes follows a very irregular pattern in many countries. In the short run, changes seem to be due to more or less unpredictable causes such as a change of political regime, the renegotiation of a large number of collective agreements during a given year, or even the exceptional importance of a certain dispute.

When the matter is considered over a longer period, no basic trend can be detected either towards an increase in the number of disputes or towards the reduction predicted by Ross and Hartman in 1960.[8] If only the industrialised market economies are considered – and they are practically the only countries for which available statistics cover a long period – it does appear that the late 1940s and early 1950s were rather agitated, that there was then a comparatively calm period up to the end of the 1960s and that the years from 1968 to 1972 were particularly turbulent. Contrary to what might be expected, the crisis that started in 1973-74 did not immediately result in a sharp reduction in the number of working days lost. The number was lower than during the period 1968-72 but above the level of the 1950s and 1960s. Between 1973 and 1980 questions concerning security of employment gave rise to an increasing number of disputes, some of which have been particularly long and severe and at times assumed new forms such as the occupation of a plant. The reason is probably that inflation, the recession and unemployment have often affected the most vital interests of the parties and thus led them to adopt intransigent attitudes. However, during the past two or three years the number of working days lost has fallen appreciably in a good many countries. This may well be due to the prolonged crisis, although events are still too recent for a confident assertion on this matter.

The distribution of lost working days by sector of activity or group of workers clearly reflects the changes in the relative importance of these sectors and groups in the national economy. Accordingly, in a number of countries, there has been a reduction in lost days in the mines and certain sectors of manufacturing industry while there has been an increase among teachers, in certain branches of the tertiary sector and in the public service.

Another remarkable fact is that there have been very few and very slow changes over the years in the relative propensity of the various countries to labour disputes. The reason is probably that the factors determining the number and length of strikes in a given country are deeply rooted in the national history and traditions and in its current values and attitudes.

The same explanation applies in the other fields of labour-management relations such as collective bargaining and the participation of workers in decisions. In other words, any national system of labour-management relations is first and foremost a product of the environment in which it has developed. It follows that the basic characteristics of labour-management systems change very slowly and that these systems can never be transplanted without adaptation from one country to another.

[1] For further details on the situation in the socialist countries of Eastern Europe, see ILO: *Growth, structural change and manpower policy: The challenge of the 1980s,* Report I, Report of the Director-General, Third European Regional Conference, Geneva, 1979.

[2] For further details on the situation in the countries of Latin America and certain countries of Asia, see Córdova, op. cit., and Schregle, op. cit. (Geneva, ILO, 1982).

[3] Concerted action has not been practised for some years, for the trade unions refuse to take part owing to a difference of opinion with the employers on a problem that has no connection with the questions normally discussed in concerted action.

[4] Schregle, op. cit., pp. 110-111.

[5] Works Constitution Act of January 1972, S. 2 (1). See ILO: *Legislative Series*, 1972 — Ger.F.R. 1.

[6] J. Schregle: "Workers' participation in decisions within undertakings", in *International Labour Review*, Jan.-Feb. 1976, p. 15.

[7] See E. Córdova: "Workers' participation in decisions within enterprises: Recent trends and problems", ibid., Mar.-Apr. 1982, pp. 125 ff.

[8] A. M. Ross and P. T. Hartman: *Changing patterns of industrial conflict* (New York, Wiley, 1960).

Part **2**

International labour standards

Introduction

Since 1919 the ILO has adopted 159 Conventions and 168 Recommendations covering a broad range of social problems. These instruments deal with basic human rights, such as freedom of association, freedom from forced labour and freedom from discrimination. They cover employment and training, conditions of work, occupational safety and health, social security, migrant workers, employment of children and young persons, employment of seafarers, fishermen, dockworkers and other occupational categories such as plantation workers and nurses. More than a quarter of the Conventions have been revised by later instruments. The application of Conventions is supervised by a Committee of Experts and a special Committee of the ILO Conference (see box).

On 1 June 1984 a total of 5,148 ratifications had been registered. The average number of ratifications per member State was 34. Average ratifications per State in the various regions were: Europe – 57 (Western Europe – 60, Eastern Europe – 50), Americas – 38, Africa – 26, Asia and the Pacific – 20. Annex 2 to this report shows the number of ratifications per member State, while Annex 3

International labour standards: Concepts and supervision *

The ILO Constitution provides for the adoption of international labour standards in the form of Conventions and Recommendations. A Convention is open to ratification by the free decision of each member State; ratification creates the obligation to make its provisions effective in national law and practice. Recommendations are not open to ratification, but are aimed at providing guidance to national policies and action.

Countries that ratify Conventions must make regular reports to the International Labour Office on the measures they have taken to give effect to the provisions of these instruments. A committee of independent experts appointed by the Governing Body of the ILO examines these reports to determine whether the provisions of the Conventions have been applied in national law and practice. The findings of this examination are then discussed by a committee consisting of Government, Workers' and Employers' delegates appointed by each general session of the International Labour Conference. The Constitution also provides for the examination of complaints and representations alleging non-observance of ratified Conventions. In addition, there is a special Governing Body

Committee on Freedom of Association to examine complaints of violation of freedom of association, which submits its conclusions and recommendations to the Governing Body. Such cases may be referred to the Fact-Finding and Conciliation Committee on Freedom of Association.

The ILO has also developed a series of practical measures aimed at helping member States to deal with questions concerning the adoption, ratification, implementation and reporting on the application of ILO standards.

A distinctive feature of the ILO's supervisory system is the active participation in it of employers' and workers' organisations. They are represented in the various ILO committees dealing with labour standards. They contribute to the adoption and review of implementing measures at the national level. And finally, they can be sources of information for ILO supervisory bodies and initiators of complaints and representations.

* The Report of the Director-General to the International Labour Conference at its 70th Session, 1984, contains a special part reviewing the functioning of ILO standard-setting and supervisory procedures.

shows to what extent individual countries have ratified selected basic human rights Conventions (on freedom of association, freedom from forced labour and discrimination).

This part will discuss some international labour standards in three important fields of labour relations. They concern freedom of association, freedom from forced labour and the protection of workers against arbitrary termination of their employment. As we saw in the first part, collective labour relations can only function meaningfully if workers and employers have the full freedom both to set up their own organisations and to undertake collective bargaining. Moreover, a basic principle governing the individual employment relationship is that there should be free choice of work: no one should be compelled to work without his consent, or under the threat of any penalty. A further dimension of the worker's free choice of work is that he should not be arbitrarily deprived of a job. To this end, standards have been adopted to define some conditions under which employers may not terminate the employment of workers.

Chapter 4 reviews the problems that arise in the application of the Conventions on freedom of association, collective bargaining and rural workers' organisations; Chapter 5 deals with the question of forced labour. Both chapters draw upon the assessments made by the Committee of Experts. These assessments do not have the force of authoritative pronouncements of law but in the great majority of cases they are accepted by the governments concerned. Chapter 6 gives an overview of the national law and practice on the matters dealt with in the Termination of Employment Convention and Recommendation. Having been adopted only in 1982, the Convention has so far been ratified by only a few countries.

Chapter **4**

Freedom of association

Three ILO Conventions in particular deal with freedom of association: the Freedom of Association and Protection of the Right to Organise Convention, 1948 (No. 87); the Right to Organise and Collective Bargaining Convention, 1949 (No. 98); and the Rural Workers' Organisations Convention, 1975 (No. 141). On 1 June 1984 96 member States (out of a total of 150) had ratified the first, 111 the second and 24 the third. The relatively small number of ratifications of this last Convention is due to the fact that it was adopted only in 1975.

The Freedom of Association and Protection of the Right to Organise Convention lays down a basic human right in providing that "workers and employers . . . have the right to establish and . . . to join organisations of their own choosing without previous authorisation". It further stipulates that workers' and employers' organisations have the right to manage their affairs in full freedom, to join federations and confederations and to acquire legal personality. The Right to Organise and Collective Bargaining Convention stipulates that in hiring or dismissing workers employers are not to discriminate on grounds of trade union membership or activities. It also states that "workers' and employers' organisations shall enjoy adequate protection against any acts of interference by each other or each other's agents". Finally, the Convention provides for measures "to encourage and promote the full development and utilisation of machinery for voluntary negotiations between employers or employers' organisations and workers' organisations, with a view to

the regulation of terms and conditions of employment by means of collective agreements". The Rural Workers' Organisations Convention confirms that the rights accorded under the Freedom of Association and Protection of the Right to Organise Convention also apply to rural workers. However, it takes a broader approach to the aim of the organisations covered. The Freedom of Association and Protection of the Right to Organise Convention considers this aim as "furthering and defending the interests of workers and employers"; the Rural Workers' Organisations Convention, in addition, considers that such organisations should be established "as an effective means of ensuring the participation of rural workers" and that such organisations should be enabled "to play their role in economic and social development".

The Committee on Freedom of Association, which is the ILO Governing Body Committee competent to hear complaints on infringements of trade union rights, has been receiving more and more complaints in recent years. The number of new cases rose from 32 in 1979 to 66 in 1980, 88 in 1981, 70 in 1982 and 76 in 1983. Although this may be due in part to a better understanding by trade union organisations of the supervisory procedures of the ILO, it remains true that the striking increase in the number of complaints shows the extent of the problems facing trade union organisations all over the world. In fact, many cases relate to violations of freedom of association that affect the whole trade union movement in the countries concerned; moreover, nearly half of the complaints contain particularly serious allegations, mentioning the death, disappearance or arrest of trade union leaders and activists. Lastly, the number – 73 during the past eight years – and diversity of the countries concerned are also tending to increase, which means that these countries belong to every region and every economic and social system.

There are two main factors to account for this situation. In several countries there have been changes of system or government after political tension led to severe restrictions on civil liberties. Those restrictions on basic rights, such as the right of assembly, the right to personal safety and freedom of the press, have had an inevitable effect on trade union rights as well. Another factor is the present economic crisis, which has led both in the developing and in the industrialised market economy countries to considerable restrictions on trade union activities, and in particular on collective bargaining. Many governments have introduced policies of austerity entailing the suspension of free wage fixing by the social partners.

The purpose of this chapter is to point out the main legal problems encountered by workers and employers in the following aspects of trade union life: the establishment of workers' and employers' organisations, the internal administration of these organisations, their activities and programmes, and the relations between trade union freedoms and civil liberties.

The establishment of workers' and employers' organisations

Although most countries recognise the right to organise, there may be some legal obstacles that prevent or restrict the establishment of workers' and employers' organisations. The law may restrict the right to organise only to certain occupations, it may require certain formalities, or it may impose certain requirements on the structure of workers' and employers' organisations.

Restrictions concerning occupations

Public officials are probably having the most difficulty in obtaining recognition of their right to organise. Although they now have this right in many countries, the law of some countries still denies them the possibility of establishing or joining trade union organisations. These include countries in Latin America (Brazil, Chile, Dominican Republic, Ecuador, El Salvador, Nicaragua and Peru, for example) and Africa (Ethiopia and Liberia). It is true that organisations set up under general civil law and acting as trade unions may exist in practice, but this legislation does not always provide all the guarantees explicitly set forth in Convention No. 87. An argument sometimes advanced for refusing the right to organise to public employees is the need to ensure continuity in public services. Certain countries, however, have been able to solve these problems by making a distinction between the right to organise and the right to strike in the public service.

Although the right of rural workers to organise is normally recognised by law, workers' organisations in rural areas are less developed than in urban areas, and sometimes even non-existent. The difficulties experienced by rural workers are often more practical than legal in nature. They are most serious for workers in the traditional sector although they also affect plantation workers. Some practical difficulties that rural workers' organisations face are widespread illiteracy, the scattered and isolated nature of peasant farms, ignorance of the law, unstable employment, mobility of seasonal workers, conflicts between different (tribal) groups, irregular payment of contributions and lack of trade union leaders. Moreover, rural workers often face heavy pressure from outside: uncooperative governments or local authorities; hostile political conditions; landowners often unwilling to accept the existence of organised labour; and, last but not least, the unequal distribution of land and other means of production. To all this must be added the fact that in several countries the law does not yet permit agricultural workers to establish trade unions or these workers are not protected by the ordinary trade union legislation (El Salvador, for example). In recent years, however, there has been some progress in the situation of agricultural workers; since 1976 members of collective farms in the USSR have joined trade unions of agricultural workers.

Restrictions concerning the registration of trade unions

Although in certain countries, especially in Western Europe (Belgium, Federal Republic of Germany, Italy, Scandinavian countries), trade unions can exist and operate lawfully without having to carry out any particular formalities, most countries have some kind of system of registration for organisations: filing of rules (France and French-speaking African countries), registration with a registrar or the labour authorities (countries in the English legal tradition and countries of Latin America).

A problem arises where the law confers more or less discretionary powers on the competent authorities to decide whether an organisation meets all the conditions laid down for registration. In that case, the application for registration could become subject to "previous authorisation" as set out in Convention No. 87. This may happen where, as in Malaysia and Singapore, the registrar can refuse registration if he considers that the trade union is likely to be used for purposes that are unlawful or inconsistent with its objectives and rules or where, as in Zambia, he considers that the organisation in question will not be able to implement all of the provisions in its constitution. Similar situations, which the Committee on Freedom of Association has had to examine in cases concerning Colombia, Costa Rica and Malaysia, arise where the registration procedure is long and complicated or where it is applied in such a way as to delay or prevent the establishment of occupational organisations.

One means that exists in many countries of protecting trade unions against arbitrary or ill-founded decisions by the administrative authorities is to provide in the legislation for appeal to the courts.

Restrictions concerning trade union structure

One of the fundamental problems affecting freedom to choose an occupational organisation and trade union structure is connected with what is commonly known as trade union monopoly. In some countries the legislation provides, whether directly or indirectly, that a single organisation shall be responsible for the interests of a given class of workers. This situation is obviously quite different from that in which the workers themselves, unconstrained by laws or regulations, have decided to be represented by a single trade union organisation.

Trade union unity imposed by law occurs in various forms. Workers in a given workplace may be prohibited from being represented by more than one organisation, as in certain Latin American countries (Colombia, Honduras and Panama). The legislation may also impose a single trade union system at every level, as in certain African countries (Congo, Sudan, United Republic of Tanzania and Zambia), Arab countries (Egypt, Libyan Arab Jamahiriya and Syrian Arab Republic), or centrally planned economies (Bulgaria, Czechoslovakia and Romania, for example). A system of trade union unity for a given class of workers may also result from the practice followed by the registrar of trade unions in certain countries in the English legal tradition (Malaysia, Singapore and Uganda). In those countries the registrar can refuse to register a trade union if there is already another organisation that, in his opinion, adequately represents the workers' interests.

Governments often justify the existence of trade union monopoly on the ground that they wish to establish a strong trade union movement that is not divided into many small and competing organisations. In such circumstances, governments can – without jeopardising the principles of freedom of association – give special rights of collective bargaining to the most representative trade union or unions and also recognise the other organisations. It is important to review the selection of the most representative trade union and to base the selection on objective and pre-established criteria. This practice is applied today in most countries where trade union pluralism exists.

The internal administration of trade union organisations

The most serious problems arising in the internal administration of trade union organisations are due in most cases to interference by the public authorities, mainly in the election and dismissal of trade union officers, in the drawing up of constitutions or in the financial administration of the organisation.

Election and dismissal of trade union officers

Public authorities can interfere in the electoral process in several ways: they can fix, by laws or regulations, conditions governing eligibility for trade union office, they can lay down the procedure for elections, or they can – directly or indirectly – try to influence the result of an election.

In numerous countries, particularly in Africa (Algeria, Burkina Faso, Libyan Arab Jamahiriya, Morocco and Niger) and Latin America (Brazil, Ecuador, Honduras, Mexico and Nicaragua) the legislation provides that a person must be a national of the country to be eligible for trade union

office. It is obvious that such provisions will create problems when there is increasing migration of workers, particularly between countries of the same region which are economically integrated. The legislation of certain countries is more flexible and allows reciprocity agreements between countries (Central African Republic and Ivory Coast), confines the prohibition to a certain proportion of trade union officers (France) or imposes conditions of residence only and not of nationality (Chile, Congo, Costa Rica, Paraguay and Venezuela).

It also happens frequently that certain occupational conditions must be met to be eligibile for posts of responsibility (as in Brazil, Ecuador, Libyan Arab Jamahiriya, Malaysia, Peru, Syrian Arab Republic and Venezuela). Restrictions of this kind can cause problems, particularly in the developing countries, where workers are not always able to find all the qualified officers necessary within their own ranks. Some countries have largely solved these problems by allowing candidatures of persons who have worked previously in the occupation or by applying the prescribed conditions only to a specified proportion of trade union officers (India, Pakistan, Singapore and Sri Lanka).

Persons who have been sentenced for almost any kind of offence are also sometimes prohibited from holding trade union office. This is the case mainly in Africa (Central African Republic and Madagascar) and in Latin America (Brazil, Colombia and Honduras). One way of avoiding so sweeping a prohibition is to define a limited number of offences that would automatically disqualify persons convicted of them for any post of trust such as that of a trade union officer (Kenya, Malaysia, Tunisia and Uganda).

Lastly, there are restrictions in some countries on the re-election of trade union officers, which may take the form of an absolute prohibition. In Mexico, for example, in the case of public servants officials cannot be re-elected, while in Guatemala,

Nicaragua and Panama officials are allowed only a limited number of successive terms of office.

With regard to electoral procedure, the existing provisions very often have no other purpose than to ensure that voting takes place normally, in observance of the rights of members, and that disputes about the results are avoided. Sometimes, however, the restrictions go so far as to give certain administrative authorities a part in the procedure, which obviously entails the risk that public authorities interfere in the internal affairs of the organisations. This is especially true when the results of an election must be approved by the ministry of labour, as in Brazil, or when the representative of the administration must supervise the voting operations or count the votes, as in El Salvador.

Lastly, the cases presented to the Committee on Freedom of Association show that the public authorities may interfere even more directly, for example when they actually make recommendations or express their opinions on candidates, refuse to recognise elected bodies or themselves appoint certain trade union officers. Similarly, when the authorities place organisations under supervision, which has occurred in certain Latin American countries (Argentina and Bolivia, for example), the right of workers to elect their officers in full freedom is possibly called in question.

Similar considerations apply when trade union officers are dismissed by decision of the administrative authorities (Brazil, Colombia, Kenya and Nicaragua) or of the single central trade union organisation (Syrian Arab Republic).

Most countries, however, avoid interference by leaving trade union organisations entirely free to organise their electoral procedure, or at least by limiting official action to ensuring a correct and democratic supervision of the vote or to cases where trade union members complain.

Drafting of constitutions

Although a number of countries, mostly in Europe, leave trade unions entirely free to draft their own constitutions, some countries oblige them, for example, to cover certain questions. The main purpose of such obligations is generally to protect the rights of members, to ensure sound administration and to prevent subsequent legal complications. In some cases, however, the right of organisations to draw up their constitutions and rules is seriously restricted or even non-existent. In many countries where trade union monopoly is imposed all unions have to conform to the constitution of the only recognised central federation. In Brazil, for example, the constitution must include certain declarations committing the union to collaborating with the public authorities, while in the extreme cases of Kenya and the United Republic of Tanzania, it is the public authorities which are authorised to draft the constitution of the central trade union organisation.

The best way of avoiding improper interference by the public authorities is probably to entrust the verification of constitutions, where this is considered necessary, to judicial authorities or to bodies that are largely independent of the administrative authorities, such as the registrar of trade unions in many English-speaking countries, with the possibility of appeal to the courts.

Financial administration

This is one of the fields in which the public authorities most often exercise some control, directly or indirectly. The purpose of official action is frequently to prevent abuses and to protect the members from the danger of financial mismanagement, for example where trade unions are obliged to submit periodical financial reports to the authorities. In some cases, however, government action goes beyond the simple rules of regular supervision. In Iraq, for example, the minimum dues of members are fixed by law; in Brazil, expenditure must be approved by the

61

authorities; in Colombia, Costa Rica, Guatemala, Honduras, the Libyan Arab Jamahiriya and the Syrian Arab Republic, the authorities can at any time demand information or verify the accounts. In some countries, such as Argentina, Barbados and the United Kingdom, governments restrict official action to cases where they have solid grounds for supposing that there have been irregularities or where they have received complaints from members.

Activities and programmes of organisations

It is probably in this field that restrictions are most common today. They are applied mainly to the following three types of activities: so-called political activities, collective bargaining and strikes. Furthermore, public authorities sometimes prohibit any trade union action by certain unions that have been dissolved or suspended.

Political activities

The legislation of a good many countries either imposes certain restrictions on the political activities of occupational organisations or prohibits them completely. In Liberia, for example, trade unions are not authorised to make financial contributions to a party or to a person seeking political office. More often the law simply prohibits the organisations from adopting the policy of a party (as in many Latin American countries, including Brazil, Colombia, Costa Rica, Ecuador, El Salvador and Guatemala) or from taking part in any kind of political activity (as in several African countries, including Chad and Somalia). The scope of such prohibitions obviously depends on the interpretation placed in practice on the term "political activities". These provisions often make it impossible for trade union organisations to speak out on matters that are clearly within their competence, such as the economic and social policy of the government. On the other hand,

provisions such as those existing in many French-speaking countries, which limit the activities of trade unions to the defence of their members' occupational interests, generally permit the unions to carry on much wider activities in practice. This more flexible conception of trade union activities is becoming commoner, since it is more in harmony with the new functions that the unions are assuming in the planning or defining of economic and social policies.

In some countries the right of workers freely to choose their own organisations is restricted. This is the case in certain political systems where – by law – trade unions are closely linked to the political parties in power, as in the centrally planned economies of Eastern Europe and several African countries.

Collective bargaining

The principle of collective bargaining is now recognised in the great majority of countries. In practice, however, collective bargaining is still often restricted or its effectiveness limited.

Collective bargaining presupposes the recognition of a workers' organisation by the employer or by an employers' organisation. What organisation is the employer to recognise? This is a question that arises fairly often and is dealt with in the legislation of an increasing number of countries, including Canada, Costa Rica, Honduras, Mexico, Pakistan, the Philippines, Singapore and the United States. Under the legislation of these countries only one organisation is accorded the exclusive right to bargain. This may be the organisation that represents a certain proportion or the majority of the workers or, where there are several trade unions, the most representative union. In other countries, some of them in Western Europe, several organisations, sometimes with preferential rights, may take part in collective bargaining.

The parties are not always entirely free to conclude the agreements they wish to. It is becoming commoner for certain questions, such as recruitment, promotion, transfer, dismissal and reinstatement of workers and more generally matters affecting the management of an undertaking, to be excluded from bargaining (in Malaysia and Singapore, for example) or for the agreements to be required to be submitted to the administrative authorities (in Greece, Libyan Arab Jamahiriya, the Syrian Arab Republic and Tunisia) or to the labour courts (in Kenya, Singapore and the United Republic of Tanzania). It can then happen – and sometimes does – that approval is refused because the authorities consider that an agreement is damaging to the economy or does not conform with official instructions on wages or employment conditions. The economic difficulties that a country is facing often lead the competent authorities to place restrictions on free wage fixing, both in developed countries (Belgium, Canada, Netherlands, provisionally) and in countries of Latin America (Brazil), Asia (Singapore and Malaysia) and Africa (United Republic of Tanzania). These measures sometimes go as far as the general suspension of collective bargaining, such as happened in Argentina and Uruguay in the recent past.

Strikes

The supervisory bodies of the ILO consider the right to strike to be one of the essential means available to trade union organisations for furthering and defending the interests of their members. This right is nevertheless restricted in many countries, although the scope and severity of these restrictions can vary greatly. At one extreme, strikes by only certain categories of workers are suspended or prohibited, while at the other all workers are prohibited from striking. A general prohibition often results from the system of settling labour disputes. This is true in many of the developing countries. In some countries, including Brazil, the Dominican Republic, the Libyan Arab Jamahiriya and Paraguay, a compulsory procedure of arbitration exists for the settlement of disputes, and the decision is binding on the parties;

in other countries, such as India, Malaysia, Mauritania, Singapore and Sri Lanka, the public authorities can impose a settlement through arbitration or a binding decision.

An entirely different situation is found in countries that prevent strikes by means of either voluntary conciliation and arbitration procedures (Canada and the United States, for example) or a system of awards that can be challenged by the parties (certain French-speaking African countries).

Some countries, without imposing an absolute prohibition, severely restrict the right to strike: suspension kept in force for long periods (Nicaragua, for example); long and complicated procedures (Chile, for example); or excessively broad definitions of the services in which workers cannot go on strike (as in Colombia, Costa Rica, Kenya, Pakistan, the Philippines and Trinidad and Tobago).

In the centrally planned economies of Eastern Europe, except in Poland, the labour legislation does not mention the right to strike. Cases submitted to the Committee on Freedom of Association show that in practice workers in these countries often experience difficulty in exercising this right.

Suspension and dissolution of organisations

Legislation generally provides that organisations can be suspended or dissolved only by decision of the trade union itself or, where the law has been violated, by a court of law. In some cases, however, dissolution or – what comes to the same thing – cancellation of registration can be pronounced by administrative authority, at times even without the possibility of appeal to the courts (Malaysia, New Zealand and Singapore).

Where the suspension or dissolution of an organisation takes place, it is usually pronounced

63

by virtue of special laws or decisions adopted by the authorities, often after a change of political regime, as has occurred during the past decade in Argentina, Chile, Turkey and Uruguay, or under a state of emergency, as in Poland.

Trade union rights and civil liberties

Most of the complaints submitted to the Committee on Freedom of Association concern civil liberties: the arrest and banishment of trade union leaders; restrictions on the right to hold meetings or demonstrations; the seizure of trade union publications; the violation of trade union premises; and discrimination in employment.

Arrest and detention

The arrest of trade unionists is by far the most frequent subject of allegations. Sometimes, the imprisonment of trade unionists is directly related to their trade union activities. For example, the Committee has had to consider cases in which workers were imprisoned because they wanted to set up organisations outside the existing trade union structure. Sometimes, too, imprisonment is due to contacts of trade unionists with international organisations of workers. Trade unionists are often arrested during a strike for a variety of reasons. There may be a general prohibition; the strike may have been called on illegal grounds; the prescribed formalities may not have been observed; or, lastly, the strike may have been called in a sector considered to be essential. Detention in such circumstances is often brief. Another occasion of arrests occurs when workers abuse their right to strike, for example by resorting to violence.

In situations where public order is disturbed, for example when the army seizes power or when martial law is being declared, measures of administrative internment or remand in custody pending

trial may be adopted, and may remain in force for very long periods. In such circumstances governments often invoke a danger to national security as a ground for bringing trade unionists before military courts, which often sentence them to heavy penalties. Certain countries also put forward subversive activities as a justification for banishing trade union leaders and activists.

Another problem that sometimes arises is that trade unionists are ill-treated or tortured during their imprisonment and in some cases even die or disappear after having been arrested. Allegations of this type have been made more and more frequently during the past decade.

Right of assembly

Arrests sometimes also occur following trade union meetings or demonstrations, for example when the persons concerned have not observed the legislation on the right of assembly.

In addition, the Committee on Freedom of Association has had to examine cases concerning the control of trade union meetings by the public authorities. A serious problem arises where the legislation requires trade unions to obtain permission from the authorities before they can hold meetings, even where these are to be held on private premises. At times, too, administrative authorities, for example representatives of the labour administration, or even the police, are present at the meetings of trade union organisations.

Seizure of publications

Although less common than cases concerning the right of assembly, cases concerning the freedom of the press have been submitted several times to the Committee on Freedom of Association. Sometimes a restriction on the freedom of the press results from more general restrictions on the right to establish trade unions, for example where trade union publications are prohibited when they do not originate from the only recognised organisation. Freedom of the press may also be violated through the general control exercised by the authorities over the means of expression: discretion to refuse authorisation to publish, establishment of censorship, obligation to pay heavy deposits for all periodicals.

Violation of trade union premises

It is not uncommon for trade union organisations to complain of acts, such as searches, occupations or closings, committed by the police at their headquarters or on other premises. While these are going on, damage may be caused or records or other property seized. Such cases raise the general problem of the limits that may be set to the principle of inviolability of trade union premises. The difficulties arise either because the protection provided by law is inadequate or because there is no obligation to obtain a warrant from a court before carrying out a search.

Acts of discrimination

Although workers are often protected by law against acts of anti-union discrimination in respect of their employment, experience shows that such acts of discrimination are far from being unknown in practice. This is not surprising, for it is very hard to guarantee absolute protection in this field: it is often difficult, or indeed impossible, for a worker to prove that a measure taken against him has any connection with his trade union activities; moreover, the mere fact that he is entitled to compensation for dismissal is seldom a sufficiently dissuasive form of protection.

It is for this reason that certain countries have reinforced the statutory guarantees in this matter:

need to obtain the agreement of an authority unconnected with the employer (the labour administration or a labour court) before transferring or dismissing trade union leaders (Colombia, France, Greece, Guatemala, Honduras, India, Norway and Venezuela); restrictive listing in the law of grounds for dismissal (Brazil and Ecuador); burden of proving the grounds for dismissal laid on the employer (Australia and New Zealand); provision of special machinery for investigation (Japan, Pakistan, Philippines and United States).

Lastly, it happens, even in countries where powerful and well-organised trade unions offer a guarantee in principle, that employers refuse to take on trade unionists. Here, too, effective protection is very difficult to ensure because it is often impossible to prove that some employers refuse to recruit workers who are trade unionists.

The foregoing overview of trade union rights throughout the world makes it clear that a staggering amount of work is still to be done before trade union rights are respected universally. More than 30 years after the adoption of ILO Conventions on freedom of association and collective bargaining, and the establishment of supervisory machinery, the task then undertaken is far from being accomplished. The problems at the present time are sometimes even more acute than 30 years ago. Immediately after the war the greatest obstacles to the free exercise of trade union rights were mainly legal restrictions on the right to organise, whereas today infringements of freedom of association are found more often in cases or countries in which all civil liberties are restricted.

Chapter **5**

Abolition of forced labour

The Constitution of the International Labour Organisation declares that "all human beings . . . have the right to pursue both their material well-being and their spiritual development in conditions of freedom and dignity". Accordingly, the Organisation has always struggled against practices that are incompatible with freedom and dignity, and in particular against forced labour. Two Conventions are the main instruments that enable the Organisation to carry on this struggle: the Forced Labour Convention, 1930 (No. 29), and the Abolition of Forced Labour Convention, 1957 (No. 105). Both have been widely ratified: the first by 126 member States, and the second by 108 (see box 5.1).

Quite a few practices related to forced[1] labour belong to the past when numerous African and Asian countries were colonised. In fact, over the past 25 years many of these countries have abolished statutory provisions that allowed the authorities – even in normal times – to call up workers to perform all sorts of duties. People were often forced to work on schemes undertaken by the government, such as the construction and maintenance of buildings and roads, the digging and

67

5.1

The main concepts and provisions of Conventions Nos. 29 and 105

The States which ratify the Forced Labour Convention, 1930 (No. 29), undertake to suppress the use of forced or compulsory labour in all its forms in the shortest possible period. The Convention defines "forced or compulsory labour" as "all work or service which is exacted from any person under the menace of any penalty and for which the said person has not offered himself voluntarily". Five kinds of work or service are, under certain conditions, exempted from the scope of this Convention: compulsory military service, certain civic obligations (such as compulsory jury service), penal labour exacted from persons convicted by a court of law, work exacted in emergencies and minor communal services. In addition, the 1930 Convention specifically prohibits two forms of forced or compulsory labour: first of all, forced and compulsory labour for the benefit of private individuals, companies or associations and, secondly, forced and compulsory labour imposed on a community as a collective punishment for crimes committed by any of its members. Finally, the Convention provides that the "illegal exaction of forced or compulsory labour shall be punishable as a penal offence, and that ratifying States shall ensure that the penalties imposed by law are really adequate and are strictly enforced" (Article 25).

The 1957 Convention does not constitute a revision of the 1930 Convention but rather complements it. While the 1930 Convention provides for the general abolition of compulsory labour, subject to a number of exceptions, the Abolition of Forced Labour Convention, 1957 (No. 105), requires the abolition of any form of forced or compulsory labour in five specific cases: (a) as a means of political coercion or education or as a punishment for holding or expressing political views or views ideologically opposed to the established political, social or economic system; (b) as a method of mobilising and using labour for purposes of economic development; (c) as a means of labour discipline; (d) as a punishment for having participated in strikes; and (e) as a means of racial, social, national or religious discrimination.

maintenance of irrigation networks, etc. They could also be forced to work on development projects, to grow certain crops, to carry loads or to supply their labour as a tax or in the service of tribal chiefs or other persons.

Examples of such compulsory labour are now becoming rarer, though certain countries, including Cameroon, Guinea and the United Republic of Tanzania, still have legislation aimed at developing agriculture and infrastructure through the recruitment of the population. In addition to these forms of compulsion found in national law, many people are still forced to work under unlawful practices. In India, for example, the authorities have not been able to eliminate debt bondage although it has been abolished by law. More frequently, however, the supervisory bodies of the ILO encounter less archaic forms of compulsory labour, imposed by national authorities either "for purposes of production or service" or "as a punishment".

Various forms of compulsory labour "for purposes of production or service" existing at present are examined by the supervisory bodies of the ILO. The most important are the general obligation to work, the use of conscripts for non-military purposes, obligations to serve related to training received, powers to call up labour outside emergency circumstances and restrictions on the freedom of workers to leave their employment. These are discussed in the first section below.

There are also various forms of compulsory labour exacted "as a punishment". The second section will first deal with compulsory labour executed by prisoners who were not convicted in court or who are placed at the disposal of private individuals or companies. It will then discuss all forms of compulsory labour, including prison labour, that are imposed on people for the following reasons: political coercion or education and the repression of political or ideological opinion, discrimination, the imposition of labour discipline, and punishment for having participated in strikes.

Forced or compulsory labour for purposes of production or service

General obligation to work

Various national constitutions impose on citizens a moral duty to work. In some countries, however, the legislation goes further by obliging able-bodied citizens who are not receiving some kind of instruction to engage in a gainful occupation; failure to do so makes them liable to the compulsory performance of specified work or to penal sanctions (Central African Republic, United Republic of Tanzania, Tunisia). A similar situation may arise under penal provisions punishing vagrancy and similar offences. In the Islamic Republic of Iran, any person who has no definite means of subsistence and who, whether through laziness or negligence, does not look for work, may be obliged by the Government to take suitable employment under pain of punishment. In Guatemala even non-wage-earning small farmers may fall under the Vagrancy Act. In the Dominican Republic similar provisions have been repealed. In the USSR the penal laws punish, in the same class as vagrancy and begging, "any other parasitic way of life". This latter notion, as defined by the Supreme Court of this country, turns upon the capacity to work of the persons concerned, and may therefore be used to compel able-bodied persons to engage in an occupation recognised as socially useful by the authorities. Similar provisions exist in other countries including Cuba, Czechoslovakia and Poland. Provisions on vagrancy have been redefined in narrower terms in several countries (Costa Rica, Ecuador, Honduras, Liberia, Paraguay, Sierra Leone, Sweden), so as to avoid abuses and confine the effects of the law to persons who not only habitually refuse to work but also have gained their income illegally.

Use of conscripts for non-military purposes

In a number of countries, particularly in Africa and Latin America, the legislation authorises the use of conscripts for non-military work of general interest or for economic and social development. Such assignments may take place either in regular military service or in arrangements that may or may not fall under the military authorities. Some of the governments concerned, however, have stated in their reports on the application of the Conventions that such assignments are confined to cases of emergency (Cameroon, Egypt, Norway) or to the vocational training of the conscripts (Cameroon, France (overseas departments), Gabon, Paraguay), or that the young people carrying out work for development or of general interest are, in practice, always volunteers (Algeria, Colombia, Ecuador, Morocco).

Obligations to serve related to training received

Sometimes newly qualified persons in a narrow range of professions, in particular young doctors, dentists and pharmacists and occasionally engineers, are required to exercise their profession for a certain period in a post assigned to them by the authorities. Elsewhere, a similar obligation is imposed on a large proportion of persons obtaining diplomas of higher, or even secondary, education.[2] In several countries the legislation to this effect has been repealed after a few years (Sudan), or, being temporary, has expired (Norway, where only dentists were concerned), or again has not been applied in practice (India). In Egypt the legislation applying to new doctors, pharmacists, dentists and engineers is reviewed regularly, and the maximum period of service has been gradually reduced. Instead of imposing compulsory service on graduates in the medical profession, several countries (Greece, Iraq, Lebanon, Syrian Arab Republic) do not allow them to practise in urban areas unless they have practised previously for a certain period in rural areas.

Powers of call-up outside emergency circumstances

In 1968 the supervisory bodies of the ILO observed that in several countries the legislation permitted the calling up of labour in circumstances that could not be said to endanger the existence or the well-being of the population. In other words, such legislation could be used to undertake public works, for example. Since then, some of the texts have been repealed (in particular, in Burkina Faso, Czechoslovakia, Kenya, Mauritius and the USSR) or are being revised (Mauritania, Morocco). It can also happen that the power to call up labour is kept in force for a long period, even after the situation of emergency is over (Pakistan).

Restrictions on the freedom of workers to leave their employment

In some cases workers cannot leave their employment without their employer's agreement or official authorisation, even outside situations of emergency. In many countries workers with an indefinite contract are not allowed to terminate their employment, even if they give notice sufficiently in advance. In Bangladesh and Pakistan, for example, any person employed by the Government, a local authority or in any service connected with transport is liable to penal sanctions if he terminates his employment without his employer's consent, even with notice. Similar provisions, covering a wide range of employments, have recently been introduced in Poland. In other countries, legislation of the same kind, which applied to certain categories of workers (Iraq, Netherlands and Spain), has been repealed during the past decade or amended so as to apply only to cases of emergency. In Bulgaria workers who leave their employment voluntarily can now take up any new employment without going through the authorities – as was required before. Provisions that prevented members of agricultural co-operatives from resigning have been repealed in Hungary; in the USSR the Presidium of the Union Council of Collective Farms – in an annex to a

---

5.2

Debt bondage

Debt bondage is a system under which labourers and their families are forced to work for an employer in order to pay off their actually incurred or inherited debts. It still affects a significant number of people in South-East Asia. A preliminary survey carried out in 1978 in eight Indian states by the Gandhi Peace Foundation in collaboration with the National Labour Institute, based on projections made from a sample of 1,000 villages, estimated that there were 2,244,000 bonded labourers in those states. Certain authorities contested the findings and even the basis of the survey, which highlights the difficulties encountered in identifying bonded labourers.[1] Despite the importance attached by the Government of India to a census of bonded labourers, as an identification process for determining the effectiveness of the relevant legislation enacted in 1976, the progress made in this connection has been slow.[2]

Debt bondage is both a social and an economic problem. One of the fundamental requirements for its solution is the worker's rehabilitation once he has been freed from bondage. In recent years, the Government of India has implemented a large-scale programme to facilitate the rehabilitation of bonded labourers who have been freed. The number of rehabilitated workers in nine states rose from 58,071 in 1979 to 115,316 in 1983. Besides the measures to free and rehabilitate bonded labourers, preventive measures have been taken to put an end to this system by ensuring that other workers do not become subjected to it and that those who have been freed do not relapse into bondage again.

A survey carried out by the Indian Statistical Institute in a district of the State of Bihar showed that most of the families who had been freed from bondage and had been granted facilities under a rehabilitation scheme became virtually bonded again within a short time. It is the application of the rehabilitation measures and not their principle that was called in question by this survey.[3]

Improved application of rehabilitation measures that would enable workers to set up on their own in economically viable conditions, help to create jobs in villages where there is a high concentration of freed labourers, with the aid of the Forest, Public Works, Rural Development and Irrigation Departments, among others, and ensure that more people knew about the provisions of the Bonded Labour System (Abolition) Act of 1976, should eventually produce better results.[4]

While the Government of India stands out because of the action it has taken since 1975 to combat debt bondage, the United Nations Working Group on Slavery pointed out, during its Ninth Session in 1983, that the exploitation of workers and debt bondage are not confined to India alone and urged that prompt and speedy action be taken wherever such abuses exist.[5]

[1] Report of the Commissioner for scheduled castes and scheduled tribes (Twenty-seventh Report), Part I, 1979-81, para. 2.22.

[2] ibid., para. 2.21.

[3] ibid., para. 2.34.

[4] ibid., para. 2.36.

[5] Economic and Social Council, Commission on Human Rights: *Report of the Working Group on Slavery on its ninth session* (Geneva, 1983; doc. E/CN.4/Sub.2/1983/27), para. 36.

---

decree adopted in 1984 – has explained that, under the Model Collective Farm Rules, these farms do not have the right to refuse a request made by a member to leave.

Illegal forms of compulsion occurring in practice

Unlawful practices such as debt bondage or the forcible recruitment or retention of workers are still found in some countries. With regard to debt bondage, India, the only country to recognise its existence, adopted legislation in 1975 intended not only to punish the guilty and to free the victims, but also to rehabilitate these workers and to provide job opportunities for them. Unfortu-nately the extent and the nature of the problems are such that, unless more vigorous means are brought into play, very many persons will remain virtual slaves (see box 5.2). In Mauritania slavery was to be abolished under a 1979 decree; after the United Nations had examined its impact, the Government asked for a mission to study the problems on the spot. These problems are also under examination by the supervisory bodies of the ILO. In Pakistan labour contractors appear to have recruited workers by force. The ILO supervisory bodies have recommended an effective system of labour inspection to protect contract labour in public works projects in this country. They have also called for a similar system to protect agricultural workers in the remote areas of Brazil, Indonesia and Liberia.

Forced or compulsory labour as a sanction or punishment

Prison labour

In certain African and Latin American countries (Colombia, Paraguay, United Republic of Tanzania (Zanzibar), Togo, Zaire), persons in prison awaiting trial or other unconvicted prisoners may be compelled to perform prison labour. In other countries, non-judicial authorities can impose penalties involving the obligation to work on vagrants and others living on the edge of society (Iceland, Islamic Republic of Iran, certain Swiss cantons, United Republic of Tanzania, Venezuela, Zaire). In several countries, however, the legislation has been amended on these points during the past decade (Austria, Dominican Republic, Hungary, Madagascar, Panama, Switzerland) or is being so amended (Finland, certain Swiss cantons, Venezuela).

The Forced Labour Convention of 1930 does not allow a prisoner to be hired to, or placed at the disposal of, private individuals, companies or associations. However, the supervisory bodies of the ILO have considered to be compatible with the Convention certain arrangements whereby a prisoner voluntarily accepts employment or service with a private employer, subject to certain guarantees as to the payment of normal wages and social security benefits, consent of trade unions, etc.[3] In recent years several countries (Burkina Faso, Canada, Honduras, Liberia, Mali, Norway) have repealed provisions under which prisoners could be placed without such safeguards at the disposal of private undertakings, though this can still be done in other countries, including Austria, Brazil, Cameroon, Colombia, France, the Federal Republic of Germany, Grenada, the Ivory Coast, Morocco and Togo. In a growing number of countries prisoners work for private undertakings both inside and outside their prison in conditions that do not differ greatly from those of free workers. Certain countries have amended their legislation so as to require the formal agreement of the prisoner (Federal Republic of Germany, though the coming into force of the amendment has been postponed) or to improve his situation in respect of wages, working conditions and social security (Brazil, France).

Abolition of forced or compulsory labour as a means of political coercion or education or of discrimination or as a sanction against workers

The Abolition of Forced Labour Convention of 1957 does not generally apply to prison labour imposed on common law offenders with a view to their re-education or social rehabilitation; but it does prohibit the imposition of such labour on persons convicted for having expressed political opinions, breached labour discipline or taken part in a strike. It should however be pointed out that restrictions on political freedoms, the right to strike, etc., do not come within the scope of this Convention except when they lead to the imposition of sanctions involving compulsory labour. In many countries, including France, Gabon, the Ivory Coast, Madagascar, Mali, Morocco, Senegal and the United Kingdom (England, Scotland and Wales), prisoners convicted of certain political offences traditionally have a special status under the law. Their status is comparable to that of persons in detention awaiting trial. It exempts them from the prison labour imposed on common law offenders but leaves them the possibility of working at their own request. During the past decade a number of other countries in Europe, the Middle East and the Americas have introduced such exemptions into their penal laws, in respect either of political offenders alone (Honduras, Iraq, Jordan, Portugal) or of both political offenders and workers convicted of participation in strikes and all other persons protected by the 1957 Convention (Haiti, Poland, Spain, Turkey). In addition, some countries (mentioned below) have

71

altogether abolished prison sentences for offences of opinion, participation in strikes or breaches of labour discipline, or amended the relevant substantive provisions in order to comply with the 1957 Convention.

Abolition of forced or compulsory labour as a means of political coercion or education or of discrimination

The scope of the 1957 Convention includes the delicate field of freedom of opinion and of political opposition. Over the past decade, a number of countries have repealed provisions under which penalties involving compulsory labour could be imposed to enforce the censorship of publications and the prohibition of public gatherings (Mauritius), the prohibition of publications whose contents, and of associations whose aims, were contrary to the basic principles of a national movement (Spain), or the prohibition of the circulation of any newspaper and the prohibition of any groups and associations pursuing political activities (Nigeria). Elsewhere, provisions have been repealed which imposed such penalties for disseminating publications or propaganda conflicting with the established political order (Greece), aimed at diminishing national sentiment (Italy), or inspired by foreign governments and likely to disturb public order (Mexico), or for the denigration of the institution of property (Austria).

In many countries in different parts of the world, however, the manifestation of political or ideological opposition and freedom of expression are still the subject of heavy restrictions enforced by penalties involving compulsory prison labour. For instance, all parties and associations professing political views other than those of a particular national movement or party are still prohibited in Algeria, Burundi, the Central African Republic, the Sudan, the United Republic of Tanzania, Zaire and Zambia. In other countries prohibitions enforced with penalties involving compulsory labour apply to groups or associations disturbing the established social order (Egypt), or advocating communist ideology (Dominican Republic, Guatemala), or to persons who carry on propaganda intended to overthrow the social order (El Salvador), to change the socialist order (Czechoslovakia, Romania) or to weaken the authority of the State (USSR); to persons who call in question, in a publication, the aims and principles of the revolution (Libyan Arab Jamahiriya), who disseminate opinions or information prejudicial to the public interest (Egypt), or who falsify the historical truth laid down by the National Academy of History (Dominican Republic).

Furthermore, administrative authorities often have wide discretionary powers to prevent persons from expressing their opinions, by enforcing penalties involving compulsory labour. It is under such powers that authorisation to appear can be refused to all periodicals (Burundi) or to newspapers (Ghana, Malaysia, Singapore); that any newspaper can be banned in the public interest (the United Republic of Tanzania); and that publications can be prohibited if this is considered to be in the interest of public order (Uganda) or they are considered to jeopardise the building of the nation (Central African Republic, Chad). Similarly, administrative authorities sometimes have wide powers to prohibit private individuals, on pain of penalties involving compulsory labour, from publishing anything that these authorities consider to be contrary to public order; from attending and addressing meetings and gatherings; or, more generally, from taking part in political activities (Malaysia, Singapore). They may also be empowered to suspend associations or to prevent their formation on general grounds such as the national interest or public order, welfare or tranquillity (Bangladesh, Ghana, Kenya, Malaysia, Singapore, Uganda).

Cases in which legislation designed to create or maintain racial, social, national or religious discrimination is enforced with sanctions involving compulsory labour appear to be rare (Republic of South Africa).

Compulsory labour as a sanction against workers

Labour discipline

Sanctions involving compulsory labour for simple breaches of labour discipline such as disobedience, refusal to work or unwarranted absence are still provided for under certain laws as a general means of enforcing labour discipline. Texts establishing a general obligation to work sometimes also punish refusal to work or unwarranted absence. In Angola the law punishes with imprisonment in a production camp the following breaches in particular: passive resistance to work, any action causing serious prejudice to the production process, leaving the job during unpaid compulsory working days imposed on workers by a disciplinary board for lack of assiduousness or punctuality, refusal to comply with trade union decisions, absence without just cause during hours of work and an inexcusable mistake. The Government has stated it will review the provisions in question.

In some countries, penalties involving compulsory labour may be imposed for failure to avoid waste of goods or materials, to conform to technical standards or to comply with general production plans (Argentina, Cuba, Ecuador, Syrian Arab Republic). Legislation imposing penalties involving compulsory labour on workers who do not fulfil obligations arising out of a collective agreement or arbitration award has been abolished in Trinidad and Tobago but remains in force in Bangladesh and Pakistan. Similar penalties imposed on workers who refused or failed to comply with a court order to fulfil their employment contracts have been abolished in Australia (South Australia), Kenya and Uganda but not in Nigeria. Other countries have abolished penalties involving compulsory labour that could be imposed on apprentices breaking or otherwise failing to fulfil their contracts (Australia (Victoria), Sudan) and on workers in the hotel industry who terminated their contracts without authorisation or committed various breaches of discipline (Cyprus).

It is persons employed in the public services in particular who are the subject of penal sanctions designed to protect the public interest. Abuse of authority by public officials is a case in which it may be considered necessary to protect the population. In essential services whose interruption would endanger the existence or well-being of all or part of the population, breaches of discipline that might lead to such danger are also frequently punished by law. Sanctions involving compulsory prison labour, however, are not always confined to cases of this sort. In some countries, they apply more generally to workers in the public sector guilty of negligence in the performance of their duties (Italy, Japan (postal and telecommunications employees), Libyan Arab Jamahiriya, Malaysia (telecommunications employees), Syrian Arab Republic, United Republic of Tanzania); to persons who impair production or service activities by failing to comply with their obligations in a state economic enterprise (Cuba); to persons in government service who engage in political activities (Japan); to officials who abandon their service without authorisation (Brazil, Iraq, Syrian Arab Republic); or to postal employees who leave their jobs without having given one month's notice (Bangladesh). Certain provisions imposing sanctions for a breach of contract likely to interrupt essential services are so worded as to prevent workers from terminating their employment, even with notice (Uganda). Elsewhere, however, the legislative authority has repealed provisions that imposed sanctions involving compulsory labour on officials or public service employees who disobeyed orders (Mauritius); on public officials and railway employees who refused to work (Netherlands); or on officials and workers of the public sector who joined certain occupational organisations (Greece).

In the merchant marine, where under certain traditions labour discipline was not always very different from discipline in the national navy, provisions permitting the forcible return of seamen to their ship have been repealed in several countries (Australia, Cyprus, Denmark, Finland,

Nigeria, Norway, Sweden, United Kingdom). Penalties of imprisonment involving compulsory labour that could be inflicted for desertion (in particular, abroad), absence without leave or disobedience have also been abolished or, in certain cases, restricted to offences that endanger the safety of the ship or of persons (Australia, Cyprus, Denmark, Federal Republic of Germany, Netherlands, Nigeria, Spain, Sweden, United Kingdom). In far more countries and territories, provisions under which compulsory labour can be imposed as a means of labour discipline in the merchant marine are still in force (Belgium, Brazil, Ecuador, France, Greece, Iceland, Italy, Poland, Somalia, Suriname and some 20 other maritime countries).

Punishment for participation in strikes

In some countries general prohibitions of strikes are enforced with sanctions involving compulsory labour. Relevant legislative provisions sometimes refer to emergency circumstances. It happens, however, that these provisions are adopted or maintained in force in circumstances where a strike would not endanger the existence or well-being of the population (Chad, Uruguay; the Government of Thailand has stated that a 1976 decree prohibiting all strikes was repealed in 1981). A prohibition of this kind may also result from compulsory arbitration procedures under which practically all strikes can be forbidden or brought rapidly to an end (Angola, Argentina, Bangladesh, Dominican Republic (legislation being revised), Ecuador, Ghana, Kenya, Malaysia, Mauritius, Nicaragua, Sri Lanka, Sudan, Syrian Arab Republic, United Republic of Tanzania, Tunisia, Zambia). In several countries provisions prohibiting recourse to strikes, enforced with imprisonment, apply to industries and services whose interruption might be harmful to the general interest or the national economy, though without creating a danger to the existence or well-being of all or part of the population (Brazil, Colombia, Dominican Republic, El Salvador, Nicaragua, Trinidad and Tobago, Zambia). There are also some countries

in which such prohibitions apply to workers in the public sector, whatever the nature of their work (Egypt (legislation being revised), Iraq, Japan, Somalia (legislation being revised)). In certain countries, however, the right to strike has been fully restored (Greece, Portugal) or the relevant legislation has been amended to eliminate the penalty of imprisonment (Gabon).

Conclusion

The forced labour Conventions are the ILO instruments that have been ratified by the largest number of countries, and it is encouraging to see the number of cases of progress noted each year by the Committee of Experts. Various forms of compulsory labour in connection with public works and services of general interest, such as the construction or maintenance of buildings and roads, reafforestation, irrigation works, transport and agricultural work, as well as work exacted as a tax, have been done away with under most national legislation in accordance with the provisions of the 1930 Convention. Effective implementation of the prohibition of compulsory labour, however, continues to be undermined by certain practices contrary to existing legislation, such as debt bondage and the use of force to recruit or retain workers.

Even more preoccupying are the provisions adopted for economic and social reasons or for mobilising or making better use of labour, which may result in work or services being exacted, under the menace of penalty, for which the workers have not offered themselves voluntarily. Several governments have invoked the need for rapid economic development to justify the adoption of legislation giving the central or local authorities broad powers to recruit or requisition labour, which are incompatible with the provisions of the Convention. Generally speaking, the problems which these governments have thought they could solve by resorting to coercion were due to geographical and structural imbalances in the utilisation of labour, the true solution to which lies in an overall employment policy.

The 1957 Convention, for its part, relates to forced labour as a means of coercion or punishment and the difficulties encountered here are due to the exacting of penal labour for production purposes on account of certain activities (expression of opinion, breaches of labour discipline, participation in strikes, etc.). Wherever the restriction of the freedoms mentioned in the Convention is enforced with penalties involving compulsory labour, there is a need to ascertain to what extent such restrictions are legitimate safeguards in a democra-

tic society or whether they are to be regarded as an unjustified infringement of the rights and freedoms in question.

---

[1] Most ILO texts on forced labour refer to "forced or compulsory labour". While the term "compulsory" may be wider and at times more appropriate than the term "forced", the latter has been traditionally used in official documents and common language. For practical purposes here, we shall here use the terms "forced", "compulsory" and "forced or compulsory" as though they were synonymous.

[2] ILO: *Abolition of forced labour*, General Survey by the Committee of Experts on the Application of Conventions and Recommendations, Report III (Part 4 B), International Labour Conference, 65th Session, 1979, para. 55.

[3] ibid., paras. 97 and 98.

Chapter 6

Termination of employment

Traditionally, in most countries both employers and workers were entirely free to terminate the employment relationship. The only guarantees available to the worker were his right (in many but not all countries) to due notice of termination and his entitlement (in an increasing number of countries) to some severance allowance.

Minimum periods of notice came to be established in many countries first by usage, then by agreement and finally by legislation. In some countries workers and employers were to give the same period of notice, but in many countries the employer had to give a longer period of notice than the worker, frequently increasing with length of service. This difference is in recognition of the fact that generally workers encounter greater difficulties in finding alternative employment than employers in replacing workers who leave. In most cases the employer did not have to give notice when dismissal was based on serious misconduct, while the worker did not have to when the employer seriously violated contractual obligations.

Then, the practice grew up in many countries, first on a voluntary, then on an agreed and finally (in many countries) on a legislated basis, of providing some income security by granting the dismissed worker a severance allowance. Usually, severance allowance or redundancy payments increased with length of service. Later, provision of income security came to rely, in industrialised market economy countries, on unemployment insurance benefits, usually independent of severance allowance entitlements which continued to apply.

A first step towards job security for workers was taken when legislation on collective agreements began to restrict the employer's right to terminate the employment of a worker. Initially, some countries applied the civil code concept of "abuse of right" to the termination of an employment contract. Afterwards, most of these countries used a more direct legislative approach by imposing limitations on the employer's right to terminate a contract of employment without valid reason – a practice which was then followed by many other countries. These limitations were thought necessary because of a growing awareness that the employment relationship was so fundamentally important to the life and well-being of workers that its termination by the employer should require appropriate justification. In addition, in the case of collective dismissals based on economic causes that were deemed to constitute a valid reason, the employer was often required to respect certain procedural rules regarding consultation of the workers' representatives and notification to public authorities.

The extent of job security provided by these rules, admittedly, was limited, since they gave protection only against dismissal without adequate reason and, in the case of mass dismissals, also gave workers' representatives and public authorities an opportunity to have a say on the matter. The resulting situation was a set of rules and procedures, varying among countries in scope and detail, which sought to balance the concern of workers for security of employment with the concern of employers for efficiency.

Requirement to justify dismissal

The requirement that dismissal should be based on a valid reason was first laid down in the Mexican Constitution of 1917 and the legislation of the USSR (1922), Mexico (1931) and Cuba (1934–38). Similar legislation was adopted in some European and African countries during the 1940s and 1950s; and, in addition, some collective agreements concluded in North America and certain European countries during the same period provided the same type of protection. The growing recognition of the need to justify dismissal formed the basis of the Termination of Employment Recommendation (No. 119), adopted by the International Labour Conference in 1963. During the following two decades, many countries – in all regions of the world – enacted legislation, at times directly influenced by the ILO Recommendation, providing for protection against unjustified dismissal. Some of these countries (such as Canada, Italy and Sweden) had previously relied on collective bargaining for the purpose, but turned later to legislation. Most countries where some such protection already existed improved or adapted the relevant legislation.[1]

Workers covered

In most countries the legislation extends protection against unjustified dismissal to workers generally, although it sometimes makes specific exception for certain sectors, such as agriculture, the maritime sector or the public service (the last of which usually offers equivalent or better guarantees).

In some countries, where the law makes no distinction between fixed-term contracts and contracts of indefinite duration, the protection apparently applies to all workers irrespective of the length of their contract. In most countries, however, such protection applies to contracts of indefinite duration.

By contrast, workers with an employment contract for a specified term or task are usually subject to special rules. If their contract is terminated prematurely, and in the absence of serious misconduct, they are entitled to their wages for the remainder of the contract period, but they receive no protection when their contract expires. Some employers tend to offer fixed-term contracts in order to avoid the obligations towards workers with contracts of indefinite duration. As a result, a number of countries have laid down limitations on recourse to fixed-term contracts.

Workers are also frequently excluded from protection during a probationary period, the length of which is usually set in the contract of employment, though it is often subject to a maximum laid down by law. Other categories of workers sometimes excluded from protection are managerial personnel, domestic workers, apprentices, close relatives of the employer, persons working in family undertakings, workers employed in small undertakings and workers who have reached the age of retirement.

Definition of valid reasons

A variety of approaches have been followed in defining the reasons deemed to justify termination of employment by the employer. In such countries as Cameroon, the Congo, Egypt, France, Gabon, the Ivory Coast, the Libyan Arab Jamahiriya, Mauritius, New Zealand, Poland, Sweden and Venezuela, the legislation is phrased in very general terms, providing protection against "unjustified" dismissal or dismissal without "just cause", or stipulating "valid reasons", "legitimate grounds", "good and sufficient cause", "real and serious reasons", or "objective cause". It is left to the bodies responsible for applying the legislation to define the concept of valid reason. Other countries define the concept of justification with a somewhat greater degree of precision. The legislation of Austria, Denmark, the Federal Republic of Germany and Norway relates the concept of valid reason both to the conduct or person of the worker and to the circumstances or operating requirements of the undertaking. In both categories of country, one kind of valid reason – serious misconduct or fault – is deemed to justify summary or immediate dismissal (i.e. without a period of notice).

In a number of other countries, the legislation defines the concept of valid reason in much greater detail, particularly in respect of the kinds of misconduct or breaches of duty that justify disciplinary dismissal. This is the case, for example, in Algeria, the German Democratic Republic, Mexico, Panama, Peru, Portugal, Spain and the USSR.

Generally speaking, the reasons that are considered to justify dismissal fall within a limited number of categories, namely, reasons related to the worker's conduct, to his capacity or ability to carry out his duties, and to the operational requirements of the undertaking. Usually, the competent body hearing appeals against dismissal will seek to determine not only what the reason for the dismissal was and whether this reason was valid, but also whether the ground invoked was sufficiently serious for dismissing the worker concerned (although generally the employer is left some discretion in assessing the seriousness of the reason).

Types of conduct for which a worker may be dismissed generally include improper performance of contractual obligations, such as neglect of duty, violation of work rules, disobedience to lawful orders, absence or lateness without good cause – most of which must as a rule be repeated or become habitual before dismissal becomes justified. Other such types of conduct include improper behaviour at the workplace, such as disorderly conduct, violence, assault, using insulting language, being at work in an intoxicated state or under the influence of drugs, committing various dishonest or untrustworthy acts, and causing material damage.

The reasons justifying dismissal that relate to a worker's capacity to carry out his duties generally include lack of qualifications for or inability to perform the job for which he was hired, as well as inability to perform his duties owing to lengthy illness or to accident. Workers may also be dismissed when the proper functioning of the undertaking requires this. Such a situation may arise from economic circumstances, such as changed market conditions (of a seasonal, cyclical or structural nature) or increased competition. The undertaking may also be obliged to reorganise, to change production technology and/or products, or to modify work methods and processes. It is often difficult to say whether dismissals resulted from events beyond the control of management or from the failure of management adequately to anticipate or adjust to such events. In practice, they are likely to result from both factors.

Many countries have legislated protection against dismissal for certain particular reasons, deemed to be invalid by their very nature. Workers can usually not be dismissed because they are trade union members or workers' representatives or because of their activities as such; sometimes dismissal of such persons is prohibited in the absence of prior authorisation. Some countries also protect workers against dismissal for having filed a complaint or taken part in court cases against the employer. Also, an increasing number of countries prohibit discriminatory dismissal for reasons of race, sex, marital status, pregnancy, religion, political opinion or social origin.

Procedural guarantees

In many countries there are procedural guarantees or rules intended to ensure, first, that some standards of procedural justice are followed by the management of an undertaking before dismissing a worker and, secondly, that redress is available to a worker who is unfairly dismissed.

Legislation, collective agreements or works rules sometimes require employers, before taking a final decision to dismiss a worker on disciplinary grounds, to investigate the allegations made against him and to enable him to defend himself against these allegations.

Certain countries require that, before a worker is dismissed, the workers' representatives must be consulted (e.g. Austria, Federal Republic of Germany, Norway, Poland, Portugal, Romania, Sweden, United Republic of Tanzania) or their consent obtained (e.g. Algeria, Cuba, Czechoslovakia, German Democratic Republic, USSR, Yugoslavia).

The legislation of an increasing number of countries requires that the worker be notified of the reason for his dismissal, either in all cases or when requested by the worker. Obligations of this kind are found, for example, in Bangladesh, Belgium, Benin, Cameroon, Chad, Colombia, the Congo, Czechoslovakia, France, the German Democratic Republic, the Federal Republic of Germany, Hungary, India, Ireland, Italy, Mexico, the Netherlands, Norway, Pakistan, Panama, Peru, Poland, Portugal, Romania, Spain, Sweden, the United Republic of Tanzania, the United Kingdom, Yugoslavia and Zaire.

Protection against unjustified dismissal can be effective only if there is an appropriate procedure whereby a worker can appeal and whereby he can obtain redress if the dismissal is found to be unfair.

In some countries, the first path open to a worker (and in certain countries the only path) is the grievance procedure in the undertaking, established by collective agreement or works rules. Such a procedure, ending with a binding decision by a jointly agreed arbitrator, is the established method in countries such as Canada and the United States.

In most countries, however, the principal avenue open to workers is a procedure of appeal to a public body, such as a court or tribunal, that has been given the competence to hear and decide such complaints. The competent authority is frequently a specialised labour or industrial tribunal (or labour chamber of a civil court). Labour or industrial tribunals are composed either of representatives of workers and employers, often with an independent president, or of independent persons alone who are knowledgeable about labour questions. In general, the competent bodies have three options when they find that a worker has been dismissed unjustifiably. They are sometimes empowered only to award compensation to the worker concerned. Their power is larger when they can order the employer to reinstate the worker or when they can choose between reinstatement and compensation. Today, a large number of countries empower the competent bodies to order the employer to reinstate the worker either in all or in some cases of unfair dismissal. This is so, for example, in Algeria, Austria, Bangladesh, Bulgaria, Colombia, the Congo, Czechoslovakia, Ethiopia, the German Democratic Republic, the Federal Republic of Germany, Hungary, India, Indonesia, Iraq, Ireland, Italy, Kenya, the Libyan Arab Jamahiriya, Mexico, New Zealand, Norway, Pakistan, the Philippines, Peru, Portugal, Romania, Singapore, Somalia, Spain, Sri Lanka, Trinidad and Tobago, the USSR, the United Kingdom and Venezuela.

Special protection related to collective dismissals or lay-offs

Dismissals and lay-offs for economic, technological or structural reasons can affect sizeable numbers of workers and create serious social and economic problems for the community. Over the past several decades, many countries have formulated special rules in respect of collective dismissals in undertakings.[2] These special rules have generally sought to give the workers' representatives concerned some say in a matter of great importance to their constituents and to give public authorities advance warning of impending job loss. The procedures established by these rules generally have aimed at two objectives: to avoid or minimise compulsory dismissals and to attenuate the consequences of job loss for any workers affected.

Consultation of workers' representatives

A number of countries have laid down legislation providing for consultation of workers' representatives before undertakings reduce their workforce. This is the case in the ten member countries of the European Community, where a directive on this subject was promulgated in 1975, and in countries such as Cameroon, Gabon, Indonesia, Kenya, Madagascar, Norway, Portugal, Senegal, Spain, Sweden, Zaire and Zambia. As already mentioned, in certain Eastern European countries, such as Czechoslovakia, the German Democratic Republic and the USSR, workers' representatives are not only consulted but also have to approve the dismissals. Sometimes, as in Australia, Belgium, Canada, New Zealand and the United States, collective agreements or industrial awards provide for notification of workforce reductions to union representatives.

These obligations frequently apply to workforce reductions of a certain size – exceeding a given number or percentage of the workforce in an undertaking – which are sometimes referred to as collective dismissals or redundancies. They often specify that there must be a minimum period between notification to the workers' representatives and implementation of the intended workforce reductions so as to allow sufficient time for effective consultation. Another obligation is usually to provide workers' representatives with appropriate information on the planned reductions, such as the reasons for the reductions, the number of workers to be dismissed or laid off, the normal size of the undertaking, the occupational classifications of the workers concerned and the period of time over which it is intended to carry out the dismissals.

Prior consultation of workers' representatives provides them with the possibility of influencing the employer's decision or the manner in which it is carried out. The degree to which they can modify management plans depends of course on the particular circumstances of the undertaking, the urgency of the measures proposed, the power of the workers and the union in the undertaking and the availability of external assistance. In many cases, negotiations may make it possible to limit the number of workers affected or even to avoid compulsory departures completely. Instead, other measures may be applied, such as early retirement, work-sharing through short-time work, attrition arrangements and internal transfers. If these arrangements are not feasible, negotiations have to concentrate on measures to mitigate the consequences of employment losses, such as additional severance pay and assistance in retraining and in finding new jobs.

Notification to public authorities

Employers are bound in a large number of countries to notify the competent administrative authorities of impending workforce reductions. After notification they are generally obliged to wait a certain period of time before carrying out the dismissals. Usually the authority to be notified is the public employment office or the labour inspectorate. The role of these authorities with respect to such workforce reductions varies.

In some countries, notification may be solely for statistical and information purposes. In others, the authorities may play a more active role: they may mediate in any dispute or difference; they may help the parties either to work out measures to avert or limit dismissals or to find new jobs for the workers concerned. In some countries, the public authorities may have additional powers: either to postpone the effective date of dismissals (e.g. Belgium, Federal Republic of Germany) or to authorise or refuse to authorise certain dismissals (e.g. Colombia, France, Iraq, Netherlands, Panama, Peru, Portugal, Senegal, Spain, Sudan and Zaire). Such powers are sometimes given to disputes settlement bodies (e.g. Congo, Indonesia, Mexico and Venezuela).

Measures to avert or minimise collective dismissals

Employers and workers now generally agree that every effort should be made to avert or minimise workforce reductions. Undertakings may provide additional work, for example by seeking to increase demand for their products or services; building up of stocks; reducing subcontracting; undertaking maintenance work in advance of the normal schedule; or carrying out in advance planned training activities. They may also distribute the available work over the existing workforce through reduction of overtime and recourse to short-time work or propose a voluntary reduction of the staff. This can be brought about by measures of attrition, including restrictions on hiring and internal transfers and by voluntary departures and early retirement.

Some governments make available large funds to help the parties to avert or minimise compulsory departures. They may set up a compensation scheme for short-time work (from public funds or unemployment insurance funds), under which workers are partially compensated for the normal hours they were not able to work. Programmes of this type have been carried out, for example, in Austria, Canada, France, the Federal Republic of Germany, Italy, Japan, the Netherlands, Norway, Switzerland and the United Kingdom and in California (United States). In some of these countries such programmes have become a major instrument of policy aimed at promoting recourse to short-time work to permit undertakings suffering from temporary difficulties to hold their

workforce together until those difficulties have passed, as well as to provide undertakings confronting longer-term problems with sufficient time to respond to these problems (through restructuring and redeployment of the workforce where necessary) in as humane a fashion as possible.

In certain circumstances some countries also make available public assistance to undertakings in difficulty. Such assistance may include provision of loans, loan guarantees, grants, public investment in the undertaking and the financing of some costs of restructuring or conversion, in particular the costs of retraining (e.g. France, Italy, Japan and United Kingdom).

Measures to attenuate the effects of collective dismissals

Frequently, collective dismissals cannot be avoided: attention then turns to what measures may be taken to attenuate the effects of job loss on the persons concerned. Such measures aim mainly at protecting the workers' income, through severance allowances or unemployment benefits or a combination of such payments, and at assisting them in obtaining new employment.

Provisions for severance allowance of some kind (sometimes called redundancy payments) have come to be included in the legislation of a considerable number of countries, are frequently included in collective agreements or are negotiated on an ad hoc basis in connection with a particular redundancy. Such allowances are usually calculated on the basis of length of service, consisting of a given number of weeks' pay per year of employment, and are usually payable in a lump sum. The payments are usually considered either as an indemnity for the loss suffered by a worker whose dismissal was not due to his own fault, or as a payment in recognition of past service.

Unemployment benefit schemes are mainly found in the industrialised countries, though they have also been set up in a few developing countries. In some countries, these benefits have been improved in recent years to respond to the lengthy periods of unemployment that have become more current during the economic difficulties of the past ten years. In some countries, the legislation or collective agreements provide for supplementary unemployment benefits in certain circumstances, in particular where loss of employment is due to economic reasons.

While financial compensation and income protection help to tide workers over a period of search for other employment, the most important issue is how to find a new job. Over the past few decades, the governments of many countries have put a great deal of effort into helping workers to find jobs. They have improved the capacities and the methods of employment services. They have taken additional measures to organise vocational training and retraining, particularly for workers displaced from declining industries or from industries subject to restructuring or technological change. Finally, they often provide financial assistance to workers who agree to be trained or retrained or who are willing to move in order to find a new job.

The main provisions of the Termination of Employment Convention (No. 158) and Recommendation (No. 166)

The question of termination of employment was discussed at the International Labour Conference in 1981 and 1982. In 1981 the discussion was based on a law and practice report – on which the preceding two sections are largely based. In 1982 the Conference had to decide what type of instrument should be adopted: a Convention or a Recommendation or both. On the basis of the 1981 discussions the Office prepared texts of a Convention supplemented by a Recommenda-

tion, which were submitted to the Committee of the Conference dealing with termination of employment.

In the Committee, the Workers' members and a number of Government members supported the adoption of a Convention supplemented by a Recommendation, while the Employers' members and a number of other Government members favoured the adoption of a Recommendation only. The latter felt that given the great diversity of law and practice on the subject, only a Recommendation would be flexible enough to be widely applied. The former felt that the importance of the subject warranted the adoption of a Convention, which could be drawn up in a manner sufficiently flexible to be widely ratified and applied. After some discussion, the Committee decided to ask a Working Party, composed of representatives of the Employers' and Workers' members, to see whether they could agree on the texts of a Convention supplemented by a Recommendation. The proposed texts finally adopted by the Committee resulted from an accommodation in the Working Party between the Employers' and Workers' groups and further discussion in the Committee.

The Conference adopted the Termination of Employment Convention, 1982 (No. 158), by 356 votes in favour to 9 against, with 54 abstentions, and the Termination of Employment Recommendation, 1982 (No. 166), by 375 votes in favour to 0 against, with 16 abstentions.

The Termination of Employment Convention applies to all branches of economic activities and to all employed persons. However, some categories of employed persons may be excluded: workers engaged under a short- or fixed-term employment contract; workers who are at least as well protected under special arrangements; and limited categories of workers for whom coverage presents substantial difficulties, as a result either of particular employment conditions or of the size or nature of the undertaking that employs them.

83

Part II of the Convention sets out a number of standards of general application. According to the basic principle governing justification for termination, the employment of a worker is not to be terminated unless there is a valid reason for doing so – either connected with the capacity or conduct of the worker or based on the operational requirements of the undertaking. Several reasons are not valid reasons for termination: union membership or participation in union activities outside working hours (or within working hours if the employer has given his consent); seeking office as, or acting in the capacity of, a workers' representative; filing of a complaint or participation in proceedings against an employer; race, colour, sex, marital status, family responsibilities, pregnancy, religion, political opinion, national extraction or social origin; absence from work during maternity leave; and temporary absence from work because of illness or injury.

Before being dismissed for reasons related to his conduct or performance, a worker must be provided with an opportunity to defend himself against the allegations made, unless the employer cannot reasonably be expected to provide this opportunity.

A worker must be entitled to appeal to an impartial body, empowered to render a decision on whether the termination was justified. Provisions are included to ensure that the rules governing the burden of proof in appeal proceedings are not unfavourable to the worker. If the competent body finds that the termination was unjustified, it is empowered to order payment of adequate compensation or other appropriate relief, if it has not the power or does not find it practicable to declare the termination invalid and/or to order or propose the reinstatement of the worker.

A worker whose employment is to be terminated must be entitled to a reasonable period of notice, unless he is guilty of serious misconduct.

The Convention also makes provision for entitlement to severance allowance or other separation benefits, as well as to unemployment benefits or other social security benefits.

Part III of the Convention deals with termination of employment for economic, technological, structural or similar reasons. An employer who contemplates such terminations must provide the workers' representatives concerned in good time with relevant information and give them an opportunity for consultation on measures to avert or minimise the terminations and measures to mitigate their adverse effects. The employer is also required to notify the competent authority of such terminations as early as possible, giving relevant information. Each country may limit these obligations to cases in which a minimum number of workers is to be affected.

In addition to the reasons mentioned by the Convention, the Termination of Employment Recommendation lists two reasons that should not be valid grounds for termination: age (subject to national law and practice regarding retirement) and absence from work due to compulsory military service or other civic obligations.

Among the recommended procedures that should be followed prior to termination, the Recommendation requires appropriate written warning in the case of repeated misconduct (where repetition is necessary for termination to be justified), and appropriate instructions, written warning and a reasonable period of time for improvement in the case of unsatisfactory performance. A worker should be entitled to be assisted by another person in defending himself against allegations regarding his conduct or performance. The Recommendation also provides for notification of the termination in writing and, if requested, a written statement of the reason for the termination. A worker should also be entitled to reasonable time off from work without loss of pay during the period of notice for the purpose of seeking other employment.

The Recommendation includes some supplementary provisions concerning termination of employment for economic, technological, structural or similar reasons.

The employer should consult the workers' representatives when he contemplates the introduction of major changes in the undertaking that are likely to entail terminations, providing them for this purpose with all relevant information on the major changes and their effects.

The Recommendation lists a number of measures that should be considered in order to avert or minimise terminations of employment, including restriction of hiring, spreading the workforce reduction over a period of time, internal transfers, training and retraining, voluntary early retirement with appropriate income protection, restriction of overtime and reduction of normal hours of work. Where a reduction of normal hours is envisaged, it is recommended that there should be partial compensation for loss of wages for the normal hours not worked.

The Recommendation also provides that the selection of workers for dismissal for economic or similar reasons should be made according to criteria that give due weight to the interests of both parties; it also states that the workers affected should have priority if the employer again hires workers with comparable qualifications.

Lastly, provisions are included in the Recommendation on how to mitigate the effects of terminations of employment for economic or similar reasons: through placement in suitable alternative employment as soon as possible, with training or retraining where appropriate, and with the assistance of the employer where possible. It is recommended that consideration be given to providing income protection during any course of training and retraining and to partial or total reimbursement of expenses connected with such training or retraining and with finding and taking up employment which requires a change of residence.

---

[1] For a review of national law and practice regarding protection against unjustified dismissal in the member countries of the ILO, see ILO: *Termination of employment at the initiative of the employer*, Report VIII (1), International Labour Conference, 67th Session, 1981, Chs. I-III.

[2] See in this connection ibid., Ch. VI, and E. Yemin (ed.): *Workforce reductions in undertakings: Policies and measures for the protection of redundant workers in seven industrialised market economy countries* (Geneva, ILO, 1982).

Part 3

Training

Introduction

Man is the initiator and beneficiary of development. He is the designer and manager of development plans and at the same time a contributor to other factors of production. Without proper planning, effective management of resources and trained people in all walks of life, it is hard to see how economic and social development can get off the ground. In addition, training not only provides man with a means of earning his livelihood but also gives him the possibility of improving his standard of living and social situation as a result of the development process.

Essentially, training aims at conveying knowledge, imparting skills and influencing attitudes (see box). This task is becoming increasingly complex owing to three major factors. First, the range of knowledge and skills needed for modern development has expanded greatly. Second, rapid advances in technology and structural changes

Main forms of training

In most cases, training is given to young school-leavers in order to prepare them for a job. They may undergo short-term *vocational preparation*, which is designed to ease the transition from school to work and enhance the employability of young people. Or they may enter longer-term (two to four years) *initial training*, which is the first complete training course for an occupation. This is often divided into two parts: *basic training*, followed by *specialisation*. Another means of making the transition from school to work is the system of *apprenticeship*. This is defined as a period of long-term training, mainly carried out within an undertaking. It is based on a contract whereby the employer assumes responsibility for giving the trainee initial training for a recognised apprenticeable occupation and whereby the trainee agrees to work for the employer.

Later in their life, workers can also take *further training*, which is any type of training subsequent and complementary to initial training. *Updating* acquaints the worker with the most recent developments — new materials, tools, processes, etc. – in his occupation. *Refresher training* restores a worker's skills, knowledge or capacity to the level for which he was originally trained. This type of training is usually given when occupational life was interrupted for a long time (e.g. because of unemployment, military service, family responsibilities). Upgrading or supplementary training provides supplementary skills and knowledge in order to increase the versatility and occupational mobility of a worker or to improve his standard of performance. This type of training frequently leads to a promotion. Through *retraining*, a worker acquires skills and knowledge needed for practising an occupation other than the one for which he was originally trained.

Forms of training can also be defined according to the place where training is given. Training may be given in training centres or in vocational schools. Training may also be provided within the undertaking. *On-the-job training* is arranged at an ordinary workplace and uses actual jobs for instruction and practice purposes. *Off-the-job training* takes place under the responsibility of the undertaking and is organised in an area (training workshop, classroom, etc.) specially equipped for training purposes. *Mobile training* "takes training to the trainee". The equipment may consist of a van, railway carriage or vessel used as a mobile training centre. Alternatively, mobile equipment (video, film projection) can be installed in any training establishment. A mobile training unit may also consist of a group of teachers or instructors who stay in an undertaking for a limited period of time. *Extension service* is a system under which technical knowledge is systematically communicated to practitioners (e.g. farmers and other rural workers) through instruction, advisory services and practical demonstrations conducted by itinerant specialists (extension agents).

have meant that training is a never-ending process; in fact, this development necessitates not only new knowledge and skills but also more creative thinking and a readjustment of a person's attitude towards his working environment. Third, as job requirements continue to change at an accelerated pace, the educational system, which is traditionally slow to react, continues to fall behind in meeting them. Increasing demands are being made on training to fill this gap and there is every reason to think that this pressure will increase in the future. This problem is becoming increasingly acute as countries, industrialised and developing alike, struggle to adapt both the education and the training system to employment goals and opportunities.

In the past, efforts to develop human resources paid too much attention to the parts – institutions with their curricula – and not enough to the whole –

a training system linked to education on the one hand and to employment needs on the other. Now, however, training is increasingly looked upon as a concerted effort emanating from a policy and supported by institutions and programmes that are efficiently run, properly co-ordinated and financed and produce a relevant output of trained resources. Various steps have therefore been taken in many countries to enact appropriate legislation and amplify signals on job requirements with a view to a better assessment of training needs, the continuous evaluation of training efforts and the introduction of the necessary mechanisms to improve the cost-effectiveness of the whole process.

In the two following chapters, the first dealing with industrialised countries and the second with developing countries, an attempt will be made to give an account of the evolving trends in the search for more effective training systems.

Chapter 7

Training in industrialised countries

Industrialised countries face two important training problems. First, they have to adapt their training policies and programmes to meet the needs of a rapidly changing economic and technological environment. Second, in this decade many countries still have to cope with an increasing flow of young labour market entrants who require training. In this chapter we shall try to show how the industrialised market economies and the centrally planned economies of Eastern Europe have responded to this challenge.

The first part of this chapter is devoted to the industrialised market economies. The second part examines the trends in the centrally planned economies of Eastern Europe.

Industrialised market economies

The current, persistent recession has affected the availability of public funds for training and has led in some cases to a critical reappraisal of the effectiveness and response of the training system to a changing economic environment.

Although there can be no doubt that interest in training has increased in recent years – as reflected in political declarations, plans, research, output, etc. – it is uncertain that this has led to a real increase in the training effort itself. It is in fact difficult to be definitive on this issue owing to the absence of reliable statistics on training at the international level and, very often, at the national level. This makes generalisation impossible and any comparison difficult, whether between countries or over a period of time.

The tempo of activities in training has varied greatly from one country to another. In Canada, for example, registered trainees increased almost fourfold between 1960 and 1979 (see table 7.1). This is due to the efforts of the federal and provincial governments whose financial assistance in training is provided for sectors facing shortages of skilled manpower at the expense of other sectors.

In contrast, in the United Kingdom the statistics on the number of apprentices and trainees in engineering and related industries and the manufacturing industry show a constant and considerable decline of the training effort in these sectors (see table 7.2).

The critical reappraisal of training policies has focused on two main basic issues: a shift from specialised training to training for broad skills and qualifications and a greater emphasis on training geared to the needs of enterprises.

General knowledge, rather than specific skills, is needed for the application of new technologies. In other words, understanding and mastery of the overall production process are becoming more important than the execution of specific tasks. In addition, governments, usually supported by trade unions, favour broader and more flexible training programmes, in particular for young entrants into the labour market. Some countries are therefore experimenting with training curricula that cover two specialisations. Such an approach has the advantage that young people entering working life are better equipped to upgrade their skills or to undergo retraining later on.

Many countries also try to focus their attention on training oriented towards employment needs. An example of this trend is the Canadian initiative called the National Job Market Intelligence Service, which carries an inventory of job requirements, educational and training profiles needed and career prospects for the vacancies. A new initiative called the Canadian Occupational Projection System (COPS) aims at projecting skill needs in industry.

Another example is the United States where specialised government services try to reduce the mismatch between the demand for and supply of skills. The occupational profiles established on the basis of surveys and research have become an instrument for decision-making in the organisation and financing of training activities.

Many governmental authorities also try to convince the private sector of the importance of training and upgrading manpower during periods of economic recession, in order to constitute an adequate reserve for periods of economic expansion. It is not clear, however, whether their attempts are successful, particularly at a time when enterprises usually try to reduce their overall costs.

In some countries, training has also become an important means of assistance to the most disadvantaged sectors of the population. Apart from unskilled youth, other population groups such as single women, the handicapped and migrants have benefited from measures designed especially for them. For example, in France, since 1974, single women with dependent children have been given priority of access to state-financed training programmes. At the same time, women over 26 years

Table 7.1
Training activities (all occupations) in Canada,* 1960-79

Year	New registrations	Total registrations	New registrations as a percentage of total registrations
1960-61	7 375	26 918	27.4
1961-62	7 748	27 695	28.0
1962-63	8 239	28 765	26.6
1963-64	10 040	31 256	32.1
1964-65	12 422	36 155	34.4
1965-66	15 532	44 067	35.3
1966-67	17 160	50 804	33.8
1967-68	14 991	53 587	28.0
1968-69	18 423	59 298	31.1
1969-70	15 850	60 362	26.3
1970-71	17 073	62 594	27.3
1971-72	18 295	64 825	28.2
1972-73	21 847	68 963	31.7
1973-74	24 535	76 625	32.0
1974-75	28 625	86 011	33.3
1975-76	28 722	95 734	30.0
1976-77	27 655	101 591	27.2
1977-78	28 966	106 659	27.2
1978-79	30 398	113 496	26.8

* Not including the Province of Quebec.
Source: Statistics Canada: *Publicly supported vocational training involving the private sector*, Cat. No. 81-238.

of age have in special cases benefited from measures under the scheme providing training-cum-employment contracts for special categories of the population. Special re-entry training programmes have been organised for women wishing to resume work once their children have grown up. In 1980, 14,000 women received this type of training in France. Despite initiatives of this sort – those in France being cited as an example – it must be admitted that on the whole training has been of much greater benefit to men than to women, even making allowance for their respective shares in the working population.

Training of immigrant workers has also been a major concern in many Western European countries as well as in Canada and the United States.

Apprentices and other trainees in manufacturing and engineering and related industries in the United Kingdom, 1964-83 (in thousands)

Year	Engineering and related industries			Manufacturing		
	Appren- tices	Other trainees	Total	Appren- tices	Other trainees	Total
1964	162.9	52.0	215.0	240.4	148.9	389.3
1965	166.9	55.1	222.0	243.3	145.3	388.6
1966	170.4	–	–	243.7	–	–
1967	171.6	96.9	268.5	242.6	201.9	444.5
1968	171.0	98.0	269.1	236.2	209.6	445.8
1969	161.5	96.6	258.2	232.1	205.3	437.3
1970	151.2	87.2	238.4	218.6	202.1	420.7
1971	145.0	73.7	218.7	208.1	173.8	381.9
1972	128.9	64.4	193.3	186.9	159.7	346.6
1973	105.8	67.6	173.4	155.5	157.0	312.5
1974	94.7	68.9	163.6	139.6	156.6	296.2
1975	98.1	64.9	162.9	155.3	135.2	290.5
1976	96.3	49.3	145.5	148.4	116.3	264.7
1977	101.4	55.9	157.3	153.1	125.1	278.2
1978	107.4	52.7	160.1	156.2	116.3	272.5
1979	106.2	48.0	154.2	155.0	111.3	266.3
1980	101.3	40.5	141.8	149.5	90.0	239.5
1981				147.6		
1982				123.7		
1983				99.0		

Source: United Kingdom, Department of Employment: *Employment Gazette* (London), various issues.

Lately the emphasis of special training programmes for migrants has shifted towards prevocational and vocational training of second-generation migrants, i.e. youth, children of migrant workers who may have been educated partly in the country of origin and who have difficulty in adjusting to host country training systems.

Youth training programmes

Many youth training programmes have recently been set up in industrialised market economy countries in order to cope with the youth unemployment problem, which – because of its extent, duration and persistence – has become quite preoccupying. In 1983 about 40 per cent of the roughly 11 million unemployed in the European Community were under 25 years of age, a percentage that had hardly changed since 1980.[1] In Canada and the United States, the percentage of unemployed youth is also very high.

In the European Community, the United Kingdom has one of the largest percentages of young people leaving the educational system without having received apprenticeship, technical or vocational training. At the end of the 1970s, about 44 per cent of those in the 16–17 age bracket had left the educational system without being employed or registered for any training. The corresponding figures for France and the Federal Republic of Germany were 19 and 7 per cent.[2] But in the United Kingdom a growing number of young people are continuing their studies beyond compulsory education, amounting to an increase of more than 36 per cent between 1972 and 1981.

Though often criticised, the Youth Opportunities Programme (YOP), which started in 1978, was the most important initiative in the United Kingdom among all the measures to combat youth unemployment: it opened up more than 1 million training opportunities for unemployed youth. One of the most praiseworthy aspects of the programme was its emphasis on the least skilled youth, those encountering the greatest difficulty in finding a job. In the autumn of 1983, the United Kingdom took new initiatives, which resulted in the launching of the Youth Training Scheme (YTS). This scheme provides one year of vocational training combined with job experience to any young people in the 16–17 age group who are not pursuing their studies and are unemployed. The YTS is above all a training activity, whereas the previous YOP was mainly intended to provide occupational experience.

In Canada, the situation is quite different. The country has a high unemployment rate (around 11.5 per cent in 1982) and at the same time an acute shortage of skilled manpower. According to estimates, Canada will be obliged to train every year, up to 1985-86, 10,000 skilled workers more than it has been training in the past.[3] This number is in addition to the 20,000-25,000 skilled immigrants expected to arrive in Canada each year.[4] Traditionally, these immigrants contribute to Canada's pool of skilled manpower; thus, 73 per cent of Canada's skilled workers were born outside the country and 87 per cent are over 40 years of age. However, immigration is slowing down[5] and it is not certain whether Canada has equipped itself with the structures and programmes necessary to fill the gap.

The Canada Manpower Training Programme (CMTP) is the most important federal programme dealing with manpower. It contains two options: training in institutions and training in industry, the latter being divided into two schemes: the Canada Manpower Industrial Training Programme (CMITP) and Critical Trades Skill Training (CTST). This last scheme is particularly intended for youth; 70 per cent of the participants are less than 25 years of age. The new Training Act adopted by Canada broadens still further the scope of these schemes and creates new ones geared particularly to youth training and to preparation for working life.[6]

In the United States three cumulative factors – a decline in productivity growth, a shortage of skilled manpower and a very high unemployment rate – have resulted in greater attention being given to manpower training. The most important government measure taken in recent years in this area was the Comprehensive Employment and Training Act (CETA) of 1973. The target groups at which the programme set up under this Act was aimed were the unemployed, the underemployed and, in general, economically disadvantaged persons. The CETA programme was mainly designed to create jobs and did not deal with the improvement of skills of persons already employed.

In 1977 the Youth Employment and Demonstration Projects Act (YEDPA) amended the CETA with a view to broadening the effort to combat youth unemployment. A variety of measures, programmes and projects were adopted mainly to help youth in difficulty to enter working life. Some schemes provided an opportunity to study and at the same time to acquire work experience in an enterprise. Others provided young people with part-time work and an income permitting them to continue their vocational training. In 1980, the youth employment and training programme assisted 463,000 young people at a cost of almost US$700 million.[7]

As table 7.3 shows, the CETA programme did reach disadvantaged groups, such as minorities, girls and the unemployed, but it also came under criticism. The placement of CETA trainees became a controversial issue. In fact, only relatively few trainees were able to find non-subsidised employment in the private sector. It appeared that business enterprises were not favourably inclined to employing these trainees, whom they considered relatively underqualified and therefore not very productive. The training content of the CETA programme was considered too slim and of too short a duration. Moreover, the relations between the CETA programme and the private sector were not always close.

The CETA programme, however, was discontinued, and replaced in October 1982 by the Job Training Partnership Act (JTPA). The legislation leading to the creation of JTPA reflects the new attitude towards training since it stipulates that most training activities must be geared to employment. Seventy per cent of the resources for this programme are devoted to this purpose.[8]

In June 1982 about 40 per cent of all the unemployed in France were under 25 years of age. In addition about one-third of the young people who leave the educational system every year do so without obtaining a diploma (more than 250,000). In order to remedy this situation, the French government authorities in 1977 launched the "youth employment pacts", which combine employment

Table 7.3
Newly registered participants in youth programmes in the United States, 1980

	No. of participants	%
Total	966 586	
Men	485 532	50.2
Women	481 054	49.8
White	359 220	37.2
Black	470 538	48.7
Other minorities	136 827	14.2
Less than 16 years of age	291 108	30.1
16-19 years	604 754	62.6
Economically disadvantaged	947 747	98.0
Unemployed	214 399	22.2

Source: *Employment and training report of the President* (Washington, 1981), p. 272.

assistance measures (exemption from social security contributions) with training measures such as "introduction-to-work" training. The duration is six to eight months, including several weeks in an enterprise. The training periods are open to youth between 16 and 26 years of age and are organised by public or private training institutions in accordance with local employment needs. Questionnaires submitted to trainees four to six months following completion of the training have revealed that the average rate of entry into employment had risen substantially as a result.

The French *Plan avenir jeunes* (Plan for the Future of Youth), launched in 1981-82, distinguishes between two categories of training: entry-to-work training – reserved for the most underprivileged youth and intended to facilitate their integration into society; and job qualification training – essentially vocational training for immediate employment. Under this plan, job qualification training was provided to 50,000 young persons and entry-to-work training to 15,000 in 1981-82.

Another means of occupational integration based on alternating work and training takes the form of the "training-cum-employment contract", restricted to young people between 17 and 26 and aimed at lasting occupational integration. The training-cum-employment contract provides for training for a duration of from 120 to 1,200 hours organised by the employer or by an outside organisation. In return for this training obligation, the employer receives a subsidy for each hour of training. This formula has proved to be successful and the number of contracts rose from 26,400 in 1977 to 75,000 in 1982. Between 80 and 85 per cent of the trainees found a lasting job, while between 40 and 50 per cent of them found a job in the occupation for which they were trained.

In a report on the integration of youth, commissioned by the French Government in 1981, an approach was advocated whereby youth problems need to be looked at as a whole, that is to say with training, occupational integration, social integration, housing and leisure, all being considered at the same time. This report had a great impact on the policies adopted in France from 1982 on, which now provide for all young people between 16 and 18 paid training opportunities lasting from six to 12 months (including periods of practical training on the job). At the same time, training posts are being offered to young jobseekers between 18 and 26 years of age. Training-cum-employment contracts will also be continued for youth under 26 years of age. Finally, a plan was prepared providing for the establishment, from 1982 on, of more than 600 youth guidance centres, to be supported by local municipalities. Intensive guidance training programmes will be offered and 60 local centres equipped to deal with the problems of youth as a whole (training, employment, social and emotional problems, housing, leisure, etc.) are to be set up in populated areas having a high proportion of young unemployed persons.

In general, the industrialised market economy countries continue to be faced with certain basic issues with regard to the vocational training of youth:

95

- How can the percentage of youth who leave the educational system every year with vocational training qualifications be increased?
- What should be the mix in the training provided between general and specialised training?
- How should employers, trade unions and the youth themselves be involved in adapting training to the changing needs of the economy, society and the individual?

The answers to these issues will determine to a very large extent the direction taken by youth training policies in future.

Apprenticeship

Apprenticeship, the traditional path to a skilled trade in many industrialised countries, has evolved considerably in the past few years. As a means of initial training, apprenticeship is intended primarily for youth; nowadays, however, it has been opened up to adults as well. Generally speaking, apprenticeship is organised in such a way as to combine theoretical training in technical establishments with the acquisition of practical experience on the job. Apprenticeship was long considered to be an ideal means of preparing young people for industrial trades and crafts; and the importance attached to that form of training varies from one country to another. Thus, apprenticeship programmes are well developed in Austria, the Federal Republic of Germany and Switzerland. In France and the United Kingdom apprenticeship has also been the principal means of training in the past. On the other hand, there is less of a tradition in apprenticeship in Canada and the United States as an acknowledged training channel. In several countries apprenticeship as an institution has been much discussed and has recently come under much scrutiny; like all training systems and programmes, it has been questioned with respect to its effective response to training needs in a constantly changing environment.

In the United Kingdom apprenticeship is criticised for being too rigid, outdated and even archaic. The number of apprentices today is half what it was in 1968. Their number dropped by 20 per cent between 1978-79 and 1980-81. In 1981 the mechanical engineering industry recruited 10,000 apprentices, i.e. only half of the 20,000 new apprentices considered necessary to cover the industry's future needs.[9] Similar situations are found in other sectors such as road transport, building trades and printing. For purposes of comparison, in the Federal Republic of Germany around 50 per cent of the young people finishing their compulsory education entered into apprenticeship in 1977, whereas in the United Kingdom the proportion was a mere 14 per cent.[10]

It is not surprising, therefore, that modernisation of apprenticeship constitutes the essence of the training reform in the United Kingdom. The main elements of this modernisation are, on the one hand, the relaxation and even elimination of the age restrictions formerly placed on apprenticeships and, on the other, a more flexible application of the years-of-service requirement for apprentices. Another proposal for improving the system is to review certification procedures for apprentices and teachers. In some experimental programmes under way the apprentices, in order to qualify for occupational status, must pass examinations requiring a higher level of knowledge and skills than in the past.

In contrast to the position in the United Kingdom, the number of apprenticeships in France increased by more than 90 per cent between 1972 and 1980 (see table 7.4). This increase was due mainly to the legislation of 16 July 1971, designed to modernise apprenticeship and give it a status equal to full-time education. This particular reform was intended primarily to create an apprenticeship contract that would be recognised as a special labour contract and give apprentices all the guarantees afforded to wage earners. It also provided for the issuing of technical teaching certificates; a minimum of 400 hours of training at a recognised centre; a minimum apprentice wage climbing from 15 to 45 per cent of the minimum

Table 7.4
Number of apprentices[a] in France, 1971-80

	1971-73	1973-74	1974-75	1975-76	1976-77	1977-78	1978-79	1979-80
Independent trades	37 725	52 737	52 729	57 482	60 345	75 986	71 609	79 859
Industry and commerce	25 046	33 718	33 721	34 660	36 427	41 316	39 821	42 275
Total	62 771	86 455	86 450	92 142	96 772	117 302	111 430	122 134

[a] Estimates.

wage between the first and the fourth training semesters; and the employer's obligation to obtain approval from the departmental vocational training committee before hiring an apprentice.

More recently, the French Government has taken additional measures to make apprenticeship more attractive. For example, since 1979 the central Government has been paying all employer and worker social security contributions for apprentices working in enterprises employing fewer than 11 workers. In 1980 the Government introduced an apprenticeship tax to finance the premiums that skilled craftsmen receive for the training of apprentices.

In the United States the apprenticeship programmes provide supervised training on the job, supplemented by related theoretical studies in a training institution. Here again, there have been various attempts to modernise the approach, to broaden the concept of apprenticeship, and to make the various programmes more responsive to local labour market needs. Thus, in 1980, 12 national apprenticeship standards were registered.[11] Employers receive financial incentives to take on apprentices, particularly in occupations where skilled manpower is in short supply. Age restrictions on entry into apprenticeship have been relaxed or done away with; as a result, the average age of apprentices is considerably higher in the United States than in other industrialised countries. Moreover, the new apprenticeship system is becoming more open and flexible, and it attaches more importance to acquired skills than the older system. In spite of these reforms, the number of apprentices decreased over a number of years. By the end of 1979 there were 323,866 registered apprentices in the United States of whom 82.6 per cent were White (excluding Hispanic) and 8.8 per cent Black (excluding Hispanic); 4.1 per cent were women. At the same time, 55.1 per cent of all apprentices were registered in the building trades, 21.7 per cent in the manufacturing sector and 6.6 per cent in the services sector.[12]

The Canadian apprenticeship programme is organised at the provincial level. Under this programme, the Federal Government "buys", as it were, training posts for apprentices in the provincial training institutions and reimburses the latter for their services. The so-called interprovincial seal constitutes a very interesting arrangement whereby apprentices can take a final examination that is nationally recognised. This procedure is quite a step forward in Canada where many training and education courses are not recognised throughout the country.

Although many observers agree that apprenticeship should remain one of the principal, if not the principal, means of acquiring skills, they also recognise that apprenticeship is badly in need of modernisation. Reforms undertaken in countries such as Austria, Canada, the Federal Republic of Germany, Italy, Switzerland, the United Kingdom and the United States, have led to a greater variety of apprenticeship programmes which in turn have increased the number of training posts available to new apprentices. These reforms and the legislation adopted to modernise apprenticeship have a certain number of points in common. The most important are the continuing effort to increase the access to apprenticeship and the number of people enrolled in schemes; the relaxation, and even elimination, of age restrictions, thus permitting adult workers to become apprentices; more emphasis on previous occupational experience and training; and, in general, more flexibility so as to permit women and handicapped people to participate. Examples of such new legislation are the programme on non-traditional training for women in Canada, the craft readiness scheme and the apprentice outreach programme in the United States, and the Apprenticeship Act, 1983, in New Zealand. Many programmes, such as those in Australia, New Zealand and the United States, have also extended the number of occupations for which apprenticeships are available. In these same countries, many new apprenticeship programmes have reduced training time, on the premise that it is the acquisition of skills rather than the time spent in formal training that determines the successfulness of apprenticeship programmes.

The renewed interest in apprenticeship in industrialised countries has been stimulated by two developments. First of all, there is a marked trend in certain countries for the employers and workers to take a greater interest in training issues. Secondly, the revival of apprenticeship would not have been possible without new subsidies, tax exemptions and other benefits that provide employers with an incentive to accommodate apprentices within their undertakings.

Training for adults

Opportunities for initial training and for updating of knowledge and skills in industrialised market economy countries are important not only for youth but also for adult workers. Most of the new legislation on training is designed to give workers more opportunities for training and retraining. The measures adopted include on-the-job training, financial assistance, the elimination of age restrictions on entry into certain training programmes, and the opening up of new training opportunities for women as well as for other groups having problems of re-entry into the labour market. As in the case of training for youth, employers are being called upon to assume greater responsibility for continuous training, much of which is carried out within the enterprise – often on the job – with the link between training and specific job requirements becoming closer.

In the United States, a whole series of programmes has been set up for adults who are either unemployed or in difficult straits. These programmes are generally designed to provide training for jobs not subsidised by the Government. However, there are not many training programmes for persons in employment, particularly programmes providing updating and further training, and yet these training programmes are more and more in demand since jobs become obsolete once every eight years on an average and workers are usually obliged to change trades at least twice in the course of their working life. Numerous measures have been taken to cope with this situation, practically all involving greater responsibility for private industry and a transfer of responsibility from the Federal Government to the states. New tripartite bodies have been set up locally to get local employers more interested in training. This is usually done by providing various financial incentives to encourage private enterprises to train their own personnel. Some programmes aim at convincing the private sector to undertake training and upgrading during periods of economic difficulty and to reap the benefits from these "investments" at the time of economic recovery. These arrangements have not always been entirely successful.

Long-term unemployment among adults in the United Kingdom has led to a number of new training measures designed to help adults, either employed or unemployed, to acquire a skill, update their knowledge and broaden their qualifications throughout their careers. The most interesting among these measures is the technical institute called Open Tech, opened in 1982, which is to training what the Open University is to higher education. The purpose of Open Tech is to assist workers of all ages to attain greater proficiency as technicians and master craftsmen. It also seeks to provide adults with training or retraining opportunities, on a full- or part-time basis. No officially recognised qualification is required for admittance to the Open Tech courses and participants may adopt a flexible training schedule. These modular forms of training have been enjoying great popularity – as training that gradually builds upon existing or previously acquired skills and qualifications and thereby contributes to the development of a continuous training system.[13]

In France continuous training is the responsibility of both the State and the private sector. Its organisation has both a legislative and a contractual basis and depends both on the Government, which has implemented a system to aid the development of continuous training activities, and on the social partners, who have signed an inter-occupational agreement on training.

The main features of this system are as follows:

— The State finances continuous training activities under agreements signed at the regional level to meet specific priorities such as employment assistance, individual advancement, target groups, etc. These agreements permit both the financing of training costs and the remuneration of trainees.

— The employers must contribute to training expenses an amount equal to at least 1.1 per cent of wages; otherwise, they must pay to the Treasury the difference between this minimum obligation and the amount of expenses actually earmarked for training. The employers must submit their training plan every year to the works council for its views.

Despite the recession and lower profits, enterprises have maintained on the whole a relatively high rate of contribution, i.e. 1.63 per cent of the payroll. The great majority of training courses concern further training and adaptation to new technologies. The most delicate problem, however, is that of small enterprises, which have not yet benefited from the advantages of continuous training. Several organisations representing occupational groups and chambers of commerce and industry have nevertheless set up organisations to collect the contributions of small and medium-sized enterprises for such purposes but are experiencing difficulty in spending these funds because these enterprises do not always see an immediate or pressing need to send their employees to training courses.

Occupational reintegration of unemployed adults is also sometimes carried out through training. The National Employment Agency has created training courses designed to upgrade the skills and knowledge of jobseekers who cannot apply for certain openings because they do not possess the required qualifications. During these training courses, the employer undertakes to reserve these jobs for the unemployed participating in the retraining activities. Apart from the activities financed under the employment pacts, the number of unemployed adults trained each year rose from 90,000 in 1974 to approximately 110,000 in 1980, while the number of people seeking work increased fourfold during the same period. In 1983, the funds earmarked for the training of jobseekers over 26 years of age were increased considerably, mainly to finance training-cum-employment contracts for the long-term unemployed.

The employment pacts, lastly, are intended to prevent dismissals rather than to cope with their consequences. Under this scheme, the government can sign training agreements with undertakings where employment is threatened, to finance retraining activities through the National Employment Fund. These retraining activities may aim at redeployment within the same firm or to others. The training courses may be organised either by the undertaking itself or by a public or private training institution. In 1980 some 10,000 persons attended such courses.

There are a number of problems with these programmes. To begin with, internal or external job openings must exist for those who have been retrained, which is not always the case; secondly, the job opening must be foreseen sufficiently in advance – in fact, several months before the redundancy occurs – and this raises the need for a warning system within the firm and for a better identification of the role to be played by the works council in this respect.

One of the main priorities of the vocational training policy in France, as reaffirmed on many occasions, is to correct social inequalities. Among the measures that have been introduced for this purpose are courses for social advancement and training leave.

The social advancement courses, which are offered free of charge, are financed by the central Government and local communities. They are generally given by public institutions coming under the Ministry of National Education and lead to diplomas in technological fields. These courses are usually held in the evening or on Saturdays. Since 1974 an attempt has been made to modernise them, by adapting them better to the needs of adults, by improving guidance and preliminary selection procedures and by introducing a credit point system so as to avoid the need for final examinations. The record shows that 510,000 persons participated in these courses in 1980, 150,000 by correspondence, and the average duration was 310 hours a year. Despite its success, this system of social advancement has come under criticism because the drop-out and failure rate is somewhat higher than was expected when the programme was introduced. The social partners have thus been advocating that the system be gradually replaced by paid training leave.

Not many people have taken up the training leave introduced by the 1970 joint inter-occupational agreement, and confirmed by the Act of 1971, because full pay is not usually maintained during the leave. Only 40,000 persons benefited from training leave in 1981, roughly the same figure as in previous years.

It would appear that the effort to overcome social inequality through vocational training is having little impact since, too often in practice, the training given benefits those who have already received some training. In the absence of leave with full pay, few individuals are in a position to take training courses leading to a diploma and hence to possible occupational and social advancement.

Japan is without doubt one of the countries where continuous training is most developed. The training concept is totally integrated into the life and work organisation of enterprises. Continuous training in fact plays a key role in industrial strategy, whether it is intended to improve the versatility and mobility of workers or to support the activities of quality circles or total quality control systems. Continuous training takes many forms: it may be given internally within the firm – usually during working hours at a centre specially set up for this purpose – or within the working team, where it is the responsibility of supervisory staff. In fact, continuous training fulfils two functions: first, it complements through practical skills the basic knowledge and scientific and technical understanding acquired at vocational secondary schools; second, it meets the need for an adaptable workforce within the enterprise. As in most other countries, small enterprises are in a more difficult position to provide continuous training than large firms.

Training and structural and technological change

When rapid economic and technical change takes place, it becomes highly important to provide not only initial training but especially continuous training that aims at constantly adjusting the imparted knowledge and skills to structural and technological change.

The introduction of new products and production processes, the rise or decline of certain industries, and the creation of new enterprises have made it necessary for workers to change jobs and even occupations as often as three or four times in the course of their working life. They should thus have the means to acquire the necessary new skills at any time and age.

With the introduction of more sophisticated technologies, industry often needs fewer unskilled or semi-skilled workers. It has been estimated that in the United Kingdom the number of unskilled and semi-skilled jobs has decreased by 1 million over the past ten years, and that an additional million will disappear by the year 1990. Technology also has an impact on the nature of the knowledge and skills demanded; thus the proportion of manual workers, which amounted to 62.5 per cent in 1961, had fallen to 53.7 per cent by 1978, and it is expected to reach a level below 50 per cent by 1985.[14]

Traditional trades in the United Kingdom have gone down along with the traditional industries (such as textiles and shipbuilding) with which they were associated. On the other hand, the demand for technicians has considerably increased, and industry is increasingly looking for people with analytical abilities, and for workers capable of participating in the introduction of new processes instead of merely performing a narrow job or of just producing a single product. In other words, employers are trying to find a greater number of technical personnel along with highly skilled workers sufficiently versatile to carry out a variety of tasks.

Several training initiatives have been taken in recent years in order to meet this requirement. The United Kingdom has been very active in this area. In 1982, the Computing Services Industry Training Centre (COSIT), was set up to study present and future needs for skilled personnel in various lines of work related to electronic data processing (EDP), and to make sure that the requirements for training personnel were met. The "threshold scheme" is another example. As a result of that measure, 1,500 young people were trained for EDP jobs in 1980-81.[15] The information technology centres, set up in 1983, provide still another example. These centres, which constitute the focus of new technical training programmes, are in the first instance open to unemployed youth. In addition, the education authorities in more than ten municipalities are engaged in pilot projects to reintroduce technical courses into schools.

The development of new technologies is raising an increasing number of problems for enterprises: either they are forced to retrain their personnel, or they are unable to find the skilled manpower they need on the labour market. In order to assist them, the French government authorities have set up retraining programmes and sector-specific upgrading courses. Enterprises that need restructuring because of the introduction of automation may be reimbursed for part of their training expenses if jobs are in danger. This aid, which can reach up to 70 per cent of the expenses, is provided by the National Employment Fund and may be supplemented by the European Social Fund.

In order to cope with certain shortages of skills, particularly in the areas of EDP and information technology, France has decided to provide initial and continuous training for engineers and technicians. Thus, in 1985-86, it is planned to double the number of engineers trained in these areas. Training courses have been set up in collaboration either with the Agency for the Development of Information Technology (ADI), which advises and finances training institutions, or with the Agency for the Development of Automation (ADEPA), which advises and subsidises enterprises wishing to introduce new technologies. However, as was already mentioned in the chapter on information technology in Volume 1 of this report, it is difficult to determine the precise impact of these technologies on employment, skills and working conditions.

The ease and rapidity with which training systems can respond to changing training needs will depend on a wide variety of factors such as the type of organisation; the institutional network in which they operate; the role played by industry and the social partners in training; available resources; the readiness and open-mindedness of teachers and instructors; the way in which programmes and training standards are established; the links between training and school education and – last but not least – the motivation of governmental authorities, employers and the workers themselves.[16] However, in most countries the training systems do not seem able to respond as quickly as is desirable to changing training needs as a result of the introduction of new technologies.

It would be well to emphasise, however, that these mismatches resulting from the introduction of new technologies cannot be attributed to inefficiencies in the training system alone. In some countries, adaptation to new technologies requires less time. This is the case in Japan (see box 7.1) and a few other countries where the basic educational level is high, where initial training is mainly geared to the acquisition of broad basic knowledge including an understanding of the role of industry and the skills and attitudes which it demands, and where in addition continuous training is solidly established at every level of skill.

Management development

In industrialised countries at present management development is a matter of considerable importance. A number of studies have shown that the number of persons who place themselves in the management category has been increasing in recent years. This is probably due to the fact that technological change has led to a relative increase in the number of persons required to perform management functions and that enterprises tend to

assign management status to an increasing proportion of their personnel.[17]

Management itself has also become a widely recognised field of study. In the early 1950s Europe had few training institutions for management or business administration aside from a few business colleges, and post-university training in this area was relatively rare. The present situation is completely different because there is now a great variety of institutions, including universities, institutions of higher learning, training institutes and centres, apart from consultancy organisations.

University-type institutions are no longer concerned solely with full-scale programmes leading to a degree in management, but also offer short-term executive development programmes, post-university programmes and programmes on specific or specialised aspects of management. In addition, many institutes of higher education now include management subjects in the curricula of traditional disciplines such as medicine, agriculture and engineering. The Danish Project Management Society, for example, helps institutes of higher education to organise traineeships that provide students with an opportunity to acquire management knowledge and experience during their studies.

Recent studies in the United States, Japan and other countries have shown that successful and well-managed enterprises tend to spend more on management training and development than other enterprises do. Also, their contacts with universities and management training centres tend to be closer and more productive. A wide variety of training and self-development methods have been developed and applied over the past ten to 15 years, in order to adapt training to the needs and possibilities of both the individual and the organisation. These include action learning, self-development groups, modular-training packages, learner-controlled instruction, instruction-free training, group projects and others.

7.1

Vocational training in Japan

The industrial expansion of the 1960s brought about a situation of skill shortages contrasting with the labour surplus observed during the previous decade. Moreover, manpower requirements shifted from simple manual skills to broader technical knowledge. In 1969 the Vocational Training Law was amended to encourage employers to provide training to their workers. This law set up a public system for vocational training and a semi-public, authorised, vocational training system. The public system provides "basic training", divided into three levels: general training (basic skills), advanced training (skilled workers level) and special advanced training (highly skilled workers/technicians level). It is also responsible for providing "upgrading training" to help employed workers to improve their skills; "updating training" to enable workers to acquire additional skills required for their occupations; and, finally, "occupational capabilities redevelopment training" for those who need to change jobs. These different programmes are delivered in general vocational training centres and advanced vocational training centres. Besides this, a unique institute of vocational training has the dual function of training vocational training instructors and of conducting research on vocational training issues. The same vocational training programmes as those mentioned under the public system can be provided by employers' organisations or trade unions when they meet the prescribed standards and are duly authorised by the governor of a prefecture. National and prefectural authorities can then provide some financial and non-

financial support to these authorised programmes in the form of training facilities, instructors, subsidies to cover part of the operating costs, etc.

Two important aspects of vocational training development in Japan need to be emphasised. The first is that the level of general education of those undergoing vocational training has constantly risen, and every year a larger proportion of trainees taking basic training programmes are graduates from senior high schools, i.e. persons who have completed six years of secondary education. The second is that the majority of employers provide training for their staff and in particular for their newly recruited personnel, either through their own facilities or, in the case of a small enterprise, through vocational training provided collectively. Most of the training is off-the-job training within the enterprise, a relatively small percentage consisting of on-the-job training. At the same time, however, undertakings also provide an opportunity to acquire skills and aptitudes on the job, through job rotation, through the system of promotion and wages, through the integration of the worker into a group where coaching is offered and through participation in quality and productivity circles. This process of training through unconventional means, not recognised as training as such, is largely influenced by the climate of consultation in industrial relations. This "learning by experience" – which can hardly be measured – may in the end prove to be an effective way of producing some of the occupational skills required in Japan.

103

Enterprises in Canada and the United States have become particularly interested in developing their management talent and this has created a thriving market for new training packages. They have also become more sophisticated in choosing the most appropriate package and evaluating its effectiveness. The increased sophistication in needs analysis and impact evaluation has come about recently primarily because more packages are based on tested principles of how to change the behaviour of people in organisations and how to make use of such a change for achieving better organisational performance. The growing interest in management topics is not limited to enterprises but extends to the general public as well. This is particularly so in the United States where improved management is seen as an important method of improving productivity. For example, since 1981 there has always been at least one book on management on the *New York Times* bestseller list.[18] This increased interest in management techniques in turn seems associated with a steady increase in the number of students majoring in undergraduate and graduate programmes in business management.

The variety of management training initiatives caused the United Kingdom in 1971 to designate a dozen regional management centres as focal points and provide support to other management institutions in their respective regions. About 200 private organisations offering management courses are covered by this arrangement. The universities certify qualifications by issuing their own degrees. Qualifications in other institutions are generally certified by the Council for National Academic Awards (CNAA). In addition, a certain number of representative professional institutions exercise a certifying function in specific areas such as marketing, personnel management, etc. The British Institute of Management (BIM), while it does not certify qualifications, is the principal professional organisation for managers. Together with the Confederation of British Industry (CBI), the BIM has created an Advisory Panel on Management Education (APME) which analyses management training problems.

In France, management personnel account for approximately 15 per cent of all trainees and slightly less than 14 per cent of training hours financed by undertakings. A survey conducted by the National Foundation for Management Education (FNEGE) in 1979 estimated that approximately 30 per cent of the overall training budget of undertakings is devoted to management training. Continuous training in management in France is mainly carried out by training institutions, consultants and training services within undertakings. The training institutions can be classified in three main groups: university institutes; private institutions; and establishments run by the chambers of commerce and industry, which have two large complexes in the Paris region and 17 business schools in the provinces.

The governmental authorities responsible for the orientation of management development in France are the Ministry of National Education, the Ministry of Vocational Training and the Ministries of Research and Industry and of Commerce. The National Council of French Employers (and its offshoot, the Association for the Upgrading of Industrial and Commercial Management Personnel), as well as the chambers of commerce and industry, also play a very active part in orienting the programmes. The National Foundation for Management Education has been designated as the focal point for all the parties concerned. Although its original function was to assist training institutions in acquiring permanent teaching staff, it has since extended its field of activities and now also assists training institutions in adapting their programmes, diagnosing their organisational problems and strengthening their links with enterprises as well as their international influence.

The training of entrepreneurs and training for entrepreneurship in small enterprises and among the self-employed are certainly the areas that have been most emphasised in recent years. This is due to the important role played by these sectors in economic, social and political life. Small enterprises can be found in practically all sectors of the economy: not only do they account for over 80 per cent of all enterprises in some countries, they often employ more than 40 per cent of all workers. The increased attention is also explained by the specific training needs of small enterprises – very different from those of large firms – and by their unsatisfactory access to training corresponding to their needs.

Many industrialised market economy countries provide special technical and financial assistance to small enterprises and make available to them training programmes for management personnel. Such programmes have been in existence for several years in France and the Federal Republic of Germany. Belgium and the United Kingdom recently took measures to grant financial subsidies – instead of unemployment benefits – to the unemployed, enabling them to set up small businesses and attend training courses. Most often these initiatives combine training opportunities with tax exemptions and credit on easy terms. The Belgian Government has launched a project to train women as managers for small and medium-sized enterprises. In Ireland the ANCO (the Irish government authority responsible for training) has a programme for aspiring entrepreneurs to enable them to set up in business on their own. This programme combines 20 weeks of training courses with practical training.

Beginning in 1977 the United Kingdom Government authorities set up a New Enterprise Programme (NEP) and, a few months later, another programme, the Small Business Programme (SBP), designed to train individuals to become self-employed or to manage small enterprises. The results of these programmes have usually been satisfactory: a large number of participants in these programmes have succeeded in setting up enterprises or in taking over enterprises in liquidation; the enterprises have created new jobs filled by formerly unemployed workers; they begin to make profits within a reasonable time; the survival rate is increasing; and, finally, the savings in unemployment benefits usually more than offset the programme expenses. The best results seem to be obtained when the training programmes take account of the concrete problems encountered by the entrepreneurs, are closely linked to the projects of the participants and effectively assist them in carrying them out. The objective, however, is that the training and aid programme or, in other words, the preferential treatment should cease as soon as possible and that the heads of enterprises should be in a position to survive in the business world. These programmes are tending to increase in number, even if the number of participants is still limited.[19]

In the United States the situation is somewhat different because an increasing number of persons have their own businesses, giving rise to a growing demand for management training. The demand for training is also due to the fact that the small enterprise sector has an average failure rate of about 50 per cent after two years of activity, largely because of a lack of qualifications, skills and experience in management. A growing number of institutes of higher education and universities in Canada and the United States have set up programmes and award special degrees for managers of small enterprises. Assistance to small enterprises is nothing new in the United States, where programmes of this sort have existed since the early 1950s. One prominent example is the Small Business Administration (SBA), created in 1953 to assist small enterprises and protect their interests. For the past ten years or so the Small Business Institute (SBI) has been providing management assistance, consultancy services and various forms of technical assistance to small enterprises through the intermediary of universities and colleges.

Centrally planned economies of Eastern Europe

Generally speaking, the centrally planned economies of Eastern Europe seek to adapt their training systems to structural and technological change and at the same time to satisfy a growing demand for education and training. The main features of these training systems are greater institutionalisation, in particular where the initial training of youth is concerned; a marked interest in broad training programmes; the high priority given to programmes designed to upgrade skills and knowledge; and, finally, a determination to make vocational training an integrated part of compulsory education, and thus available to everyone before entering working life. Achievement of these objectives will require more resources for training and more effective and efficient programmes.

Training in the USSR is provided through two main channels: technical and vocational education, and initial and further training within enterprises.

Technical and vocational education prepares pupils for 1,400 different occupations. This system, directed by the State Committee for Vocational and Technical Training, consists of 7,250 institutions. During the period 1976-80, nearly 11.5 million skilled workers were trained in these institutions, accounting for two-thirds of the country's newly trained manpower. The training system within the enterprise provides initial training, upgrading and retraining, mainly to adults in the form of practical training supplemented by courses on theory. In 1980 roughly 38 million workers attended courses under this system. For approximately 6 million of them, it was their first training. The training capacity of the two systems taken together was increased between 1976 and 1980 by approximately 22 per cent.[20]

In Czechoslovakia the training of youth, following their general education, is provided in 1,950 technical and vocational training centres with a total attendance of 373,000 students [21] (1979). In Bulgaria the vocational training of youth is carried out mainly by the country's 152 secondary vocational training schools connected with the large industrial enterprises. In 1980 training of this type was given to 85,000 students, preparing them for entry into 149 different occupations. This system accounts for 60 per cent of the total vocational training given in the country.[22] In addition, Bulgaria has·392 vocational training centres which entertain close relations with industrial enterprises.

Reforms of educational and training systems

Over the past ten years, the centrally planned economies of Eastern Europe have introduced a series of reforms designed to improve their educational and training systems. These reforms were intended to facilitate the access of youth to training of every type and at all levels, by making secondary education compulsory; and to diversify training programmes and make them more flexible so as to respond to structural and technological changes.

These were the aims that inspired the educational reform in Czechoslovakia in 1976 and the measures taken between 1976 and 1981. In Czechoslovakia today 50 per cent of young people finishing their compulsory education are registered in institutions providing both full secondary education and vocational training. The objective of compulsory secondary education for all is expected to be achieved by 1985. This secondary education combines general education with the acquisition of occupational skills.

In 1980 the Bulgarian Government adopted various measures to reform technical education and vocational training and set up a unified national continuous training system. Under this reform,

prevocational training and basic vocational education have been given at technical and vocational training institutions since the 1982-83 school year. In addition, young people are being given practical training during the final year of their secondary education. The Ministry of Education was made responsible for carrying out the reform in co-operation with regional and local authorities and state enterprises.

In the USSR decisions made by the Government in 1977 and 1979 have clarified how the training of youth in technical education and vocational training establishments should be carried out. These decisions also led to a reorganisation of in-plant training in order to make it more responsive to new technologies and production processes. These reforms are based on improved co-ordination between training and employment; a review of programmes; a strengthening of training infrastructure; and greater integration between secondary general education and training. Individual practical training is considered to take second place to group training in enterprise workshops specially set up for this purpose. At present a new reform of general education and vocational training is being considered. The main goal of this reform is to bring closer general polytechnical education and vocational training. The reform includes an increase of the length of study from ten to 11 years. There is also an arrangement for introducing vocational training in general education in order to provide all new workers with proper training before taking on their first job. In the USSR it is expected that by 1990 all young people who do not continue their general education beyond the ninth year will have completed general secondary education and acquired vocational skills.

All these measures are likely to raise the general education and training of workers to a level higher than that required for carrying out their jobs. However, some specialists consider that this will make it easier for workers to adapt their skills when so required by technological progress.

In recent years, centrally planned economies in Eastern Europe have paid increasing attention to the evaluation of training results. A number of studies have been carried out to determine the efficiency and effectiveness of institutional training as compared with enterprise training. The conclusions of these studies show that enterprise training results in faster short-term productivity gains and wage increases while institutional training offers better long-term prospects of reaching higher qualification levels and enables workers to adapt more easily later on to technological change.

One of the structural changes having an impact on the training systems of these countries is the steady decline in the agricultural population, which is offset by increased employment in the services sector. This phenomenon is particularly pronounced in Bulgaria and the USSR, although the same trend can be observed in the other centrally planned economies of Eastern Europe. The decline in the agricultural population is occurring at the same time as increased mechanisation of agriculture, resulting in greater demand for skilled labour in that sector.

Although industrial employment has hardly increased over the past ten years, the extension of mechanisation and automation in this sector has also resulted in greater demand for skilled workers and technicians. At the same time, this had led to changes in the nature of skills required: work is becoming more and more intellectual in nature, while manual skills are diminishing in importance.

The vocational training measures adopted in the USSR since 1977 have been accompanied by a parallel effort to standardise the level of general education; to obtain a more balanced mix of subjects in general and vocational education; to make a clearer distinction between general education, specialised education and practical training; and, finally, to reduce the length of weekly courses to 36–38 hours. In addition, changes have been made in the list of occupations for which recognised technical and vocational training courses are available. This list has been extended to a number of occupations related to electronic data processing and automation. On the other hand, other occupations have been regrouped, thus making them include broader qualifications so as to increase the mobility of workers and facilitate their adaptation to change, particularly with respect to work organisation. Research has been under way in the USSR since 1970 that is expected to result in a classification of occupations according to the following criteria: socio-economic importance of each occupation; the working conditions and technical requirements involved in the occupation; the nature and organisation of the work involved; the educational, training and qualifications levels required; and the psycho-physiological aptitudes needed.

Training within enterprises

In-plant training has continued to develop, but research carried out in the USSR shows that not enough of this type of training is available. Recently created enterprises are sometimes faced with a shortage of skilled manpower. An analysis of delays in the starting up of new enterprises and production units in 1978 attributed this to a lack of trained manpower in 14 per cent of the cases. Other studies conducted between 1973 and 1978 confirmed this finding.

Therefore it is not surprising that the USSR has adopted a number of measures since 1979 to improve the efficiency and effectiveness of training in enterprises. These measures included the setting up of a system for planning and financing training in enterprises and the introduction of standards with respect to training methods, teachers and targets. The various ministries were assigned additional responsibilities, particularly as regards further training. The USSR State Committee for Labour and Social Affairs and the USSR State Committee for Vocational and Technical Training were assigned a supporting role for the

methodological aspects and the design of programmes. The measures taken tend to improve
further training and to increase the number and
quality of the participants. In respect of standards,
the objective is to make further training available to
all workers at least once every five years. The
training plans of the various enterprises are also
required to include a definition of objectives with
respect to the training of women.

Teacher training

In recent years, the training and further training
of teaching staff of the various training institutions
and structures have been given high priority. In
1976 some 448,000 persons, including adminis-
trators, teachers and ancillary staff, were engaged
in technical and vocational education alone in the
USSR. Between 1971 and 1975, the number of
teachers in this system increased fivefold; and a
special university infrastructure had to be set up to
train them. In 1978 more than 62,000 students
attended technical and vocational courses for the
training of trainers in the industrial and technical
fields.[23] Nevertheless, this number is still too low,
because every year graduates from other higher
institutions as well as skilled workers, technicians
and engineers enter the teaching profession without necessarily having had previous pedagogical
training. For all these groups special programmes
are organised to upgrade their knowledge and
teaching ability.

Management training

Management training has been receiving
increasing attention in the centrally planned
economies of Eastern Europe in recent years. The
main reason for this increased interest is a desire to
improve economic efficiency, to overcome manpower shortages and to increase productivity
through the introduction of more advanced technology in countries and regions very unequally
endowed with skilled manpower. Any estimate of
management training needs in the USSR must take
into account the fact that 15 per cent of the

economically active population, amounting to
more than 18 million individuals, exercise management functions. Although the number of
persons in top management remains more or less
stable, the number of middle managers and
supervisors is increasing rapidly.

In the USSR management development falls in
general into three categories: basic training,
training connected with career advancement, and
further training. In many cases, basic training in
administrative and management techniques is
combined with general or specialised education.
For example, engineering education usually
includes courses in economics, administration and
management. In addition, there is a network of
institutions and organisations that provide training and further training in management techniques
to senior management. This is the main task of the
Academy of National Economy, under the Council of Ministers, and of the sectoral institutes for the
advanced training of managers and professionals.
About 1 million managerial personnel receive
management training every year in these institutions. It is estimated that from 1975 to 1980, 7
million managers and professionals attended management training courses in the USSR. A special
department of the Ministry of Higher and Specialised Secondary Education is responsible for co-
ordinating all the institutions administering this
training. There are also the regional institutes for
management personnel attached to the governments of the various republics of the USSR.

Middle-level managers are trained either in
specialised centres, of which there are 83 in the
country, connected with various kinds of activity,
or at courses organised within the respective
enterprises. Management training for middle-
level managers is also given by the training
departments of the institutes of higher education.
These training courses generally last six months,
three of which are spent in classrooms.

In the German Democratic Republic the highest authority for management development is the

Central Institute for Socialist Management of National Economy created in 1966. This institute co-ordinates research on management and trains the top-level managers of the Party, of the state ministries (including the ministers themselves and their deputies), and of large state enterprises with more than 5,000 workers. It is also responsible for the training of a reserve of management and supervisory personnel who may be called upon to assume high functions. One of its most important activities is to organise discussion groups regularly, which are usually attended by a large number of top managers. At a lower level, there are 14 different institutes for socialist management in the universities and technical institutes, which are responsible for a large part of the country's management training. Each institute covers various industrial branches, trains the top managers of large and medium-sized state enterprises, and in general the managers of the second level of the hierarchy and the reserve staff for such posts. Managers belonging to the third level of the hierarchy, i.e. managers of medium-sized and small enterprises, are trained in branch industrial academies attached to the various enterprises. Small enterprises are sometimes grouped together to form academies for training socialist management. Supervisory personnel at lower levels, and

in particular foremen, attend courses given by the enterprise academies which can be found in a number of state enterprises.

Towards the end of the 1960s, the Hungarian Government set up the first National Management Development Centre. Over the past ten years, more than 6,600 managers have come to this centre, to participate either in one-year courses for middle management or in training sessions of from three to five weeks set up for higher management personnel. In addition, this centre provides consultancy services to enterprises on a contractual basis.

Similar management development centres exist in Bulgaria, Czechoslovakia, Poland and Romania. Generally speaking, the emphasis given to certain areas of management varies from country to country and in some cases, like the USSR, within the same country. Thus some centres place more emphasis on quantitative methods and systems analysis while others tend to base their curricula on more traditional areas of management. There has also been more emphasis than in the past on the case study method, on management games and, more generally, on training methods calling for greater participation.

[1] I. Hargreaves: "Unemployment in Europe", in *Financial Times* (London), 17 Jan. 1983, p. 11.

[2] A. Pike: "Britain's antique apprentice system", in *Financial Times* (London), 2 Sep. 1980, p. 21; and "Sorcery among Britain's apprentices", in *The Economist* (London), 12-18 Dec. 1981, pp. 80-81.

[3] "Seasonally adjusted U.S. jobless rate up to 41-year peak", in *Financial Times* (London), 7 Aug. 1982, p. 2.

[4] J. Bagnall: "Urgent priority to job training", in *Financial Post* (Toronto), 16 Jan. 1982, p. 3.

[5] Employment and Immigration Canada: *Annual report to Parliament on immigration levels, 1980* (Ottawa, n.d.).

[6] See for example, Economic Council of Canada: *In short supply: Jobs and skills in the 1980s* (Ottawa, 1982), pp. 81-82.

[7] *Employment and training report of the President* (Washington, United States Government Printing Office, 1981), pp. 35-38.

[8] "US Job Partnership Act", in *Public Administration News* (St. Paul), Nov. 1982, pp. 1322-1399.

[9] R. Taylor: "Skilled hit by slump", in *The Observer* (London), 29 Nov. 1981, p. 8.

[10] "Wanted: A plan for skilled people", in *The Times* (London), 2 Dec. 1981, p. 8.

[11] *Employment and training report of the President*, op. cit., p. 45.

[12] ibid., p. 284.

[13] For additional information on Open Tech, see Manpower Services Commission: *An Open Tech programme: A consultative document* (London, 1981), and idem: *Open Tech Task Group report* (London, 1982).

[14] idem: *A new training initiative: A consultative document* (London, 1981), p. 2, and *MSC Manpower Review 1980* (London, 1980), p. 19.

[15] idem: *Annual Report 1980-81* (London, 1981).

[16] K. H. Ebel: "The microelectronics training gap in the metal trades", in *International Labour Review* (Geneva, ILO), Nov.-Dec. 1981, p. 730.

[17] See for example, *Management education: A world view of experience and needs*, Report of a committee of the International Academy of Management (London, British Institute of Management, 1981).

[18] These include R. T. Pascale and A. G. Athos: *The art of Japanese management* (New York, Simon and Schuster, 1981); W. Ouchi: *Theory Z: How American business can meet the Japanese challenge* (Reading, Massachusetts, Addison-Wesley, 1981); and T. J. Peters and R. H. Waterman, Jr.: *In search of excellence: Lessons from America's best-run companies* (New York, Harper and Row, 1982).

[19] P. A. Neck (ed.): *Small enterprise development: Policies and programmes*, Management Development Series, No. 14 (Geneva, ILO, 1977).

[20] USSR, Central Statistical Directorate: *Narodnoe khozyaistvo SSSR v 1980 g.*, Statisticheski Ezhegodnik (Moscow, Statistika, 1981).

[21] Federal Statistical Office, Czech Statistical Office, Slovak Statistical Office: *Statistická ročenka Československá socialistické republiky, 1979* (Prague, SNTL, ALFA, 1979).

[22] *Opportunities for industrial personnel and their utilisation by the developing countries*, Technical paper for UNIDO (Bulgaria, 1981).

[23] A. A. Bulgakov: *Professionalno-tekhnicheskoe obrazovanie v SSSR na sovremennom etape* (Moscow, Vysshaya Shkola, 1979), pp. 214–219.

Chapter 8

Training in developing countries

The numbers of young people who will enter the labour market in the developing countries are enormous. This means that these countries' training task is not just one of adjusting existing training systems or of taking temporary measures. Even though most of them now have institutions that can provide basic training,[1] the main task is to build up and strengthen the training infrastructure, particularly in the least developed countries. However, because of a number of financial constraints, the emphasis will have to be on efforts towards a fuller utilisation of existing training capacities, in centres and in enterprises, and on the use of innovative, low-cost training approaches.

The quality, amount, content and relevance of general education have a powerful influence on the nature, scope and effectiveness of training activities. Many developing countries find that the educational models and systems they have inherited or adopted are inappropriate to their cultures and to their social and economic needs. Since about 60 per cent of their population is over 15 years of age and a high percentage has had no access to education, new contents and methods of training have to be found to transmit useful skills to large numbers of illiterates, semi-illiterates and school drop-outs.

A few sectors urgently need training facilities, such as small enterprises, handicrafts and the informal sector. These sectors have benefited little from existing training programmes. However, it is precisely these sectors that produce many consumer goods and services, provide jobs for a large part of the active population and still offer considerable potential for expanding employment.

Women have few training opportunities and have difficulty in qualifying for jobs in the more modern sectors of the economy. Young drop-outs or illiterate youth continue to have very few opportunities to acquire skills or other qualifications. However, there is a growing awareness of these problems, partly because of the economic and social pressure exerted by these sectors and population groups.

Many of the training problems are in fact common to all developing countries. Each country's response to these problems, however, is often determined by historical factors and by its level of economic development. We shall therefore discuss the training problems facing each developing region – Africa, Latin America and Asia – separately despite the fact that certain issues and approaches may be common to all.

Africa

The broad objectives of African development policies are laid down in the Monrovia Declaration of Commitment of the Heads of State and Government of the Organisation of African Unity (OAU), adopted in 1979. This Declaration emphasises the objective of "national and collective self-reliance", which can only be achieved if African nations mobilise all their resources and if

111

they collaborate with each other. The Lagos Plan of Action – which followed this Declaration – states that the principle of self-reliance should apply in the first place to human resources, and that training in all sectors and at all levels is one of the ways of achieving this objective.

In particular, it calls for co-operation among African countries in the setting up and utilisation of specialised subregional and regional training and research institutions. However, it also states unequivocally that responsibility in the training area is first of all a national one.

Almost all African countries face a whole series of training problems, related to three socio-economic phenomena:

– a growing social demand for education and training;
– the continuing existence of large-scale under-employment and an almost general increase of unemployment, particularly of youth;
– the governments' concern to increase the participation of all strata of the population in the development efforts.

Africa's training situation at the time of independence has been analysed in great detail.[2] The training systems inherited from the colonial Powers were rudimentary at best. Since that time training has gradually acquired its own identity under the pressure of economic necessity and population growth. It is now clear that the African continent wishes to integrate the elements of its own traditions into its development, taking account of its own socio-cultural environment and meeting its own development needs, and thus gradually free itself from inherited or imported education models.

African governments are striving to reduce or do away with a whole series of imbalances. Some of these imbalances are geographical in nature, such as the great discrepancy between the training capacity available in the large cities and that in the provinces. Equally important differences exist between the major sectors of the economy, and between the modern and the traditional sector. These imbalances have been growing because the primary sector has had to continue absorbing the great majority of the population, while the industrial sector has been expanding much more slowly than expected. The tertiary sector is expanding, but existing education and training systems are not always able to meet the qualitative demands of this sector.

Moreover, some African countries do not yet have fully developed policies for the development of human resources. Over the past 30 years many have set up their own training institutions and facilities, often within the framework of bilateral and multilateral technical co-operation pro-grammes, but issues of co-ordination, continuous upgrading and the linkages of these institutions with employment policies in general are important problems that have yet to be solved. Other African countries have a legislative and institutional framework that enables employers' and workers' organisations to participate in the formulation and implementation of training policies, but such participation is often somewhat formal and not altogether effective.

In accordance with the Lagos Plan of Action, African countries have also undertaken joint activities. The main result of such collaboration in the field of training is the Inter-African Centre for the Development of Vocational Training (CIADFOR) established in 1978 at the initiative of African leaders, of which approximately 20 coun-tries are members.[3] Its main objectives are to set priorities for action among its member States and to promote the exchange of information and resources.

In Africa, where the proportion of youth is high, the main emphasis is on initial vocational training. Given the tight economic situation, governments tend to concentrate their efforts on providing directly employable skills, at the expense of more general education. Various countries have their own training centres, but they are not always used to their full capacity. Many countries have difficulties in recruiting and retraining teaching and management staff owing to inappropriate entry requirements for trainees, and in the placement of graduates. Moreover, the trainees who participate constitute only a small part of the labour force, belonging mainly to the modern sector. In spite of all these problems, various countries have achieved remarkable results in the field of vocational training.

The United Republic of Tanzania is one of the countries that have made great efforts in the training field. When it gained independence in 1961, skilled manpower and training facilities were scarce. Today the country has more than 250 training institutions and makes full use of training possibilities in other countries. This training effort has made it possible for Africans to fill many jobs formerly held by expatriates.

In order to solve problems of co-ordination, Nigeria has established two institutions with a semi-independent status: the Centre for Management Development and the Industrial Training Fund. The former is intended for supervisory and management personnel, whereas the latter is mainly responsible for financing the training of workers and technicians through a levy on wages and salaries paid by enterprises. The demand for skilled personnel in Nigeria is so great that industrial enterprises are obliged to develop their own training facilities. This is the case, for example, in the automobile industry, where the rate of turnover of manpower in some plants is estimated to be 100 per cent every two or three years. These workers, once they have been trained at the technician and skilled-worker levels, often establish their own small enterprises and workshops, and contribute in this way to the expansion of economic activity in the country.

Egypt is encountering serious problems in obtaining qualified technicians and skilled workers, mainly as a result of the massive migration of skilled labour to neighbouring Arab countries. Technicians are trained in technical institutions following completion of secondary education. Skilled workers are trained in secondary technical schools or under apprenticeship schemes. Apprenticeship includes one year in a training institution and two years of on-the-job training alternating with study periods. Many other training channels exist for skilled workers. These are organised either by the ministries or by ministerial departments, in particular the Productivity and Vocational Training Department of the Ministry of Industry and Mineral Resources, the Ministry of Housing and Reconstruction, the Ministry of Manpower and Vocational Training and the Ministry of Transportation and Communications, or by large state-run or private enterprises, which have their own training facilities. More emphasis is being placed on accelerated training but the absence of national standards for skills constitutes a major problem. Enterprises establish their own qualifications standards upon hiring, and these standards vary widely from one enterprise to another.

The Ivory Coast has for some years been developing a programme for continuous vocational training. The promotion, management and supervision of this programme have been entrusted to a public – but largely autonomous – body, the National Office for Vocational Training (ONFP). Training activities are financed by a levy on private enterprises. During the 1979–80 period about 10,000 employees, or approximately 5 per cent of all employees of public and private enterprises, participated in at least one vocational training course. An analysis of these courses showed that the manufacturing sector is more active in the training field than the other two sectors (agriculture and services). Participation by the services sector is much less, apparently because of the small size of enterprises in this sector; agriculture is represented only to a very limited extent. A particularly important achievement in the Ivory Coast was the setting up of a study and

113

research service within the ONFP, responsible for studying the relationship between training and employment. Decision-makers now have available to them the analyses and information they require for future planning in the field of education and training.[4]

Other countries are also encountering many problems in their efforts to adapt training to development needs. One of the problems is that their educational systems are still modelled largely on those of industrialised countries. The shortage or absence of qualified and experienced instructors is another problem. Finally, the lack of co-ordination between the planning and implementation of training programmes has made it more difficult to meet training needs adequately. In addition to these problems of relatively long standing, new problems are emerging. For example, many enterprises require workers with much higher qualifications than before, and the expansion of the public enterprise sector has put pressure on such enterprises to absorb more than their share of manpower, often with little or no relevant training.

The scarcity of skilled labour in Africa is particularly acute at the technician and high skills levels. A study by the Economic Commission for Africa (ECA)[5] showed that not one of the least developed countries of Africa possesses a training infrastructure for technicians at the medium or advanced level. This of course explains why there are so few technicians in these countries.

People in rural areas, where the vast majority of the population lives, have benefited much less from training than those living in urban areas and working in the modern sector. There are several reasons to explain this. Training needs are more difficult to assess in rural areas, and training activities are more expensive because they have to be tailor-made if they are to be effective. Some African governments are now allocating more resources to rural training and are introducing new programmes and approaches specially adapted to

rural conditions. This is the case, for instance, in Kenya.

Another study by the World Bank describes Africa's dilemma with regard to the development of its human resources in the following terms: "The increases in investment in human resources needed to sustain economic growth over the next 20 or 30 years will jeopardise the fiscal and economic health of many African countries in the next five to ten years."[6] While this dilemma is not fundamentally different from that of other developing regions, it is particularly serious in the case of Africa. It means that Africa, which is already devoting a large share of its resources to education and training, is far from meeting its needs, while the chances of increasing this effort to any significant extent are slight owing to the limited resources available.

Consequently, it is to be expected that the training systems in Africa will evolve in two directions. First, there will be an emphasis on making training available to a larger proportion of the population, including people in rural areas, the urban informal sector and especially unskilled youth who have either dropped out of school or had no access to education. Second, there will be more emphasis on increasing training efficiency. This will only be achieved by better planning and improved organisation; by giving higher priority to the training of teachers and instructors; and by making a more intensive use of existing training facilities and infrastructures.

At the time of independence, most African countries did not have sufficient supervisory and management personnel since their modern sector was very weak, and important posts were occupied by expatriates. To make up for this shortage, many decided to introduce accelerated training courses in management theory and techniques. Management and productivity centres were set up, and management consultancy training services were offered to local enterprises, both public and private. National universities set up faculties and departments of advanced business administration. Several advanced training institutes were established. Many young Africans were sent to study industrial management and business administration in Europe and North America.

There are now roughly 230 management institutes in Africa, including universities, that provide training in management and public administration. About 60 of them provide training for persons already holding managerial posts. The need for top managers continues to be great and many persons in these posts require further training.

Numerous countries have set up local institutions, particularly to train supervisory staff and shop foremen for both the public and the private sector. Some countries, such as Algeria, Egypt, the Ivory Coast, Mali, Nigeria, Senegal and Tunisia, have their own training staff and specialists. Other countries, such as Somalia and the Sudan, which had successfully set up their own institutions, have lost some of their trainers through emigration. In still another category are those countries which do not have sufficient management trainers. It is therefore understandable that many countries with management training institutions felt it necessary, towards the end of the 1970s, to define more precisely their needs for management personnel, both quantitatively and qualitatively. Studies along these lines were conducted by Egypt, Nigeria, the United Republic of Tanzania and Zambia, among others.

There is increasing co-operation among various regional institutions in Africa. The National Institute for Productivity and Industrial Development (INPED) in Algeria organises programmes for management trainers from French-speaking countries. The Centre for Management Development in Lagos also organises courses for management trainers and consultants from other African countries. Finally, the Eastern and Southern African Management Institute (ESAMI) and the

8.1

Training-through-consultancy programme at the National Productivity Centre (NPC) of Ethiopia

This programme was developed in response to a specific request from the Minister of Industry, who was keen to increase production, reduce down-time and scrapping, and improve product quality in several dozens of factories through better maintenance. NPC lacked sufficient consultants to keep up with growing problems in the factories and it found managers hesitant to carry out consultants' recommendations. NPC decided to increase the number and capability of consultant-managers in the maintenance field, from within the companies.

The programme gradually starts with short seminars for top managers and policy-makers, during which hundreds of maintenance problems are aired. Then maintenance managers from within the companies participate in courses and work in closely supervised teams on consultancy assignments. Certificates of completion (not attendance) are awarded to members of the teams when their recommendations are "signed off" by plant management. NPC documents and closely monitors the implementation of recommendations in the plants.

Rather than just evaluate the programme at the end, NPC uses continuous evaluation to adjust and improve the programme as it expands. Evaluation has documented savings of at least eight times the cost of the programme, in which more than 1,000 people received training and 20 maintenance management consultants were certificated. NPC finds that managers' attitudes towards maintenance have changed. Co-operation between production and maintenance departments in most plants is better. Down-time has been reduced by between 7 and 15 per cent; record-keeping and plant layouts are better. In 1982 four of the participating enterprises documented annual savings of more than US$1.2 million from increased production, prolonged machine life, increased numbers of spare parts produced locally and reduced rejection of production. In the same year, NPC expanded the programme to 143 factories.

115

Pan-African Institute for Development (PAID) organise regional seminars and courses.

Methodologies applied to management training in Africa have also evolved, particularly in the most prominent institutions. Most programmes formerly were more theoretical than practical in character and orientation; however, there has been a recent tendency to stress the practical side, utilising participative techniques and case-studies. In addition, the training content has been considerably improved.

8.2

Promotion of small enterprises in the African construction sector

In Kenya the National Construction Company (NCC), now a semi-public corporation, was set up in 1967 to provide African contractors with credit facilities, advisory services and training. It was also to help contractors obtain work, especially from the public sector. By 1978-79 NCC was giving loans to 53 African contractors, whereas when the NCC started, very few African contractors existed.

In Swaziland the Small Enterprises Development Company (SEDCO), created in 1970, had objectives similar to those of the NCC, except that it covered all types of small-scale industries, not just construction. The extension of SEDCO's training, advisory and loan services to the construction industry arose in response to the initiative of a few Swazi contractors. In 1980-81 assistance was given on contract totalling seven times the amount of the loan fund, which then stood at approximately US$434,000.

In Botswana the Botswana Enterprise Development Unit (BEDU) was created in 1974. Although similar in principle to SEDCO, it does not possess the autonomy of a corporation, because it is a line department of the Ministry of Commerce and Industry. It has provided advisory and training services to contractors, but because it is a government department its financial help has been rather limited.

In 1973 the Ghana Bank for Housing and Construction (GBHC) started operations in order to finance and carry out housing and various kinds of civil engineering schemes. Another objective of the Bank is to develop and promote efficiency in the construction industry generally. The GBHC has been more successful in achieving its financial objective than in improving contractor efficiency.

Experiences with these schemes have been examined in various case-studies and served as the basis for *Guide-lines for the development of small-scale contractors*, published by the ILO in 1983.

that the National Productivity Centre (NPC) of Ethiopia has had under way since 1979 to help scores of manufacturing companies solve maintenance problems (see box 8.1).

The small enterprise sector received little attention during the years following independence. The institutions that had been created especially to aid small enterprises were devoting only a small part of their activity to management and the promotion of entrepreneurship; their efforts were concentrated mainly on identifying, formulating and carrying out small business projects, and on organising credit schemes. Management training for small enterprises was therefore most often obtained under rather informal conditions and on an ad hoc basis. To remedy this situation, a certain number of management institutions developed specialised courses with counselling services for small enterprises. In addition, vocational training institutions are now also involved in programmes designed to promote entrepreneurship and to assist in the setting up of new enterprises. Finally, governments and semi-public companies carry out such programmes as well, for example in the construction sector (see box 8.2).

Latin America and the Caribbean

Many countries of Latin America and the Caribbean have long been engaged in manpower training activities, some already possessing vocational education and training institutions before the turn of this century. A number of these countries have created national training institutions or systems that today enjoy a well-deserved reputation for excellence.

Generally speaking, training situations fall into two categories. Most of the countries have national institutions, dating back in some cases to the 1940s and 1950s, that were set up to meet the demand for

116

At present, the need for more thorough training and long-duration courses in management is recognised by most countries. Africa has begun recently to introduce management training aimed at specific economic sectors. Specialised management training programmes are to be found particularly in the construction, transport and energy sectors, in addition to a very wide sector consisting of small enterprises. A good example of the evolution of management training in Africa is the training-through-consultancy programme skilled manpower created by economic and industrial development. Other countries strengthened their training infrastructures by creating new training institutions, but without placing them under the authority of a national co-ordinating body. In these countries the institutions come directly under the various ministries. Initially, institutional mechanisms were created to ensure the necessary co-ordination, but afterwards they were gradually replaced by national organisations with some degree of autonomy.

For many years it was difficult to carry out any form of human resources planning in Latin America and the Caribbean owing to the purely indicative nature of national planning. This explains why governmental bodies had to develop their own planning machinery that would enable them to adapt training as rapidly as possible to the constantly changing demands of the labour market. For that purpose, national training institutions often had to undertake their own research on quantitative and qualitative vocational training needs. However, the assessment of these needs is still being carried out under conditions that are not entirely satisfactory; and the problem of insufficient co-ordination between employment, job requirements, education and vocational training persists.

Vocational training institutions have usually been assigned a broad range of tasks: they are responsible for the further training of workers who are already employed; for the initial training of youth, including those who have not received formal education or who have dropped out of the school system; for the training of women; for the training of marginal groups; for providing advisory services to enterprises; and for the training of instructors.

Faced with these tasks, training institutions have been obliged to assign priorities to their activities. While priorities may vary considerably between countries, most national training institutions tend to give highest priority to providing further training to already employed workers in order to increase productivity in enterprises. This is followed by training for the unemployed, assisting enterprises in setting up their own training facilities, and setting up sectoral vocational training programmes.

Rural vocational training has expanded quite rapidly, particularly in activities related to the industrial sector, i.e. in large agro-industrial complexes and industrialised farming. It was not until quite recently that vocational training became concerned with the very heterogeneous group of activities consisting of subsistence farming and rural non-farm activities. For this mixed group the institutions followed initially a training strategy based on cash crops; afterwards they began to give a higher priority to the training of small farmers and their families in managing their farms. In other words, such training is concerned with rural enterprise development as a whole, in which the motivation of the family head, his wife and friends, the acquisition of technical and management knowledge and a knowledge of their socio-economic environment all play a role. With time, organisations engaged in rural training necessarily became specialised, and new institutions adopting this broader approach to training have been set up.

In view of the very serious socio-economic situation in the suburban areas of many cities, several countries have attempted to set up programmes specially designed for marginal groups. National training institutions have often been entrusted with these tasks. The Ecuadorian Vocational Training Service (SECAP) has set up a pilot training programme in the suburbs of Guayaquil. This programme is intended for the poorest strata of the population, and assists them in acquiring the necessary know-how for improving their living and housing conditions and at the same time increasing their chances of finding employment. Programmes with similar objectives exist in a number of other Latin American and Caribbean countries.

117

In Latin America and the Caribbean, as in most developing regions, more than half of the unemployed are young people. Thus in Argentina youth unemployment has been estimated to account for 72 per cent of total unemployment, in Colombia and Panama for 74 per cent, and in Venezuela for over 61 per cent.[7] In most cases the unemployed youth have had no job experience and have few if any skills.

For this reason many countries in the region have shown interest in setting up training programmes specifically designed for the unemployed, and more particularly for young people between 14 and 24 years of age. In Brazil the Ministry of Education and Culture has set up a socio-economic action programme for the under-privileged urban population. The principal aim of this programme is to improve both the quality and the quantity of schooling at the basic community level, offering at the same time vocational training opportunities to unemployed youth. In 1981 a budget of 1,000 million cruzeiros (approximately US$8 million as at December 1981) was allocated for this programme. Part of this money was used to finance schooling and training infrastructures for underprivileged groups. This action programme is being carried out jointly with the Ministry of Labour and in close collaboration with the country's most important national training institutions.

In Colombia the National Apprenticeship Service (SENA) has been working for more than ten years on a mobile programme to train urban and rural populations. Such training programmes are intended primarily for unemployed youth, for whom they provide badly needed initial training. In 1979 the mobile urban programme covered 93,000 workers and the mobile rural programme more than 200,000.[8] Colombia is also one of the countries that has been most active in developing training programmes for the urban informal sector. These programmes aim at generating employment and improving productivity and production conditions. They started as pilot projects and have since been extended to promote small enterprise development.

In Venezuela 18,000 apprentices completed training between 1979 and 1983 and at the end of that period 15,000 apprentices were following courses. The programme of the National Institute for Educational Co-operation (INCE) covers 157 industrial trades and 35 trades in the tertiary sector (commerce, banking, hotels and tourism, etc.). The programme of in-plant training sponsored by INCE trained 220,000 workers and supervisors between 1978 and 1983. INCE is also carrying out a training programme addressed to underemployed people living in the poorer areas of big cities. Through voluntary instructors, trained by INCE, short courses (40 to 300 hours) are organised aiming to train men and women in skills which allow them to increase their incomes. This programme provided courses in 176 different occupations which, in the 1977-83 period, were completed by 480,000 trainees.

The management training capacity in Latin America and the Caribbean has expanded considerably during the past decade, following a parallel increase in the demand for such training. Most countries have set up a rich variety of management training institutions for supervisory and management personnel in government administrations, and both state-run and private enterprises. Some are institutions for public administration, others are management centres and still others are productivity centres.

Other training institutions are linked to professional associations such as the associations for marketing personnel, for personnel managers and for labour relations. Certain institutions were created on the initiative of international foundations and religious groups. Several of the large international vocational training institutions, such as INA in Costa Rica, INCE in Venezuela and SENA in Colombia, also offer management training and training for medium-sized and small enterprises. The quality of management develop-

Personnel policy in Centrais Eléctricas de Minas Gerais, Brazil

Centrais Eléctricas de Minas Gerais (CEMIG) of Brazil developed an innovative staff selection and development system that seems to account, at least in part, for good bottom-line results and high morale. A typical management problem in utilities is that of maintaining an organisational *esprit de corps* in the conditions under which they operate – routinised work, monopoly position, no radical changes in products, and so on. These can all lead to ossification. CEMIG's answer is based on a study of a physician/psychologist who compared the internal structures of organisms and organisations. He compared an organism's nervous system with the personnel function of an organisation (other authors have advocated the information system or the finance department for this role). He noted that the personnel function could help the individual to integrate into the organisation and thus was responsible for reducing and eliminating conflicts between the objectives of individuals and those of their organisation and, by extension, those of different departments. CEMIG adopted this philosophy, and applied it to its selection procedures. These include a battery of tests evaluated by psychologists, sociologists and anthropologists. The personnel profile is updated during the career of each individual. These profiles are matched with job descriptions and are used as the basis for preparing short lists of candidates for promotion or transfer for presentation to the chiefs concerned, as well as for identifying candidates for training, counselling and so forth.

ment training varies greatly from one country to another and between institutions in the same country. Efforts to improve the performance of management development and consultancy services have not always been successful, but some government organisations provide examples of good staff development (see box 8.3).

Although public and private efforts to improve management training are far from negligible, the results are still inadequate for covering the needs of Latin American and Caribbean countries. Management training is more or less satisfactory in the manufacturing sector, but not in other sectors such as transport and construction. Small enterprises are receiving increased attention, and a large share of management training efforts will probably be concentrated on this sector in the future. Generally

speaking, however, management development has not enjoyed the same degree of support as vocational training activities.

Asia and the Pacific

Many countries in the Asian and Pacific region have made great efforts to expand and modernise their vocational training activities. A good example is provided by India, where vocational training activities have expanded enormously over the past 30 years (see box 8.4). Countries have enacted new legislation on training, and in particular on its financing. Moreover, they have tried to make training available to a larger proportion of the population. The Philippines, for example, has eliminated the age-limit for apprentices, and has adapted many programmes to new developments, such as rapid urbanisation and the growing demand for the training of women and of illiterate or semi-literate people.

The Bangladesh authorities are particularly interested in close relations between Government and industry and have given greater power to the National Council for Skill Development and Training (NCSDT), which co-ordinates the whole vocational training system. Bangladesh provides prevocational training, and it has an apprenticeship system and teacher training facilities. It has also considerably improved its training network in rural areas. For instance, it has taken the initiative to train local artisans to become master artisans capable of assuming trainers' responsibilities. There are, too, an increasing number of private organisations in Bangladesh that offer accelerated training over periods varying from three to 12 months for persons wishing to obtain jobs in the Middle East.

In Papua New Guinea perhaps the most prominent initiative has been the extension of a programme to prepare youth for apprenticeship. This programme, known as pre-employment technical training, has resulted in more and better

8.4

Vocational training in India

Vocational training as it now stands in India is the result of some 30 years of effort and investments. The craftsmen training programme was one of the early initiatives in the 1950s aimed at providing youth between the ages of 15 and 25 with off-the-job training in both engineering and non-engineering trades in the industrial training institutes. This programme, which lasts one to two years, is now delivered in more than 1,100 such institutes and centres.

The rapid growth of the industrial sector, including the expansion of small-scale industries which took place in the 1960s, resulted in a scarcity of technical personnel and called for new policy decisions to increase the flexibility of the vocational training system. The craftsmen programme was therefore strengthened by the introduction in 1961 of an apprenticeship scheme implemented in large and medium-sized industries. Apprentices in 138 designated trades acquire skills under this scheme over a period of one to three years. At the same time, seven central instructor training institutes were established to respond to the need for trainers.

The demand for higher skill levels in specialised industrial fields led to the launching of the advanced vocational training programme which started with the Advanced Vocational Training Institute in Madras in the late 1960s. The Madras institute served as a pilot scheme and became a model for the setting up of similar institutes in Bombay, Calcutta, Kanpur, Hyderabad and Ludhiana. The programme was further expanded at state level, first in 16 industrial training institutes and then gradually extended to another 75. At the same time, advanced training in electronics and process instrumentation was introduced at the Hyderabad and Dehra Dun central institutes. New approaches are now being tested to improve the quality of training using broad-based basic training in the mechanical, electrical/electronics and heat engine trades group followed by modular training based on the ILO modules of employable skills training programmes.

The advanced vocational training programme constituted a major change in the concept of training in India, from the traditional "once-for-all" institutional training to lifelong training with skills being upgraded to meet the needs of rapidly changing technology. This scheme was also instrumental in establishing both institutional and informal relationships with industry.

Liaison between the industrial training programme, the advanced vocational training programme and industry is the responsibility of consultative committees at various levels. Local committees are attached to each industrial training programme to study specific needs of industry in the area and make suggestions to state councils of vocational training empowered to authorise the starting up of new training courses. At the national level, the tripartite consultation process rests with the National Council for Vocational Training which monitors the extent to which the programmes respond to prevailing and future skill requirements.

India chose to develop a specific vocational training programme for women providing both basic and advanced training. There are three vocational training institutes offering advanced skill training to women, located in New Delhi, Bombay and Bangalore. Besides these, there are 123 industrial training programmes run exclusively for women by state governments.

The entire vocational training system is headed by the Directorate-General of Employment and Training under the Minister of Labour and Rehabilitation. It is responsible for policy formulation, the whole training process, the setting up of training standards and the organisation of the programmes.

The success of the vocational training experience and the training expertise developed in India can be judged by the fact that this country, besides responding to its own domestic requirements for trained personnel, is now helping other developing countries to train their personnel either by admitting foreign trainees in its own institutions or by providing expertise to help those countries to organise their vocational training systems.

prepared youth entering apprenticeship. Alternating training is becoming more widespread in this country, particularly for technicians. There is for instance an arrangement under which trainees are taken in charge by employers for six months per year over a period of three years.

The serious shortage of skilled manpower in Indonesia, particularly in the modern sector, caused the authorities to re-examine their training systems and to restructure technical education and vocational training. One result of this re-examination is that informal sector activities such as handicrafts are now included in the formal vocational training system, reflecting a desire to make this traditional sector part of the development effort. In a similar vein, the Philippines now also offers apprenticeship in traditional handicrafts.

Trade testing and skill certification are attracting the attention of many countries in the region, particularly Malaysia, the Philippines, Singapore and the Solomon Islands. The development of national certification standards and procedures in Indonesia and Papua New Guinea has made it possible to recognise experience and skills acquired outside the formal apprenticeship system.

The higher priority given to rural development has led to a number of rural vocational training measures, among which mobile training units appear to be gaining in popularity. These units are mainly found in India and Indonesia. Measures taken to assist rural artisans include supplementary training qualifying them for training tasks and encouraging them to accept apprentices. This is the course followed by India in its efforts to overcome the shortage of instructors willing to teach in rural areas. Through this approach, deficiencies in theoretical knowledge are to a large extent compensated for by manual skills.

The interest shown in Asia for the modular approach to training sometimes takes a highly original form. In Indonesia, for example, young people, after completing primary education, have an opportunity to participate in a modular vocational training programme over a period of four years. Certificates are issued at various training stages, making it possible for apprentices to use their acquired skills at all times. A modular approach of the same type has also been adopted in Singapore as the basis of full-time and part-time training programmes. This approach is becoming more and more popular, particularly for updating, upgrading and retraining. Initially, the modular approach was adopted for the purpose of imparting immediately usable skills, meeting the needs of trainees with different levels of previous training and overcoming the scarcity of qualified instructors. Gradually, it has been used more widely and today it serves as a basis for continuous training programmes, as is the case in Singapore.

The Republic of Korea has established a special status for the highest degree of qualification of master craftsman, "postgraduate master craftsman". This level is said to be equivalent to a Ph.D. and is granted at the end of seven years of training, i.e. a period identical to that required for the training of graduate engineers.

In Asia apprenticeship is by tradition a recognised and respected method of acquiring skills. It takes the most varied forms. It may be compulsory, as in India, where plants or enterprises with more than 500 workers are obliged to have manpower training centres. In Pakistan factories and enterprises with more than 50 workers are required to take on a specified number of apprentices. Although the legislation varies considerably between countries, provisions requiring enterprises to accept a certain quota of apprentices as part of their personnel are not exceptional in Asia. In the Republic of Korea, trainee quotas are established in January of each year for enterprises with more than 300 workers.[9] In countries such as Indonesia and Thailand, on the other hand, apprenticeship arrangements are voluntary, and not required by legislation.

Arrangements for prevocational training and vocational preparation for apprenticeship have been developed in Thailand in particular. These are intended for young drop-outs and unemployed youth. The system includes programmes lasting from three to 11 months, with alternating periods in training establishments and enterprises. In Hong Kong prevocational training lasts three years. In industrialised countries (see Chapter 7), age restrictions have long been an obstacle to the development of apprentice training. In Asia and the Pacific the level of education required for entry into apprenticeship is established by law, and generally linked to the compulsory school-leaving age. However, there is usually not only a minimum age of entry into apprenticeship but also a maximum age. The maximum age conditions have been eliminated in recent years in Malaysia, Papua New Guinea, the Philippines and Singapore. In addition, financial incentives and subsidies have also helped to develop apprenticeship, particularly in those sectors and occupations where a shortage of skilled manpower exists.

China has identified low productivity, an outdated technology and the rate of population growth as some of the main obstacles to development. Its development and modernisation plans give highest priority to industry, agriculture, defence, science and technology. China also places great emphasis on the acquisition of skills and their effective use in order to increase productivity. Its rate of industrial growth remains lower than desired, because competent supervisory and management personnel are in short supply. In addition, it seems necessary to modernise its vocational training programmes, to design instruction methods corresponding to the new training goals, and to assign a high priority to the training of vocational training teachers and instructors.

Various measures have been taken to overcome the weaknesses of the Chinese training system. This is illustrated by the recent creation at Beijing of the China Enterprise Management Association (CEMA). Together with newly created university departments of management, it is organising training courses for industrial management personnel. The training undertaken by CEMA covers only a relatively small proportion of the requirements; however, the courses have mainly used mass methods not only for initial but also for further training. Enterprises have been selected from four priority sectors to try out and develop new methods of training management personnel.

Generally speaking, the management training situation in Asia and the Pacific is as varied as the region itself, since countries with advanced technologies exist side by side with others where the notion of management is almost unknown.

A study recently carried out in Indonesia estimated the number of senior managers in that country at approximately 130,000; among these, more than 100,000 were in need of further training. The demand for management training projected over a period of five years revealed a need for the training of more than 47,000 public sector supervisors and managers per year, to which should be added the very considerable requirements of the private sector. In contrast to this situation, small

countries in the Pacific region are having almost insurmountable problems in finding a few nationals with a sufficiently high educational level to be trained for posts presently occupied by foreign managers.

Although management principles can be transmitted relatively quickly and easily, the process of acquiring experience is very slow. That is why several countries of the region are examining ways to accelerate the process of acquiring managerial experience. For this purpose, some countries in the Pacific area have devised an individual training system in which each trainee is assigned to a manager or a supervisor. In Bangladesh training given in institutions is linked to practical training which includes analysing and solving problems encountered in real life. This formula has the double advantage of developing a continuous management training capacity within the enterprise and at the same time of avoiding the risk of creating a gap between the management development institutions and the clients they are supposed to serve.

The diversity of management needs today is much greater than in the past, and this has led to a significant increase in management training courses for sectors other than the manufacturing sector. For example, Bangladesh and India now have specialised management training institutions for the road transport industry, whereas the Management Development and Productivity Centre in Thailand provides training and offers consultancy services in the area of public utilities, particularly in the water supply sector. A particularly successful example of management training in the water supply sector is provided by the Philippines (see box 8.5). The need for specific management training is now also recognised in the areas of energy, distribution and construction (particularly for small construction firms).

Problems of flexibility to meet changing conditions have been the subject of studies, carried out particularly in the sector of government-run

---

8.5

Specialised management training organised by the Local Water Utilities Administration in the Philippines

The Local Water Utilities Administration (LWUA) in the Philippines has helped hundreds of municipal water authorities to improve their performance in the past few years. LWUA was established to break the vicious circle of poor service that most countries are caught up in. LWUA was able to break this circle in hundreds of municipalities by shielding the local water authorities against excessive local political influence and by helping them to operate in a business-like manner.

For this purpose, LWUA set up a model management training programme for its own staff and for the staff of its clients – the municipal water authorities. LWUA recruits fresh graduates (to avoid having to help mature engineers unlearn bad habits) who go through a two-month "cadetship training programme" before being fielded. A few years later, the "battle-scarred" engineer returns for a four-month advanced course designed to close the gap between theory and practice. In addition, LWUA uses a variety of other methods to provide staff members with new knowledge at various points of their careers and, in particular, to give them an opportunity to change work attitudes and outlook. It uses overseas fellowships as a reward for good performance and to broaden a person's outlook, but not as a substitute for staff development.

An unusual feature of LWUA, which perhaps accounts for much of its success, is the management advisory service it provides. Every month, each municipal water authority is visited by a team of two LWUA advisers who sit down with the general managers to solve pressing problems and to draw up a plan of action, which the advisers monitor on subsequent visits. This service for the 200 or so municipal water authorities under LWUA's wing is based on a "management audit check-list" including a set of development indicators that reflect the characteristics of well-managed water authorities. Progress toward business-like efficiency is measured by the month-by-month accumulation of points on this check-list. The junior advisers learn their skills largely by being teamed up with senior advisers. This one-on-one training and field experience is supplemented by monthly meetings using case-studies and lectures.

Client training at LWUA is at least as important as internal staff development and the management advisory service. It aims at three audiences: policy-makers, water authority managers and technicians. Seminars for policy-makers are designed to help members of community boards, who often suddenly find themselves, for the first time in their lives, making policies for a complex public utility. The seminars are credited with helping these board members to find innovative solutions to the age-old water supply problems of their communities. The periodic seminars for management teams from different authorities are considered by LWUA to be among the most stimulating in its client training programme. The technical training courses cover water quality surveillance, leak detection and repair, equipment operation, and maintenance. In addition, LWUA runs a certification programme to increase the number of qualified operators throughout the country. One of the most innovative programmes is the programme of pre-construction seminars organised to bring together contractors, construction inspectors, local officials and interested members of the community prior to any large-scale construction project.

123

enterprises. Bangladesh, Indonesia, Pakistan and other countries of the region have taken measures to improve the performance of enterprises in the public sector by introducing improved management and control techniques.

Thinking on management often focuses on the notion of productivity, which has reappeared in many Asian countries. Productivity is not looked upon simply as a means of making people work harder; it is now recognised as a management responsibility. This approach has of course a great impact on the demand for training, and in particular for further training. Countries such as Indonesia and Singapore have therefore worked out a comprehensive plan for the training and development of management personnel. The economic successes of Japan and the Republic of Korea are often taken as models. It is therefore not surprising that countries such as Malaysia and Singapore are following closely the policies adopted and applied by these two countries.

The Japanese approach to human resources development policy and productivity has aroused great interest among management training institutions and leaders in most other countries. However, the initial enthusiasm for these models of economic performance has been tempered by the realisation that these results were achieved in a context and environment radically different from those prevailing in other countries of the region.

It is in the area of small enterprises that Asia has achieved the most interesting results. Countries such as India and the Philippines have created small enterprise planning units at ministerial level and have set up institutional support structures and training programmes specially designed for small enterprises.

It is increasingly clear that their lack of financial resources for training is one of the principal obstacles to the development of small enterprises. The Republic of Korea and Malaysia have created training and consultancy services for small enterprises within financial and industrial institutions, particularly those concerned with the development of small enterprises. In Indonesia a similar scheme has been put into effect with the support of the Bank of Indonesia (see box 8.6).

India has created institutions at district level which provide aid to small enterprises, including assistance in the establishment of contracts with local commercial banks. It also promotes the practice of subcontracting between large and small enterprises, which in certain cases opens up new credit lines. In Burma support services are usually intended for co-operatives made up of small producers.

The diversity of approaches to assisting small enterprises has led to the creation of a large number of autonomous or semi-autonomous institutions endowed with highly qualified personnel capable of offering high-quality services. Although Asia has a long tradition in the matter, entrepreneurship is not evenly distributed among all the social groups (see box 8.7). That is why countries such as India, Malaysia and the Philippines have set up special programmes to promote entrepreneurship precisely among those groups that appear to be largely lacking in it.

Measures to finance training differ greatly from one country to another in Asia and the Pacific, even though special training levies and subsidies are becoming more and more common. In Hong

---

8.6

Indonesian credit programme for small enterprises

Indonesia has a loan programme for small enterprises in urban and rural areas. In 1981 it was growing at the rate of 1,000 loans per day, with a disbursement of more than US$4 million per day. By 30 June 1980, i.e. some seven years after its launching, this so-called KIK/KMKP programme of the Bank of Indonesia had provided more than 218,000 loans to individual businesses and at least 400,000 to groups of businesses. Repayment performance was satisfactory. This programme proves a number of points that may be of interest to other countries:

- it is possible to launch medium-term credit (of an average amount of about US$2,000) through commercial banks;

- it is possible to reach rural areas: 70 per cent of all credit was granted in non-urban areas;

- it is possible to provide finance to sectors other than agriculture or manufacturing: more than 30 per cent of all term lending was for the trade and distribution sector.

Kong, for instance, construction enterprises have to pay out 0.25 per cent of the value of their contracts for training. Other countries, such as Nepal, have chosen to subsidise all or part of the wages of apprentices or, as is the case of the Philippines, to provide financial support to enterprises that have set up training programmes. The Philippines is stepping up its training efforts considerably, especially in the construction, textiles, electric power, mining, transport, agro-industrial, and hotel, catering and tourism sectors. These sectors are reimbursed for their training expenses.

Many countries in Asia and the Pacific still face considerable quantitative and qualitative manpower shortages that constitute serious obstacles to their development. Future training programmes in this region will probably be directed mainly towards increased training opportunities for population groups formerly isolated and cut off in rural areas; improvement of training efficiency; development of training in maintenance; and increased training of technicians.

8.7

Entrepreneurship development in Gujarat (India)

Reputedly, one of the most successful programmes in developing viable small enterprises is the entrepreneurship development programme of Gujarat State in India. Started in 1969 to provide capable entrepreneurs with financial backing, the programme has expanded to over 35 centres and encompasses all components of entrepreneurship support: selection and training for entrepreneurship development, managerial and technical skills training, project identification, assistance in securing finance, provision of infrastructure and raw materials, institutional and political support, and progress evaluation. The programme has trained more than 6,000 entrepreneurs, who have started more than 1,900 industrial units, while 1,800 are in the process of starting. Untrained entrepreneurs failed in business six times as frequently as the ones it trained (21.4 per cent as against 3.6 per cent); and the businesses of the trained entrepreneurs were more often profitable (76 per cent as against 57 per cent). It costs about US$150 to train each person, and much of this cost is subsidised.

Each person who enters the programme is screened by tests and interviews to ensure that he possesses traits associated with successful entrepreneurship. The tests are largely based on McClelland's theories of achievement motivation. People possessing certain traits and possibly with some commercial or industrial experience are accepted. Those with industrial experience are offered an evening programme lasting 90 days, while those without such experience, for example, recent graduates and the educated unemployed, attend a six-month full-time course which includes practical training and work experience.

Each programme is conducted in the local language and covers four main topics: achievement motivation, product selection and project development, business management, and practical work

experience. First, the trainees spend five days on achievement motivation; here the programme attempts to increase the trainee's capacity to take initiative, his desire to achieve results, and his ability to define realistic goals. Then, the programme moves on parallel tracks in which the trainee investigates a viable industrial opportunity while learning the techniques of management. Trainees talk with many people who have industrial and commercial experience to find commercial opportunities and then produce reports covering product line, market mix and commercial feasibility. The business management syllabus, which is covered while the trainees search for business opportunities, includes all important aspects of managing and developing a small or medium-sized enterprise.

Over the years the programme has developed both performance indicators and standards that are used to manage all the centres. These performance indicators may well become models for similar projects elsewhere. Various input and output indicators are used, such as the number of new entrants, the percentage of drop-outs, the number of new business projects identified, how many get financial backing, how many survive and how they grow. Even in rural and backward areas, the project leader is expected to identify at least 50 potential new entrepreneurs for each programme, which must have less than 10 per cent of drop-outs; otherwise the trainer is considered not to be doing his job properly, or the selection was made wrongly. Fifty per cent of the trainees must prepare a project report for a viable business by the end of the programme; and over 90 per cent of these must get financing; otherwise the programme may be at fault. At least 65 per cent of the trained entrepreneurs in urban areas, and at least 45 per cent in rural areas, are expected to start industries and be surviving profitably after two years.

Some special problems in the Asian Arab countries

Asian Arab countries have some special training problems. While the scarcity of skilled manpower is a serious impediment to accelerated development, the oil-rich countries have tended to rely more on importing skilled labour than on training their own nationals. This is true for both workers and managerial staff. The great majority of trained manpower is imported, in particular from other Arab countries, resulting in a drain on the latter's reservoir of trained human resources.

These countries, while reaping the benefits of remittances, find themselves faced with a situation where the planning of training activities is becoming increasingly difficult. For, on the one hand, it is hard to determine whether existing resources can continue to meet local and other countries' needs and, on the other, it is felt that the phenomenon of migration may not continue indefinitely and hence the expansion of training facilities may be unwarranted or, worse still, these countries might be faced with a problem of reverse migration.

Another great problem for Asian Arab countries is the lack of high-level management personnel. Although no comprehensive study is available of the management needs in all countries of the region, a number of studies conducted in Bahrain, Democratic Yemen, Iraq, Jordan, Kuwait, the Syrian Arab Republic, the United Arab Emirates and Yemen have brought out the following points:

- Productivity in all sectors is suffering, not only because of inadequate training and experience, but especially because of a shortage of qualified management personnel.
- The problems which management and supervisory personnel have to face vary considerably from country to country. For example, in Saudi Arabia and the United Arab Emirates, top managers have to deal not only with large and widely different investments, but also with workers from many different countries and cultures; in some cases, like the United Arab Emirates, workers from as many as 30 different countries are employed in various organisations.
- The introduction of new technologies is accompanied by an urgent demand for technicians and specialised management personnel.
- Planning, the definition of goals and the establishment of control procedures are areas in which management training is needed.

Basic management training in the Asian Arab region is provided by some universities giving courses in either business or related subjects, such as accounting, and offering degrees at the bachelor or more advanced level. Iraq has the largest number of such faculties in the region. The standard of training varies considerably from one country to another and often within the same country. Some of these faculties offer short-term programmes for management development, such as the College of Industrial Management at the University of Petroleum and Minerals in Saudi Arabia. Others, such as the College of Administrative Sciences at the United Arab Emirates University, have plans to introduce such programmes in the future.

Of the 12 countries of the region,[10] six have management institutions which aim at upgrading the professional competence of practising managers. Two centres exist in Iraq: the National Centre for Consultancy and Management Development and the National Computer Centre. In Saudi Arabia, the Institute of Public Administration caters mainly to the training needs of the public sector. This is also the case of the National Institute of Public Administration in Yemen. The Management Development and Productivity Centre in the Syrian Arab Republic is mainly concerned with state-owned enterprises. In Jordan, one institute is geared to civil service training, the Institute of Public Administration, and two are active in management development for private and state-owned enterprises, the Jordan Institute of Management and the Royal Scientific Society.

Apart from these national institutes, some regional institutes, such as the Arab Planning Institute and the Arab Organisation of Administrative Sciences, hold management development seminars from time to time on an ad hoc basis. Thus, few centres in the Asian Arab region cater for the needs of private, mixed or state-owned enterprises as distinct from training for the civil service and public administration. It is not surprising, therefore, that a number of large enterprises have introduced their own training activities, in several cases in co-operation with private Arab and foreign consulting firms. However, in a recent survey conducted by the ILO, some of the managers interviewed expressed disappointment with the services provided by commercial consulting firms, considering that they were expensive or inappropriate. The multitude of small and medium-sized enterprises in the private sector, however, find themselves in a situation where their management development needs remain largely uncovered or only partly met on an ad hoc basis.

[1] UNDP: *Programme implementation evaluation*, Report of the Administrator, Governing Council of the UNDP, 31st Session, Geneva, June 1984 (New York, 1984, mimeographed: doc. DP/1984/18).

[2] ILO: *Education for development*, Report III, Fifth African Regional Conference, Abidjan, September–October 1977.

[3] Similar institutions also exist in Latin America and the Caribbean and in Asia and the Pacific: the Inter-American Vocational Training Research and Documentation Centre (CINTERFOR), and the Asian and Pacific Skill Development Programme (APSDEP).

[4] See, for example, E. Duhy Zeze: *La formation professionnelle continue en Côte d'Ivoire* (Abidjan, 1981).

[5] ECA: *Feasibility study mission report on the establishment of an African institute for higher technical training and research*, Internal document (Addis Ababa).

[6] World Bank: *Human resources in Africa: A continent in rapid change* (Washington, IBRD, 1982, mimeographed: doc. TCDC/AF/4) p. 65.

[7] ILO: *Year Book of Labour Statistics, 1981* (Geneva, 1982).

[8] CINTERFOR/OIT: *Anuario Estadístico de la Formación Profesional en América Latina* (Montevideo, 1981).

[9] ILO: *A study of apprenticeship in Asia and the Pacific* (Islamabad, 1981), pp. 62 and 151.

[10] Bahrain, Democratic Yemen, Iraq, Jordan, Kuwait, Lebanon, Oman, Qatar, Saudi Arabia, the Syrian Arab Republic, the United Arab Emirates and Yemen.

127

Conclusion

Most countries at present see the major objective of training as being to impart the necessary knowledge, skills and attitudes for meeting the needs of modern society. At the same time, training should cater for the aspirations and needs of its various beneficiaries: men and women, youth and adults, able-bodied and disabled, migrants, refugees and other disadvantaged groups. There is also a growing realisation that if a training system is to be effective, its component parts – training legislation, guidance and counselling, levy systems, training institutions and programmes, etc. – must be mutually supportive and co-ordinated.

Above all, the system must be responsive to a changing socio-economic environment. Part III of this report has dealt with some of the major changes that are occurring in society and the way in which various countries are responding to them. To recapitulate, demographic changes will have a greater impact on training systems if only because of the sheer number of young people who will need training for employment. In addition to Canada, Japan, the USSR and the United States, the issue of youth training is likely to be acute in Europe at least until 1990 and will continue to present a major problem for developing countries where over 50 per cent of the population is under 21 years of age. This is happening at a time when Third World countries are faced with financial constraints that will make it difficult to expand training facilities to any great extent. Other measures will have to be found, such as more intensive and effective use of existing facilities, in-plant training programmes, self-development methods and distance training.

High unemployment in many parts of the world has forced industrialised and developing countries alike to strengthen the link between training and employment programmes. The past decade has seen a number of innovative schemes launched together with a more intensive search for better methods of linking manpower planning with training needs assessment. In fact, rapid changes in job requirements, both quantitative and qualitative, have focused the attention of policy-makers on shorter-term plans that can better reflect the training implications of these changes.

All countries, though to varying degrees, face the major problem of responding to accelerated technological developments and in some cases to profound structural adjustments. This has brought to the fore the need for continuous training, upgrading and retraining of workers for newly emerging occupations or ones for which they were not initially trained.

Another problem is the division of financial and other responsibility for training between government and enterprises. This question has been the subject of a number of legislative measures most of which tend to provide incentives to enterprises to shoulder an increased burden rather than to impose compulsory measures.

Most countries also find it difficult to strike a balance in their training effort between regions and between sectors. Issues of the proper mix between rural and urban, industry and services, modern and traditional, are being increasingly debated. The imbalance is also marked within the sectors themselves, e.g. while vocational training is relatively well advanced in most countries in the construction sector, management development for that sector has lagged behind. Similarly, while entrepreneurship and management development programmes for small enterprises have been introduced in many countries, vocational training for that sector has been overlooked.

The financing of the ever growing cost of training constitutes a major problem for most countries. Two courses have been adopted. First, in many parts of the world the reliance on institutional training is being reduced in favour of on-the-job training and self-development methods; in certain countries the cost of training institutions is being kept down by using them on a two- and even three-shift basis. Secondly, many countries have set up levy systems or have provided tax and other incentives designed to encourage the private and public enterprise sectors to assume a greater share of the financial responsibility. These measures have contributed greatly to the expansion of training efforts in both industrialised and developing countries.

Training methodology is also swiftly changing. New participative methods are being increasingly used in the management development field that aim at analytical problem solving and at changing attitudes. The development of modular programmes, training packages, programmed learning and computer-assisted education has made training more flexible and increased its accessibility to various target groups. Coupled with this, there is a growing realisation that since the training content itself needs to be constantly updated, special attention must be paid to the training and upgrading of trainers and also to improving the management of training institutions.

Part 4

Conditions of work

Introduction

Many people throughout the world have to work in unpleasant conditions, putting up as best they can with dirt, danger, noise, fatigue, stress, monotony and – often – a feeling of not being in control of their own work situation. In fact there are millions of workers for whom deplorable conditions and danger are inseparable from the job. For instance, agricultural labourers and construction workers put in long hours at heavy jobs, and coalminers frequently work in a poorly lit, noisy and dusty environment. For such workers, working conditions need to be improved not only through higher wages and shorter working hours, but also by efforts to reduce accidents and health hazards as much as possible and to improve the organisation of work.

In this part we shall not deal with wages – some aspects of which were already discussed in Volume 1 of this report. However, we shall examine occupational safety and health in Chapter 9 and trends in working time in Chapter 10. Although labour inspection covers, in principle, the application of all labour legislation, in practice it deals chiefly with occupational safety and health and other aspects of working conditions. Labour inspection will therefore be the subject of Chapter 11. In Chapter 12, we shall discuss a particular aspect of work organisation: the concept of quality of working life, which has become a major concern in the industrialised countries.

Chapter 9

Safety and health

Today, every three minutes somewhere in the world one worker dies of an occupational injury or illness, and in every second that passes at least three workers are injured. It is estimated that each year 180,000 workers meet their death and 110 million are injured in occupational accidents. This shows, in stark terms, the occupational safety and health problem at present, which is the subject of this chapter.

Virtually all work includes some hazards; many are obvious; others are insidious and slow to manifest themselves. Workers may be exposed to the dust-laden air of a mine, to the fumes and gases in a chemical extraction plant, to the freezing temperatures of cold storage; to the high level of radiant heat of a steel rolling mill; to artificial humidification in cotton mills; to the loud noise of testing aircraft engines; to vibration from pneumatic drills; to certain paints which contain solvents that can be absorbed through the skin; to rays from electric welding; to tropical heat or to attack from wild animals (snakes, etc.). They may be struck by falling bricks and masonry on a demolition site, or receive an electric shock from a wet switch; their work on conveyor belt production may be boring and tedious; they may suffer physical stress working in tree felling or over-excitement working as firemen or as riot policemen.

What do we mean by occupational safety, by occupational health and by related words such as accidents, hazards, risks, etc.? Simply put, "safety" is the absence of danger and "occupa-tional safety" the absence of danger at work. By danger, or the risk of danger, we mean the degree of exposure to a hazard and by a "hazard" we are thinking of a situation or a condition which has the potential of causing an accident. An "accident" is regarded as an unforeseen event that may cause personal injury or property damage or both. So occupational safety is concerned with injury and property damage at work. Similarly, occupational health is concerned with illness and disease arising from work.

Perhaps an additional concept should be defined here, namely, that of being "safe". What is "safe"? To quote one definition: "A thing is provisionally categorised as safe if its risks are deemed known and in the light of that knowledge judged to be acceptable." As an example we may regard travelling by train or walking across a field as "safe" because we believe we know what the risks are and judge them to be acceptable. And by "risk" we are thinking of the degree of exposure to hazards; these could be a derailment of the train or being struck by lightning or attacked by a bull. So also at work, we regard activities as safe if we judge the risks involved in carrying out the work to be acceptable. Most efforts in the field of occupational safety and health are concerned with reducing the occupational risks to the level defined above as acceptable.

It is not always easy to determine to what extent accidents are the direct consequence of the working environment and of the working environment only. Many accidents occur at the workplace because safety equipment is lacking or the factory and its machinery are poorly designed. The working environment may be so noisy that it is impossible to hear warning signals. The temperature may be such that workers easily become tired and are unable to concentrate on the task in hand, or inadequate ventilation may result in the build-up of toxic fumes and again lead to accidents. Also, the workers themselves may be a contributory factor in some accidents if they have not received adequate training or have little experience of the task.

It may be even more difficult to establish a link between the working environment and the health of workers. Since workers spend about three-quarters of their lives outside the working environment, their health is determined mainly by their living conditions and habits. Poor housing, low levels of hygiene, educational shortcomings and malnutrition, as well as the possible misuse of drugs, alcohol and tobacco, therefore influence the workers' health and can also affect their responses to occupational risks.

The particular relationship between work and health makes it difficult to collect statistics on this aspect of working life. The most reliable statistics are on accidents where the link between accident and death or injury can be clearly established. However, information on occupational diseases is often sketchy and fraught with problems of statistical definition. As a result, the analysis of trends given in this chapter will be mainly qualitative in nature.

In this chapter we shall try to show the main facts about occupational safety and health and to explain why work still leads to so many accidents and diseases. We shall discuss the problems of developed and developing countries in two separate sections, because their differing economic and social environments lead to quite different consequences for occupational safety and health. The chapter will conclude with some remarks on legislation and institutions.

The industrialised countries

This section begins with the subject of occupational safety. It provides statistical information on industrial accidents, followed by a discussion of the main issues concerning accident prevention. Secondly, it gives a qualitative analysis of recent developments concerning occupational diseases. Finally, it discusses the discipline of ergonomics (i.e. the scientific study of the relationship between man and his working environment) which aims – among other things – at improving the safety of workers.

Occupational safety

Data on industrial accidents usually distinguish between fatal and non-fatal injuries. They are often not comparable between periods, countries and industrial sectors since coverage, data sources and statistical definitions may differ considerably. Data are mainly collected for the medium-sized and large enterprises in the mining, industry and construction sectors, while little information is available on the agriculture and services sectors. The statistics of occupational injuries are generally based on industrial accident compensation data or on a compulsory accident-reporting system. However, the statistical definitions of non-fatal injuries used by these sources may vary considerably. Some countries report injuries only when the worker was not able to work for more than two or three days. Other countries – and in general compensation schemes – report every day of work incapacity.

Another factor limiting comparability between countries and sectors has to do with the concept of "persons at risk". For purposes of comparison a calculation is often made of so-called "frequency" rates, defined as the number of injuries (multiplied by 1 million) divided by the number of man-hours worked. The latter number usually does not accurately reflect the number of "persons at risk" because, for example, the office workers of an enterprise run other (and often fewer) occupational risks than its factory workers.

Figure 9.1
Deaths and death rates as a result of fatal industrial accidents, United States, 1933–80

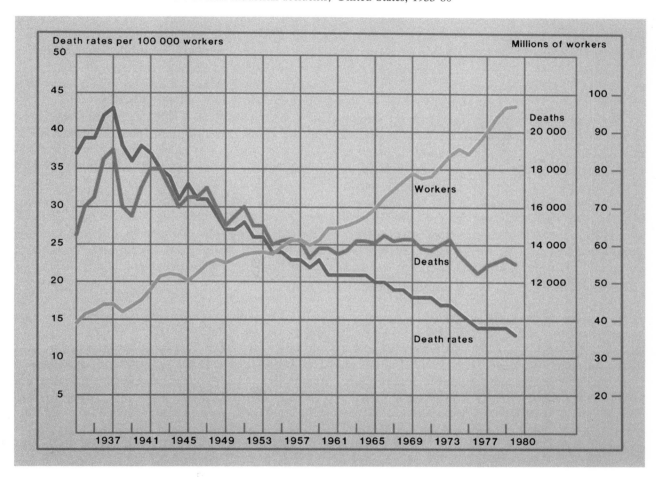

137

In spite of these difficulties, it is possible to make some comparisons over time, based on data from the ILO *Year Book of Labour Statistics*. Two trends emerge from this analysis.

First, there has been a significant reduction in total fatal accidents over the past ten to 20 years; in some countries this has been as much as 30 to 50 per cent. A typical example is the number of occupational accidents in the United States, where death rates as a result of fatal accidents have declined steadily over the past 50 years (see figure 9.1).

Secondly, despite recent efforts, injuries to workers have not declined significantly and have

even, in certain instances, increased, not only in absolute numbers but also in rates per exposed worker. In 14 industrialised countries reporting data to the ILO, the total numbers of persons non-fatally injured for 1979 and 1980 taken together were 5 per cent higher than those for 1976 and 1977. This occurred during a period of stagnant employment. Although some of these increases may be due to better reporting procedures, it is difficult to be optimistic about the trend in non-fatal occupational injuries.

The size of an enterprise is an important factor in the number of accidents. Accident rates tend to be significantly higher in small and medium-sized enterprises than in large factories. For example, a recent study of the metal trades in the Federal Republic of Germany shows that enterprises employing between 50 and 199 workers averaged 130 accidents per 1,000 workers as against 93 accidents per 1,000 workers in establishments with more than 1,000 employees.

Accident fatality rates have declined significantly in the industrialised countries. Sixteen countries (Austria, Canada, Czechoslovakia, Finland, France, German Democratic Republic, Federal Republic of Germany, Hungary, Japan, Luxembourg, Netherlands, Spain, Sweden, Switzerland, United Kingdom and United States) provided data on fatality rates to the ILO which were sufficient for an analysis of the 1971-80 decade, with those for manufacturing and construction being most frequently available. For the countries taken together, the unweighted average fatality rate fell by 16 and 20 per cent in manufacturing and construction respectively between 1971-75 and 1976-80. Some individual decreases were very large, with the fatality rates in both manufacturing and construction reduced by half in Japan while Austria, Canada, the German Democratic Republic, the Netherlands, Sweden and the United Kingdom experienced decreases exceeding 30 per cent in at least one of the two sectors. Only three countries reported higher fatality rates and only one showed a significant increase.

Without exception, fatality rates were much higher in construction than in manufacturing. The difference was particularly striking in Canada, Japan, the United Kingdom and the United States where the fatality rates for the late 1970s in construction were more than four times those in manufacturing. Throughout the 1970s mining continued to be even more dangerous than construction, with fatality rates often five to eight times higher than those in manufacturing.

While fatality rates have fallen, there is no ground for complacency. The absolute number of annual fatalities due to occupational accidents in manufacturing and construction, and indeed in the whole economy, remains high. Fifteen countries alone (Austria, Czechoslovakia, Denmark, Finland, France, Federal Republic of Germany, Hungary, Ireland, Japan, Netherlands, Norway, Sweden, Switzerland, United Kingdom and United States) altogether reported around 16,300 fatalities annually in 1979 and 1980. The three largest market economies (Federal Republic of Germany, Japan and United States) each reported annual deaths exceeding 3,000 in 1979-80.

Several factors contributed to the reduction in fatal accidents: a growing awareness of hazards and the need for prevention, fewer workers exposed to dangerous work, and increased mechanisation and automation. In the 1970s and early 1980s the safety of machinery was improved in both centrally planned and market economies. Machines came with better guards for dangerous parts or with built-in safety devices. In other instances, the introduction of automation, including the use of robots, led to the elimination of dangerous work. There was a growing awareness too that new machines were more powerful and that the consequences of an accident would be more serious. Finally, new legislation was enacted in a number of countries – for example, Denmark (1975), France (1976), the Netherlands (1980), Norway (1979), Sweden (1977) and the United Kingdom (1974) – requiring machine manufacturers, vendors or suppliers to ensure that the machinery and substances placed on the market would not present risks to safety or health. Along with better guarding of machinery there was renewed interest in provision of personal protective equipment. Breathing apparatus, eye protectors, protective clothing, among other equipment, were the subject of research and innovation.

Accidents continued to be frequently associated with the handling of materials, falls of persons, falling objects and impact against objects. For example, these four factors alone accounted for 57 per cent of reported industrial accidents in the

Figure 9.2
Occupational injuries by parts of body (percentage distribution)

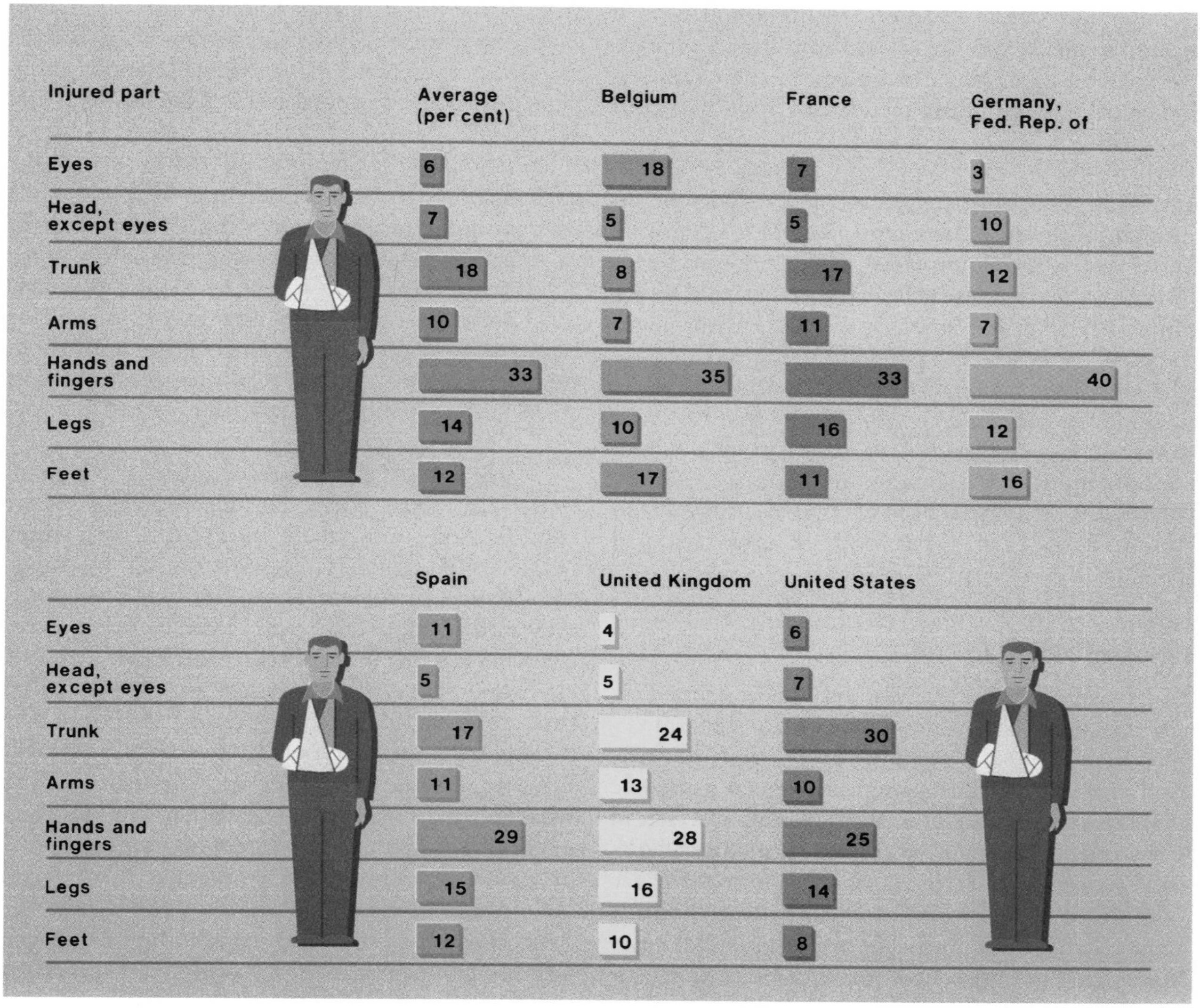

Injured part	Average (per cent)	Belgium	France	Germany, Fed. Rep. of
Eyes	6	18	7	3
Head, except eyes	7	5	5	10
Trunk	18	8	17	12
Arms	10	7	11	7
Hands and fingers	33	35	33	40
Legs	14	10	16	12
Feet	12	17	11	16

	Spain	United Kingdom	United States
Eyes	11	4	6
Head, except eyes	5	5	7
Trunk	17	24	30
Arms	11	13	10
Hands and fingers	29	28	25
Legs	15	16	14
Feet	12	10	8

United Kingdom in 1978. Injury of hands and fingers was the most common occupational accident, followed by injuries of the trunk, legs and feet (see figure 9.2). The human element was certainly present, but it would be wrong to conclude that careless, unsafe acts of workers were the sole, or principal, cause of these accidents. Accidents occurred too because workers were not able, or did not know how, to perform the job safely.

In the 1970s and early 1980s it was increasingly realised that organisational factors play a major part in accident causation. For example, supervisory pressure to increase production or payment-by-results systems designed for the same purpose may induce workers not to use protective devices. Techniques such as the fault-tree accident analysis were developed and used to predict the combination of events and circumstances that could lead to an accident. Moreover, it was recognised that fragmented, repetitive, unskilled work paced by the machine had given rise to harmful levels of fatigue and stress. Workers on night shifts were found to need extra breaks and appropriate welfare services and facilities, for otherwise their reduced level of concentration could lead to errors and accidents.

While the ultimate costs of accidents lie in human suffering, there are also high economic costs borne by enterprises and society at large. Direct costs to firms include the wages paid to the injured worker for time not worked, medical and hospital expenses, and payment to compensate for the loss of use of a part of the body. Indirect costs include the monetised value of time lost by other (non-injured) workers, damage to plant and equipment, and damage to human capital. Economic costs have been estimated in developed countries at 1 to 4 per cent of gross national product.

Occupational health

Statistics of occupational diseases as defined by national legislation can provide only limited information on the relationship between occupation and disease. Legislation and social insurance systems of most countries still make a distinction between occupational and non-occupational diseases; only a limited number of disorders are considered to be caused by the working environment. Statistics of notifiable or prescribed diseases under factory inspection, occupational health or social insurance legislation constitute the main type of information on work-related diseases. However, if expertise in occupational health is lacking in the country, many occupational diseases will not be found, and these diseases will not be recorded as occupational. If there is no health supervision of workers, including systematic periodical examinations, occupational diseases will also escape detection. Undoubtedly, occupational diseases tend to be under-reported in many countries. Epidemiological surveys are more accurate, but they are usually representative of

only a small group of workers. They are often designed to study the health of certain categories of workers and to identify relationships between work and diseases. These and other ad hoc surveys in different countries have shown a surprisingly high incidence of occupational diseases.

In practice, it is often not possible to establish a clear dichotomy between occupational and non-occupational diseases. It is probably more correct to distinguish between diseases caused by work and diseases aggravated by work. There are those for which a single cause can be identified (for example, lead poisoning). But a large number of work-related diseases (for example, chronic bronchitis) are due to multiple factors.

Many diseases due to mixed causes and characterised by long latent periods tend to escape identification until acute symptoms and signs manifest themselves. Diseases caused by long-term exposure to low levels of toxic substances may not develop until years later. Workers may change jobs and be exposed to different levels of exposure. Finally, recent research shows that many factors interact in causing diseases. For example, it is difficult to isolate work-related stress from stress caused by events in the personal life of workers, their individual characteristics or their psychological attitudes. Moreover, some workers have undoubtedly contracted diseases from exposure to substances not yet identified as hazardous. And changes in national legislation raising the number of compensable occupational diseases can invalidate comparisons over time even within a country.

While these factors make it very difficult to compile accurate statistics on occupational diseases, it can hardly be disputed that some workplaces are unhealthy. The past 15 years or so have witnessed a proliferation of new chemicals in workplaces. Estimates of new chemicals entering the market each year in excess of one ton range from 200 to 1,000. This proliferation has raised concern over the adverse effects of occupational exposure to chemical hazards, especially as most of the chemicals newly introduced have not been tested for their toxicity. Occupational exposure limits have been established for only a small number of the toxic substances encountered in workplaces. For example, the ILO[1] lists 1,178 substances for which occupational exposure limits have been established in a score of countries. It is unlikely that the list will be extended much in the near future, because of the time and the high cost involved in toxicological research. It is estimated that some 80 years will be needed to assess the toxic properties of about 40,000 new chemical substances according to current toxicological research methods.

Research showed that exposure for long periods to concentrations hitherto regarded as inoffensive could cause disorders and even cancer. As a result, the criteria for determining the limits of exposure were revised and, in general, those limits were lowered. Possibly, the most conspicuous case concerned vinyl chloride monomer which can cause angiosarcoma of the liver. Its exposure limit was reduced in Sweden, for example, from 100 ppm to 1 ppm (parts per million).

In industrialised countries, the capacity to test for chemical toxicity has been strained to the limit by the speed with which new, untested chemicals are introduced into the workplace. This dangerous gap has prompted the development of new, faster techniques to assess toxicity, for example, in the United States. The OECD and the CMEA have also intensified their activities in this area. Another problem, which came to light more clearly in the 1970s but has yet to be solved satisfactorily, relates to research findings that simultaneous exposure to two or more chemicals may have additive or even multiplicative effects on their toxicity. A useful contribution in this field comes from the the International Programme of Chemical Safety set up by WHO, the ILO and UNEP.

Pneumoconioses, lung diseases resulting from exposure to noxious dust, and occupational asthma have remained serious problems attracting increasing attention. The hazards related to asbestos exposure perhaps received more attention than any other occupational health problem during the past 15 years or so, particularly when epidemiological research confirmed that asbestos was the cause of mesothelioma (a cancer of the pleura or peritoneum). Significant progress was made in controlling occupational exposure to asbestos in individual countries, as, for example, in the Federal Republic of Germany, Spain and the United Kingdom. The Council of Ministers of the European Communities also recently agreed upon measures to deal with asbestos hazards.

During the 1970s there was generally more noise and vibration in factories, because more powerful machines – often with a large number of moving parts – were installed, sometimes concentrated in a limited space. Excessive noise damages the ear and adds to physical and mental strain. Considerable efforts were made to reduce the ill effects of noise, with most developed countries adopting noise standards limiting exposure. Extensive exposure to vibration causes osteoarticular lesions and impairment of the nervous system, blood vessels and muscles.

Increasing recourse to non-ionising radiation, which includes ultra-violet, visible, infra-red and radio-frequency electromagnetic radiations of different wavelengths, has exposed a growing number of workers to the dangers of burns, conjunctivitis and possibly skin cancer. This is the result of greater use of radioactive materials and of medium- and low-powered radiation sources such as X-ray machines in various industries (atomic energy, aircraft manufacturing, chemicals, coal-mining, electronics, metal trades, petroleum, plastics).

There has been heightened concern among the general public, partly generated by a number of alarming disasters, that some industrial health hazards can imperil the surrounding community. Public opinion has become more and more mobi-

9.1

Future research priorities for occupational safety and health in the United States

The National Institute for Occupational Safety and Health (NIOSH) in the United States recently developed a list of the ten main work-related diseases and injuries. Three criteria were used: the frequency of occurrence of the disease or injury, its severity in the individual case, and its amenability to prevention. The list is intended (1) to encourage deliberation and debate among professionals about the major problems in this field of public health; (2) to assist in setting national priorities for efforts to prevent health problems related to work; and (3) to convey to a diverse audience the concerns of the NIOSH and the focus of its activities. The list will be reviewed periodically for necessary updating as knowledge increases and as conditions change and are brought under better control.

Ten main work-related diseases and injuries, United States, 1982

1.	*Occupational lung diseases*	Asbestosis, byssinosis, silicosis, coal workers' pneumoconiosis, lung cancer, occupational asthma.	5. *Cardiovascular diseases*	Hypertension, coronary artery disease, acute myocardial infarction.
2.	*Musculoskeletal injuries*	Disorders of the back, trunk, upper extremity, neck, lower extremity; traumatically induced Raynaud's phenomenon.	6. *Disorders of reproduction*	Infertility, spontaneous abortion, teratogenesis.
3.	*Occupational cancers (other than lung)*	Leukemia, mesothelioma; cancers of the bladder, nose and liver.	7. *Neurotoxic disorders*	Peripheral neuropathy, toxic encephalitis, psychoses, extreme personality changes (exposure-related).
4.	*Amputations, fractures, eye loss, lacerations and traumatic deaths*		8. *Noise-induced loss of hearing*	
			9. *Dermatologic conditions*	Dermatoses, burns (scaldings), chemical burns, contusions (abrasions).
			10. *Psychological disorders*	Neuroses, personality disorders, alcoholism, drug dependency.

Source: *Morbidity and Mortality Weekly Report* (Atlanta, Georgia), 21 Jan. 1983.

142

lised by the installation of chemical, nuclear and other establishments in densely populated areas.

It is important to establish which diseases and injuries are most serious, in order to determine future research priorities in the field of occupational health. A report recently published in the United States has given an indication of these priorities, which are likely to be valid for other industrialised countries as well. It states that the three main work-related diseases and injuries are occupational lung diseases, musculoskeletal injuries and occupational cancers (see box 9.1).

Ergonomics

Though ergonomics has often been described by the simple phrase "fitting the work to the worker", the past 20 years have seen the growth of a much broader concept of ergonomics. Ergonomics has come to be regarded as the scientific study of the relationship between man and his working environment. It takes into consideration not only the physical environment in which man works, but also his tools, materials, and the method and organisation of his work. In other words, it is concerned with the whole man, not just his physical dimensions but also his mental processes, his emotions, his relationships with other workers and his ability to deal with information of all kinds.

At the beginning of the 1960s ergonomic research concentrated on the design of machine controls, levers, knobs, buttons, on the visual displays carried by instruments, on workplace layout, on seats and benches, on the design of hand tools, on manual handling and on heavy workloads. Other factors related to occupational hygiene were added later, such as noise, vibration, lighting and temperature. Finally, the whole of the working environment came to be studied, with job design and organisation, stress, monotony and fatigue all added. The science of ergonomics adopted the systems approach or the systems concept and applied it to the relationship between man and machine.

Starting from the complete redesign of crane control cabins in the 1950s, this systems approach has been used in numerous situations – for the design of control rooms of oil refineries and power stations, for the design of large machines and extensive plant used in motor car and lorry manufacture, for the design of ships' bridges and aircraft control systems and, most recently, for the extremely sophisticated design of complete spacecraft control systems.

The place of ergonomics in every sphere of activity is firmly established.[2] There are two reasons for this. First, ergonomics increases productivity, because it takes full advantage of man's abilities, while allowing for his limitations. Second, ergonomics makes work safer, because it prevents him from working outside the optimum range of his abilities and making errors that might lead to accidents and injuries.

The developing countries

Generally, the state of occupational safety and health in developing countries is much poorer than in industrialised countries. In some developing countries, conditions have become worse in certain respects. Competition for scarce resources within the context of economic slow-down has limited the application of corrective and preventive measures, such as ergonomics, for improving ocupational safety and health.

Occupational safety

Statistics on occupational accidents in developing countries are rarely available, and the few that are have to be used with circumspection. Even comparisons over time for the same country may be invalidated by improvements in reporting or increased coverage of disability compensation arrangements. Generally, the statistics supplied are minimum figures, as a number of accidents escape reporting.

Twenty-four developing countries (seven in Africa, 12 in Asia and the Pacific, five in Latin America and the Caribbean) provided sufficient data to the ILO *Year Book of Labour Statistics* to permit a calculation of average annual rates of fatal injuries for 1971-75 and 1976-80 for the manufacturing and construction sectors. Unlike for developed countries, where fatality rates are going down, no such trend was discernible for these 24 developing countries. Almost half of them reported higher fatality rates for 1976-80, with significant increases recorded for both manufacturing and construction in four countries, and for construction only in another two. If better reporting partially accounts for higher fatality rates in some countries, it is also true that a real increase in fatality rates occurred in some countries.

While it may be risky to compare fatality rates between countries and sectors on the basis of ILO statistics, some in-depth studies show that rates of fatal accidents are several times higher in the developing than in the industrialised countries. They also show that the sectoral pattern of fatal accidents is similar to that in the industrialised countries: much higher rates in mining and construction than in manufacturing.

In most developing countries the number of non-fatally injured persons increased during the late 1970s, often faster than the labour force. The labour force grew at annual rates of between 2 and 3 per cent during the 1970s in the various regions. In contrast, the average annual growth rate of non-fatally injured persons during 1976-80 was 5.3 per cent for the 21 developing countries which reported data to the ILO. Thus, the number of injured persons per 1,000 members of the labour

143

force rose appreciably in those 21 countries as a group, a disquieting development.

While machines in industrialised countries became safer to operate during the 1970s and early 1980s, the same cannot be said of developing countries where the use of machinery is rising with industrialisation. Many modern, large enterprises in developing countries have high safety standards. However, some modern establishments still have problems with imported machinery and indeed whole processes and plants. While designed for safe use in industrialised countries, such plant or machinery may become inappropriate or unsafe in developing countries, because of differences in the physical, psychological and social environment.

To cut costs, new machines have been imported into developing countries without the safety equipment that is standard in the exporting country. Second-hand machinery bought by medium-sized and small firms often comes with dilapidated or missing safety guards, if there were any originally.

Machinery is often poorly maintained. Many factories which were safe initially have rapidly deteriorated after only a few years of operation because of lack of maintenance. Also, safety guards have sometimes been perceived as hindrances to faster production and removed in an attempt to increase output.

Machines are also employed outside the manufacturing sector. Stationary machinery in a manufacturing complex is generally safer than the same piece of machinery when moved from one place to the other, as in construction. In mining, the most common accidents are cave-ins due to poor timbering or dangerous tunnelling techniques. In the Indian subcontinent up to 200 men can be found working at each coal-face. They are exposed to the hazards of roof-falls as the coal-face moves slowly forward, leaving unsupported roof.

There are also great problems in the agricultural sector where about half of the developing countries' labour force is working. It is estimated that 33,000 fatalities and 8 million non-fatal injuries occur in agriculture each year (these figures exclude China). The main causes of fatalities are machines, especially tractors; in fact, in some countries they account for half the total fatal accidents. Experience in the industrialised countries shows that a large proportion of these could have been prevented by the use of a safety cab. Other accidents are due to animals, such as buffaloes, horses and snakes; falls; and fire and chemicals. Recent years have also seen a growing number of traffic accidents involving people on their way to work.

Frequently, personal protective equipment is not supplied. When it is, however, it may be very uncomfortable in a hot and humid tropical climate. And many developing countries lack the expertise for testing such equipment.

Difficult working conditions have sometimes aggravated the situation. For many workers working hours are long and inconvenient. A number of countries increasingly resort to piece work, which results in a faster work pace. Poor housekeeping, particularly in smaller firms, and the poor living conditions of many workers also contribute to accidents. Malnutrition, substandard housing and poor sanitation weaken the general health of workers, make them more vulnerable to a bad working environment and reduce their alertness to occupational hazards.

Many workers are ignorant of the hazards in their workplaces and of the means to protect themselves from those hazards. Illiteracy and insufficient familiarity with industrial work compound the problem. The weak financial position of workers prompts them to accept hazardous jobs and poor working conditions.

Virtually all of the above factors apply with greater force to small enterprises and informal activities in both urban and rural settings. Living space is often used as working premises during the day and is substandard for both purposes. Guarding of machinery is often unknown. Proper maintenance of machinery and equipment is as exceptional as good housekeeping of premises and provision of personal protective equipment. Working hours are often long and arduous. Many employers are financially constrained and not knowledgeable about much needed improvements in working conditions and the working environment. In addition, they seem unaware that a safer, healthier workplace contributes directly to higher productivity. The young, the unskilled, the least experienced and educated, unable to obtain jobs in the modern sector, gravitate to the small-scale and informal sectors. They are not likely to refuse risky work or to press hard for safer conditions.

Occupational health

Statistics on occupational diseases in developing countries are in an embryonic stage. In these countries, the discrepancy between statistics on occupational diseases and data based on epidemiological studies carried out at the enterprise level is much greater than in industrialised countries. This is due to various circumstances that characterise developing countries: a smaller list of. recognised compensable occupational diseases, a shortage of doctors and other health personnel trained in diagnosing occupational diseases, the lack of monitoring equipment and the absence of systematic reporting of recognised occupational diseases. Notwithstanding the virtual absence of reliable statistics in developing countries, there is no doubt that occupational diseases are much more common and, above all, more serious.

The situation is worst in agriculture. The greatly increased use of such chemicals as pesticides, herbicides and insecticides and the use of "treated" seeds and of fertilisers have brought chemical hazards into an area of work ill-equipped to deal with them. The result has been many

known cases of poisoning, leaving workers disabled in one form or another. For example, in one Middle Eastern country several thousand cases of mercury poisoning due to the use of treated seeds were reported to WHO. In another case it was reported that a small Asian country had experienced 900 fatalities and 14,000 hospital admissions from pesticide poisoning, most of them being related to occupational exposure. A field survey in another Asian country showed that 40 per cent of spraymen had toxic symptoms of varying degrees from pesticide poisoning.

Agricultural work has also other health hazards. Working long hours in the heat can cause, especially when nutrition is not adequate, serious loss of salts resulting in chronic general fatigue. Repeated contact with animals, insects and certain plants frequently exposes workers to various zoonoses and allergies, some of which are particularly serious.

In mining, in spite of rapid labour turnover, 10 to 12 per cent of workers have contracted some form of pneumoconiosis. In some smaller mines, pneumatic drilling in dry conditions still prevails because of technical difficulties, and ventilation installations have not always kept pace with production increases. Sometimes the existence of occupational hazards is unknown: for example, the presence of free silica in the ore is not identified, so that the most elementary precautions are not taken.

Mechanisation has led to excessive noise levels, and surveys in developing countries have registered particularly high levels, for example, in shipyards, boilerworks, cement factories, sawmills and textile factories. In most countries, tests are not carried out for hearing impairment caused by noise, which commonly is not even registered as an occupational disease, though independent investigations indicate its prevalence.

Poor working and living conditions also make workers more susceptible to occupational diseases. For example, heat precludes the use of a good deal of personal protective equipment, including safety glasses. In tropical conditions the skin absorbs more toxic chemicals than in temperate climates, so that exposure limits established for industrialised countries cannot be applied in some developing countries. Endemic parasitic diseases not only are a public health problem but may also be work-related. Schistosomiasis – caused by parasitic worms found in tropical and subtropical regions – is a frequent consequence of the construction of dams and irrigation systems.

The threat to health is often more acute in the small-scale and informal sectors. Toxic substances are used in production processes, not infrequently without informing the workers of their toxicity. Recycling of materials is an important activity and poses special problems, such as poisoning from recycling of batteries and mercury poisoning from dismantling of fluorescent strips to get the metal caps. It is also a common practice to burn away the plastic casing of wire to obtain the metal inside – a process that can release carcinogenic fumes. The concentration of lead in the atmosphere in some lead retrieval and battery factories has reached 200 times the exposure limit. The use of toxic solvents, particularly benzene, without any protective measures has also been found in many countries. Most cases of benzene poisoning have been discovered in small, badly ventilated workshops where the concentration of benzene does not drop to the maximum exposure limit even outside working hours and, in the course of the day, may be as high as 200 ppm or more.

In medium-sized and large enterprises many new technologies have been introduced. While the transfer of technology during the 1970s and early 1980s from industrialised to developing countries has contributed to economic growth and higher productivity, it has also brought with it some health hazards. One highly controversial aspect is the export of hazardous processes from industrialised countries, as occupational health standards rise and compliance becomes more costly, to developing countries, where the laws are not so rigorous or their enforcement so strict. This situation has also led to the continued use of known toxic substances in developing countries (see box 9.2).

Ergonomics

The role and potential of ergonomics for the improvement of working conditions and environment in developing countries are increasingly recognised. The application of ergonomic principles in countries such as Algeria, Brazil, India, Indonesia, Mexico and Tunisia has shown the important contribution made by ergonomics to the improvement of work layout, work processes, work methods and work organisation and to the elimination of negative effects of the transfer of technology. The work of experts has also shown that ergonomics can improve not only health and safety but also productivity; moreover, the application of ergonomic principles need not involve expensive or sophisticated methods.

These principles are used for example in the design of factory buildings, but their use could be greatly expanded. When factories are constructed in tropical zones, the same designs of buildings are often used as for the cooler industrialised countries. The same is true of the plant and process arrangement. The result is that the factories and plants impose unnecessary discomfort and stress on the workers. There have been some improvements recently, such as steel rolling mills in a hot dry climate built without walls to allow maximum air movement through the mill, and factory walls constructed of huge louvres which are kept open during the dry season and closed when the monsoon begins. But these are the exceptions: the idea of designing a factory for the climatic conditions and the people of a developing country is only slowly being accepted.

The basic cause seems to lie in training courses that teach students to design factory buildings for industrialised countries only. But some pioneer work has been started and elements of the subject

9.2

The transfer of technology

The transfer of technology takes various forms. It includes the building of complete factories and plants, the design and importation of machinery and equipment, the financing of major industrialisation projects, the provision of foreign experts as consultants and the training of local personnel. The developing world receives more and more such technology and in general benefits considerably from its transfer.

Experience has shown, however, that an uncontrolled transfer of technology to developing countries can lead to an unacceptable level of occupational accidents and diseases if appropriate modifications are not adopted to prevent undesirable and harmful effects. These risks arise if such transfers do not take into account differences in social and climatic factors, in local levels of skill and training and in the size and constitution of workers.

Many things are taken for granted when technology is transferred. One has to do with the maintenance level required to make the plant function according to specification. It is assumed that in the developing country local skill and ability will meet maintenance standards and requirements. But this may not be so. A failure to achieve the designed standards of maintenance can lead to breakdowns, accidents and injury to health. For example, a sulphur refining plant designed to European standards of maintenance was set up in a developing country where those standards could not be achieved. The resulting leaks of sulphurous fumes, etc., caused extensive bronchial and other complaints among the workers.

Much concern has also been expressed about the "export of hazards". Some production processes or parts of them are transferred from industrialised to developing countries where environment standards and hence production costs are lower. It is claimed that in the dye industry, for example, certain carcinogenic intermediaries are manufactured in developing countries, thus entailing a serious health hazard for the workers producing them.

More common than the export of hazardous processes has been the continued use of known toxic substances. For example, the use of carbon disulphide, formerly widespread, has been declining in industrialised countries, while it has been rising in developing countries. Similar developments have been cited for asbestos and vinyl chloride monomer. The use of heavy metals in various chemicals in manufacturing has a direct link with the numerous cases of poisoning that are not generally covered by national statistics but come to light in the course of plant-level surveys.

are now taught in universities in major towns of several developing countries, such as Calcutta, Denpasar and Singapore, or through extension classes (Singapore), local community work and some radio and TV programmes directed specifically to the rural population. For instance, in Bali (Indonesia) such programmes have been shown on the 5,000 television sets provided by the Government in rural areas. In addition, village headmen, doctors, engineers and medical and technical students have been given introductory training in ergonomics, with health centre staff helping to conduct the training. Students have also been asked at times to deliver lectures in villages. Since 1976 ergonomic models have been installed in several villages for demonstration purposes. In the Philippines, the Institute for Small-Scale Industries has helped traditional and other small industries to modernise their work processes.

Developing countries are also becoming more interested in standardisation. For example, within the International Organisation for Standardisation (ISO) 14 developing countries are participating in the preparation of international standards in ergonomics, anthropometry and biomechanics.

Conclusion

In the early part of the Industrial Revolution in what we now call the industrialised nations, the safety and the health of the individual worker depended very largely on himself – on his attitude of mind, knowledge and skill and, besides, on a good deal of luck. The laissez-faire philosophy of the time held that accidents, injuries and damage to health were a natural by-product of industry and that preventing them was the responsibility of the individual worker.

Alerted by grim information about factory conditions, public opinion began to press for the inclusion of various protective provisions in factories Acts and other laws, including workmen's compensation Acts, that made it compulsory for employers to provide compensation to workers who had suffered injury or damage to health. Employers also started to provide machine guards and personal protective equipment.

In the third phase of the struggle for a safer and healthier workplace the aim was to influence the minds of the men and women who worked in factories. It came to be realised that "the best safety device is a careful workman". Leaflets, posters, talks, newspaper articles, radio and television explained what health and safety hazards workers could be exposed to and how they could deal with them. This phase, like the two earlier phases, is of course continuing today.

The latest approach – developed by the leading safety and health organisations – is to "manage out" accidents. This means that safety and health should be dealt with from the top and are the responsibility of senior management in the organisation. It is the direct, active and personal involvement of senior management (and, through them, line management and supervisors) that counts.

Legislative action began in the industrialised nations in the middle of the last century. By the end of the century such occupational diseases as phossy jaw (deformation of the jaw), anthrax (formerly a fatal disease contracted from the skins of infected animals), certain lung diseases and poisoning due to arsenic, lead and mercury, were so prevalent that corrective action was demanded and obtained. Phossy jaw, due to the use of white phosphorus in the match trade, was the first industrial disease to be abolished by international action following the Berne Convention of 1906.

During the first decades of this century occupational health standards were mainly of an administrative nature in that they prohibited the exposure of certain categories of workers to a given occupational hazard, or prohibited the use of a given hazardous substance without prior authorisation. Later on, preventive standards required

increasingly high levels of professional competence on the part of medical personnel and industrial hygienists. The plant physician soon found himself involved in a number of complex obligations and became aware that his efforts in the field of preventive medicine would be ineffective unless there was a parallel improvement in the working environment. In countries where there are frequent conflicts between management and workers, the powers and duties of the plant physician can obviously be defined only by legislation; where this is done, the plant physician will be able to act according to professional criteria to meet present-day needs and adapt himself to them.

There are, of course, other ways in which legislation affects the development of occupational health. For instance, obligations imposed by legislation stimulate the training of specialists and guarantee them equitable conditions of remuneration, which is an important factor, especially in the developing countries; health protection at the workplace can be made a permanent obligation whereby all concerned must comply with certain minimum standards, which cannot be altered merely because of other in-plant priorities or economic fluctuations; furthermore, each national occupational safety and health law has now become part of the widespread network of international standards and, even if only partly enforced, still contributes to international social progress and the development of ideas and recognised principles.

The ILO has produced 25 Conventions on occupational safety and health, dealing with occupational diseases, accidents, labour inspection, guarding of machinery, medical examinations, etc. The most recent, the Occupational Safety and Health Convention (No. 155), was adopted in 1981. It defines, for the first time, the basic right of workers to refuse to commence work, or to cease work, in the event of danger. Article 13 states that "a worker who has removed himself from a work situation which he has reasonable justification to believe presents an imminent and serious danger to his life or health shall be protected from undue consequences in accordance with national conditions and practice". The adoption of this principle under national legislation is likely to have a profound impact on safety and health policy within enterprises.

Occupational safety and health services are often absent in small enterprises, particularly in developing countries. It has proved difficult to organise such services for employees of small factories and other underserved population groups. However, attempts are being made to provide these people with some degree of protection through health examinations or through primary health care programmes.

The effectiveness of safety and health services in medium-sized and large enterprises depends largely on the priority they are given by management. Over the past 20 years the role of safety officers (also called safety advisers, safety engineers, safety professionals, etc.) has become more important in these enterprises. Moreover, many industrialised countries and some developing countries have passed legislation to set up safety committees. These committees are now given greater responsibilities and they are often attached to influential managers.

In some countries the legislation provides for the appointment of workers as safety representatives. In the United Kingdom, for example, safety representatives are drawn from trade unions, provided with basic training and given the right by law [3] to investigate potential hazards and dangerous occurrences, to investigate complaints by any employees they represent relating to their health, safety or welfare, to examine causes of accidents, to make representations to the employer on specific or general matters affecting the health, safety or welfare of employees, to carry out inspections, to represent employees in consultations at the workplace with inspectors of the Health and Safety Executive and to receive information from inspec-

tors in accordance with the Health and Safety at Work Act.

Where they exist, occupational health services are usually set up by the employer; sometimes a group health service may be used. These services have several functions: (1) to assist as part of a multidisciplinary team in assessing unhealthy working conditions and to propose preventive or remedial action; (2) to examine whether workers are fit for their work; (3) to provide first-line medical aid for injured workers; and (4) in some cases to provide general medical diagnosis and treatment of non-occupational illness. In some countries this last function may include the worker's family and cover other aspects of medical care.

While the physician is usually paid by the employer, his loyalty is to his patients – the workers – and detailed medical records, etc., are normally not made available to the employer. There is now a movement in some parts of the world to have all the safety and health personnel employed by and directly responsible to the safety and health council of the enterprise or of the industry, such councils being semi-autonomous and composed of workers' and employers' representatives.

Occupational safety and health institutes are public or semi-public bodies usually linked to ministries of labour or health or to social security organisations. Their main tasks are to assist labour inspection services and to advise employers on safe working practices. Many developing countries have recently set up such institutes, often in collaboration with the ILO. At the moment there are about 50 altogether, half of them in developing countries.

Safety councils are often voluntary organisations engaged in accident prevention and the promotion of safe and healthy working conditions. They are supported by the employers and workers, and may also have the support and active

149

participation of the government. The councils carry out a great variety of activities (see box 9.3). They also collect data on accidents and injuries and issue statistics periodically. Some of the longer established councils, such as the National Safety Council of Chicago, provide a large amount of most informative statistics on injuries and illnesses.

Some of these well established councils, for example those in the Federal Republic of Germany, the USSR, the United Kingdom and the United States, have been in existence for many years. Newer councils are found in other parts of the world, including a number of developing countries.[4]

The Inter-American Safety Council (IASC) is a private international organisation with headquarters in the United States and 3,200 affiliate enterprises all over Latin America. IASC offers technical services and guidance and a wide range of educational services and training material.

Each of the Latin American countries has its own national safety council (with slightly different names in some countries), sustained through voluntary contributions from large enterprises.

For example, in Brazil all employers pay a contribution to sustain a private organisation called Social Services for Industries, which offers a wide range of services, including occupational safety and health, with specialised units in each of the states. Moreover, all employers contribute with a fraction of the accident insurance premium to maintain another private organisation, the Brazilian National Foundation for Occupational Safety, Hygiene and Medicine (Fundacentro), linked to the Ministry of Labour and dealing only with occupational safety and health.

150

9.3

The National Safety Council of India

The National Safety Council of India was established in 1966 on the initiative of the Union Ministry of Labour and Rehabilitation as an autonomous national body to generate, develop and sustain a movement of safety awareness at the national level. The Council was set up because the number of industrial accidents was increasing at an alarming pace as a result of rapid industrialisation after independence. It was realised that enforcement of legal safety provisions and other government steps alone were not adequate. It was therefore essential to have a national body to develop a voluntary safety movement in the country with the full involvement of managements, trade unions and workers and the full support of the Government.

The Council has four categories of members: corporate members (organisations and institutions); corporate trade union members; life members; and individual members.

The Council's activities and the services it provides to members include organising conferences, seminars and symposia; carrying out training programmes including in-plant courses mainly for middle and upper levels of management; maintaining a library of films available on loan; undertaking safety audits, surveys and studies; providing an information service; holding national safety competitions; organising a national safety day campaign each year to commemorate the founding of the Council; issuing a national safety calendar; providing publicity material, technical literature and periodicals; and liaising with national and international bodies (including the ILO).

---

[1] ILO: *Occupational exposure limits for airborne toxic substances: A tabular compilation of values from selected countries,* Occupational Safety and Health Series, No. 37 (Geneva, 2nd (revised) ed., 1980).

[2] Widespread recognition of the relevance of ergonomics is clear for example from the fact that, even in the field of standardisation, two international standards on the subject have been issued and several others are in preparation.

[3] Safety Representatives and Safety Committees Regulations 1977.

[4] Argentina, Brazil, Chile, Colombia, India, Mexico, Nigeria, Singapore, Sri Lanka, Tunisia, Uruguay, Venezuela.

Chapter 10

Working time

Working time is one of the basic elements of conditions of work. How much time workers are called upon to spend on the job and how that time is organised can significantly affect not only the health, well-being and earnings of the workers directly concerned but also the successful operation of the enterprise and the economic and social situation of the country. Because of these wide-ranging effects, working time issues tend to be controversial. They are particularly so in the industrialised market economy countries in the present circumstances of economic difficulties, high levels of unemployment and consequent efforts to find ways of protecting or creating jobs.

Most of the current discussions on working time focus on the question whether reductions in working time are an effective means of reducing unemployment (this question was discussed in Chapter 2 of Volume 1). Topical and controversial as this issue may be, other policy considerations should not be forgotten. In a longer historical perspective, the limitation and the reduction of working time have been pursued with two main objectives in view.

The first is social protection. It has long been recognised that the limitation of working hours and the provision of adequate opportunities for rest are essential for the health, safety and well-being of workers. Hence, almost all countries have adopted legislation or other statutory measures setting maximum normal hours of work, imposing restrictions on overtime and requiring minimum periods of weekly rest. The great majority have also set minimum standards on annual holidays with pay.

The second objective is the improvement of working conditions and the quality of life through increased leisure. Shorter hours or longer holidays can be seen as a benefit gained by workers from technological advances, productivity increases and progress generally. The question is often posed in terms of a choice between higher income and greater leisure and is often considered appropriate for negotiation between employers and trade unions. In many countries, as is fully realised, improvements have initially been achieved through collective bargaining and have eventually been confirmed or extended by legislation.

The idea of reducing working time in order to expand employment opportunities is by no means new. It was extensively discussed during the depression years of the 1930s and indeed formed the basis for the adoption of the ILO Forty-Hour Week Convention, 1935 (No. 47). The economic difficulties of recent years have drawn fresh attention to this basic idea and have engendered many variations on the theme.

The main purpose of this chapter is essentially descriptive: to give an overview of the current state of law and practice concerning working time in different parts of the world, to highlight trends in actual working time and to identify major problems and trends.

The term "working time" is very broad, and encompasses a wide range of topics. Some of these relate to the period over which working time is taken into account. This may be the day or the week, but it also may be a year or even a whole working life. In the last two cases, annual holidays, public holidays and the age of retirement would have to be taken into account. Other topics relate to the organisation or arrangement of working time: for example, shift work, night work, various forms of flexible hours. Still others relate to special arrangements or measures to meet particular needs: for example, part-time work and paid educational leave.

While all of these topics are important, it would hardly be feasible to cover all of them in a single chapter. This chapter will therefore concentrate on two fundamental topics: weekly hours of work and annual holidays with pay. Other questions, such as shift work and overtime, will be discussed more briefly in relation to recent developments in certain countries or regions.

Normal hours of work

The key concept in dealing with hours of work is that of normal hours. A convenient definition of this term may be found in ILO Recommendation No. 116: "Normal hours of work shall mean, for the purpose of this Recommendation, the number of hours fixed in each country by or in pursuance of laws or regulations, collective agreements or arbitration awards, or, where not so fixed, the number of hours in excess of which any time worked is remunerated at overtime rates or forms an exception to the recognised rules or custom of the establishment or of the process concerned."[1]

Time worked beyond normal hours constitutes overtime or exceptions. Weekly hours that are temporarily less than normal hours with a corresponding reduction in pay (usually due to adverse business conditions) constitute short-time work-ing or "partial unemployment". Weekly hours that are substantially less than normal hours and are worked on a regular and voluntary basis can be considered part-time work.

Normal hours of work are the reference point for wage determination and the basis for calculating overtime or short-time work. The level of normal hours is therefore a fundamental policy issue. This level may be established by statutory measures or by collective agreements or simply by practice. In almost all countries, the level may not exceed specified legal limits; but it may, of course, be lower. In other words, legislation sets the maximum but the level as fixed by collective agreements or other means is usually lower. In some countries there are also limits on total hours – the sum of maximum normal hours and maximum overtime.

In assessing and comparing normal hours, two benchmark figures should be kept in mind: 48 hours a week and 40 hours a week. The former is the original standard established by the Hours of Work (Industry) Convention, 1919 (No. 1), and the Hours of Work (Commerce and Offices) Convention, 1930 (No. 30). The Reduction of Hours of Work Recommendation, 1962 (No. 116), called for immediate steps to bring the normal working week down to 48 hours, where it exceeded that level, without any reduction in wages. It is thus reasonable to regard the 48-hour week as the basic standard required for the protection of workers all over the world. Although some allowance may be made for the particularities of certain occupations (for example, those involving substantial periods of mere presence), normal hours longer than 48 can in general be considered excessive. The 40-hour week, originally proposed in 1935 by Convention No. 47 in the context of massive unemployment, was affirmed in 1962 as a social standard by Recommendation No. 116. It can be regarded as an objective to be reached progressively in the light of the economic and social conditions prevailing in different countries.

Over most of this century, national action on hours of work has focused on these two figures: first, the establishment and consolidation of the 48-hour week – in other words, the eight-hour day with a weekly rest day – and then, the movement towards the 40-hour week. At present, normal hours fixed by law or collective agreement in the great majority of countries fall in the 40–48 range, though there are important exceptions in both directions.

The following paragraphs give an overview of the present situation in most member States of the ILO. This information is subject to a number of qualifications. Firstly, different countries regulate hours of work in different ways: some primarily through legislation or other statutory action, some primarily through collective bargaining and some through a mixture of the two. An attempt has been made to indicate, wherever appropriate, both the statutory maximum and the general level as determined by collective agreement or practice. Secondly, in many countries there are significant sectoral variations, as established either by law or by collective agreement or practice. To give a full picture would require a comprehensive study. Most of the information below relates to industry, though some indications are given of the position in commerce and offices. Agriculture, maritime navigation, civil aviation and other activities with special conditions are not covered. Thirdly, there are often variations for particular occupations or categories of workers: for example, longer normal hours for occupations characterised by intermittent work, shorter hours for arduous jobs, shorter hours for young workers. The information refers to the main provisions, not to such departures from them. Finally, national legislation often excludes certain categories of undertakings or workers: for example, very small enterprises, family undertakings, domestic servants. Such exclusions are especially common in developing countries and may cover a very large proportion of the workforce. The provisions cited often apply only to the more organised sector of the economy.

With these reservations, the position regarding normal hours of work in different parts of the world can be summed up as follows.

In the majority of developing countries, the maximum level of normal weekly hours fixed by laws or regulations remains 48. This is the standard in virtually all of Latin America, most of Asia and the Pacific, and much of Africa.

A number of countries in each region have, however, fixed lower limits. Thus, many African countries formerly under French administration prescribe a 40-hour week. Originally laid down in the old labour code for French overseas territories, this standard has been retained in national labour legislation. Since its application has always been subject to a number of exceptions and qualifications, the standard working week in some branches of activity and occupations may be longer. Other African countries with maximum normal hours below 48 include Burundi, Ghana, Lesotho, Mauritius, Rwanda, São Tomé and Príncipe and the United Republic of Tanzania (all 45), and Algeria and Angola (both 44). In Latin America and the Caribbean, countries with a standard below 48 include Cuba, the Dominican Republic and Honduras (44), and Ecuador (40). A common pattern in this region is the establishment of lower levels for night work than for day work. Many countries with the 48-hour standard for day work prescribe 42 hours for night work and 45 for mixed day and night work. Others have night work standards below 40. In Asia and the Pacific, the developing countries prescribing normal hours below the maximum of 48 include Democratic Yemen and Mongolia (46), Burma and Singapore (44), and Indonesia (40). A number of Islamic countries of the Middle East provide for reduced normal hours during the month of Ramadan (usually 36 instead of 48).

The maximum level of normal hours may vary according to sectors. Normal hours in commerce and offices, for example, are lower than in industry in some countries but higher in others. Longer

153

hours are particularly common in retail trade and services, where the work is sometimes classified as intermittent. In the public service, on the other hand, normal hours of 40 or less are often the rule. A number of countries have specific regulations for particular industries or branches of activity and some prescribe lower normal hours for particular categories such as young workers.

In recent years there has been no widespread movement towards reducing the maximum levels of normal hours. While a handful of countries have in fact reduced them and two or three have increased them, in the great majority of the developing countries the statutory levels have remained stable for many years. Lower normal hours have been established by collective agreement or practice in some industries or individual firms but these are usually concentrated in the most modern sectors and are applicable to small numbers of workers. With the exception of a few countries, in particular former British territories in Africa, the Caribbean and the Pacific, collective bargaining has, by and large, not aimed at the reduction of normal hours.

Legal provisions on working time usually have a limited impact in developing countries. First of all, only a few sectors of the economy are covered by this legislation. And, even within these sectors, the provisions often do not apply to family undertakings or undertakings below a certain size. Thus, large segments of the workforce – such as workers in agriculture other than plantations or similar establishments, in small industrial workshops, in petty retail trade and services, and in the informal sector – are excluded from coverage. Secondly, formal coverage does not necessarily mean effective protection. Economic pressures to work long hours, with or without overtime compensation, are strong and enforcement of legal provisions is often weak. Labour inspectorates suffer from insufficient staff, inadequate training and small resources. Workers are often unorganised and have difficulty in seeking and obtaining legal redress.

In these circumstances, the general reduction of normal hours is a less urgent problem than the need for effective measures to ensure at least a basic level of protection to a greater number of workers.

In the industrialised countries, on the other hand, a widespread and substantial reduction of normal hours has taken place over the past 25 to 30 years. The objective of the 40-hour week has been reached or approached in most of them and has been surpassed by several others. Most often, the reductions were achieved through collective bargaining; in some countries, they were subsequently consolidated through legislation. The present position can be summed up as follows.

Virtually all of the industrialised countries have normal hours, determined by law or by collective agreement or practice, in the 40-44 hours range. About half of them have general levels of 40 hours or less.

In Canada and the United Sates, the 40-hour normal working week is provided for in federal legislation and has been the general standard for many years (although some provincial legislation in Canada fixes higher levels). In both countries, large numbers of workers, especially but not exclusively office employees, have normal hours below 40, many of them between 35 and 37½.

The 40-hour week has been established in New Zealand since the late 1930s and in Australia since the late 1940s. It is provided for in legislation or arbitration awards and remains the general standard. Workers in a few branches of industrial activity and most office workers in Australia have shorter hours, 35 to 38. In New Zealand, shorter hours have been fixed in the public service (37½) and in mining.

The legal standard in Japan was fixed at 48 hours in 1947 and has not been amended. Almost all workers, however, have shorter hours through collective agreements or practice. Normal hours tend to vary with the size of the enterprise. They are usually below 40 in the larger firms; around 42 in the medium-size ones; and around 45 in the smaller ones.

In Western Europe, the 40-hour week has gradually become the prevailing standard. It is provided for by law in Austria, Belgium, Finland, Luxembourg, Norway, Spain and Sweden. Several other countries – the Federal Republic of Germany, Greece, Ireland, Italy and the Netherlands – still have a legal standard of 48 but almost all workers have a 40-hour week through collective agreements or practice. In Denmark and the United Kingdom, neither of which has general legislation on hours of work, a normal working week of 40 hours or less is the usual standard established by collective agreements or practice.

The first country to establish the legal standard of normal hours at a level below 40 was France. In 1981, the normal working week was reduced to 39 as the first step towards a target of 35. In several other countries, a substantial proportion of the workforce has normal hours below 40: Belgium, Luxembourg and the United Kingdom. In Belgium, the majority of workers have normal hours below 40, many of them 38 or less. Recent figures for the United Kingdom indicate that a large number of manual workers have normal hours of 39 or less and that the majority of non-manual workers have normal hours of 37 or less. Normal hours below 40 have also been established in particular sectors or for certain types of work, such as shift work, in various countries.

The remaining Western European countries in which normal hours exceed 40 include Cyprus, Portugal, San Marino, Switzerland and Turkey. In Cyprus, hours of work are governed mainly by collective agreements and there is considerable sectoral variation. The most common level is 41-42 hours but a sizeable proportion of workers have normal hours of 38-40 and a smaller proportion 43 or more. The legal standard is 48 in Portugal, San Marino and Turkey. Legislation in Portugal, however, prescribes 42 hours for office employees and collective agreements in certain sectors provide for normal hours of 45 or less. In Switzerland, the general legal standard is 45 hours, though there are some sectoral variations. Normal hours established by collective agreements range from 40 to 45, the most common being 43-44; progressive reduction to 40 is envisaged in several branches of activity.

In the planned economies of Eastern Europe, the 40-hour week has been widely adopted as an objective but has not yet been applied to workers in general. Normal hours have been reduced in several stages since the late 1950s. The general standard now ranges from 41 to 44. It is 41 in the Byelorussian SSR, the Ukrainian SSR and the USSR; 42 in Hungary and Poland; 42½ in Bulgaria and Czechoslovakia; 43¾ in the German Democratic Republic; and 46 in Romania. In Yugoslavia, the normal working week is 42 hours but a daily break of 30 minutes is counted as part of working hours.

It is noteworthy that the planned economies of Eastern Europe give priority to the reduction of hours to workers employed in arduous or hazardous occupations or under unhealthy conditions (such as harsh climates); to young workers; and to women with family responsibilities. Shorter hours are also common in shift work and work deemed to be stressful.

In the USSR, for example, the working week is 36 hours where the conditions of work are detrimental to health; it is also 36 hours for young workers between 16 and 18, and 24 hours for those under 16. In Poland, the level is 36 for workers in arduous jobs and for young workers under 16. In the German Democratic Republic, workers on the two-shift system have a 42-hour week and those on the three-shift system, a 40-hour week; young workers under 16, a 42-hour week and mothers of young children (under certain conditions), a 40-hour week. In Bulgaria, normal hours for workers employed in unhealthy conditions may be 30, 36 or 41. In Czechoslovakia, the standard is 40 hours for young workers over 16 and 36 for those under 16; standards of 41¼ hours and 40 hours are prescribed for workers on two- and three-shift systems respectively. Shorter hours for shift work and work in unhealthy conditions are also applied in Hungary.

Annual holidays with pay

The right of workers in general to annual holidays with pay is of surprisingly recent origin. Before the 1930s, annual holidays were the privilege of employees such as managerial staff, office workers and public servants. It was only after the Second World War that this right was extended to all manual workers. Annual holidays are now one of the most important aspects of conditions of work – and probably one of the most appreciated by workers. Over the past three decades, holidays and related entitlements have been vastly improved in both developing and industrialised countries.

This progress has been reflected in ILO standards. The earliest instrument, the Holidays with Pay Convention, 1936 (No. 52), provided for an annual holiday with pay of at least six working days (usually constituting one working week) after one year of continuous service. A minimum of two working weeks was called for by the Holidays with Pay Recommendation, 1954 (No. 98). The latest instrument, the Holidays with Pay Convention (Revised), 1970 (No. 132), sets a minimum standard of three working weeks.

The great majority of countries have legislative or statutory provisions setting minimum holiday entitlements for employed persons in industry, commerce and offices, and sometimes agriculture. These are often supplemented by collective agreements or practice. The essential element of the entitlements is the basic holiday: that is, the length of holiday to be granted after one year of service. In some countries, longer holidays are provided for by law, collective agreement or practice for workers meeting specified criteria (such as age, length of service, arduous duties) but this approach has become less important as the basic holiday has increased. An appropriate benchmark for the basic holiday is three working weeks, as laid down in Convention No. 132.

This minimum standard has now been reached in most industrialised countries. However, in many of them the basic holiday, as established by law or collective agreements, is three or four weeks.

In Western Europe, the general level has risen to four or even five weeks. Several countries have recently adopted legislation extending the basic holiday to five working weeks: Denmark, France, Luxembourg and Sweden. Those providing for four weeks include Belgium, Finland, Greece and Iceland; Austria and Norway grant four weeks plus one and two days respectively. The United Kingdom has no general legislation on holidays with pay but most workers now have four weeks. In Spain, the legal minimum is now 30 calendar days. Legislation in the Federal Republic of Germany sets a minimum of three weeks but the majority of workers are entitled under collective agreements to five weeks or more. In Ireland, the legal entitlement is also three weeks. The legal minimum in the Netherlands is three weeks but most industrial workers have four weeks or more. In Switzerland, federal legislation prescribes two weeks but most cantonal legislation three weeks and some collective agreements four weeks. Italy has a statutory minimum of ten working days but many collective agreements provide for four weeks. Recent legislation in Portugal provides for three weeks. In Turkey, the legal minimum is 12 days (2 weeks); in San Marino, ten days; and in Cyprus, two weeks.

A number of countries provide for increases in holidays with length of service. Examples include Austria (a fifth week after 20 years); Finland (a fifth week after three years); Italy (five, ten and 20 extra days after five, 15 and 25 years respectively); and

Turkey (a third week after five years and a fourth after 15 years). Several countries also provide for longer holidays for young workers and a few longer holidays for older workers.

In Eastern Europe, the basic standard is between two and three weeks. Increases with length of service and longer holidays for young workers and other categories are common. Two countries – the German Democratic Republic and Yugoslavia – prescribe a minimum of 18 working days. The Byelorussian SSR, the Ukrainian SSR, the USSR, Hungary and Romania all provide for a minimum of 15 days and longer holidays for various categories. The minimum in Bulgaria is 14 working days, rising to 16 after ten years and 18 after 15 years of service. In Poland, it is also 14 working days, rising to 17 after three years, 20 after six years and 26 after ten years. In Czechoslovakia, it is two weeks, rising to 18 days after 11 years, 19 after 14 years, 21 after 17 years and 24 after 20 years; the basic holiday is longer for young workers, older workers and certain other categories.

Among the other industrialised countries, Australia generally has a standard of three weeks under state legislation, with longer holidays for certain special categories such as continuous shift workers, workers with irregular hours and workers in remote areas. The general standard under collective agreements is four weeks. In New Zealand, the general legal entitlement is three weeks. Legislation in Japan provides for a basic holiday of six working days with an increase of one working day per year of continuous service, starting after two years, up to a maximum of 20 days. An unusually large number of public holidays – 16 or 17 – are widely granted. In Canada, federal and provincial legislation generally prescribes a minimum of two weeks with, in some cases, increases of one or two weeks after a specified number of years of service. Collective agreements frequently provide for increases with length of service, sometimes rising up to seven weeks. In the United States, there is no general legislation on annual holidays with pay. Salaried employees tend to have more favourable entitlements than hourly paid workers. Under collective agreements or in practice, most salaried employees have a basic holiday of two weeks; the majority of hourly paid workers have one week but a substantial proportion, two weeks. Increases with length of service are the usual pattern, often up to three or four weeks after five to 15 years. Some major collective agreements, however, provide for holidays of five, six or seven weeks for workers with long service, usually 20 to 30 years.

In the developing countries, the situation is extremely varied. Most countries have laws or regulations providing for annual holidays with pay. As in the case of hours of work legislation, the scope may be limited. Agriculture is often not covered and in the other sectors small undertakings and family enterprises are often excluded. Even where the legislation does apply, enforcement is again difficult: ensuring that workers receive the holiday pay to which they are entitled is a particular problem. In the more organised sector, however, annual holidays with pay are virtually universal.

Most developing countries provide for a basic holiday of around two weeks and a substantial number, three weeks or more. Only a handful still have a basic holiday of around one week. Increases with length of service are fairly common; longer holidays for young workers somewhat less so.

In Latin America and the Caribbean, several countries have legislation providing for a basic holiday of three weeks or more: Uruguay (20 days) and Brazil, Cuba, Panama and Peru (all one month). A minimum of 15 working days is prescribed in Bolivia, Chile and Colombia. The majority of countries have a basic standard of two weeks, 12 working days or 14 or 15 calendar days: Antigua and Barbuda, Argentina, Costa Rica, the Dominican Republic, Ecuador, El Salvador, Haiti, Jamaica, Nicaragua, Suriname and Venezuela. Increases with length of service are provided for in Argentina, Bolivia, Chile and Ecuador. In Guatemala, the minimum is 15 days in commerce, ten days in industrial enterprises with at least ten workers and six days in other enterprises. The basic holiday is relatively short in a few countries but provision is made for increases with length of service. Thus, in Mexico the basic entitlement of six working days rises by one day each year up to 12 days and by two more days for every five years of service. In Paraguay the same basic entitlement rises to 12, 20 and 30 working days, after three, eight and 12 years of service respectively. In Honduras, the minimum of ten working days increases to 12 after two years, 15 after three years and 20 after four years.

In Africa, a considerable number of countries have adopted legislation establishing a standard of three weeks or more. Several of them provide for a basic holiday of around four weeks: Algeria, Angola, Benin, Burkina Faso, Djibouti, Gabon, Guinea, the Ivory Coast, Madagascar, Mali and Togo. An entitlement of 21 working days is prescribed in the Congo and Kenya. The countries with a standard of three weeks include Cameroon, the Central African Republic, Chad, Egypt, Mauritania, Morocco, Niger, Senegal and Uganda. Most of the other African countries for which information is available provide for a basic holiday of around two weeks. Increases with length of service are prescribed in a number of countries. Examples of countries in which the progression starts relatively early and leads to a substantial increment include Ethiopia (a basic holiday of 14 days rising by one day a year up to a maximum of 35 days), Liberia (two weeks after two years, a third week after three years and a fourth after five years) and the Sudan (increases of five days each after three, eight and 15 years). Other countries providing for increases with length of service include Benin, Burkina Faso, Burundi, Cameroon, the Central African Republic, Djibouti, Egypt, Mauritania, Morocco, Niger, Tunisia and Zaire.

In the developing countries of Asia and the Pacific, the level of the basic holiday tends to be lower than in the other regions. A few countries do have legislation prescribing three to four weeks. These include Bahrain, Democratic Yemen, Iraq and the United Arab Emirates. In the majority of countries, however, the basic holiday is around two weeks and it is less than two weeks in several. Collective agreements in Singapore, where the basic legal entitlement is one week, often provide for a basic holiday of two weeks rising progressively to a maximum of four weeks after 20 years of service. Increases with length of service are granted in some countries: Bahrain, Democratic Yemen, Iraq, Kuwait, Malaysia, Qatar, Saudi Arabia, Singapore and the Syrian Arab Republic. Longer holidays for young workers are required in Burma, India and the Islamic Republic of Iran. In many Asian countries, extensive public or festival holidays and casual leave are widely granted.

Trends in actual working time (IMEC countries)

The main components of hours actually worked are normal working hours and overtime. Hours actually worked also include minor items such as time spent at the place of work waiting or standing by, as well as the time corresponding to short rest periods at the workplace including tea and coffee breaks. The definition of hours actually worked excludes hours paid for but not worked such as paid holidays, paid public holidays,[2] paid sick leave, meal breaks and time spent in travel to and from work.

Statistics on hours of work are mostly obtained from payroll data supplied by a sample of establishments. Other sources are household sample surveys or social insurance statistics. The data from these various sources are not fully comparable in view of differences in scope, coverage and methods of data collection. The only way to make these data comparable is to adjust them for these differences. This was recently done for the OECD countries, where radical reductions in working

Table 10.1
Actual hours worked in full-time and part-time employment: Selected OECD countries, 1960-81 (percentage average annual growth rates)

	1960-70	1970-73	1973-76	1976-79	1979-81
Belgium [a]	−0.9	−2.2	−3.1	−0.8	2.0
Canada	−0.8	−0.5	−0.7	−0.6	−0.6
Finland	−0.4	−1.1	−0.6	−0.3	−1.1
France	−0.5	−1.0	−1.1	−0.8	−0.2 ★
Germany, Fed. Rep. of	−0.9	−1.5	−0.8	−1.2	−1.2
Italy	−0.6	−2.2	−0.8	−0.1	−0.1
Japan [b]	−0.8	−1.8	−1.6	0.3	−0.3
Netherlands [c]	−1.4	−2.0	−1.7	−1.9	0.9
Norway	−1.1	−2.4	−1.1	−1.5	−0.6 [e]
Sweden	−0.9	−1.7	−0.7	−1.6	−0.7
United Kingdom	−0.1	−0.3	−1.1	−0.9	−2.9
United States [d]	−0.5	−0.2	−1.1	−0.2	−0.6

[a] Manual workers in manufacturing enterprises. [b] Employees in enterprises with 30 or more employees. [c] Employed persons in the private enterprise sector, excluding agriculture and fishing. [d] Employees (wage and salary earners). [e] The 1981 data for France and Norway are estimates.
Source: OECD: *Employment outlook* (Paris, 1983).

time have taken place since the beginning of the 1960s (see table 10.1).

Over the period 1960-81, the figures show a decline of 20 per cent or more for several countries (Belgium, Netherlands, Norway and Sweden), while Finland and the United States show declines of only just over 10 per cent. In 1981 Japan was the only OECD country where the average worker worked for more than 2,000 hours per year. Belgium, Norway, Sweden and the United Kingdom had the lowest annual hours, at about 1,500 or less. Annual hours in France, the Federal Republic of Germany, Italy, the Netherlands and the United States were in the range up to 1,750 and in Canada and Finland between 1,750 and 2,000.

Table 10.1 further shows that the first half of the 1970s saw a rather faster decline in average hours than in the 1960s. The rate of decline slackened off noticeably during the period of moderate recovery in 1976-79; Japan even recorded a slight increase.

Since the second oil shock, there has been no general tendency for a return to a sharper rate of decline, except in the United Kingdom; average working time in Belgium and the Netherlands even increased.

As noted earlier, the reduction of normal hours per week has been the main factor behind the long-run reduction of working time. This was achieved through collective bargaining rather than through legislation. A second factor is the increase in paid holidays [3] which has accounted for a large part of reduced working time since the beginning of the 1970s. Lastly, average working time per person was reduced because more and more people have part-time jobs. This trend was already discussed in the first volume of this report (Chapter 2).

Problems and issues

The pace and the nature of changes in the next few years will no doubt vary widely from country to country. But it does seem likely that further reductions in working time will be made in much of the industrialised world. Movement towards the 40-hour week and the four-week holiday can be expected in many of the countries where these standards have not yet been attained. The further spread of working weeks below 40 hours in a very gradual way seems probable in the industrialised countries of Western Europe, North America and the Pacific and the extension of the fifth week of annual holiday in Western Europe. The issue of reducing working time is, at all events, certain to remain a major concern and a major source of controversy.

It seems equally certain that a preponderant role will be played by collective bargaining not only in determining whether, to what extent, in what forms and at what rate working time will be reduced but also in making the necesssary adjustments to any such changes. The experience of the past few years, even in countries with a tradition of legislation on these matters, has suggested that the

159

10.1

Reduction of working time: The case of France

France was one of the first countries to establish by law the 40-hour week. Legislation for this purpose was adopted in 1936. Its practical application, however, has been subject to qualifications and difficulties. These included the use of a system of "equivalences" by which in certain occupations – characterised by periods of mere presence – workers were required to work more than 40 hours and – most importantly – the use of systematic, indeed institutionalised, overtime. Mainly as a result of long overtime hours, the 40-hour week remained until the late 1960s essentially a legal benchmark. The "standard" or ordinary or usual working week ranged between 44 and 48 hours. Basic wage rates were fixed low so as to incorporate an element corresponding to overtime premiums. In fact, the maximum limit on working time was determined not so much by legal provisions on normal hours as by those on total hours.

While the statutory hours of 40 remained untouched, regulatory action was taken on several occasions from 1967 to 1979 to lower the limits on maximum total hours. The permissible average over 12 weeks was reduced from 60-54 to 50-48 and then in some branches to 46. The maximum in any week, except for special cases requiring prior authorisation, was reduced from 60-57 to 52-50. Moreover, the "equivalences" for certain occupations were reduced or even abolished by decree or by collective agreement.

Moves to reduce actual hours of work began in the late 1960s. Discussions held in 1968 between the Government and the main employers' and workers' organisations led to a general agreement calling for the gradual reduction of hours through industry- or enterprise-level negotiations. In 1975, a new national framework agreement was signed calling for the progressive achievement of the 40-hour week, again through industry- or enterprise-level negotiations. By the end of the decade, the "standard" week was most often in the 40-42 range and the 40-hour week had become fairly widespread.

Developments took a fresh turn in 1981 when a new Government, committed to working time reduction, came to power. In July 1981, the national employers' organisation and most, though not all, national trade union federations agreed on a reduction of statutory weekly hours to 39, reductions in maximum hours, the generalisation of the fifth week of annual holidays and a number of other measures. An extremely significant – and controversial – feature of this agreement was the inclusion of provisions for "modulating" – that is to say, averaging – the 39-hour week over the year. This would give the employers more discretion in the use of overtime and make for greater flexibility in a number of other respects.

A main point of contention was the question of wages. Should real wages be maintained or reduced in proportion with the working time reduction? After a series of sharp conflicts, the Government expressed clearly its view that the reduction should not entail any reduction in wages. This principle, however, would not necessarily apply to future reductions towards the 35-hour week.

By the summer of 1982, the reduction to 39 hours had been widely implemented. According to sample surveys, the overwhelming majority of enterprises had applied the reduction in hours without any cut in pay. Statistics on actual hours of work showed a marked decline; while such statistics are generally difficult to interpret, in this case the drop in actual hours seemed attributable to the reduction in normal hours. (The employment effects of this measure were discussed in Volume 1, Chapter 2.)

---

complexity of the problems and the variety of the specific situations found in modern economies make collective bargaining at different levels a flexible and effective method of dealing with working time issues. The negotiations may take place within a framework of national policy or they may be conducted at the sole instance of the parties; they may serve to apply legislation or they may precede statutory measures or they may be unrelated to any governmental action; they may address basic points or they may focus on modes of implementation. But the need for negotiations and for a certain decentralisation of decisions – in other words, the need for employers and trade unions at the industry, enterprise and plant levels to find solutions appropriate to their own circumstances – is becoming increasingly recognised.

This emphasis on negotiated solutions is closely related to the new issues that are emerging. Concern for the familiar questions of normal hours and annual holidays has been nearly equalled by concern for questions pertaining to the management and organisation of working time. There is a growing tendency to approach the reduction and the organisation of working time in an integrated way. It is likely that many future decisions on the former will be linked to measures affecting the latter. This is, for example, the case for France, which provides a clear illustration of this approach (see box 10.1).

A common strand running through the discussions in different countries seems to be the difficulty of finding the right balance between the

Figure 10.1
Weekly working time by main sectors: France, 1968–82

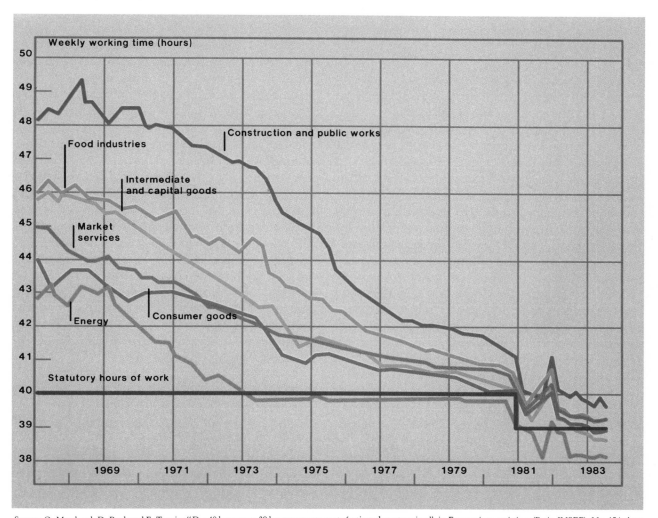

Source: O. Marchand, D. Rault and E. Turpin: "Des 40 heures aux 39 heures: processus et réactions des entreprises", in *Economie et statistique* (Paris, INSEE), No. 154, Apr. 1983, p. 3.
Data are corrected for seasonal variations.

need to safeguard and extend hard-won advances in conditions of work and the need to give employers enough flexibility to meet changing economic and technological conditions. Some of the key issues are outlined below.

First, the question of regulating, limiting or reducing overtime is not a new issue in countries where systematic or extensive overtime has been a long-standing practice. But it has drawn renewed attention in the context of proposals to reduce hours of work. Fears have been expressed that a reduction of normal hours without stricter control of overtime may amount to an indirect wage increase rather than a true reduction in working time. The employment effects of a reduction might be nullified by recourse to overtime. But it has been argued from another standpoint that the possibility of overtime is indispensable for firms to cope with shifts in business conditions and that flexibility in its use is all the more important if standard hours are reduced. A further problem may be that workers accustomed to overtime pay as a regular part of remuneration may object to any loss of earnings.

Even if action to control overtime is contemplated, its concrete form may still be open to debate. Premium wage rates are almost universally applied but they seem to serve more as compensation for the extra effort of the worker than as a real deterrent to employers. Other methods used are the obligation to grant compensatory time off in addition to overtime pay, the legal restriction of the circumstances in which overtime may be worked, the requirement of prior authorisation by the labour inspectorate under prescribed conditions and the imposition of limits on the amount of overtime or on the total hours of work that may be worked in a day, a fixed number of consecutive days, a week, a month or a year. Which measures or combination of measures would be most effective and least detrimental to production requirements? Some recent discussion has emphasised compensatory time off but the practice seems to be tending more towards a limitation of overtime, coupled with greater discretion for employers in using it. Statutory action in this area would, however, run counter to the tradition of some countries and is therefore unlikely in the near future.

Like overtime, shift work is not a new issue but has attracted considerable attention in recent years. Whether shift work is increasing is difficult to judge, not only because of inadequacies in the data available, but also because of the difficulty of separating long-term trends from fluctuations in economic conditions. What does seem clear is that the range of activities and occupations in which shift work is applied has been expanding as a result of technological change. These also seems a distinct possibility that reductions in hours of work will foster the extension of shift work as a means of maintaining or intensifying productive capacity.

At the same time, concern about the possible adverse effects of shift work, and particularly continuous shift work, for the workers has led to moves either to restrict the use of continuous shift work or to improve the working conditions of shiftworkers. The former objective is, of course, extremely controversial but the latter has been pursued in many countries both through collective bargaining and through legislation. Measures to improve the working conditions of shiftworkers have included the reduction of working time, sometimes the granting of additional holidays, and the development of new rotation schedules designed to minimise the disruption of normal living patterns. Moreover, some large enterprises have introduced a fifth team in their continuous shift schedule. This innovation is likely to spread, especially where normal hours of work are reduced. Employers have also tended to accept the reduction of working time more easily if workers accept greater flexibility in regard to shift work. Some have argued that more shift work may be indispensable if the reduction of working time is to have positive employment effects.

The related question of night work has been under review mainly through a re-examination of existing legislation prohibiting the night work of women in industry. A number of industrialised countries have rescinded this prohibition and, while this has met with some reservations in trade union circles, more such action can be expected.

Some of the other emerging issues can be grouped under the general heading of the diversification of working time patterns. It may be too soon to speak of a trend but there has undoubtedly been a movement away from a standard work schedule characterised by fixed starting and finishing times, daily hours, weekly rest days and the like. Changes in technology, in management techniques, in the economic environment and in the composition and attitudes of the workforce have led to a questioning of traditional practices. The eight-hour day, the uniform working week, the payment of overtime rates for all hours exceeding the normal limits in a given day or in a given week, the establishment of single schedules for all or well-defined portions of the workforce, even the notion of full-time employment – these and other long-established patterns are apparently beginning to break down. The newer patterns designed to replace them include such practices as the averaging of hours over relatively long periods, the annualisation of hours, flexible rostering, the variable weekly rest day, the individualisation of work schedules, staggered hours, the compressed week, different forms of flexible or à la carte hours and part-time work.

Developments and proposals along these lines have often provoked controversy and sometimes led to conflict. Some of them have been advocated on grounds of increased operational flexibility, others as responding to the needs and preferences of individual workers. They have been criticised and sometimes strongly opposed by trade unions as jeopardising the protection gained for workers after hard struggles. For example, some schemes permit exceptionally long hours in any given day or week, thus negating the protection offered by hours of work regulations. The door may be opened to disguised overtime work without payment of overtime rates. Time-clocking may be introduced where it did not exist or had been abolished. Enterprises may secure productivity increases while workers gain only cosmetic improvements. The individualisation of schedules may lead to fragmentation of the workforce and make it more difficult to check abuses. The encouragement of part-time work may reduce the availability of full-time jobs. It may also create a large group of workers who are deprived of various benefits and may thus undermine the conditions of all workers.

These are legitimate concerns. They do not mean that changes in working time patterns will, or should, be halted. What they do imply is the need for safeguards. In this respect, too, the necessity of negotiations at different levels has become increasingly apparent.

163

---

[1] Reduction of Hours of Work Recommendation, 1962 (No. 116), Paragraph 11.

[2] The number and distribution of paid public holidays vary considerably between countries and can have an important impact on the number of hours actually worked.

[3] Statistics on paid holidays are difficult to collect, because ascertaining the number of days actually taken requires either recall by a person being questioned or access to employee records relating to a period of time. Paid vacation entitlement may differ from the number of days actually taken because (i) entitlement is carried over from one period to another; (ii) people receive pay in lieu of entitlement when they leave a job; or (iii) some people take less than their entitlement. See R. Turvey: "Statistics of paid vacations", in *Bulletin of Labour Statistics* (Geneva, ILO), 1983-3, p. XXXVI.

Chapter **11**

Labour inspection

Two thousand four hundred years ago, Hippocrates had already established a causal link between rock dust and lung diseases of stone cutters. In the seventeenth century the connection between different trades and specific health hazards was well known in Europe. But it was not until 1833 that a Factory Act was passed in Great Britain, and that four inspectors were appointed, essentially to supervise the application of regulations on hours of work of children in the some 3,000 textile factories existing at the time. That was the beginning of labour inspection, an important innovation since, for the first time, government inspectors were charged with overseeing the application of labour legislation.

During the nineteenth century most European countries adopted, albeit slowly, legislation reflecting new developments in industry and more democratic and social attitudes. In 1890, representatives of 15 States attended a conference in Berlin to adopt the first international conventions on labour standards. That conference affirmed that laws in each State should be supervised by an adequate number of specially qualified officers, appointed by government and independent of both employers and workers. The first medical inspector of factories was appointed in Great Britain in 1898; in 1899 the first specialist engineering adviser was in office. Thus, the foundation of a modern labour inspection system, with general inspectors and technical and medical specialists, had been laid in a number of European countries by the beginning of the twentieth century.

The end of the First World War saw the creation of the ILO, one of whose early international instruments was the Labour Inspection Recommendation, 1923 (No. 20). At the end of the Second World War, work had been completed on an ambitious set of standards: the Labour Inspection Convention, 1947 (No. 81) – now ratified by 105 member States – and associated Recommendation. These new standards were comprehensive and far-sighted. The goals they laid down over 35 years ago are still highly valid today – so much so that quite a few ILO member countries are still not in a position to report that they have attained and maintained the norms of this Convention and its sister instrument, the Labour Inspection (Agriculture) Convention, 1969 (No. 129).

This chapter describes the purpose and functions of labour inspection and aspects of its organisation and resources in developing, centrally planned and industrialised market economy countries, and highlights some significant trends, problems and prospects in this field.

Purpose and functions

Originally, the primary duty of labour inspection was to supervise labour legislation. Inspectorates were regarded simply as law enforcement agencies, a kind of auxiliary police to safeguard nascent social progress in the field of workers' safety, health and welfare. But though supervision is still one of the major responsibilities of any labour inspection service, today, in most countries, its purpose is much broader. The primary duties of practically every modern system of labour inspection, as laid down in Convention No. 81, are:

(a) to secure the enforcement of the legal provisions relating to conditions of work and the protection of workers while engaged in their work, such as provisions relating to hours, wages, safety, health and welfare, the employment of children and young persons, and other connected matters;

(b) to supply technical information and advice to employers and workers concerning the most effective means of complying with the legal provisions;

(c) to bring to the notice of the competent authority defects or abuses not specifically covered by existing legal provisions.

Today it is generally considered better to prevent than to punish. This change of attitude is reflected in the more recent Convention No. 129, which states that inspectorates must be associated with the preventive control of new methods or processes that appear likely to constitute a threat to health or safety. In many countries national laws require not only that new plants or processes be registered, as for instance in much of French-speaking Africa, but also that plans for new plants and products be submitted in advance to the labour inspectorate for approval, as in the centrally planned economies, the Federal Republic of Germany, India, Japan, Peru, Sweden, the United Kingdom, English-speaking African countries and others.

Emphasis on preventive as against corrective means of intervention is gaining ground. Of course, "traditional" inspection, i.e. the various aspects of technical supervision, still contributes substantially to the prevention of accidents and health hazards, particularly if accompanied by comments and advice to employers and workers. However, experts are concerned about the reduction of actual inspection work in favour of other duties. In some Scandinavian countries and the United Kingdom, for instance, they feel that the predominance of prevention over control has become too strong and that there is a need to strike a better balance.

Enforcement powers of labour inspectors vary greatly from one country to another. They may be general and apply to all labour and social legislation, as for instance in Belgium, Bulgaria, France, Greece and most Latin American countries. They may be restricted to certain fields, such as safety and health, work of women and children, etc., as in India and the United Kingdom. Or, conversely, certain matters such as wages may be expressly excluded from the inspectorate's tasks, as in the Federal Republic of Germany. Inspectors may have specific responsibilities with regard to certain employers, e.g. in the case of public works contracts, as in Ghana, Tunisia or the United States. This is an important feature since labourers on public works are, by law or practice, frequently exempt from minimum standards of protection. Enforcement powers may also be limited to particular sectors of the economy, typically excluding mining and transport. While in this case other inspectorates, e.g. mining inspectorates, may have been established, certain sectors are sometimes not protected by any external labour inspection, e.g. offshore oil industries or public sector activities such as railways, postal services, or the armed forces. However, some countries such as the United Kingdom and the Nordic countries have extended labour inspection to the public sector, and specifically to public administration systems; this is an important new development.

Advice, information and publicity in most labour inspection systems today go far beyond the mere supplying of technical counsel on safety and health matters. Clearly a modern inspectorate must command high technical expertise to be accepted as a partner by industry and the trade unions. The latter, particularly, often ask the experts of the labour inspectorate for assistance. Some countries, however, following the French pattern, rely more on a corps of generalist inspectors with broad enforcement functions. Others, like the Federal Republic of Germany, have created a dual system, with a more generalist state labour inspectorate, and a more technically specialised inspectorate. Many inspectorates experience difficulties in striking a proper balance between enforcement on the one hand, and advice and information on the other. The social partners tend to expect a degree of flexibility and judgement not commonly found in any public service system. Some countries have attempted to solve the inspectors' dilemma: in Brazil, for example, an inspector has to draw employers' attention to the legal consequences of their action (or lack of it) before contemplating prosecution. In most countries, it is in practice left to the individual inspector to decide which remedial measure to take; and in times of economic difficulties, there is the temptation, often backed by public policy, to rely too much on advice and information and refrain from "unpopular" enforcement measures. This would not, of course, apply to cases of immediate danger to life and limb, but in some countries it does jeopardise the effective enforcement of laws and regulations dealing with workers' health and welfare.

Participation in standard setting is a time-honoured function of labour inspection. It can provide ideas for new legislation and regulations by notifying the competent authority of defects or abuses not specifically covered by existing legal provisions and by proposing to that same authority improvements in laws and regulations. In a large number of countries the labour inspectorate is represented on national tripartite advisory bodies, to which it can bring its knowledge of problems and deficiencies at the workplace so as to ensure that new laws and regulations are applicable in practice. Labour inspectorates are also often called upon to express their professional opinion or to make proposals for draft legislation on matters of employment, social security, etc. Much as the association of labour inspectorates in the field of standard setting highlights the importance gov-

ernment authorities attach to their services, such demands can place a considerable burden on the ever small resources of inspectorates. This is particularly true in cases where inspectors are required to make statistical surveys, e.g. on wages or strikes, or to establish cost-benefit analyses in advance of new regulations or even to make recommendations involving legal consequences, as for instance in Norway.

Collaboration with the social partners is an important aspect of labour inspection. Most systems have made appropriate arrangements for promoting co-operation between the labour inspectorate and employers and workers or their organisations, in the form of conferences or joint committees at the plant, local, regional or national level. The effectiveness of any action by the labour inspectorate depends largely on the collaboration of employers and workers. National tripartite committees therefore exist in countries as varied as Belgium, Czechoslovakia, Italy, the Ivory Coast, Nigeria, Pakistan, Switzerland and the United Kingdom. National legislation in many countries provides for the establishment at the level of the undertaking of health and safety committees, labour protection councils or similar bodies. Their role consists in actively promoting safety consciousness among the social partners, investigating accidents and means of preventing them, and generally supervising the enforcement of all measures designed to make working conditions more human. These bodies, as a rule, co-operate closely with the labour inspectorate during inspection visits; they may also be empowered by law to request the labour inspectors to be present at their meetings. Such procedures ensure that the interests of the social partners are safeguarded to the maximum.

In addition to the major functions of most labour inspection systems, other duties are sometimes entrusted to them. Where this is the case, Convention No. 81 specifically provides that such duties should not interfere with the discharge of their primary duties, or prejudice in any way the

167

inspector's authority or impartiality. In practice, such additional duties abound. Many countries have established labour research or labour protection institutes, often under the direct control of, or at least attached to, the labour inspection system. Another duty of labour inspectorates often lies in their contribution to or participation in development planning; but this may be a double-edged weapon. It is desirable because it enhances the service's capacity vis-à-vis other, better-endowed government bodies, and it can therefore give inspectorates more recognition, status and resources within the public administration; on the other hand, it can also draw slender resources away from the major functions, which may themselves already suffer from lack of political and financial support. In some countries, labour inspectors are required to carry out labour market surveys. They may be called upon to supervise the payment of contributions to safety and social security schemes. They may be asked to collect statistics on conditions of work, or they may be entrusted with a host of administrative duties. They may have responsibilities with regard to employment services, or they may supervise vocational training centres.

Opinion is divided on the role of labour inspectors in industrial relations, particularly their participation in collective bargaining procedures and the settlement of industrial disputes. In countries following the British tradition, the negotiation of agreements is left entirely to labour and management. In countries influenced by the French tradition, and in most Latin American countries, collective bargaining procedures often require labour inspectors to attend, or even chair, the relevant meetings. Such arrangements are found in Chile, France, Greece, Mexico and some French-speaking African countries. But whereas participation in collective bargaining is generally considered an acceptable additional charge since the labour inspector may contribute to the improvement of industrial relations, his possible role in the prevention and settlement of industrial disputes is controversial. In France and countries following the French system conciliation is one of the major functions of the labour inspector. International labour Recommendation No. 81 however provides that the functions of labour inspectors should not include conciliation or arbitration, on the ground that conciliation and inspection duties are incompatible. Recommendation No. 133, on the other hand, recognises the possibility of labour inspectors acting as conciliators on a temporary basis. If the ILO itself seems somewhat divided on this issue, so, indeed, is the rest of the world. At one extreme we find such countries as Cyprus, Denmark, Hungary, India, Japan and the United Kingdom, where regulations prohibit inspectors from playing any role in dispute settlement, and at the other France, Greece, Guatemala, Spain, Turkey and other countries, where disputes must be submitted to a labour inspector; and in between every variety of law and practice can be found.

Aspects of organisation and resources

As with labour administration as a whole, there are many variations in the way labour inspection systems are organised. In many countries following the British pattern, the work of the inspectorate is divided into two streams, one dealing with safety and health, usually under the aegis of a factory inspectorate, and the other with general conditions of work and employment, under a labour (or wages) inspectorate. In France and most French-speaking African countries the labour inspector is responsible for the application of all labour legislation. In either case, the private sector may play an important role in the inspection system by carrying out the highly specialised inspection of pressure vessels, lifts, cranes, etc. In most centrally planned economies, labour inspection takes place within a highly developed participative structure of administration.

While a few developing countries already had a labour inspectorate of some kind before the Second

World War, the majority have created inspection systems only fairly recently, and in a climate that was not conducive to the development of social institutions. People in favour of rapid industrialisation were not always aware of the price to pay in terms of human suffering and environmental degradation. Today a number of serious deficiencies inhibit the proper functioning of labour inspection systems in these countries. Most important is the generally weak position of labour ministries; their share in the government budget is often not more than 1 per cent, and in a few cases closer to 0.1 per cent. Lack of resources is the major organisational weakness, and reflects perhaps a lack of awareness at government levels of the importance of the work of labour inspectorates, because any effective prevention of occupational diseases and accidents contributes to the preservation of skilled manpower, overall development and social peace. Consequently, labour inspection services are very often unable to function effectively, for lack of staff, premises, equipment and transport.

It follows that the impact of these services is often extremely limited. Their field of intervention is, by and large, restricted to the wage-earning sector of the population, sometimes 30 per cent, sometimes less than 5 per cent, of the total labour force. The rural sector and the informal urban sector are rarely touched. Nor are the factories and other premises of the urban formal sector inspected regularly or thoroughly. A serious, if unanswerable, question is: in how many of the 120 developing countries of the world can an effectively organised labour inspection system – a system whose impact is measurable and that does not suffer from lack of credibility – be said to exist? In the majority of cases, and not only in the developing countries, the real impact of labour inspection is rather limited and, as a result, many existing systems do not fulfil their mission, or only partly so. This is seldom a consequence of deliberate policy. For instance, the Indian Labour Ministers' Conference in 1973 recommended that there should be one labour inspector for every 150

factories subject to inspection under the Factories Act (1948), which covers the formal sector only. But in Bihar, typically, one inspector would have to check over 1,300 factories per year. Industrialising societies often feel, though they may not say so, that they cannot afford a costly and effective inspectorate system, or rather, that they can afford to do without one, despite the human cost incurred. In some countries, polluting or highly hazardous industries, banned in their place of origin, find a safe haven, with little consideration for the ultimate, irreversible damage. Other countries which for whatever reason invest inadequately in labour inspection, like to believe that even if the inspectorate cannot effectively be present in the enterprises, it can still induce entrepreneurs (and workers) to comply with regulations. Such a policy, again by no means limited to developing countries, has in most cases proved to be of little effect, and tends to diminish the inspectorate's credibility.

Nevertheless, a growing number of developing countries agree in principle with the need for setting up an adequate and comprehensive inspection organisation able to keep abreast of the process of industrialisation. It is often easier to build up a constructive relationship between the social partners and the labour inspectorate in the developing countries because these institutions have grown up together in a relatively short period of time, and have not had to overcome entrenched traditions of the kind so often found in the industrialised market economies.

In most industrialised centrally planned economies labour inspection is part of a comprehensive system where the protection of workers is a shared responsibility between state bodies independent of the undertaking's administration and workers' organisations themselves. This may be illustrated by a prototype of this form of organisation, the labour inspection system of the USSR. This system relies on the various social and economic agencies of government (both at the central and at the local level), the trade union movement, and legal and judicial bodies and other institutions of public control.

The state organisations concerned with the development of basic labour standards, maintenance of socialist legality in regard to labour laws, and general labour inspection are:

- the State Committee for Labour and Social Affairs which is responsible for elaborating and reviewing the most important norms on labour safety, as well as supervising the activities of other state economic agencies in this field;

- the State Committee for Safety Control in Industry and Mines, which ensures the observance of government decrees on the creation of safe working conditions and safety rules (the State Technical Inspectorate);

- the Ministries of Public Health of the USSR and the Union Republics, which supervise the observance of hygienic standards and rules by state bodies, enterprises, organisations and citizens (the State Sanitation Supervision);

- the Procurator-General of the USSR and the Procurator-General of the Union Republics, which have supervisory power over the observance of labour legislation by all ministries, departments and enterprises and their officials both in industry and in agriculture.

On the workers' side the bodies responsible for the general management and co-ordination of the labour protection system are:

- the All-Union Central Council of Trade Unions, which provides the general management and co-ordination of the labour protection system operated by the trade union movement; it has wide authority for initiating legislation and for participating in economic planning and policy decisions at the national level;

- the central committees of the sectoral trade unions with their corresponding labour protection services;

- the councils of trade unions at union republic level, which co-ordinate the activities of the field inspectorates in general and provide some technical inspection services for non-industrial sectors;

- the republican committees of constituent trade unions, which undertake both general labour inspection and an increasing amount of technical inspection in their particular industries; the regional, area and town branches of these councils and committees, which undertake labour inspection services locally; and

- the trade union committees at undertaking or establishment level, which are responsible for the bulk of general labour inspection.

The labour protection services operated by the trade unions are required, among other duties, to carry out labour inspections calling for a considerable degree of specialisation. They therefore have two main groups of inspectors: technical and general (legal). Both groups of inspectors perform their functions under territorial or branch organs of the trade unions and they can give binding orders to management personnel of all ranks. Because of the numbers of part-time inspectors – trade union "activists" drawn from and acting on behalf of the workforce – workers may be said to be the eyes and ears of the trade union technical inspectors. Full-time technical staff number some 6,200. More than half work for the industrial trade unions, the rest for various councils of trade unions.

The labour inspectorate is completed by about 1.5 million "voluntary" inspectors, who are ordinary workers or supervisors in enterprises or other establishments and who accept additional responsibilities for part-time supervision of the application of the less specialised standards of labour welfare, hygiene and safety within their own work sections. In the USSR general supervision of labour legislation is also carried out by local government.

In addition to these various services, the branch ministries also play a part in the protection of workers by ensuring that full responsibility is borne by management. The principal characteristic of labour inspection in the Soviet Union is therefore its dual nature – supervision both by the State and by the trade unions. And whereas variations do of course exist among the centrally planned economies, this basic and unique pattern is common to almost all of them. Exceptions are Poland, Romania and, if one were to include it in this group, Yugoslavia. In Poland, following moves made to reform the trade unions since 1980, the State took over the functions of the labour inspectorate. Romania and Yugoslavia have developed independent systems of labour inspection along with greater autonomy in other policy fields.

Each industrialised market economy country has adopted an organisational pattern for its labour inspection system that reflects its historical evolution, particular economic conditions and customary administrative methods. Stratified like any branch of the civil service, labour inspectorates have followed the practice of establishing offices throughout the national territory. Most countries of this group have a central or main labour inspection body and, generally speaking, this forms part of the ministry responsible for labour and social affairs. Apart from this common feature, organisational patterns vary greatly depending on whether a country has a centralised or decentralised administrative structure. Federal States obviously belong to the latter group. Typically, mining, transport, agriculture, defence and public administration are specialised sectors of activity often outside the responsibility of the general labour inspection system, whose activities, because of its nineteenth-century origin, are still largely industry-oriented. But, throughout the 1970s, many countries of this group made genuine efforts towards a comprehensive reform of their systems. The United Kingdom, for example, amended its Factories Act in 1974, bringing practically all inspection activities under one central body, the Health and Safety Executive, and giving inspectorates wide powers in all sectors of public and private activity. In Norway the

comprehensive Workers' Protection and Working Environment Act came into force in 1977. Similar reforms of the organisation, scope and functions of labour inspectorates in the past decade were undertaken for example in Denmark, France, the Netherlands, the United States and other industrialised countries. Sweden chose a somewhat different, but equally effective, approach: the functions of the labour inspectorate are carried out by the Workers' Protection Board, under the Ministry of Health and Social Affairs, with a general mandate to cover all sectors of activity.

In countries with more than one inspectorate, the labour inspection system is organised in one of two ways. Specialisation may be according to economic sectors each of which has its own inspectorate, or according to the nature of inspection, that is, social, medical, chemical or technical, with further subdivision possible, e.g. boilers and pressure vessels, radiation, etc. It is not possible to say that one organisational structure is better than another. Where the system seems rather fragmented, such as in Belgium, co-ordination may be provided by a Higher Council for Safety, Health and Amenities at the Workplace. It is essential that inspectorates should be able to act according to uniform principles and procedures applicable to the whole country; and this is what the comprehensive reforms in the past decade, of often century-old organisation structures, have mainly endeavoured to achieve.

A number of labour inspection systems in the industrialised market economies have of late felt the need not only to change the basic laws under which they operate, but also, and partly as a consequence, their whole way of operating. While labour inspectorates have made great efforts to adapt their role and functions to changes in the world outside, changes within the organisation have often trailed behind. Inspectorates have seldom been able to modernise their organisational structure, planning and information system, methods of work, etc. Their internal organisation

Table 11.1
Characteristics of labour inspection in selected IMEC countries (early 1980s)

Country (and year of latest available statistical data)	Inspectors	Establishments (incl. construction sites) in the purview of the inspectorate	Inspection visits [1]	Percentage of establishments covered	Notifications (written observations, notices, citations, legal proceedings) [2]
Austria (1982)	240	192 000	102 000	53%	16 700
Denmark (1982)	293	140 000	71 000	51%	34 600
France (1982, Labour Inspectorate only)	3 100	over 1.1 million	329 000	29%	870 000 [3]
Federal Republic of Germany (1982, State Labour Inspectorate only)	3 400	1.8 million	535 000	33%	357 000 [4]
Japan (1981, Labour Standards Inspectorate only)	3 000	over 3.5 million	210 000	6%	106 000
United States (1980, Occupational Safety and Health Administration only)	1 400	over 3 million	60 000	2%	128 500 [5]

[1] This column includes repeat inspection visits. Some statistics include the number of first inspections also, e.g. France: 190,000; Federal Republic of Germany: 347,000; Japan: 174,000.   [2] Caution should be exercised when comparing the figures in this column as the methods of intervention vary considerably from country to country.   [3] Total number of written communications.   [4] Average number of inspection reports.   [5] Violations only, does not include mere citations.

is often characterised by outdated management approaches; inadequate planning, information, reporting; substantial differences in structures within the national system, in internal and external work methods, etc.; lack of co-ordination between policy and implementation, between headquarters and the field offices, between the field offices themselves, and between various planning and administrative units; and finally, rigid allocation of duties to functional groups. How can a way out be found? The case of the Netherlands may be as informative as it is innovative: here a comprehensive organisational development project was started in 1976, a process not finished to date. Steps in this process, undertaken by all staff of the inspectorate and all its units, central and decentral-ised, were: comprehensive problem diagnosis, development of proposed solutions, democratic (staff) decisions on implementation. Problem analyses were discussed with the social partners, the Ministry of Finance, and others. A report was issued and sent to Parliament and the media. Finally, a plan for implementation was decided upon, encompassing five major areas: personnel and organisation; scope of activities; objectives and tasks; work methods; information. Although much remains to be done, it seems that the energy invested in this project for organisational overhaul of a traditionally rigid public service system has produced significant results. Other countries, such as Norway and the United Kingdom, have initiated similar processes.

Trends, problems and prospects

Major trends in labour inspection over the past decade necessarily reflect at least some of the significant social, technological and economic developments of that period. In the 1970s, by and large, there was a favourable climate for programmes of social reform, and in a number of countries with developed but traditional labour inspection systems it was workers' representatives in particular who forcefully pushed the idea of making work more human.[1] This vision of humanisation covered in principle all aspects of working life and, inevitably, also had an impact on the agencies entrusted with supervising and improving the physical and the psychological working environment. Thus, a number of countries promulgated ambitious and comprehensive Acts for the protection of workers, in order to change the basically end-of-nineteenth century industry-oriented foundations of existing legislation. But passing an Act is one thing; bringing it to life is quite another. Moreover, in the 1980s, the climate has changed. Today, the economic situation is the single most pressing concern of everyone, including labour inspection experts. The opinion is gaining ground, even among the workers themselves, that the worst "working environment" is not to have a job at all.

In a number of countries this has led to an increasingly restrictive interpretation, and even a withdrawal, of reforms in labour inspection. New legislation designed to give more substance to the reforms has been delayed, or quietly abandoned. Proposals for reform that "missed the boat" by 1980 cannot find political backing today, however clearly the need for change is written on the wall. No matter how serious and well documented the case for labour inspection reform may be, it will be subjected to rigorous cost-benefit or other economic scrutiny. The ambitious legislation of the 1970s, proclaiming that workers' safety, health and welfare should carry greater weight than financial considerations, while not abrogated, will cease to be followed up with equal ambition, and this, perhaps, is the single most important trend, as it conditions all other developments.

The second major issue is labour inspection's role vis-à-vis new technology, certainly in the industrialised world, but increasingly also in developing countries. Many experts believe that labour inspectorates will be more affected by information technology than by any other single factor. And how can labour inspectors hope to deal effectively with companies, employers, academics and specialists who are working on the frontiers of, and with, new technology? In dealing with programmed electronic systems, microbiology, genetic manipulation, control engineering, how can labour inspectors keep pace with changes in technology and science? How can they assess the problems – assess, in particular, what they do not know about them – keep up with current thinking, foresee developments, and influence such developments where necessary and in the right way, all the while giving advice to those who ask questions and expect answers? How can they maintain within the inspectorates up-to-date technical expertise to ensure that their response is knowledgeable and authoritative and matches that of safety experts in private industry? How can they make sure that the best of the old traditions are maintained while they adapt to new needs? This will demand a degree of flexibility and responsiveness almost unknown in this sector of public administration. There is the need for inspectors to have specialised knowledge of particular industries and processes, in contrast with the need to deploy existing staff resources economically in decentralised, regional or local systems. There is the problem of how to organise and distribute limited expertise in specialised disciplines or narrow fields of experience as against the need of inspectorates to have at their disposal a very wide range of specialist knowledge. As ever, this is also the problem of resources: how to use them effectively in such a way as to ensure an acceptable balance between professional priorities and the expectations,

173

demands and fears of employers, trade unions and the general public?

New technology has a further implication: it will significantly reduce the number of traditional jobs in industry over the next decade, and the properties and qualities of a large number of jobs will change substantially. Clearly this tendency may have the potential of impoverishing conditions of work, although it may also enrich them (see Chapter 7, in Volume 1). It also seems evident that with low-priced information technology, opening up ways for increased automation of hazardous work processes and thereby removing workers from certain risk areas, a reduction in "traditional" accidents is likely (while, of course, a new risk factor, that of robotics, is being introduced, as yet a little explored dimension). Thus, with a foreseeable reduction in industrial activity on the one side, and with still largely industry-oriented legislation and activity of labour inspectorates on the other: what kind of jobs will inspectors inspect in ten, in 20 years' time, and how will they go about it? Trade unions – and not only trade unions – are greatly concerned about the effects that this potential workplace improverishment may have on society beyond the enterprise, and they expect guidance from the labour inspectorate.

Another problem that inspectorates face today is how to deal with the dangers associated with the "scale-up" factor in production processes, that is, increased volumes of storage and transport units of highly volatile materials, such as liquefied natural gas, liquefied petroleum gas, chlorine, etc.; bigger-sized units, higher pressure, etc. within process industries; the growing number of highly toxic chemical substances in production systems; bigger-sized structures of various kinds, dams, oil rigs onshore and offshore, bridges; the nuclear industry, etc. Inspectors are faced with the problem of how to draw an acceptable and defensible balance between necessary precautions and the changing needs and expectations of society, and how to minimise risks, without

unduly restricting industrial development. As already mentioned in Chapter 9, there are tens of thousands of chemicals regularly used in modern industry. Some are clearly dangerous, while others may hide dangers not to be detected for years to come. What is certain is that the development and use of new chemicals, compounds and substances clearly outpace the ability of labour inspectorates (or other competent authorities) to regulate them on an individual basis. For example, between 1970 and 1977 the National Institute for Occupational Safety and Health (NIOSH) in the United States identified 25,000 toxic substances used in local industry. By the end of 1978, the Occupational Safety and Health Administration (OSHA) had issued standards for fewer than 25 of them. But whether or not the long-term effects are understood, systems for safely handling and working with these substances and feasible methods of control must be developed.

Labour inspectors must further endeavour to balance "hardware" solutions – i.e. more stringent levels of emission control, stricter limits to maximum exposure of dangerous substances, more complex interlocked guards, more sophisticated precautions against radiation, fire, accidents, etc. – against alternative, if complementary, "software" strategies, e.g. influencing employers to refine and tighten management systems; pointing out to managements that they are ultimately responsible even if top management can delegate legal responsibility in labour protection matters. Such considerations also apply to the public sector. For example, in the United States, OSHA has recently negotiated with the Government's Office of Personnel Management a plan to include safety and health considerations among the performance criteria of all federal managers, so that federal government supervising personnel would be evaluated, in part, on the health and safety of their employees. With few exceptions, such concepts have yet to spread to the private sector.

One of the serious problems labour inspectorates are discussing today is whether it is possible or even desirable to maintain uniform standards of inspection for all enterprises, public utilities, administrations, etc. In principle, inspectors must apply the law regardless of general or specific economic considerations and of the size and nature of the respective undertaking. In practice, two sets of difficulties arise: what level of standards to apply in respect of small enterprises on the one hand, and unprofitable or economically failing medium- and large-sized undertakings on the other. In both cases observance of prescribed standards can seriously jeopardise employment, since expenditures on safety, health and particularly welfare are presented as being at the cost of other more necessary investments. In times of severe economic recession, social demands are quickly brushed aside, and even established social rights are threatened. In a country such as Greece, 98 per cent of manufacturing industry workshops employ less than 50 people, and many of these establishments are characterised by old (and unsafe) buildings, outdated machinery and tools, and old-fashioned production methods. Most face such economic difficulties – and this, of course, is true for many other countries [2] – that they can just maintain their level of employment, but not even the minimum labour protection standards. A modern ventilation system in a small textile factory, or in an aluminium manufacturing shop with 20 workers, costs more than all the machinery in place. Yet an aluminium dust explosion or constant inhalation of free-floating fibres could cost the lives of all the people working in such a shop. If the labour inspector demands the necessary changes, the people will be out of a job. If he connives, and an accident happens, he and his inspectorate will be the target of public outcry. In practice, this is often a "no-win" situation; and the resulting consequences are drastic. Some modern foundries in the United Kingdom, for instance, with high investments in safety, health and welfare, have been known to close down because production, under these circumstances, had become too costly; on the other hand, some age-old small foundries typically still found in the West Midlands, with unsafe and unhealthy working

conditions, continue to operate. It cannot be the labour inspector's task to contribute to unemployment; and, of course, he must intervene in cases of immediate danger – but when is a dust explosion imminent?

A more serious trend resulting from this dilemma is that trade unions fighting, as it is their duty to do, for the betterment of their members' lot, often face hostile opposition from their own members when doing so. For example, it is an extremely dangerous job to refit a large passenger ship in whose interior asbestos was extensively used when it was built 30 years ago. But with the high rate of unemployment in the shipbuilding industry of Western Europe, the unions in this case are subject to extreme pressure by their rank and file to dismiss their objections. And the labour inspector, typically in such a situation, risks falling between two stools. To what extent must he take economic considerations into account? Certain countries have tried to give an answer: in the United Kingdom the concept of "reasonable practicability" gives the inspectorate an important degree of flexibility. In the Federal Republic of Germany the law prohibits the use of "disproportionate measures"; in other words, the cost of safety measures should be in proportion with the hazards they prevent. The policy in Norway is that an analysis of all the consequences must precede even individual measures or sanctions, if economic costs are foreseeable. Whatever common sense, law or policy may dictate in principle, in practice the dilemma of the labour inspector is seldom easily solved.

The trend towards cost-benefit analyses of improved standards in labour protection merits special attention. Research in the United States is particularly advanced in this field. Cost calculations vary considerably, depending, for instance, on whether one relies on engineering controls or – which is usually less costly – personal protection devices. Industry cost calculations are, furthermore, often inaccurate. During the debate on new vinyl chloride standards, the United States industry estimated, in 1975, that 2 million jobs would be lost and the cost to the economy would be between US$65,000 million and $90,000 million. Yet when the standard was passed, industry very soon developed new technology to control vinyl chloride, and production rose to record heights. No worker was laid off, new plants were opened, and the total cost came to about one two-hundredth of that predicted.

There are a number of reasons why such cost estimates may be inaccurate. Once standards are set, industry often finds cheaper control solutions than originally thought feasible. Improved maintenance may lead to savings. Productivity increases may occur. Measures to control one hazard may control others simultaneously. With larger production volumes, costs go down. And so forth.

Benefits may be even more difficult to predict, however. There is no acceptable monetary equivalent to loss of life. But some of the costs of not controlling hazards have been estimated in the United States. In 1980 that country's industry as a whole paid an estimated US$11,000 million in workers' compensation. The National Safety Council estimated the cost of accidents at work alone at over $20,000 million annually. The cost of bad health due to occupational risks may be much higher. Costs include health care and health insurance; lost productivity and buying power; losses from absenteeism; low productivity, equipment damage and waste of material due to unsafe operations. Industry figures in the United States show that the number of workdays lost annually owing to occupational accidents is ten times that lost owing to strikes. If a more effective labour inspection system and, therefore, improved working conditions were to result in reducing this figure by one day per worker per year, it is estimated that perhaps $15,000 million would be added to the output of goods and services in the country.

Today's labour inspector has stepped out of the semi-closed system of government, employers and workers and their definable relations. More

---

11.1

Hazard evaluation and labour inspection in the United Kingdom

In the United Kingdom, inspectors give each establishment a rating based on their judgement of six different factors: safety, health, welfare, maximum potential hazard for workers and for the public, and management's ability to maintain standards (see figure 11.1). For every year without a general inspection, the computer automatically adds three points to the rating figure. The Health and Safety Executive can thus immediately establish the updated rating for every establishment under its purview. The higher the total number of points, the more urgent it is that the establishment be inspected. Workplaces that have been recently visited and negatively assessed would have a rating comparable to enterprises that have not been visited for a number of years. A critical line is drawn at, say, 43 points; all establishments with higher ratings would be subject to a general inspection at least once a year. One way to improve the effectiveness and efficiency of labour inspection would be gradually to bring down this critical line and to bring more and more establishments within the scope of regular annual inspections.

---

and more he has to accept, to define, to expand or to limit his role vis-à-vis the general public. Minamata, Flixborough, Seveso and Harrisburg have become synonyms for the ubiquitous threat of man-made disaster, and this has significantly sharpened the interest of the general public in major hazards associated with production. There have always been similar incidents, for instance, with boiler explosions in the last century. But the spread of knowledge and interest has given rise to much more media scrutiny and questioning of the labour inspector's responsibility, not only at the workplace but also towards the population as a whole. To fully recognise and satisfy public awareness, demands, fears and expectations is a new dimension in labour inspection and, in technical terms, a very difficult problem. It is difficult to explain that there is no such thing as absolute safety; and that even relative safety could not be ensured if funds were unlimited. In labour protection, the law of diminishing returns applies with force. These and other considerations have given rise to much public interest in what constitutes an acceptable risk.

Figure 11.1
Model form for hazard evaluation by the labour inspector (HSE, United Kingdom) *(slightly modified)*

1. To give your assessment of an employer, a proprietor or, if need be, a non-wage earner, please choose among the following that which corresponds to the actual level in the field of:

   (Please choose only one assessment)

Very good	-0	a. SAFETY
Good	-1	
Satisfactory to good	-2	b. HYGIENE
Satisfactory to insufficient	-3	
Insufficient	-4	c. WELFARE
Completely insufficient	-5	

Assessment Note		TOTAL
	×4	
	×4	
	×1	

2. If the worst were to happen, what would be the size of the problem, whether an isolated accident or a long-term hazard for the health of threatened workers and the general public?

   a. Workers

Tick off	×4	TOTAL
Negligible	0	
Weak	1	
Great	3	
Catastrophic	5	

   b. General public

Tick off	×3	TOTAL
None	0	
Small	4	
Great	5	

3. What confidence do you have in the ability of management to maintain acceptable standards in the near future?

Tick off	×4	TOTAL
Total confidence	0	
Great confidence	1	
Reasonable confidence	2	
Little confidence	3	
Hardly any	4	
None at all	5	

GLOBAL RATING BY THE INSPECTOR

(Form to be completed as soon as possible after the visit)

Unconsciously we all understand and perhaps accept the concept of "acceptable risk". But it is an interesting fact, as one authority recently noted, that the public tends to over-react to such relatively minor disasters as fires and explosions, with minor effects on their surroundings, and that it demands a large space between production sites and inhabited areas, hospitals, schools, etc. On the other hand, storing, production processes or transport involving, for instance, chlorine, a highly dangerous toxic chemical entailing great hazards, by and large leaves the general public complacent; similarly toxic chemicals can often be found stored, etc., in close proximity to residential areas. The exigencies on nuclear reactor safety are tremendous, in technical and cost terms. In the Federal Republic of Germany, for instance, such power stations must be capable of withstanding a crash of a fully loaded fighter aircraft. Protection measures for chemical reactors are, as a rule, nowhere near as stringent, and – to stick to the example – a single-seat private aircraft crashing on such a plant would be likely to produce a major disaster.

The fact that labour inspectors have an important future role to play in the analysis and prevention of potential major hazards has recently been recognised by, for example, the European Economic Commission's "Seveso Directive".[3] In spite of some difficulties, the countries of the Communities have translated this directive into law and practice, and their labour inspectorates are adjusting to these exigencies. In the United Kingdom, for example, the Health and Safety Executive (HSE) operates an innovative computer-based system of priority visiting of workplaces according to inherent hazard evaluation. All premises are given a rating number based on the degree of risk and the ability of management to control the hazards, whether inside or outside the workplace. High-risk enterprises are then inspected quite frequently, low- or no-risk enterprises perhaps only once in three or five years (see box 11.1). Other inspectorates are choosing different approaches, for instance by using multi-disciplinary teams of inspectors. In quite a few cases, inspectorates have the official responsibility to monitor and control the general environment, as in most of the *Länder* of the Federal Republic of Germany. Contacts with the general public go even further in, for instance, Czechoslovakia, where households and leisure activities (both very accident-prone) come under the responsibility of the labour inspectorate. At the other end of the spectrum, in some countries, such as Sweden and the United Kingdom, even the armed forces are subject to labour inspection – stopping just short of the front line.

This chapter has raised a number of questions that labour inspectors face and to which, of course, it did not have ready answers. That, typically, is also the situation of many of today's labour inspectorates. But if inspectors cannot easily furnish the answers, the social partners expect that they (and the government) can at least provoke an informed discussion and dialogue based on objective rather than emotional arguments. Such a discussion is indispensable before difficult decisions about priorities and policies are discussed and agreed upon. Such a dialogue would also ensure that the new technologies and developments do not dictate the pattern of social progress, or at least that undesirable or unacceptable hazards are known and controlled before new production processes are introduced.

[1] The International Labour Office, at the request of member governments, has since 1976 organised a series of high-level tripartite consultancy missions to evaluate the effectiveness of labour inspection in selected industrialised countries. This programme has filled a keenly felt need for international exchange of experience and information, as well as being an advisory service at the national level. The initiative for it came from the Workers' group of the ILO Governing Body.

[2] Almost all labour inspectorates face the problem of how to establish an effective presence in small-scale enterprises. For instance, in the Federal Republic of Germany 92 per cent of all establishments subject to inspection fall into the category of 1-19 employees, accounting for 40 per cent of the total labour force. If the category of 20-200 employees is included, the figure rises to 99.3 per cent, accounting for over 60 per cent of the labour force. It often seems that the discussion on improved safety, advanced inspection techniques, etc., concentrates on the remaining 1 per cent of large-scale enterprises where modern labour inspection philosophy accompanied by regular, often weekly, visits guarantees to the extent possible a good working environment. But the problem is how to organise an inspection system that has an effective impact on safety policies or thinking in small-scale enterprises, for it is in the latter that workers' safety and health is usually most threatened. One of the explanations given for the effective observance of standards in, for instance, the USSR is the fact that no small-scale enterprises exist in that country: in Moscow, typically, the 2,000-odd barbers work within one single organisation, where safety and health standards can effectively be controlled. Unfortunately, in labour inspection, small is not beautiful.

[3] The "Seveso Directive" is designed to ensure safe handling of certain substances (in small or large quantities) that carry the risk of a disproportionately large hazard for the general public, by requiring enterprises to:

(1) declare to the labour inspectorate the use, storage, handling, transport, etc. of such hazardous substances;

(2) establish a safety analysis of how technically to avoid such hazards; and

(3) to make containment and emergency plans for the event of a hazard occurring.

Chapter 12

Quality of working life

One of the most striking lessons of the past decade is that many people in industrialised countries, and particularly women, have shown a strong desire to work. Even though unemployment is not as stigmatised as in the past, a large majority of those presently on unemployment rolls would certainly prefer to work rather than to be unemployed. Moreover, evidence is growing that unemployment is seriously detrimental to mental and physical health. Notwithstanding widespread complaints about the "collapse of the work ethic", work has retained and even strengthened its central role in life.

In retrospect, we can see that social changes – including the desire of many women to have a career of their own – together with economic motivations have generated a strong and steady rise in the demand for employment. However, the new entrants to the labour market do not have the same characteristics as the previous generation of workers who are leaving the labour market. The new entrants are better educated, economically less dependent on their work, more ready to challenge authority and more likely to demand that their work provide them with social rewards in addition to a pay cheque. In short, many modern workers want good jobs rather than any jobs, and they define the quality of their jobs in ways that go far beyond pay levels. Their jobs are a part of their lives – sometimes the most important part – and do not merely provide the means to live.

During the 1960s, workers from various countries and backgrounds began to express their desire for better jobs in ways which managers, trade unionists, public policy-makers and academic analysts could no longer ignore. Absenteeism and labour turnover rose; existing management productivity techniques seemed less effective, and insistent – if ill-defined – demands for workplace democracy, equal treatment, greater job satisfaction and other "new" issues were increasingly heard. This turbulent situation was part of a broader movement to change society. Many workers, especially the young and the well-educated, were concerned about the protection of the environment and a better "quality of work". Some of them even rejected the existing social order. The tensions between old and new visions of society ultimately became explosive, as the events of May 1968 in France and the autumn of 1969 in Italy demonstrated. While only a part of these social changes related directly to work, by the end of the decade there was a feeling that work and workplace were ready for change. Perhaps it was no coincidence that an international conference held in 1972 at Arden House, New York, introduced a new term that was almost universally accepted afterwards: the quality of working life.

It may be that if jobs had changed as rapidly as the characteristics and expectations of workers, there would have been no need for a new term. There have, of course, been changes in some sectors because the industrialised societies have become increasingly "post-industrial", with the majority of their labour forces in office and service-oriented jobs. Unfortunately, many of these jobs are neither interesting nor well-paid. The skills and training required are often poorly matched with the general education and expectations workers bring to the job. In fact, analyses of changes in work content suggest that there has been a modest downgrading of skill requirements since the beginning of this century.[1] Moreover, there is evidence that one of the most critical aspects of job content, which might be called responsibility, autonomy or discretion, has not changed during the past few decades.[2] While some of the studies which suggest a lack of change in skill requirements can be questioned, it is beyond doubt that skill requirements have not changed nearly as rapidly as the characteristics of the labour force.[3]

It would be misleading to claim that the majority of workers are highly educated and their skills underutilised. Surveys suggest that a solid majority of workers are reasonably satisfied with their jobs.[4] Younger workers may be frustrated because they have failed to acquire skills that are valued by potential employers. None the less, there is a broad consensus that "something" is wrong in many modern workplaces. A poor "quality of working life" has been blamed for low motivation and productivity, absenteeism, a harsh industrial relations climate and many other problems. At the same time, a host of solutions have been proposed: industrial democracy, new forms of work organisation, group production methods, quality circles, etc.

In recent years, these proposals for improved quality of working life have led to new scientific research, the setting up of new institutions and new bargaining efforts. Very recently, certain technological developments have raised new questions and led to new actions. Before exploring these points, it may be helpful to clarify the concept of "quality of working life".

The concept of quality of working life

Modern ideas about the quality of working life have their roots in a number of theoretical developments and empirical discoveries stretching back over half a century. One early set of studies has been particularly influential. It related to women assembling telephone equipment at the Hawthorne plant of the Western Electric Company in the United States in the 1920s. In an attempt to increase productivity, improvements were made in such conditions as lighting, the length of rest breaks and the length of the working day. Indeed, productivity increased considerably. But the productivity increases remained even when the women returned to their original workplaces with the poor work environment, presumably because they interpreted the changes as evidence of management's interest and good will. The experiment demonstrated that the "human factor" was probably more important than the physical and economic conditions under which work was carried out. The Hawthorne studies and a host of subsequent research formed the basis for what has come to be known as the "human relations school of management". Two ideas are central to the work of this school: the key role of social relations among workers in determining work norms and productivity ("group dynamics"); and a view of management emphasising leadership qualities and communication with the workers. Another important research finding associated with the human relations school is the power of participative decision-making to generate motivation and commitment on the part of the workers. A "democratic leadership style" was therefore seen as superior to the "autocratic" styles observed among many managers.[5]

A second important development that has greatly influenced ideas about the quality of working life was the coalmining studies carried out by researchers from the Tavistock Institute,

London, in the early 1950s. These studies examined the impact of a technological change – the long-wall mining method – on the organisation of work. It was discovered that the new method broke up the closely knit and relatively autonomous small groups which had worked together using the previous technology. As a result, morale and productivity dropped. The researchers then tried to recreate the same kind of closely knit groups by looking carefully at the organisational implications of improvements in the new technology. This proved to be a considerable success, with the result that both productivity and morale shot up. The experiment led to other investigations about the possibilities for "organisational choice", and ultimately to a school of theory and practice usually referred to as "socio-technical systems".[6]

These two developments are concerned primarily with the contributions of psychologists and other social scientists to productivity and organisational effectiveness and to the improvement of the psychological conditions in workplaces. A third equally critical development is the link between the socio-technical systems approach and the Scandinavian conceptions of industrial democracy. The theoretical and practical implications of this development are considerable. Research on work organisation in enterprises began to involve trade unions and to take into account their concerns. At the same time, programmes began to expand into the entire industrial relations arena with the result that institutional development, collective bargaining and even legislation became the concerns of practitioners who previously had restricted their interest to the level of the enterprise. Moreover, some ideas from other fields – for example, the working environment – led a broadening of concerns beyond work organisation and socio-technical systems. A new, broader term was therefore needed. "Quality of working life" began to be used in the early 1970s. By the middle of the decade, it had taken the place of "humanisation of work" – its major competitor – and became the dominant generic term for a loosely connected set of concerns in areas such as work organisation, working conditions, the working environment and shop-floor participation.[7, 8]

There is no single commonly accepted definition of the term "quality of working life". But there are a number of characteristics that are found in all or almost all approaches related to this concept. They are the following:

(a) a participative approach to the introduction of improvements. In a way, this does not define the quality of work concept because each enterprise, group of workers or individual can use a definition that expresses its or his own priorities. However, the process of participation is almost always considered to be desirable in itself. Thus one major result of most quality of working life programmes is that they promote greater participation and consequently greater responsibility and involvement of the workers concerning decisions directly affecting their own work;

(b) an attempt to take into account simultaneously both technical and organisational considerations. In other words, one tries to design jobs that are optimal from both a technical and a human point of view, rather than to make them fit in with pre-existing equipment and operating procedures. Other elements of this characteristic are an emphasis on both organisational effectiveness and human needs, and a belief that in at least some circumstances both employers and workers can benefit;

(c) an emphasis on making the content itself of work desirable instead of just the surrounding conditions or the terms of employment. Ideas like co-operation, feedback, completion of a significant task, opportunities for learning and self-expression, use of multiple skills, self-management, etc., are frequently at the heart of quality of working life experiments, projects or programmes.

These characteristics of the quality of working life approach find their concrete expression in the application of a number of techniques, such as job rotation, job enrichment, semi-autonomous work groups or quality circles. At times, an approach to work improvement with a different history and somewhat different methods – prominent examples are ergonomics and organisation development – uses some of these same techniques or lends its own techniques to the quality of working life. Thus most work improvement practitioners, whatever their dominant speciality, read about and use the tested techniques of others.

Institutions dealing with quality of working life

In the early 1970s, some countries started to create specialised institutions, large-scale research programmes and even in a few cases legislation. This institutionalisation of the quality of working life approach was based on a number of earlier developments. First, pioneering research and enterprise-level experiences had led to a consensus of opinion that much was already known about improving the quality of working life and that it was time to promote the rapid diffusion of existing knowledge and experience. In 1974 the Swedish Employers' Confederation, for example, was able to report on the results from 500 shop-floor projects undertaken during the previous decade.[9] A second reason for the move toward institutionalisation was the growing conviction, especially in Scandinavia, that worker representation at high levels was insufficient for achieving industrial democracy. As early as 1964 a report of a co-operation project between Norwegian employers' and workers' organisations concluded that "on the whole worker representation at the top level cannot be regarded as an effective means of achieving industrial democracy".[10] The movement in favour of worker participation and industrial democracy thus began to push for improvements at the shop-floor level.

Interest in the quality of working life (QWL) arrived after a long period of prosperity and rapid economic growth. There was considerable speculation that QWL was a fad or luxury that would disappear should economic difficulties appear and dominate the industrial relations scene. In the late 1970s and early 1980s, however, the predicted collapse did not take place, though there were certainly some setbacks. In some cases, the resilience of QWL concepts and interests can be attributed to the continuing relevance of the reasons for their emergence. More important in many cases, however, was the application of QWL methods in the rapidly expanding field of "information technologies" (see also Chapter 7 of Volume 1). The resources that poured into technology promotion provided a welcome source of funds and a strong new rationale for the process of institutionalisation which had already started.

A whole range of institutions are now concerned with quality of working life.[11] In some cases, entirely new institutions have been created while in others existing institutions have partly or wholly changed their approaches or their focus of concern.

Public institutions

A few countries have established a single institution with a central role in public policy and action concerning the quality of working life. In some countries, this "institution" is in fact a unit or department within the government, but more commonly it is semi-independent and has a tripartite board of directors. Countries with such central institutions include Belgium (Institut pour l'amélioration des conditions de travail – Institute for the Improvement of Working Conditions), Canada (QWL Unit, Labour Canada), France (Agence nationale pour l'amélioration des conditions de travail – National Agency for the Improvement of Working Conditions), the Federal Republic of Germany (Bundeszentrum Humanisierung des Arbeitslebens – Federal Centre for the Humanisation of Working Life), the Netherlands

(Commissie voor Ontwikkelingsproblematiek van Bedrijven – Committee on Development Issues of Enterprises, Social and Economic Council), Sweden (Arbetslivscentrum – Centre for Working Life), and the United Kingdom (Work Research Unit, Department of Employment).

We shall describe one such institution in detail for purposes of illustration. The French National Agency for the Improvement of Working Conditions (ANACT) [12] was established by an Act of 1973 and has a tripartite governing body composed of representatives of employers, of the most representative national trade union confederations and of various government departments, in addition to a number of independent experts. The main activities of the agency include the collection, analysis and dissemination of information; the encouragement and the execution of research; the organisation of model programmes or pilot projects; and the promotion of training activities.

In a few countries, institutions for promoting the quality of working life have been established that have less than national scope. For example, in the United States there are at least 25 such institutions, which are often mainly engaged in consultancy work. In addition, a number of institutions are national in scope but do not have a legal mandate as a central co-ordinating body.

Funding programmes

Several countries have established a public agency that funds research and practical projects to improve the quality of working life. Such agencies often have considerable funds at their disposal, because the enterprise-level costs of the projects they sponsor are often high and because their mandate often includes extensive work on occupational safety and health. Perhaps the best-known funding programme is the "action programme" on humanisation of work set up by the Federal Ministry of Labour and Social Affairs and the Federal Ministry of Research and Technology in the Federal Republic of Germany. Its budget was DM13 million in 1974, its first year, and DM134 million in 1981. Other funds include the Swedish Work Environment Fund, the Fund for the Improvement of Working Conditions (Fonds pour l'amélioration des conditions de travail) in France, and the Fund for the Humanisation of Working Conditions (Fonds d'humanisation des conditions de travail) in Belgium.

Research institutions and university departments

This is by far the largest category of the institutions. The size of these institutions and the degree to which quality of working life is a major concern for them vary widely. They have sometimes played an important role in the development of the ideas and practices now called quality of working life, as is the case with the Tavistock Institute in London and the Work Research Institute in Oslo. While most of these are non-profit-making organisations, many also offer consultancy services. In some cases the research staff independently undertake consultancy work in addition to their work for the institution.

Productivity and management centres and consultancy groups

This is also a relatively large category of institutions and appears to be the most rapidly expanding group. In most cases, the quality of working life is only one of many concerns. There are, however, some exceptions. For example, the national productivity centres in both Belgium and the Netherlands have been entirely converted into quality of working life institutes.

Employer- and union-sponsored institutions

It is not surprising that institutions sponsored by employers' organisations and trade unions have devoted increased attention to quality of working life issues since in many countries these issues are

185

closely connected with collective bargaining. In Norway and Sweden, organisations sponsored by both the employers' organisations and trade unions were in existence for a time. However, this category of institutions is usually not primarily devoted to the quality of working life. They provide services to their sponsoring organisations in the form of research, policy development, information exchange and consultancy services. In some cases the positions they take, in contrast, for example, to institutions with tripartite boards of directors, are quite polarised. It is thus not clear whether they are primarily interested in promoting the quality of working life or in defending the interests of particular groups.

International institutions

A number of international institutions have an ongoing mandate for the quality of working life or have recently become concerned with this field. In a few cases new international institutions have been set up, such as the European Foundation for the Improvement of Living and Working Conditions, established by the EEC in 1975, with its headquarters in Dublin.

The work of the ILO in this field can be said to have begun with measures to limit excessive working hours in 1919: it was expanded and reinforced by the launching of the International Programme for the Improvement of Working Conditions and Environment (PIACT) in 1976.[13] Today work consists mainly of preparing and revising relevant international labour standards; providing technical assistance to member States; organising tripartite meetings; conducting action-oriented studies and research; and acting as a clearing-house for information on conditions of work.

Legislative frameworks

While an improvement of traditional working conditions has depended heavily on labour legislation, the use of legislation to improve the quality of working life is relatively rare and often controversial. Two examples, based on somewhat different approaches, will serve to illustrate some of the advantages and weaknesses of a legislative approach. The Norwegian Workers' Protection and Working Environment Act, which came into force in 1977, contains a special section on job design and work organisation. The Act states that jobs should be so designed as to give employees a reasonable degree of freedom and reasonable opportunities for developing and maintaining their skills and competence. The purpose of the Act is not directly to require that everyone should have meaningful work. Instead, it is based on the idea that participation at the plant and shop-floor level can improve the quality of jobs. Through its various provisions, the Act promotes mechanisms at the enterprise level through which employees can play an active role in designing their work and in developing their skills. In turn, it is expected that greater worker involvement will lead to improvements not only in job content but in all aspects of the working environment. Thus the Act is part of a strategy for improvement in which legislation lays the groundwork for change but does not attempt directly to specify the changes themselves. Consistent with this strategy, the Norwegian Government supports various institutional and research activities to help local enterprise-level action.[14]

A second example[15] is the 1972 Works Constitution Act in the Federal Republic of Germany. This Act contains two important provisions on job design and work organisation. First, under section 90 of the Act, the employer has to inform the works council in advance of any plans concerning the construction, alteration or extension of manufacturing, office or other facilities, or changes in technology, the work process or jobs. Sections 90 and 91 of the Act require that job design, tasks and the working environment take due account of accepted scientific principles underlying a humane approach to work.

The legislative approach to improving the quality of working life is associated in both

Norway and the Federal Republic of Germany with particularly broad definitions of the improvements being sought. In Norway, the conception of the "working environment" places considerable emphasis on occupational safety and health, and it is assumed that co-determination and industrial democracy are intimately related both to the working environment and to work organisation. In the Federal Republic of Germany, the "humanisation of work" covers occupational safety and health, ergonomics, workplace design and the working environment, in addition to work organisation questions. Here, too, the idea of co-determination is seen to be closely related to all these subjects. Such modern legislation therefore differs from earlier approaches in that it covers the entire field of working conditions and environment as well as many aspects of industrial relations.

Enterprise-level quality of working life projects: Goals, techniques and results

Interest in the quality of working life has always been based on the success of action at the enterprise level. Broader concerns at the national level have drawn from the success of practical, narrowly defined interventions at shop-floor level. The early experiments have gradually become experiences and a mass of case-study information is now available about what was done and what resulted.

While literally thousands of articles and books have been written about quality of working life experiments, a relatively small number of highly publicised programmes in particular enterprises have been especially influential. For example, while over 1,000 projects were reported in Sweden by 1975, most of the publicity and interest have been focused on the Saab (see box 12.1) and Volvo

motor-car firms. Even within these two firms, the experiences at Volvo's Kalmar plant and Saab's Södertälje plant are by far the best known. In these plants, it was possible to design assembly work so that the workers could be organised in groups and build entirely a major component of the car, such as an engine, co-operatively and at their own pace. Automobile assembly-line work has continued to be an important area for quality of working life projects. Well-documented experiences at Volkswagen, Fiat, General Motors' Tarrytown plant, etc., were followed by other manufacturers. In fact, many of them are engaged in at least some experimentation. Early and extensively publicised projects at Philips and Olivetti have also had widespread influence on the assembly of electrical goods. The same holds true for electrical appliances. Projects at Siemens and Bosch, for example, have explored the potential for longer work cycles and enriched jobs. There were also early demonstrations that in plants using process technologies the problems of controlling complex continuous operating systems could be effectively dealt with by work groups: for example, fertiliser at Norsk Hydro, paper pulp at Hunsfoss, petrochemicals at Imperial Chemical Industries (ICI), or even pet foods at the Gaines Pet Foods Topeka plant. Other well-known names include Skandia Insurance (office work), Rushton mines (coal), Harmon industries (automobile parts) and Alcan (aluminium). It is of course impossible to list all influential cases, which vary by country, industry, goals and techniques used, but this short list of prominent projects should help to evoke the kinds of enterprise-level experience which are described below in terms of goals, techniques and economic and human results.

Goals

The goals of quality of working life projects have almost always been both economic and social. The collaboration required for carrying out these projects usually takes place only if employers and workers accept both sets of goals. In spite of this mutual acceptance, the economic and social

12.1

Engine production in the Saab-Scania Factory

A shop for the assembly of engines (at Saab-Scania), put into operation in 1972, was the first large-scale example in the automobile industry where the traditional line production was replaced by several parallel subsystems. The arrangement has worked well, and this basic idea has inspired many others within the European motor-car industry and in other fields. The assembly of the engine, which requires approximately 30 minutes, is done by small groups working in parallel loops (see figure A). There are seven such loops, of which five are regularly used. The sixth is used for training purposes, and the seventh can be put into operation when production capacity has to be increased.

In this system, the so-called parallel grouping has been used to good advantage. The groups can work at different speeds without upsetting the overall flow. The normal manning level is three operators per loop, but the work can proceed even if two of the three are absent. At times when considerable capacity increases are needed, up to six operators can be assigned to each loop. Moreover, the number of loops in operation can easily be varied.

Let us look at another example of parallel flows from the motor-car industry. This is the Saab-Scania body factory at Trollhättan in Sweden where, in order to achieve advantages similar to those mentioned above, an inter-related production system with numerous work stations in a chain has been replaced by a series of parallel work groups, each of which carries out the entire sequence of tasks

on the body. The work consists primarily in welding and grinding. The introduction of the new system means that all the tasks needed to complete the work on already assembled bodies are performed at each of about 20 stations. At each station there are two workers who work together. It takes 45 to 60 minutes for them to finish the job, depending on the model. In the old arrangement, incorporating a fixed-speed assembly line, the task cycles were three minutes per working station.

As regards work organisation, the parallel stations have been organised in production teams or production groups. Each group consists of seven ordinary group members, of whom six work at one of the three stations (see figure B). The seventh member is the contact man for the group and handles indirect jobs integrated in the group's total responsibility – for example, quality control. This role rotates among the members on a weekly basis. Figure B also shows that the bodies pass a quality control point after leaving the area of the group. If necessary, the bodies can be returned for adjustment to the particular group responsible for the fault.

In this project, the following advantages have been achieved with the help of parallel grouping:

– jobs with natural borders have been created; one stage in the manufacture of bodies is begun and completed at a single work station;

Figure A   Engine assembly – three of the seven loops at the Saab-Scania plant

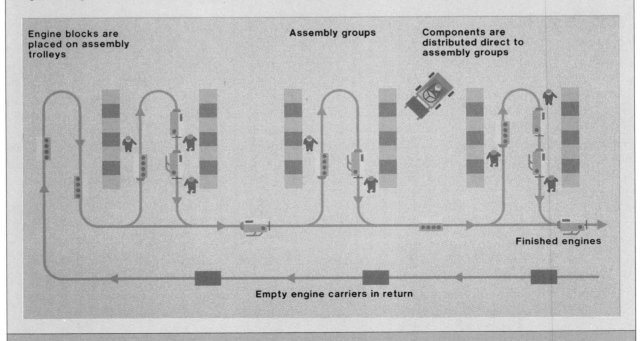

Engine blocks are placed on assembly trolleys

Assembly groups

Components are distributed direct to assembly groups

Finished engines

Empty engine carriers in return

12.1 (continued)

– production groups have been formed with complete responsibility for production, including the quality of their own work, plus auxiliary tasks such as materials requisitions, maintenance of their own equipment, etc.

Capital investment costs for the changeover – about 10 million crowns (US$2 million) – were amortised in less than three years. The greatest advantages of the new system from the industrial engineering and financial viewpoints have been:

– greater production reliability;

– more efficient use of manpower, due to the elimination of bottlenecks that sometimes occur in traditional line assemblies if the output of the different work stations is not synchronised;

– a reduction of costs for adjustment and quality control of about 20 per cent;

– the capacity of the system to absorb fluctuations in production targets which is difficult to accomplish in a line assembly.

Source: R. Lindholm and S. Flykt: "The design of production systems: New thinking and new lines of development", in G. Kanawaty (ed.): *Managing and developing new forms of work organisation* (Geneva, ILO, 2nd (revised) ed., 1981).

Figure B   Three of the parallel stations

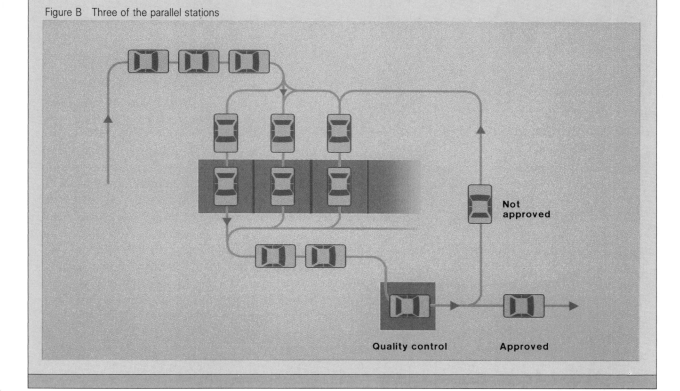

189

goals of quality of working life projects have often been stated separately.

Typical of the economic results that are sought in quality of working life projects are an increase in total production or productivity; better product quality and reduced waste; reduced absenteeism and labour turnover; greater operational flexibility; and reduced costs of supervision. Often a project will be started because of an overriding economic problem such as excessive absenteeism or declining product quality. In other cases, the goal may be merely to facilitate the introduction of a new technology that is seen as necessary or inevitable.

Together with the economic goals, there are two problems – related to the protection of workers' interests – that have also received high priority. First, labour will generally not participate in quality of working life projects unless it can share in the economic benefits. In fact, this is one of the main reasons why employees are interested in participating. A second and much more delicate problem is the use of the quality of working life label for activities intended to weaken the need for trade union representation.

Typical of the social benefits expected in quality of working life projects are the "psychological job demands" formulated in Norway in the 1960s:[10]

(a) variation and meaning in the job;

(b) continuous learning on the job;

(c) participation in decision-making;

(d) mutual help and support from fellow workers;

(e) meaningful relation between the job and social life outside; and

(f) a desirable future in the job – not only through promotion.

Most of the other sets of social goals that have subsequently been developed contain similar items. One additional point that has become particularly important in recent years is the problem of excessive work intensity or occupational stress on the job.[16] The increased stress for manual workers is often the result of simply speeding up an assembly line or assigning larger production quotas; however, this is usually not justified, even bearing in mind the legitimate economic goals of the enterprise.

Techniques

There is an essential distinction between the form and the content of techniques for the improvement of quality of working life. In other words, there is a distinction between, on the one hand, the methods used to develop improvements and to ensure their general acceptability and, on the other, the actual changes in tasks, working methods, organisational patterns and workplaces.

This section lists a number of improvements that have been introduced in various quality of working life projects and discusses the various means whereby these improvements have been identified and produced.[17]

Reducing the operator's dependence on the machine

It is particularly stressful and demotivating for a worker when his pace of work is determined by a machine or assembly line. Not only does the worker have to repeat the same tasks over and over; he is unable to adjust the pace of his work to temporary fatigue or to personal daily rhythms of activity.

Possible improvements include the use of buffer stocks between operations or providing a means for workers to personally control the speeds at which machines operate or lines move. Other improvements at the level of the machine can be made to reduce the mental and physical loads associated with full-time machine operation. The increasing number of office workers whose jobs are linked to office machines with video display units (screens) also tend to find their work stressful, especially when they have a full-time, monotonous job in a word-processing or key-punch centre. In some cases this has led to agreements specifying a maximum number of hours at the terminal or increased rest breaks.

Job rotation

One simple technique for increasing the amount of variety at work is to exchange workers among jobs. Where the tasks involved are simple, there are few training costs and no changes need to be made in the equipment and work processes. However, the substitution of one boring task for another has few long-term benefits.

Job enrichment

A much larger number of the social goals listed above can be accomplished if new and qualitatively different tasks and activities are added to an individual's job. For example, many inspection tasks – whether of raw materials or finished products – can be incorporated into jobs instead of being left to a separate group of inspectors. In some situations, this may mean that the worker can repair defective items after finding a problem through inspection. Another possibility is to include in the worker's job the task of setting up, adjusting and even maintaining or repairing the machines he uses at work. Some variety during the working day can be provided by making the worker responsible for maintaining an adequate stock of parts or equipment. Even if none of these things can be done, a worker can be given the possibility of completing a task that requires a longer time and greater skill variety.

Perhaps the most important aspect that can "enrich" a worker's job is responsibilities that go beyond mere lists of activities to be carried out. These responsibilities may include scheduling, safety, cleanliness of work area, reporting, communicating with other workers, etc. Particularly in offices and the services sector, workers may be given the opportunity to set priorities, plan their work and choose their work methods.

Work groups

The enriching of individual jobs has two important limitations. First, it fails to take advantage of the desire of people to work together and the motivational potential of collaborative work. Second, the limitations of the individual – in skills, training, physical capacity, etc. – may be such that he cannot effectively carry out on his own the entire set of activities required. In co-operative work, the weaknesses of one individual can be compensated by the strengths of another. Moreover, groups can make internal adjustments to compensate for differing preferences, temporary problems, variations in the nature of the work, absences, etc. Groups can therefore take on larger and more meaningful responsibilities, including some supervisory responsibilities. On the other hand, the technical and organisational changes that are necessary to facilitate group work are usually more extensive, more expensive and more dif-

ficult. For these reasons, the design and operation of work units involving semi-autonomous groups have excited great theoretical interest, but applications are considerably less common than for the simpler methods of work improvement. Most of the landmark quality of working life projects mentioned earlier in this chapter involve the use of such groups.

In industry, the adoption of group work has often accompanied the design of an entirely new plant or production unit, so that it has become associated with the development of "new factories".[18] In the well-known case of the Volvo assembly plant at Kalmar, for example, the working arrangements required a special modular hexagonal floor plan, innovative equipment to facilitate assembly transport, a computerised scheduling system and other innovations. On the other hand, in office work the main changes are not in equipment but in organisational arrangements and procedures. There are greater variations in the ways decentralisation and delegation of authority can be handled and in the forms of co-operation within groups. For these reasons, organisational change in offices is often more ad hoc and gradual than in manufacturing, and terms like "job enrichment" or "semi-autonomous work group" may not have exactly the same meaning.[19]

Other techniques

A number of techniques have at least occasionally been labelled "quality of working life" though their origins are sometimes quite different. For example, the introduction of a Scanlon plan (a company-wide bonus system with a particularly extensive suggestion scheme) is given as one example of a quality of working life project in the United States.[20] Another example of an innovation commonly called quality of working life is the use of quality circles. As originally introduced in Japan, quality circles are also essentially a suggestion scheme. Their purpose was primarily if not exclusively economic. Their influence on the content of work was limited, because the suggestions that were accepted usually concerned only product quality. However, recent applications of quality circles outside Japan have sometimes gone further because new participative mechanisms were set up and were used to solve problems that go beyond group-level quality control. Thus a technique that was initially not included in the quality of working life projects has come to be seen as one of the possible techniques in this field. The same evolution is typical of a number of techniques in the fields of personnel management and organisational development. An entirely different form of quality of working life technique goes beyond shop-floor or enterprise-level concerns and focuses on action at the level of an entire community. Perhaps the best-known case of this sort is that of Jamestown, New York,[21] in which an area committee was successful in promoting economic expansion by encouraging worker participation and quality of working life projects in numerous enterprises. Of course, at this level the economic and social issues are somewhat different. In particular, community-level initiatives have often been directed at increasing productivity in order to prevent the closing down of poorly performing enterprises or to attract new industry.

Techniques used in the centrally planned economies

In the centrally planned economies, both the nature of labour problems and the institutions that deal with them differ somewhat from those found in industrialised market economy countries. None the less, several of the techniques mentioned above, such as job enlargement, job enrichment and job rotation, are commonly applied in centrally planned economies as well. There are, however, also a certain number of techniques and developments that are different enough to warrant a brief description.[22] The most significant new development in the 1970s was the widespread introduction of a group method of organisation usually called work brigades. These brigades tend to be relatively large, having as many as 50 to 60 or even in exceptional cases 100 members. They include workers with different occupations and

levels of skill, as opposed to the usual case with semi-autonomous work groups. The brigade elects a team leader, or brigadier, but there is often a foreman as well. In terms of human goals, the brigades aim at greater participation, development of multiple skills, greater co-operation among workers and the reduction of monotonous work (frequently achieved by using techniques very similar to job enrichment). In terms of economic goals, there are reports of greater operational flexibility, higher work quality and 10 to 15 per cent productivity improvements. Centralised methods for the introduction of brigades have meant that in the USSR, for example, 48.6 per cent of the total industrial workforce were members of these work groups by 1980.

A very different approach is that of social development planning. This widespread and usually obligatory practice, which began in the 1960s, calls for the development of enterprise-level plans on the social structure of the enterprise; improvement of working conditions and protection of the health of workers; development of welfare facilities and improvements in living conditions of workers; and individual and group socialist education. The plans are developed in collaboration with management and party and workers' organisations. An interesting characteristic is the frequent use of sociological studies on organisation, psychological climate and workers' attitudes.

A final example is the use of work organisation standards and models of work organisation. Standards have been developed for a variety of commonly found workplaces and work stations. They provide guidance and requirements on such topics as equipment and physical layout of work stations; workers' qualifications and responsibilities; operating procedures; performance and quality standards; and safety and health. Work organisation models are also very commonly used. In the USSR, for example, 3,500 models have been developed and introduced at 6 million work stations. They often provide for group or brigade work methods, changes in management systems, changes in payment systems, upgrading of workers' skills and related training, and improved working conditions. The introduction of participation is always emphasised.

Economic results

As noted in the discussion of the definition of quality of working life, most projects in this field have both economic and human objectives. Even when the objectives have seemed to be essentially social, there are usually provisions specifying that there should be no economic losses. The measurement of possible economic benefits or losses, however, poses numerous problems. For example, quality of working life projects are often introduced at the same time as major technological changes, so that it may be difficult to attribute costs or benefits solely to the project. Even when there are no technological changes, such methodological requirements as control groups are usually not present, casting in doubt the validity of possible conclusions. Perhaps most restrictive of all is the problem that many enterprises do not wish to release precise economic information to potential competitors.

In spite of all these difficulties, a significant amount of information is available on the economic results of quality of working life projects.[23] In the following discussion of this information, it is assumed that the changes brought about by the quality of working life projects are fairly comprehensive.

The starting up of any project in an enterprise entails costs, and quality of working life projects are no exception. One immediately identifiable cost is any investment that may be required in plant, machinery and stocks. For example, the use of buffer stocks to break the direct link between man and machine requires more working space, changes in machines and equipment and a larger inventory. For more extensive projects, such as the introduction of semi-autonomous groups, the additional cost for plant and equipment may range from an additional 10 per cent to as much as 30 per cent. If the improvements are made after the plant is already built and the equipment installed, the costs may be even higher. Additional personnel costs are also likely to occur. The time spent by employees on designing new work systems is a cost, as is the time required to train them for any new tasks or for the multi-skilling arrangements that are common in group work. When a new work system starts to operate, productivity may be expected to dip, because the employees have to get used to the new system. If tasks are upgraded, wage costs may go up as well. There are many reports of increases of up to about 10 per cent, some of increases of up to 20 per cent and a few reports of even higher increases. There may also be higher productivity-linked bonus payments. Finally, the consultants who help with setting up many quality of working life projects also need to be paid.

In spite of the many costs associated with quality of working life projects and in spite of some definite failures, nearly all large-scale reviews indicate that most are, on balance, economic successes. Some of these benefits tend to counterbalance directly the costs identified above. For example, the higher cost of machinery, floor space and stocks may be outweighed by substantial increases in the actual operating time of machines and/or in the total production associated with machine operation. In addition to direct increases in production, costs associated with output of poor quality or waste of raw materials are often reduced. In addition, machines may be better maintained, and thus have a longer life. Corresponding to the possible increases in personnel costs, there may also be significant cost reductions. A reduction in absenteeism, for example, reduces the costs of keeping replacement workers on hand and of possible disruptions in production. Reductions in employee turnover also have important cost effects. The costs of severance, recruitment, placement and initial training may account for a large proportion of labour costs. In many cases, quality of working life projects have reduced requirements for supervisory personnel. In the case of semi-autonomous work groups, supervision time has been reduced by as much as 75 per cent.

While all or nearly all costs of quality of working life projects are usually measurable, there are often benefits that are measured less easily. In particular, investments in giving employees multiple skills and in creating flexible production systems may enable enterprises to produce a greater variety of products, to take better account of specific customer requests, to adjust more rapidly to changing market conditions, to introduce technological improvements, or to overcome such problems as variations in the quality of raw materials. These benefits have been found to increase in technologically advanced environments and in some cases these flexible systems may even be technologically necessary. Moreover, participative approaches are generally recognised to be very successful in overcoming resistance to technological change among workers.

On the other hand, it is certainly true that a significant number of quality of working life experiments have been economic failures. In some cases, the projects were started to try to pull an enterprise out of a desperate economic situation and were unable to do so: this hardly seems a fair test of their economic viability. In other cases, the innovations were apparently poorly planned and haphazardly introduced. Still other cases created personnel or industrial relations problems that vitiated any possible benefits. One common complaint is that the changes introduced were not comprehensive enough to generate the results expected. In general, it is therefore advisable to examine carefully the possible difficulties and advantages – in terms of technology, product market, personnel and industrial relations and other factors – before asking management and labour to commit themselves to a project.

Human results

Since improvements in job satisfaction, morale, motivation and related behaviour are always among the goals of quality of working life projects – usually the most prominent goals – it is not surprising that most projects report very positive human results. However, there are great difficulties in measuring and comparing such results. Some of these difficulties may be summarised as follows:

(a) measurement is necessarily subjective (e.g. using questionnaires) or indirect (e.g. as indicated by absenteeism or turnover). The validity of methodologies used is therefore always subject to challenge and conclusions are rarely definitive;

(b) attitudes towards work are determined by the individual's priorities: one worker may emphasise pay, another companionship, and yet another responsibility. Even the same individual may have different evaluations of different aspects of the same project;

(c) it is difficult to measure the strength of the reactions of different individuals. In the case of economic results, a monetary cost is always directly comparable with a monetary gain (assuming they can be measured in practice). In the case of people, however, one person's dislike of a project can only be compared with another person's positive reaction by making bold assumptions about the strength and measurability of their reactions; and

(d) psychological reactions may be quite variable over time. As the early Hawthorne experiment showed, even the fact of participating in an experiment may be sufficient to give a temporary positive reaction.

Nearly all case-studies concerning the quality of working life indicate that most of the workers directly involved in the projects prefer the new work system to the old one. Studies that have collected more detailed information, however, suggest that this overall improvement conceals a much more qualified response. Especially when accompanied by technological change, quality of working life experiments often "leave behind" a certain number of workers who find it difficult to adapt to new technologies, new work demands or the human problems of working co-operatively in groups. Usually these workers – perhaps 10 per cent in a typical project – can be transferred to jobs not affected by the project. For the remaining workers, there are usually both positive and negative effects. For example, when specialised inspection jobs are eliminated through the self-inspection of work, workers experience a gain in the variety and responsibility of their tasks but can no longer aspire to become inspectors. The increased responsibilities for groups may mean that everyone's job is more interesting, but the likelihood of being promoted to a supervisory job is thereby reduced.

While the above considerations tend to show certain limits to the possibilities for uniform improvement of all aspects of working life, it should be repeated that the vast majority of experiments are successful on balance. Many of them are in fact victims of their own success. Numerous cases are reported of limited experiments that aroused the jealousy of workers who were not involved and that in spite of their apparent success ended up being dropped or restricted to a very limited number of workers.

Quality of working life in perspective: Some current and future issues

Quality of working life and new technologies

The quality of working life and technological change have often been seen as closely linked.[24] Indeed, the socio-technical school argues that it is always necessary to consider technology in any serious attempt to improve the content of work. The past four or five years have seen heightened interest in the implications of new technologies – especially microprocessor-based technologies – for work and workers. This interest is a subset of the major national concerns about the implications of new technologies for employment, competitiveness in national trade, productivity and social change in general. (See also Chapter 7 in Volume 1.)

The ways in which microprocessor-based technologies are affecting tasks and jobs are complex and differ. For example, where the technological advance relates to isolated machines, such as automatic packaging machines, numerically controlled machines or simple robots, the tasks that are left for workers to perform tend to be fragmented, unskilled and fast-paced. More integrated types of automation are associated with different kinds of problems. In some cases, automation has been carried so far that workers are faced with simple monitoring jobs. Usually, however, the realities of production do not allow for complete automation. In these cases, the design of automated work systems requires that the tasks to be carried out by workers should be carefully integrated with those carried out by machines. Because most of the tasks carried out by workers in these systems relate to process control, planning and communications, it is particularly important to ensure that the "social side" of the design operates well. Nevertheless, many of the design procedures that have been commonly promoted as desirable for workers turn out to be adopted on grounds of efficiency, especially in advanced technological environments.

There has long been a concern that automation would "polarise" the labour force, separating it into a small group of highly skilled programmers and technicians and a larger group of unskilled or semi-skilled workers. Experience has shown that there are indeed cases in which this happens, but there are counter-examples as well. In-depth case-studies demonstrate that design decisions concerning technology and work procedures are more critical than the mere fact of introducing technology. One problem, however, is that designers do not often see the quality of working life as an important objective.

Even where there are carefully planned attempts to take into consideration the quality of working life, a number of serious problems often arise. For example, the new jobs frequently require qualitatively different skills than existing jobs. Acquired skills, crafts and trades may suddenly have their value destroyed, and older workers may find that employers prefer younger persons with less experience but more general education. Younger workers without a relatively high education may find the minimum requirements of new jobs an impossible hurdle.

In short, experience with the introduction of new technologies shows first of all that quality of working life approaches are relevant, and secondly that new technologies usually advance faster than the design of work systems to operate them. The challenges for engineers and systems designers, for management, for trade unions and for government programmes are many and extensive.

Trade union participation

The reaction of trade unions to the quality of working life has depended very much on the specific industrial relations situation in individual countries. In a few countries – Denmark, the Federal Republic of Germany, Norway and Sweden should be mentioned – the trade unions became involved early in efforts in this field. Their demands helped to shape the content of projects and programmes (and it is important to note that approaches and contents of programmes vary among these countries). They provided the political support necessary to ensure that government funding was available and that legislative changes were made. In other countries, trade union reactions were mixed: often indifferent, sometimes hostile and in a few cases positive and active. Perhaps the most negative attitudes have been found in the United States.

There are several reasons why trade unions may be hesitant about quality of working life projects:

(a) Trade unions considered that for decades they had been the leaders in improving the quality of working life through their struggle for higher wages, greater job security, improved safety and health, etc. They resented the devaluation of their past contribution and the challenge to their continuing leadership on the ground that quality of working life was "something new" or more important.

(b) Early quality of working life projects tended to be promoted using academic or otherwise unfamiliar jargon. Trade unions saw little reason to become involved in socio-techniques, organisational development, industrial democracy or other programmes that sounded academic, foreign or unrelated to day-to-day trade union concerns.

(c) The co-operative flavour of quality of working life projects seemed to go against deeply held trade union beliefs about adversarial collective bargaining or the primacy of class struggles in trade union action. There was genuine fear of co-optation.

(d) There were some bitter experiences with unscrupulous use of the quality of working life label to promote programmes that were anti-union.

(e) Some programmes seemed to reserve financial benefits for the employer while offering "psychological benefits" to the worker.

(f) Few trade unions had the necessary expertise to co-operate effectively in quality of working life programmes, because for a long time they had considered work organisation issues as the exclusive domain of management. As a result, they could not guarantee that these programmes would be beneficial to workers and would not weaken the trade union.

Many of the above problems continue to limit the interest of trade unions in quality of working life initiatives. However, an increasing number of trade union leaders have drawn attention to the possible benefits of quality of working life projects as well as to their possible pitfalls. They recognise that trade unions should not leave full responsibility for job design process to management because quality of working life relates not merely to personal satisfaction but also to "hard" issues such as the quantity of employment, skills and training, job evaluation and pay, and the pace of work. Interest has thus often turned away from the issue of "whether to participate" towards the issue of "under what conditions to participate". Many quality of working life projects now take place under the shelter of written agreements that guarantee full participation of the trade union, an equitable share in any increase in production or reduction in costs, and the right to withdraw from the experiment.

Quality of working life: A passing fad or a central concern?

So much has been written about the quality of working life, from so many perspectives, that it can easily seem to be a dominant new development. However, this is clearly not the case if we define quality of working life in the way we did at the beginning of this chapter. For example, it has been estimated that in France only 3.2 per cent of wage earners have been directly affected by experiments related to new forms of work organisation.[25] While most experiments that have been carefully analysed have shown positive results, they have not led to a dramatic change in the way work is organised and carried out. Of course, many of the ideas may have influenced jobs in unsystematic ways which have gone unmeasured.

On balance, however, it would seem that the number of workplaces and of workers affected is very small. Whether or not technological changes will alter this situation is not yet clear; it is, however, clear that technology is having a much greater impact on work than quality of working life initiatives.

Yet the underlying concerns are clearly serious and it is certain that the quality of working life approach has something to offer. It is significant that, while the initial enthusiasm may have waned, the interest and the activity have by no means died out as they might have been expected to in a period of recession. In fact, government programmes, institutions, collective agreements and even legislative provisions have expanded in number and scope. If anything, the persistent economic difficulties and structural problems have heightened the feeling that some far-reaching changes may be needed in conceptions about work and work relationships. Low productivity, poor quality control, absenteeism, turnover and the like are preoccupations increasingly shared by unions as well as management. Worries about international competitiveness, structural adjustment and lasting unemployment have led to growing concern about such factors as dissatisfaction, alienation and stress, and to wider interest in the potential contribution of new approaches. This interest has been further stimulated by the introduction of new technology and the prospect of radical technological changes that may pose such questions still more dramatically.

---

[1] See K. I. Spenner: Temporal changes in work content", in *American Sociological Review* (Albany), Dec. 1979, pp. 968-975.

[2] J. S. Brown: "How many workers enjoy discretion on the job?", in *Industrial Relations* (Berkeley), May 1975, pp. 196-202.

[3] See ILO: *Growth, structural change and manpower policy: The challenge of the 1980s*, Report I, Third European Regional Conference, Geneva, October 1979, pp. 22-24. In particular, it is noted that: "In the Federal Republic of Germany, for instance, it is expected that each year from 1977 to 1982/83 about 40,000 to 60,000 school-leavers qualified to attend university will take the trainee positions generally sought by less qualified students. What one observes, then, is a top to bottom displacement, or bumping process, which thrusts a large number of workers at each level down into jobs below their

qualifications and expectations. In France many young people who have worked hard and made sacrifices in order to obtain a CAP (a first technical degree at the secondary level, qualifying them for a specific occupation) find themselves in only semi-skilled or unskilled jobs, where they are assigned tasks which do not use their qualifications."

[4] J. E. Thurman: "Job satisfaction: An international overview", in *International Labour Review*, Nov.-Dec. 1977, pp. 249-267.

[5] These developments can be found in any standard text. See, for example, E. H. Schein: *Organizational psychology* (Englewood Cliffs, Prentice-Hall, 3rd ed., 1980).

[6] A good recent review of the history of socio-technical ideas is E. Trist: *The evolution of socio-technical systems: A conceptual framework*

and an action research program, Occasional paper No. 2 (Toronto, Ontario Quality of Working Life Centre, 1981).

[7] A number of reviews of quality of working life are of particular interest to the international reader. See L. E. Davis and A. B. Cherns (eds.): *The quality of working life* (New York, Free Press, 1975); J. R. Hackman and J. L. Suttle (eds.): *Improving life at work: Behavioral science approaches to organizational change* (Santa Monica, Goodyear Publishing Company, 1977); A. Alioth, M. Elden, O. Ortsman and R. Van der Vlist: *Working on the quality of working life: Developments in Europe,* International Series on the Quality of Working Life, Vol. 8 (Boston, Martinus Nijhoff Publishing, 1979); ILO: *Making work more human,* Working conditions and environment, Report of the Director-General, International Labour Conference, 60th Session, 1975; ILO: *New forms of work organisation* (Geneva, 1979); ILO: *Policies and practices for the improvement of working conditions and working environment in Europe,* Report III, Third European Regional Conference, Geneva, October 1979; K. Newton, N. Leckie and B. O. Pettman: "The quality of working life", in *International Journal of Social Economics* (Bradford), Vol. 6, No. 4, 1979; Y. Delamotte and S. Takezawa: *Quality of working life in international perspective* (Geneva, ILO, 1984).

[8] Delamotte and Takezawa, ibid., present a particularly complete analysis of quality of working life, proposing both expanded and restricted definitions of the field and exploring the historical process of problem recognition, resource allocation, technology development and programme implementation.

[9] Swedish Employers' Confederation (SAF): *Job reform in Sweden: Conclusions from 500 shop floor projects* (Stockholm, 1975).

[10] P. Dundelach and N. Mortensen: "Denmark, Norway and Sweden", in ILO, *New forms of work organisation,* op. cit., Vol. 1, p. 23.

[11] L. Stoddart (ed.): *Conditions of work and quality of working life: A directory of institutions* (Geneva, ILO, 1981).

[12] ANACT: *Agence nationale pour l'amélioration des conditions de travail,* National Agency for the Improvement of Working Conditions (Montrouge, n.d.).

[13] J. de Givry: "The ILO and the quality of working life. A new international programme: PIACT", in *International Labour Review,* May-June 1978, pp. 261-271; ILO: *Evaluation of the International Programme for the Improvement of Working Conditions and Environment (PIACT),* Report VII, International Labour Conference, 70th Session, 1984.

[14] B. Gustavsen: "Improving the work environment: A choice of strategy", in *International Labour Review,* May-June 1980, pp. 271-286.

[15] W. H. Staehle: "Federal Republic of Germany", in ILO, *New forms of work organisation,* op. cit., Vol. 1, pp. 79-106.

[16] Research indicates that fast-paced but boring jobs are often as stressful as challenging ones, and that manual workers show at least as many stress symptoms as managers or office workers.

[17] The various techniques for improving quality of working life are the subject of a vast literature. See especially J. R. Hackman and M. D. Lee, Work in America Institute: "Redesigning work: A strategy for change", in *Studies in Productivity: Highlights of the Literature,* 9, 1979; J. R. Hackman and G. R. Oldham: *Work redesign* (Reading, Mass., Addison-Wesley Publishing Company, 1980); G. Kanawaty (ed.): *Managing and developing new forms of work organisation* (Geneva, ILO, 2nd (revised) ed., 1981); G. I. Susman: *Autonomy at work: A sociotechnical analysis of participative management* (New York, Praeger Publishers, 1976), in addition to the references in note 7 above.

[18] S. Agurén and J. Edgren: *New factories: Job design through factory planning in Sweden* (Stockholm, SAF, 1980).

[19] A. Hepworth and M. Osbaldeston: *They way we work: A European study of changing practice in office job design* (Farnborough, Saxon House, 1979). See also D. Birchall and H. Valerie: *Tomorrow's office today: Managing technological change* (London, Business Books, 1981).

[20] P. S. Goodman and E. E. Lawler III: "United States", in ILO: *New forms of work organisation,* op. cit., Vol. 1, pp. 143-173.

[21] Jamestown Area Labor-Management Committee: *Commitment at work,* The five-year report of the Jamestown Area Labor-Management Committee (Jamestown, n.d.).

[22] Modern methods of work organisation used in the centrally planned economies are a very complex subject which has received relatively little discussion outside the countries concerned. Space permits only a very brief sketch in this chapter. Some basic references include H. Hanspach and A. Schäfer: "German Democratic Republic", in ILO, *New forms of work organisation,* op. cit., Vol. 2, pp. 3-23; A. S. Dovba et al.: "USSR", ibid., pp. 79-111; ILO, *Policies and practices . . .,* op. cit., Ch. III; A. Prigozhin and A. E. Louzine: "Automation in USSR industry", in F. Butera and J. E. Thurman (eds.): *Automation and work design* (Geneva, ILO, 1984); L. Héthy: "Automation and work organisation: Policies and practices in countries with centrally planned economies", in *Automation, work organisation and occupational stress* (Geneva, ILO, 1984).

[23] A systematic review is provided in A. G. Hopwood: "Economic costs and benefits of new forms of work organisation", in ILO, *New forms of work organisation,* Vol. 2, op. cit., pp. 115-145.

[24] A full review of the implications of automation for the quality of working life, with emphasis on industrial work, is provided in Butera and Thurman, op. cit. For a brief review, see J. E. Thurman: "New technology and work design: Implications for worker attitudes and industrial relations", in *Changing perceptions of work in industrialised countries: Their effect on and implications for industrial relations,* Working paper of an International Symposium (Vienna, April 1982) (Geneva, International Institute for Labour Studies, 1983). Further information is also provided in the chapter in this volume on new technologies.

[25] European Foundation for the Improvement of Living and Working Conditions: *New forms of work organisation in the European Community - France* (Dublin, n.d.).

Part 5

Women at work

Introduction

The increasing number of women working outside the household in paid employment has brought about a qualitative change in their political, legal, economic and social status. This is one of the most remarkable features of this century, the precise economic and social causes of which have not yet been closely analysed. The vast human resource potential of women, their actual and "hidden" economic contribution and the changing social perceptions of women's work are in the process of transforming the world of work for both men and women. It is increasingly recognised that a more rational use of the potential of women could accelerate the pace of economic and social progress and thereby contribute to the overall welfare of humankind. But owing to various economic and social factors, such as discrimination against women, this potential remains underutilised in most countries of the world.

The ILO established the principle of non-discrimination in the Declaration of Philadelphia, adopted in 1944 and incorporated in its Constitution. The Declaration affirms that "all human beings, irrespective of race, creed or sex, have the right to pursue both their material well-being and their spiritual development in conditions of freedom and dignity, of economic security and equal opportunity". In 1958 the International Labour Conference, recognising the need for comprehensive instruments to protect workers against inequalities based on race, colour, sex, religion, political opinion, national extraction or social origin, adopted the Discrimination (Employment and Occupation) Convention (No. 111) and Recommendation (No. 111). The Convention (ratified by 107 member States, see Annex 3) covers all forms of discrimination, exclusion or preference that have "the effect of nullifying or impairing equality of opportunity and treatment", whether they are the result of legislation or of existing policies and practices.

The 1970s saw new developments in policy thinking and legislation on discrimination. Convention No. 111 refers to the elimination of discrimination on grounds of sex, but a number of declarations and standards go further and refer explicitly to marital status. This idea was expressed in, for example, the ILO Declaration on equality of opportunity and treatment for women workers and Plan of Action with a view to promoting equality of opportunity and treatment for women workers, both of 1975; the United Nations Convention on the Elimination of All Forms of Discrimination against Women of 1979; the decisions and resolutions of the World Conference on International Women's Year (Mexico City, 1975); and the World Conference of the United Nations Decade for Women: Equality, Development and Peace (Copenhagen, 1980).

The ILO's most recent contributions were the Workers with Family Responsibilities Convention (No. 156) and Recommendation (No. 165) of 1981. According to the Convention, each ILO member State "shall make it an aim of national policy to enable persons with family responsibilities who are engaged or wish to engage in employment to exercise their right to do so without being subject to discrimination and, to the extent possible, without conflict between their employment and family responsibilities". These instruments apply to men and women workers with responsibilities in relation to their dependent children and to other members of their immediate family who clearly need their care or support.

Discrimination against women, where it exists, has its roots in a variety of technological, economic, social and political developments. The rapid technological and scientific progress that is imperceptibly changing the world of work is closely linked to the changing division of labour between and within nations, and within households. In other words, technological progress produces changes at both the macro-economic and the micro-economic level. While there has been some progress towards eliminating discrimination in countries that have taken steps to generate employment for women, adopted new legislation on equality and introduced special measures to eliminate discrimination between men and

women at work and the workplace, women in many countries encounter obstacles that are specific to their status as workers. Though these problems have many facets, at their core lie unequal access to employment, education and training, concentration in certain occupations and unequal pay. Moreover, women are hardly represented in planning and policy institutions or in international, national and local bodies where decisions about work and life are made.

It is the aim of Part V to examine the relationship between these various developments and discrimination against women. In Chapter 13 – on women in the labour force – we shall see that women's contribution to economic development is often grossly underestimated. Chapter 14 tries to document to what extent working women have equal employment opportunities and whether they receive equal treatment in respect of working conditions. The main issues discussed are : unemployment, education and training, occupational patterns, pay differentials, and special protective legislation.

Chapter **13**

Women in the labour force

The labour force is conventionally defined as comprising all persons who furnish the supply of labour for the production of economic goods and services. In practice, this definition raises many specific problems, especially problems involved in measuring women's work.

It is increasingly recognised that activities typically performed by women are systematically excluded from labour force and national income statistics. Social perceptions in many economies tend to disregard the work of women, and such a bias tends to influence the ways in which statistical information on women's activities is collected.[1] Methodological problems, such as the time reference period used in surveys (one day to one week, thus excluding seasonal fluctuations or intermittent employment), operational problems, such as the sex of census takers and respondents (mostly males interviewing, presumably, male heads of households), and definitional problems regarding economic activities, all contribute to an underestimation of women's activity rates in the official data of many countries.

Up to 1982, several recommendations by the United Nations and the ILO specifically linked work to a primary and remunerated occupation contributing to the national product. Although census practices vary greatly among countries, most tend to under-report the many unpaid activities of women that are nevertheless economic and contribute to household and national income. The underestimation of women's economic work is most acute in areas with a low degree of market penetration, typically the small farming subsistence sector in developing countries. This underestimation has serious consequences for women and their families, for development policies and strategies and for the value systems that form the basis of socio-economic decisions.

Detailed surveys, including empirical observation and activity and time-use charts, although limited in number and scope, help to supplement inadequate official data and provide a more accurate picture of women's economic contribution. The problem of accounting for women's work is particularly acute in two areas: unpaid family labour and household work.

Unpaid family workers are found in all economic sectors in many countries but play a particularly important role in the agricultural sector of developing countries. Rural women are not only active in primary agricultural production but are also largely responsible for small animal production and are engaged in a variety of non-farm activities, such as processing, storage and marketing of agricultural produce. In the Andean countries, for instance, which are considered to be a male farming region, national census data report a small participation of economically active women in the agricultural sector (ranging from a low of 3.4 per cent to a high of 13.8 per cent for the six countries between 1972 and 1976). However, detailed investigations in three regions of Peru and Colombia show that women are heavily involved in agricultural work, which includes not only field work but a number of related off-farm activities such as processing and marketing of agricultural and animal produce.[2]

The main difficulty of accounting adequately for unpaid family labour lies in the fact that such work is carried out in conjunction with household work and that the borderline between the two is often hard to draw. Indeed, in low-income households virtually all members (men, women and children) make significant contributions to meeting the family's basic needs.

It is the women mainly who take care of household activities, even if both men and women spend the same amount of time on economic activities.[3] In developing countries women spend much time and effort in preparing food, in carrying water over long distances and in gathering fuel for household needs. Various time-use surveys indicate that a rural woman's typical day includes some 12 to 16 hours of work, which is a serious threat to her health. In industrialised countries women generally work less but still do most of the household work, such as cooking, cleaning, shopping and taking care of children.

Domestic work remains mostly unpaid and is generally not regarded as an economic activity, although this is controversial. An ILO study has reviewed the numerous methodological problems involved in evaluating household work, from the standpoint of production, income, human investment and time use.[4] The economic nature of household activity becomes more evident when it is or can be replaced by goods and services that have an economic price. Indeed, part of the post-war growth of the services sector, particularly in the industrialised countries, can be explained by the fact that some activities traditionally carried out exclusively within the household are now also performed by the market sector.

The distinction between economic and non-economic activities, or between labour force and non-labour force activities, based on the concept of national product, gives rise to confusion and widely divergent applications. In an attempt at clarification, the Thirteenth International Conference of Labour Statisticians held by the ILO in 1982 adopted a new definition of the "economically active population", based on the United Nations system of national accounts, in which the production of economic goods and services includes all production and processing of primary products, whether for the market, for barter or for own consumption, the production of all other goods and services for the market, as well as own consumption of these goods and services by households that also produce them for the market.[5] Subsistence workers and unpaid family workers are considered to be in self-employment, but household duties are not considered to be an economic activity. The new definition of economic activity should in future substantially improve the recording of women's work.

Wide variations are observed in female labour force participation rates between countries and regions, urban and rural areas, and age groups. The most recent ILO estimates show that in 1980, out of a total of about 1,800 million workers, women accounted for over 600 million, or more than one-third. The highest female participation rates for ages 15 and over, according to these estimates, are found in the USSR (about 60 per cent) and in other European centrally planned economies (about 57 per cent), the lowest in Latin America (about 24 per cent) and North Africa (about 4 per cent). It is also interesting to note that in almost all parts of the world women's participation rates increased considerably between 1950 and 1980, with the result that in 1980 women constituted a much larger part of the labour force than in 1950. The changes between 1975 (the start of the Women's Decade) and 1980 do not show a uniform pattern. While female labour force participation rates increased in most European countries, North America and Oceania, they dropped in other continents.

The great majority of women workers live in the developing countries, and as table 13.1 shows, about two-thirds of them work in agriculture. In

Table 13.1
Composition of world labour force, by sex and main sector of activity (1970 and 1980) (in percentages)

		Agriculture		Industry		Services		Total	
		1970	1980	1970	1980	1970	1980	1970	1980
Developing countries	Female	73.6	66.3	12.5	16.3	13.9	17.4	100.0	100.0
	Male	62.8	55.7	17.7	21.6	19.5	22.7	100.0	100.0
Industrialised market economies	Female	11.4	7.7	25.4	25.8	63.2	66.5	100.0	100.0
	Male	12.0	8.5	44.6	45.9	43.4	45.6	100.0	100.0
Industrialised centrally planned economies	Female	31.7	21.5	29.6	33.1	38.6	45.4	100.0	100.0
	Male	27.7	19.4	44.2	50.3	28.1	30.3	100.0	100.0
Total [a]	Female	54.3	47.8	17.9	20.8	27.8	31.4	100.0	100.0
	Male	49.2	43.5	25.7	28.8	25.1	27.7	100.0	100.0

[a] Including 124 countries having more than 1 million inhabitants.
Source: ILO Bureau of Statistics.

the industrialised market economies, on the other hand, about two-thirds work in the services sector, one-quarter in industry and less than one-tenth in agriculture. In the industrialised centrally planned economies one-fifth of women workers are in agriculture and the remainder in industry and the services.

Between 1970 and 1980 the proportion of women working in agriculture declined all over the world, while the proportion in the services increased. This contrast was particularly marked in the industrialised centrally planned economies. The number of women working in industry doubled in the developing countries and continued to be very high in industrialised centrally planned economies, but remained almost the same in the industrialised market economies.

Developing countries

Women in rural areas

Rural women in the developing world, and particularly those who are poor, invariably work hard at a variety of tasks, with little time for leisure and little control over productive resources or even over their own income or labour. Yet they often must assume a large share of the responsibility for the survival of their families, through direct production for consumption, income earning, providing health care, etc. Women constitute a substantial part – in some countries the majority – of the agricultural labour force, including workers on plantations; they are engaged in home-based production of modern as well as traditional products, sometimes working for a contractor under the putting-out system; and many migrate from impoverished rural areas to work in the urban informal sector as traders, or in export processing zones as industrial workers.

Women in rural areas throughout the Third World are typically farmers. In sub-Saharan Africa, subsistence farming is essentially a female activity, and women are the primary labourers on small farms, where they contribute two-thirds or more of all hours of work. Food production (as well as processing and often marketing) is essentially a female responsibility – a situation that also prevails in the Caribbean.

A more complex picture emerges in Asia. In India, while overall female labour force participa-

205

tion has been falling in the face of surplus labour (see Volume 1, Chapter 1), more and more women are becoming agricultural wage labourers because of growing landlessness.[6] Between 30 and 40 per cent of the agricultural labour force is composed of women. In Bangladesh, where women are still presumed to be secluded, they are increasingly seen in the fields, and poverty forces them to come forth for other hard work, such as road construction; these activities are in addition to their long-standing, essential but largely invisible work behind compound walls in seed selection, processing, winnowing and threshing.[7] In China, the female labour force in rural areas has greatly increased over the past 25 years, as women's participation in agricultural work and in many non-farm activities has been strongly encouraged, both to increase production and to combat discriminatory practices and prejudices. A new dimension is emerging with the recent shift toward family farming and the promotion of family-based domestic sidelines.[8] In south-east Asian countries, such as Indonesia, women are very active in the rice fields, a crop which usually requires intensive farming.

In Latin America, women work more in agriculture than is commonly thought, even without counting such activities as processing done in the fields and services provided to field workers. Andean agriculture, often considered a male farming system, as noted earlier, is in fact better characterised as a family farming system.[2]

There is a large proportion of female labour in the plantation sector as well. Working as tea pluckers, as rubber tappers or as casual workers on coconut plantations, women in Malaysia and Sri Lanka, for example, constitute more than half of the labour force; but they receive lower pay than men for the same work, face extra burdens because of inadequate child-care facilities and the long distances between home and work, and often see others collecting their pay.[9] Despite a high rate of trade union membership on the part of women plantation workers, their particular needs and interests have seldom been given attention by the union leadership.

In addition to agricultural work, many women are engaged in home-based production, either full-time or in slack seasons to increase family income. In some cases such production is traditional; in others it is relatively new – particularly where traditional sources of production and income have been lost with modernisation and commercialisation; in still others it is the result of the promotion of "income-generating activities" designed to allow women to increase their cash income without disturbing their domestic responsibilities. Sometimes the result is a good income for women. In many cases, however, the returns to labour are very low. And at its worst, such home-based production definitely involves exploitation, as in the case of the lace-makers in Narsapur (see Volume 1, p. 19). Secluded women in poor households working at home rolling beedies (popular cigarettes)[10] or crocheting lace[11] for contractors under the putting-out system do not receive anywhere near the minimum wage, nor do they control their own labour, let alone the labour process or marketing. They constitute an invisible labour force, dependent on traders and intermediaries who control the work. Wages (or piece rate payments) may be very low, yet they account for a substantial proportion of the income of poor households. Data on such workers are very scanty, but the beedi industry in India alone employs between 2 and 3 million women. And this system has begun to encompass the manufacture of some modern products, such as electronics assembly units.

Access to and control over resources

Land is obviously the principal asset in rural areas: access to credit, extension services, technologies and even co-operative organisations is generally linked to land titles. Yet even where women perform the bulk of agricultural work, as in much of sub-Saharan Africa, they seldom have full title (but rather, land use rights). Where rights are collectively held, it is almost invariably the

13.1

Participation and organisation of rural women

Various initiatives in Bangladesh, India, Nepal and the Philippines, with which the ILO is associated, have stimulated through grass-roots discussions and awareness-raising workshops the women's resolve to organise themselves. Rural women have started to discuss their common problems, to voice their concerns and needs, to negotiate with government officials and employers, to undertake collective or individual employment and income-earning activities. For example, in the state of West Bengal (India) various "Gramin Mahila Sramik Unnayan Samitic", or village-level rural women workers' development organisations, have been formed through the intervention of a non-governmental organisation. The women have been quick in using their collective power to discuss with officials development issues from their point of view, such as employment and income-earning opportunities, access to land, credit facilities, health and education problems, discrimination, etc. The development of wasteland through rural women's organisations is being given particular consideration.

male head of household who participates in the peasant association. In family farming systems, women have even less access to basic assets. The provision of land rights and access to related resources (credit, technology etc.) would alter the production relations, which are now characterised by the unequal bargaining position of the women. In many societies (particularly in Asia and Latin America), the process of agricultural growth and modernisation is leading to pauperisation and increasing landlessness, thus drawing more and more women into agricultural wage labour even where overall employment opportunities for women are shrinking. In North Africa and the Middle East, a little-heralded effect of male migration to the oil-producing countries of the region is the increase of female-headed households and women's participation in agricultural labour. And in sub-Saharan Africa, while land in itself may be relatively abundant and accessible, women usually neither own nor control improved cultivable land. However, in many parts of the developing world women are beginning to organise themselves and to raise these issues within their communities and nations (see box 13.1).

Forests are another resource that is very important to women in rural areas, as a source of fuel, food, fodder and livelihood. Reduced access to forests, which may occur because of drought, deforestation or changes in land tenure or forest policy, can have a devastating effect on family welfare. But it is the women who are most dependent on this resource, and whose work and income are at stake. When fuel is not readily available, families either have fewer cooked meals or have to work harder to find fuel or have to earn cash to buy fuel and/or cooked food.

There is increasing evidence that the income of household members is not automatically pooled, and that it does matter to family welfare who earns and, particularly, who controls "household" income. For example, a case-study in India has found that increasing women's wages has a visible effect on child nutrition.[12] Therefore, increasing women's income and entitlement to or control over resources can be an important means of improving the welfare of households in rural areas.

207

Changing division of labour between men and women

While domestic work is almost universally considered to be the domain of women, great variations are found in the division of labour between men and women in non-domestic activities (and even the domestic division may eventually change). Social and economic development affects men and women in specific ways, producing significant changes in the division of labour between men and women. In many developing countries great changes have occurred in agriculture during the past three decades, which have profoundly but differently affected the work of rural men and women in various income groups. The introduction of new technologies, changes in the agrarian structure, the spread of commodity production and growing inequality in rural areas have displaced women from many traditional activities, while at the same time increasing women's workload in certain agricultural tasks.[13]

Labour mobility and the changing patterns of work and employment that accompany economic growth are often detrimental to women workers in rural areas. Modernisation has done away with many traditional income-earning opportunities, and rural development policies and programmes do not generally recognise women as producers. This is happening at a time when the incomes of poor households are dwindling, forcing women in many countries to provide for an increasing share of their family's needs. In the struggle for survival, women face great obstacles, such as their limited mobility due to family responsibilities and social and cultural restrictions.[14] In Africa growing labour displacement towards cash crops is leaving rural women increasingly on their own to produce food with no means of improving productivity. The best arable land is usually allocated to cash crops. Yet concern is growing about falling per capita food production. This should logically lead to support for Africa's food producers – the rural women. ILO research has indicated that women's productivity can be increased by using improved technologies (see box 13.2).

In green revolution areas in Asia, agricultural modernisation has increased the demand for casual labour while marginalising small tenants and dispossessing smallholders of their land. Male tasks have been more commonly mechanised than those of women, thereby decreasing male employment opportunities and income and pushing women into agricultural wage labour. Women are also seeking needed income in the informal sector or as home-based workers, or they may migrate to look for work elsewhere. Landlessness and poverty have dramatically increased the number of women working as casual labourers. Improved transport facilities and the spread of manufactured goods threaten many petty commodity trade activities undertaken by women and men without opening up new employment opportunities for women, as jobs in the modern sector are seldom available to them. Permanent or seasonal male out-migration in Asia, west and southern Africa is affecting farming practices. In Lesotho, for instance, the plight of migrant workers' families is such that the departure of able-bodied men to the mining industry in South Africa calls for additional work by women, and is hardly compensated by insecure and meagre migrant remittances.[15] Strained family bonds and reduced household income are leaving women in a very vulnerable position. In Malawi about a quarter of rural households are headed by women, and this rate is even higher among the lowest income groups. Rural development programmes and extension services have failed to reach these women, who in the absence of male workers are unable to increase agricultural productivity.[16] In some countries, such as Ghana, Malawi and the Sudan, female-headed households constitute between one-fourth and one-third of all rural households, while in other countries the proportion is estimated at between 5 and 20 per cent (about 12 in Indonesia, 17 in Mauritania and 13 in Panama, for instance).[17]

Increasing rural poverty has also precipitated female out-migration as a means of supplementing family income.[18] Export processing zones in Asia (e.g. in Malaysia, the Philippines and Singapore) have increasingly attracted a young and docile female labour force for export-oriented industries relying on a cheap but intensive labour process.[19]

Women as industrial workers

Rapid industrialisation, while expanding employment opportunities, has not fully benefited working women, since they often lose traditional sources of income without getting new jobs. This has happened for example in such newly industrialised countries as Brazil, India, Mexico and Nigeria. Various studies show that women are increasingly confined to homework (as in the textiles, clothing and tobacco industries) and in marginal service jobs in the urban informal sector where employment is casual and irregular and where incomes are very low.[20] It is also characteristic of most developing countries that mainly young unmarried women (in the 20-25 age group) obtain employment in the formal sector.[21]

13.2

Technologies for rural women

The introduction of improved technologies usually increases woman's productivity and reduces the strain, drudgery and physical injuries associated with her tasks. A recent survey[1] of rural women's production methods in three African countries (Ghana, Kenya and Sierra Leone) revealed that rural women are the main producers of processed products not only for home consumption but also for both the rural and the urban market. The technologies they use are mainly traditional ones characterised by low productivity, as well as being unsafe and unhygienic. And yet there are a number of simple improved low-cost technologies that could alleviate these problems. A handbook[2] on upgraded and improved technologies catalogues some of these technologies. The woman's decision to buy such equipment depends mainly on its price (which may be high compared with her cash income), and the benefits that she expects from it. The following table gives a few characteristics of some traditional and improved technologies, and indicates the benefits from improved technologies.

[1] E. Date-Bah, Y. Stevens and V. Ventura-Dias: *Technological change, basic needs and the condition of rural women* (Geneva, ILO, 1984).
[2] ILO: *Upgraded and improved technologies for rural women's activities in West Africa* (Geneva, 1984).

Improved technologies for rural women

Activity	Traditional technology	Improved technology	Improvements in relation to traditional technologies	Activity	Traditional technology	Improved technology	Improvements in relation to traditional technologies
Cooking	3-stone method	Improved stoves of different types: mud, ceramic, metal, ceramic-lined, insulated metal stoves, etc.	Save fuel (20 to 50% savings in fuelwood), time and labour; reduce smoke (stoves with chimneys); safer and more hygienic	Fish smoking	Stands and mud/metal ovens	Improved ovens: Altona type, Kagan oven	Save fuel and time; safer and more hyienic; greater capacity (fuel savings of up to 100%; capacities up to 10 times that of traditional ovens)
Water collection	Traditional wells: hand-drawn buckets	Wells/boreholes with hand/power-operated pumps, solar pumps	Reduce physical strain and improve water quality	Shelling (maize, ground-nuts)	By hand	Hand/pedal/engine-operated shellers	Save time and labour (outputs of up to 500 times that of traditional method)
Food processing Milling/ crushing/ grating	Mortar and pestle, stone mills	Hand/pedal/engine-operated, buhr mills, palm kernel crushers, cassava graters	Save time and labour (outputs of up to 100 times that of traditional methods); reduce strain	Grain threshing	By foot/hand	Hand/pedal/engine-operated threshers	Save time and labour (outputs up to 25 times that of traditional method); eliminate injuries
				Grain dehusking	Mortar and pestle	Hand/engine-operated dehullers (plate and roller types)	Save time and labour (outputs of up to 500 times that of traditional method); reduce physical strain
Oil pressing	Pressing by hand or foot (wet process-ing)	Hand/engine-operated: screw presses, hydraulic presses (dry processing)	Higher extraction efficiency (up to 100% more oil than traditional methods), save fuel, labour and time	Rice parboiling	200 cc drums	Solar parboiling unit	Eliminate need for fuel

209

Why do certain employers prefer to recruit young unmarried women as employees? Some studies indicate that this preference is based less on the job requirements than on social perceptions. Women are supposed to have dexterity, speed and endurance in certain assembly-line jobs in old industries such as clothing or new industries such as electronics. They are considered to be more dis- ciplined and docile than male workers, and ready to accept low wages. In some cases young girls have been dismissed when they reached the legal age at which they would be entitled to adult wages.

The fact that women are concentrated in the traditionally "female industries" and in low-skilled jobs keeps their wages low, hinders their upward mobility and makes them prone to long periods of unemployment in times of economic and technological restructuring. It is well known that in "female industries", such as textiles, clothing, electronics, food and beverages, wages are usually lower than in other industries.

What is the impact of new technologies on women's jobs? While technological progress over the years has widened women's employment opportunities in the modern sector, it has had the effect of frequently displacing them into low-skilled and low-status occupations. This trend is illustrated by the commerce, finance and services sectors where their employment at first expanded enormously but may now be affected in two ways: those who are already employed may lose their jobs or see the content of their jobs change, while those who are looking for jobs may not find one corresponding to their qualifications. This situation, combined with high rates of unemployment, may cause serious setbacks to the emancipation of women through work. It appears that even in newer industries, such as electronics, the dynamics of technological change require higher levels of technical skills, generally not accessible to women.[22] In plants located in several industrial estates and export processing zones, young, inexperienced rural women are considered to be the best choice,[23] since they are believed to be more patient and diligent and to have keener eyesight and more nimble fingers than men.

In developing countries lack of skills leads women to seek employment as domestic servants, an occupation in which they are often exploited and which offers low wages and uncertain and long hours, with no paid leave or other social benefits. Other occupations in which women find themselves are those of barmaids, hostesses and receptionists, which are outside the reach of labour regulations. Sometimes young girls under the minimum age of admission to employment work as domestic servants or entertainers under harsh conditions and often without adequate pay, food or shelter.

The number of women working in offices and commerce varies from country to country. In developing countries secretaries and teachers are still occupational categories filled by both men and women. There is, however, a trend for these occupations to become more feminised. This is true of first-grade teachers in Asia and secondary-level teachers in Africa, where the number of women occupying such posts rose from 22 to 29 per cent and from 25 to 33 per cent respectively between 1975 and 1980. Community, social and health services in many countries show a high concentration of women since welfare services are considered to be a female sphere of activity. But even in these occupations women hold jobs in the lower echelons, while the higher echelons are almost exclusively occupied by men. This is particularly true of the health sector where women are usually nurses, etc., but not hospital managers, surgeons or research technicians.

There are occupations, however, in which there is a neat division of labour between men and women. For example, it is mainly women who are engaged in the retail trade of certain African and Asian countries, while men dominate the wholesale trade and commerce.

In the public service sector women usually have reasonable opportunities to reach responsible positions, owing to the scope of labour legislation and other regulations. Although their numbers are still very small, in some countries they work in ministries of health, education and social affairs at intermediate levels and in various government departments and agencies.[24]

Industrialised market economies

In industrialised market economies labour force participation rates of women have increased over the past 20 years, even during periods of economic recession. On an average, women now account for about 40 per cent of the labour force, and a considerable proportion of them are working part-time.

The number of agricultural workers has declined substantially over the past few decades. Landless agricultural labourers and unpaid family workers – many of whom are women – experience hardships and are below the poverty line in several countries. In other countries unpaid women farmers have a working week as long as that of workers engaged in full-time jobs outside the house, say, in a factory or an office; e.g. they work between 20 and 30 hours in Denmark, 25 hours in Belgium, over 38 hours in the United Kingdom, between 42 and 45 hours in France, between 43 and 47 hours in the Federal Republic of Germany and 45 hours in Ireland. If the hours spent on housework are also counted, some of these women may well work as many as 70 hours a week. Farm work usually takes priority over housework and women are regarded as helpers available for many tasks during the day.

In 1980 women constituted about one-quarter of the industrial labour force. While previously there were many women working in labour-intensive industries, such as textiles, clothing and food processing, there are now much fewer employment opportunities, either because of technological developments or because of restructuring. Instead, they have turned increasingly to jobs in such capital-intensive industries as electronics, where the assembly work is generally tedious. The introduction of information technology in some sectors has affected the employment opportunities of both men and women.[25] A Canadian study of the banking sector shows for example that the introduction of electronic data processing and automatic cash tellers has had negative results on future employment opportunities for both men and women. Although job losses have not been quantified, it was found that job openings declined and a number of vacancies were left unfilled despite an increase in the volume of business. A study in the United States showed a similar pattern: while the use of new technologies enabled some com-

panies to expand business, employment opportunities did not keep pace with the expansion. But both studies also show that many of the new jobs that are being created require different types of skills that are possessed by men rather than by women. A study in the United Kingdom[26] showed that in 60 per cent of the workplaces surveyed in West Yorkshire more men than women were employed and that most of the women's jobs were affected by automation, while only 17 per cent of men were threatened with displacement. Here again, job losses for women were higher, although not counted in precise numbers. The many new jobs being created through new information and communication technologies are in scientific and technical areas, for which men are usually better qualified than women.

More than two-thirds of all women workers are found in the services sector. They are concentrated in such occupations as domestic servants, sales personnel, nurses and teachers (particularly in primary schools). The banking, communications, hotel and tourism sectors also employ many women, but their numbers vary according to the country.

It is likely that some "female" occupations in the services sector will be hard hit by technological developments, and in particular information technology. In the Federal Republic of Germany it has been calculated that 25 per cent of office jobs in the private sector and 36 per cent in the public sector will become superfluous. A report of the Equal Opportunities Commission in 1980 in the United Kingdom estimated that 21,000 secretarial jobs will be lost by 1985 owing to new electronic technologies, and 170,000 by 1990.

Over the past ten years women have gained greater access to jobs in the public sector. Regulations, guide-lines, legal provisions and measures of "positive discrimination", such as quota systems, have been prepared in a move towards more equal representation of women in the public service. Large discrepancies remain, however, espe-

211

cially in higher echelons. In the United States, for example, where women account for nearly half of federal civil servants, they hold only 6.2 per cent of the upper-grade posts (grades GS 14 to 18); in the Federal Republic of Germany, out of 6,454 higher-grade posts in the federal public service in 1977, 423 were held by women, of whom one held a post of director in a ministry, three held posts of ambassador and one held a post of secretary of state.[27]

Centrally planned economies

Women constitute on an average between 45 and 50 per cent of the labour force in the centrally planned economies and a large part of those employed in industry: 49 per cent in the USSR, 48.5 per cent in Bulgaria, 41.6 per cent in the German Democratic Republic and 30 per cent in Czechoslovakia. They are employed in almost all industrial occupations except those involving extremely strenuous work.

They tend to be concentrated, however, in food processing, light industry – such as textiles and clothing – and the metal trades, particularly the first two groups. In the USSR, for example, 82 per cent of all workers in light industry and 53 per cent of those in food processing are women.[28]

In 1980 more than half of Bulgarian women industrial workers were employed in machine building, metalworking, light industry and the food industry. Their number in radioelectronics, in the electro-technical industry and in the instrument-making industry is growing rapidly.[29] Statistics from the German Democratic Republic show that in 1983, 65.5 per cent of all workers in light industry were women, and 46.3 per cent in the electro-technical industry.[30]

With the progress of technology, the structure of the female labour force changed and women's employment in machine maintenance increased considerably. Women's share of the total work-force engaged in the monitoring of mechanised and automated equipment is also rising. This had led to greater productivity and to improved working conditions. In the USSR a larger percentage of women than before are employed in such highly skilled work as job setters, motor operators, machine assembly fitters, operators of metalworking machines, tool operators and electricians. For instance, women account for 78.8 and 40.3 per cent respectively of flow-line operatives and tenders of automatic machines.[31] In the Soviet Union 40 per cent of all research workers and 50 per cent of all engineers are women.[32]

On an average, women constitute about three-fifths of all workers in the services sector, though the proportion is reaching two-thirds in the USSR. There are several service sector occupations in which more than 70 per cent of the workers employed are women. In 1982, 96 per cent of all nurses in Hungary were women; and for other occupations the percentages were as follows: pharmacists: 75 per cent; primary-school teachers: 79 per cent; kindergarten teachers: 100 per cent; typists: 100 per cent; wage clerks: 92 per cent; librarians: 85 per cent; beauticians: 97 per cent; hairdressers: 84 per cent; and sales personnel: 79 per cent.[33] In 1976 women in Bulgaria made up 73 per cent of the personnel in health services and 68 per cent of the personnel in education, culture and art. In 1981, in the USSR 82 per cent of all employees in health services, physical education and social security were women; the corresponding percentages for public education and culture were 74 and 73.

Almost half of the agricultural labour force are women. The large majority work on state and co-operative farms while some are family workers on individual agricultural plots. They are employed in a wide range of agricultural activities, but particularly in livestock and crop farming. In the USSR there are special schools that train female agricultural personnel – for instance, tractor drivers, machine operators and other skilled workers. As a result, 50 per cent of all agricultural workers with a specialised education and about 40 per cent of agronomists, livestock experts and veterinary specialists with higher education are women. Women account for 49 per cent of the workforce on collective farms and 45 per cent on state farms. The introduction of shift work on a number of co-operative and state farms has made it possible for women generally not to work more than eight hours a day.

[1] R. Anker: "Female labour force participation in developing countries: A critique of current definitions and data collection methods", in *International Labour Review*, Nov.-Dec. 1983; L. Benería: "Accounting for women's work, The sexual division of labour in rural societies", in idem (ed.): *Women and development* (New York, Praeger, 1982); R. B. Dixon: "Women in agriculture: Counting the labor force in developing countries", in *Population and Development Review* (New York), Sep. 1982.

[2] C. D. Deere and M. León de Leal: *Women in Andean agriculture: Peasant production and rural wage employment in Colombia and Peru*, Women, Work and Development, 4 (Geneva, ILO, 1982).

[3] K. Uno: *A note on time-budget surveys in 24 countries* (Geneva, ILO, 1983; mimeographed).

[4] L. Goldschmidt-Clermont: *Unpaid work in the household: A review of economic evaluation methods*, Women, Work and Development, 1 (ILO, Geneva, 1982).

[5] ILO: *Report of the Conference*, Thirteenth International Conference of Labour Statisticians, 1982.

[6] M. Mies, assisted by K. Lalitha and K. Kumari: *Indian women in subsistence and agricultural labour* (Geneva, ILO, 1984; mimeographed World Employment Programme research working paper; restricted).

[7] A. A. Tahrunnessa and S. A. Zeidenstein: *Village women of Bangladesh: Prospects for change*, Women in Development Series, 4 (Oxford, Pergamon Press, 1982).

[8] E. Croll: *Women in rural development: The People's Republic of China* (Geneva, ILO, 1979); and idem: *Changing patterns of rural women's employment, production and reproduction in China* (Geneva, ILO, 1984; mimeographed World Employment Programme research working paper; restricted).

[9] See R. Kurian: *Women workers in the Sri Lanka plantation sector: An historical and contemporary analysis*, Women, Work and Development, 5 (Geneva, ILO, 1982); and N. Heyzer Fan: *A preliminary study of women rubber estate workers in Peninsular Malaysia* (Geneva, ILO, 1981; mimeographed World Employment Programme research working paper; restricted).

[10] Z. Bhatty: *The economic role and status of women in the beedi industry in Allahabad, India*, Social Science Studies on International Problems, Vol. 63 (Saarbrücken, Breitenbach, 1981).

[11] M. Mies: *The lace makers of Narsapur: Indian housewives produce for the world market* (London, Zed Press, 1982).

[12] S. K. Kumar: *Role of the household economy in child nutrition at low incomes: A case study in Kerala*, Occasional Paper No. 95, Department of Agricultural Economics (Ithaca, New York, Cornell University, New York State College of Agriculture and Life Sciences, 1978). See also A. S. Carloni: *The impact of maternal employment and income on the nutritional status of children in rural areas of developing countries* (Rome, FAO, 1983).

[13] Benería, op. cit.

[14] Z. Ahmad: "Rural women and their work: Dependence and alternatives for change", in *International Labour Review*, Jan.-Feb. 1984.

[15] E. Gordon: "An analysis of the impact of labour migration on the lives of women in Lesotho", in *Journal of Development Studies* (London), Apr. 1981.

[16] G. H. R. Chipande: *Labour availability and smallholder agricultural development – The case of Lilongwe Land Development Programme (LLDP) (Malawi)* (Geneva, ILO, 1983; mimeographed World Employment Programme research working paper; restricted).

[17] N. H. Youssef and C. B. Hetler: *Rural households headed by women: A priority concern for development* (Geneva, ILO, 1984; mimeographed World Employment Programme research working paper; restricted).

[18] P. Phongpaichit: *From peasant girls to Bangkok masseuses*, Women, Work and Development, 2; and N. Heyzer: "From rural subsistence to an industrial peripheral workforce: An examination of female Malaysian migrants and capital accumulation in Singapore", in Benería, op. cit.

[19] E. Eisold: *Young women workers in export industries: The case of the semi-conductor industry in south-east Asia* (Geneva, ILO, 1984; mimeographed World Employment Programme research working paper; restricted).

[20] ILO: *Social aspects of industrialisation*, Report VII, International Labour Conference, 69th Session, Geneva, 1983.

[21] A. Fuentes and B. Ehrenreich: *Women in the global factory* (New York, Institute for New Communications, 1983), pamphlet No. 2.

[22] *Women in industry in developing countries* (Geneva, ILO, 1978, doc. ILO/W.6/1978; mimeographed).

[23] R. Maex: *Employment and multinationals in Asian export processing zones*, Multinational Enterprises Programme Working Paper No. 26 (Geneva, ILO, 1983).

[24] ILO: *General Report*, Report I, and *The effects of structural changes and technological progress on employment in the public service*, Report III, Joint Committee on the Public Service, Third Session, Geneva, 1983.

[25] D. Werneke: *Microelectronics and office jobs: The impact of the chip on women's employment* (Geneva, ILO, 1983); A. Dirrheimer: *La microélectronique et la formation professionnelle des femmes*, Colloque "Formation professionnelle des femmes en Europe et nouvelles technologies", Paris, 24–25 Jan. 1983.

[26] Equal Oportunities Commission: *New technology and women's employment: Case studies from West Yorkshire* (Manchester, 1982).

[27] ILO: *Recruitment, training and career development in the public service*, Report II, Joint Committee on the Public Service, Third Session, Geneva, 1983.

[28] L. Rzhanitsyna: *Female labour under socialism: The socio-economic aspects* (Moscow, Progress Publishers, 1983), p. 36.

[29] *Women and work* (Sofia, Committee on Social Information and the Women's Movement, 1980).

[30] *Statistical pocket book of the German Democratic Republic, 1983* (Berlin, Staatsverlag der Deutschen Demokratischen Republik, 1983).

[31] A. Biryukova: *Soviet women: Their role in society, the economy, the trade unions* (Moscow, Profizdat, 1981), p. 17.

[32] *The equality of women in the USSR* (Moscow, 1983), p. 17.

[33] Központi statisztikai hivatal: *Adatok a nők helyzetéről* (Budapest, 1982), pp. 13 and 16.

213

Chapter 14

Women, job opportunities and conditions of work

In many countries working women are discriminated against in various direct and indirect ways in the economy and society. A situation of factual discrimination exists in the modern sectors of the developing countries and in most industrialised market economies, where women are more likely to be unemployed than men; this is described in the first section of this chapter. Often at the root of such discrimination and inequality between men and women is the fact that women have less access to education and training – a problem that is particularly acute in the developing countries and is discussed in the second section. Even if women have equal access to education and training, they may still be concentrated in certain "female" occupations, a problem that will be examined in the third section. These occupations often have less favourable conditions of work: they are frequently less well paid and provide fewer career opportunities with the result that on average men tend to earn more than women. Moreover, it can happen that men and women do not receive equal pay for work of equal value – a fundamental principle laid down in Convention No. 100. Both issues are analysed in the fourth section. In the fifth and last section, we shall discuss the question of working conditions and special protective legislation for women.

Unemployment

Volume 1 of this report showed that unemployment in the industrialised market economies increased sharply from an average of about 3 per cent in 1973 to more than 9 per cent in 1983. In almost all these countries unemployment among women is higher than among men, though in some countries female unemployment did not rise as fast as male unemployment. The question of unemployment in developing countries is more complicated. A large proportion of workers in the developing countries are underemployed, i.e. they work only part of the year or of the day, and they have a low income. There is a relatively small proportion of workers who are "openly" unemployed. They are usually attached to the modern sector and their unemployment is generally recorded by government employment agencies. In the centrally planned economies there is normally full employment, both for men and women. Some employment problems remain, however, particularly as regards matching the supply of labour with demand (both in the short and in the long run) and utilising human resources to their full productive potential (see Chapter 3, Volume 1).

Industrialised market economies

The official unemployment figures in the industrialised market economies do not always accurately reflect the underutilisation of human resources. As was explained in Volume 1, the figures may be overestimates because a large group of workers (including women) are in clandestine employment. However, on balance, they probably underestimate the actual underutilisation of human resources.

First of all, some countries do not count as unemployed certain migrants and young people who – having left school – are still looking for their first job or who may be in a temporary training scheme. Secondly, there is a considerable group of "discouraged workers", many of whom are women. They have given up looking for a job because they know from experience that none is available. At the lowest point of the recession in 1982, there were roughly 1 million discouraged women workers in the United States, accounting for roughly 1 per cent of the labour force. Thirdly, unemployment may also be hidden in part-time work, which is mainly the domain of women and which has increased rapidly during the past decade. Many women freely choose to work part time, because such work enables them to combine work with family responsibilities and to keep up their occupational skills; others, however, do not have this free choice. In the United States, one of the few countries where statistics on involuntary part-time work are collected, there were more than 6.5 million non-agricultural workers involuntarily on part-time schedules in 1983. Half of them worked part time in their old jobs, while the other half had to accept a new part-time job. There is also some evidence of a shift towards a greater use of "temporary" labour, where much of the work is of a part-time nature.[1] The majority of part-time jobs carry no entitlement to employment benefits, reduce labour costs, have a low skill component and are often outside the scope of the relevant provisions of labour legislation.[2] In the long run, moreover, part-time employment for women may contribute to perpetuating discrimination in the labour market if proper wages, social security and other benefits are not provided. Part-time workers are often not only deprived of labour protection, but they also have few opportunities to become members of trade unions.

At the end of 1983 about 33 million persons in the OECD countries were looking for work – slightly over 9 per cent of the labour force. Table 14.1 shows that in 1973 – before the recession – female unemployment was in most cases higher

Table 14.1

Unemployment rates for men and women in selected industrialised market economies, 1973 and 1982

	1973		1982	
	Women	Men	Women	Men
Australia	2.8	1.4	8.4	6.2
Austria	1.8	0.6	4.6	2.8
Canada	5.1	5.8	10.8	11.0
France	2.7	1.7	11.6	5.6
Germany (Federal Republic of)	1.3	0.9	7.7	6.0
Italy	4.7	3.0	14.7	6.0
Japan	1.2	1.3	2.3	2.4
Norway	2.4	1.0	3.0	2.3
Spain	2.6	2.8	20.3	15.1
Sweden	2.8	2.3	3.4	3.0
United States	6.0	4.0	9.4	9.7

Source: OECD: *Quarterly labour force statistics* (Paris), various editions.

than male unemployment. In 1982 – at the lowest point of the recession – this general picture still applied, but with some important qualifications. In Canada and the United States the rate of unemployment among men and women was virtually the same; on the other hand, in some southern European countries (such as France, Italy and Spain), female unemployment between 1973 and 1982 had increased much faster than male unemployment. It is also in this latter group of countries that youth unemployment (and particularly among young girls) is very high (see Volume 1).

Developing countries

As mentioned above, in many developing countries a considerable proportion of workers are underemployed. Those registered as unemployed are usually workers in the modern urban sector and constitute a relatively small proportion of the labour force. It is also likely that for various reasons many women do not register themselves even though they are unemployed. Table 14.2, which shows some trends in the employment and unemployment of women, should be interpreted with these qualifications in mind.

Table 14.2
Trends in employment and unemployment in selected developing countries (1976-81)

	1976		1981	
	Women workers as % of total economically active population	Unemployed women as % of total unemployed	Women workers as % of total economically active population	Unemployed women as % of total unemployed
Colombia	37.5	43.6	38.2	49.3[a]
Costa Rica	21.5	38.0	24.3[a]	33.2[a]
Cyprus	36.8	23.6	37.7	38.7
India	11.9	12.4	12.3	14.9
Jamaica	38.2	67.1	40.1[a]	67.6[a]
Republic of Korea	38.4	19.2	38.2	20.4
Mauritius	23.5	22.1	26.6	29.4
Panama	26.9	43.5	29.0[b]	46.9[b]
Puerto Rico	34.5	23.7	36.3	24.8
Syrian Arab Republic	9.2	10.3	15.8[b]	15.7[b]
Tunisia	19.2	12.7	22.6	15.3
Venezuela	28.0	22.1	26.7	21.7

[a] 1980. [b] 1979.

Source: ILO: *Year Book of Labour Statistics, 1982* (Geneva, 1983), Chapter II, pp. 215 ff. and Chapter III, pp. 363 ff.

Table 14.3
Comparative growth in literacy among males and females: Developed and developing countries (estimates for 1970 and 1980, and projections for 1985)

Regions		Number (millions)			Change (in %)	
		1970	1980	1985	1970-80	1980-85
Developed countries:						
Population:	M	370.1	423.8	445.6	14.5	5.1
	F	414.4	465.9	485.4	12.4	4.2
Literates:	M	359.2	415.5	438.2	15.7	5.5
	%	(97.1)	(98.0)	(98.3)		
	F	396.6	451.8	473.0	13.9	4.7
	%	(95.7)	(97.0)	(97.4)		
Developing countries:						
Population:	M	775.2	1 008.0	1 150.6	30.0	14.2
	F	750.1	981.4	1 121.5	30.8	14.3
Literates:	M	468.5	683.1	815.6	45.8	19.4
	%	(60.4)	(67.8)	(70.9)		
	F	325.3	504.9	619.1	55.2	22.6
	%	(43.4)	(51.4)	(55.2)		

Data cover population at age 15 and above. The figures in brackets show literacy levels among males and females, expressed as percentages of their respective populations.
M = Male. F = Female.

Source: UNESCO data on computer printout (1983).

217

In 1981 seven out of the 12 selected developing countries indicated that women's share of unemployment was higher than their share of employment, while in 1976 this was so for only six countries (Colombia, Costa Rica, India, Jamaica, Panama and Syrian Arab Republic). The table also shows that the percentage of women in total unemployment increased in ten countries. This may be partly explained by the increasing share of women in the labour force, but it probably also means that the rate of female unemployment increased faster than that of men.

Another important trend (not shown in the table) is that women who are looking for their first jobs are particularly vulnerable. In countries for which data are available (such as Barbados, Ghana, Mauritius and Tunisia) women's share of unemployed persons looking for their first job is considerably higher than that of other unemployed persons.

Education and training

In most countries women do not have equal access to education and training (see table 14.3). In 1970 fewer than 44 per cent of women over 15 years of age in developing countries could read and write, as against 60 per cent of men. However, during the 1970s literacy rates in developing countries increased spectacularly to more than 51 per cent for women and almost 68 per cent for men, and this trend is likely to continue in the 1980s.

The attitudes of parents, teachers, employers and workers concerning education and training play an important role in influencing educational and occupational choices of young women. It appears from preliminary data compiled by UNESCO[3] and the ILO[4] that social perceptions undervalue the role of women in the labour market and for this reason schooling (primary, secondary and technical) and training are not equally accessible for girls and women. As regards education, girls are often channelled towards humanities and away from mathematics and physical sciences. Moreover, the education structures in many countries do not yet provide the same facilities to women as they provide to men for qualifying as technicians, scientists or physicists. In countries for which data are available, there has been a marked increase in the number of women in medicine and the legal professions. A recent WHO study shows, for example, that women are providers of health at the primary level but have generally not yet entered the ranks of surgeons, supervisors or deans of schools of medicine.[5]

Another important factor is the extent to which existing educational and training schemes are equipped to respond to the special needs of girls and women. In industrialised market economies the facilities include on-the-job training, formal and informal education schemes, adult education centres and retraining for women. In developing countries the problem is more basic – that of providing primary-school facilities, particularly for girls in some countries. In addition, in many rural areas girls need to help at home or on the farm, so that they drop out of school more readily than boys. In the centrally planned economies there are equal educational opportunities for both men and women and many special training opportunities for women (see also Chapter 7).

Developing countries

In the past three or four decades education has become universal, free and compulsory in a number of countries. Even though literacy levels have greatly improved, there are still millions of women who are illiterate. But there has recently been a remarkably clear advance in literacy levels among women in the developing countries (see table 14.3). Between 1970 and 1980, the increase in the number of female literates in developing

countries was 55.2 per cent, i.e. an annual growth rate of 4.5 per cent. This compares well with the developed countries where the corresponding increase was 13.9 per cent or an annual growth rate of 1.3 per cent. Moreover, projected literacy growth rates for women are considerably higher than those for men, so that literacy rates for women will be fairly close to those for men by the end of this century.

Low incomes and demanding household duties in rural and sometimes in urban areas are one of the main reasons why young girls drop out of school to help their mothers. Additional reasons are early marriage, systems of seclusion of women, and other concepts of "women's roles". To this list must be added working girls who have to earn their living from a very tender age.

Even if girls are free to undergo education and training, they may not be able to do so for various reasons. There may be a lack of schools and vocational training institutions, particularly in rural areas. They may not take advantage of education and training opportunities because of traditional attitudes preventing them from acquiring or upgrading skills that can be used in modern sector jobs. Finally, even where education and vocational training are accepted by women, they often do not acquire the skills in demand in the labour market.

Where free secondary and higher education are not available, low-income families often give priority to investing in the education of boys, from which they expect a higher rate of return than from investments in the education of girls.

Even in the urban and modern sectors of many developing countries, training facilities are often grossly inadequate to meet women's needs. For instance, in Bangladesh, about 250,000[5] women on an average are expected to enter the workforce each year, but the number participating in vocational training is estimated to be only about 20,000.[6] In Pakistan an average of 173,000[5] new

218

female entrants into the labour force is projected, for whom only 8,000[7] places will be available within the formal vocational training system. In India the yearly increase in the female labour force is estimated to be over 2 million,[5] while the annual capacity for training women covers less than 5 per cent, i.e. 95,000.[8]

In many developing countries there are numerous governmental and non-governmental institutions that provide technical and managerial training and in theory do not exclude women from entry. In practice, however, there are many constraints acting as barriers, including entry-level qualifications, age restrictions for entry, the requirement to drop out on marriage or pregnancy, etc.[9]

The greatest obstacle for the few who receive training is that women's training is oriented towards only a few occupations or professions – away from technical or industrial fields and towards the social sector, such as teaching and nursing. The following data will illustrate the point. In 1978-79, women formed only 4.8 per cent of the students receiving secondary technical education in Niger,[10] and were severely under-represented in industrial courses in the Ivory Coast.[11] Training programmes for women are often oriented towards welfare, which is to say that the curriculum is small-scale, ad hoc, fragmented and focuses on short-term objectives. These programmes do not make use of resources and inputs from other development programmes, nor do they function within the broader framework of development efforts and economic realities. Above all, they do not provide a base for viable income-generating activities, for they fail to recognise that women need cash income.

Industrialised market economies

Although school enrolment of boys and girls at the compulsory level is almost 100 per cent and post-compulsory, secondary education shows higher participation rates for girls, there are wide discrepancies among countries. For example, in some countries girls have gone beyond parity, as in Ireland (57 per cent) and Belgium (51.7 per cent). In a number of other countries (Australia, Canada, Finland, France, Japan, Norway, Portugal and Sweden) the percentages for girls and boys are near 50 per cent; only Switzerland shows a participation rate of less than 40 per cent for girls. But as one goes higher up the ladder of advanced education – at the university level – the percentage rates for girls begin to fluctuate between, for example, 25 per cent in Japan and 51 per cent in the United States.

The above (unpublished) data compiled by UNESCO indicate that during the past few decades more and more women have been participating in secondary levels of education, though equality at the university level still remains elusive in many countries. At the same time, the choice of subjects reveals wide differences between young men and women. Young women are seriously under-represented in the technical fields such as mathematics and the physical sciences. The converse is true for boys, who choose to study the humanities and the arts more rarely. These differences are most pronounced at the university level and in vocational training, and are responsible for certain jobs being labelled as "male" and others as "female". It is the choice of subjects in the education and training streams that determines gender priorities. In Austria, 80 per cent of female apprentices concentrate on only ten occupations out of a total of 225.[12] In Portugal, between 1973 and 1976, women took courses in only four of the 28 subjects offered by the 16 vocational training centres.[13] In the Federal Republic of Germany, 40.5 per cent of female apprentices in 1982 were concentrated in five occupations considered to be "female" occupations.[14] At the university level, the humanities, the arts and, in some cases, social sciences are considered to have low employment potential and are, at the same time, those for which more and more women are enrolled.

219

What are the consequences of these trends for women's labour force participation rates? While evidence shows that within countries the labour force participation rates of both men and women increase with education, this relationship does not apply between countries.[15] Available information also indicates that it is not the number of years spent in education or the duration of training courses that determines employment or promotion opportunities, but the type and content of education and training that women receive. The curricula in many schools and technical institutes do not take into account the real skill needs of girls and women in the labour market.

Centrally planned economies

In the centrally planned economies women have free and equal access to education at all levels. The educational standards of working women in the USSR have been raised to the same level as those of men. Universal education up to the age of 16 is compulsory for both boys and girls. The proportion of women in higher educational establishments is 52 per cent, and in specialised secondary schools 57 per cent; 84 per cent of women workers have secondary or tertiary (completed or uncompleted) education, while the corresponding percentage for men is 85.1; and 59 per cent of specialists with tertiary or specialist education are women. They are employed in various jobs in the physical, biological and medical sciences, pedagogy and chemistry.

In other centrally planned economies, such as the German Democratic Republic, full-time women workers with higher skills receive additional benefits when they participate in vocational training in order to upgrade their skills. Women are also given on-the-job training in enterprises under the terms of collective agreements. Directors of various enterprises and organisations are under an obligation to offer women positions that correspond to their training and skills.

In the German Democratic Republic almost 52 per cent of the students in grades 9 and 10 of the ten-year polytechnical school are girls; in grades 11 and 12 of the senior high school and in vocational training institutes whose final examinations lead to university entrance qualification, more than 50 per cent of the students are girls. Women account for over 70 per cent of the students in engineering and technical schools. At universities and similar institutions, the proportion of female students is 52.5 per cent.[16]

The equal access to polytechnic education and training provides a firm basis for equal opportunities in selecting a career. At present, almost all female school-leavers who do not go on to a higher educational establishment take up vocational training. Agriculture is an important example of equal access to education and training for girls and women. Recent data show that 83 per cent of women farm workers have undergone some form of training and obtained a certificate.

In Hungary there was a significant increase in women students in tertiary education between 1970 and 1981 (see table 14.4). In 1981 half of all students in tertiary education and in vocational secondary schools were female. The proportion of girls in secondary schools was even higher, 65.2 per cent, while that of skilled worker trainees was 32.1 per cent. There are a few occupations and professions in which women are strongly concentrated, i.e. in pharmaceuticals and public health, commerce, clothing, services, leather and textiles. In addition, there are very few males training to become kindergarten or primary-school teachers.

However, for all the progress made by women in the field of vocational training and further training, it would be wrong to assume that all the problems have been solved. There is, to begin with, the problem of women's continuous vocational training and retraining. The goal of ensuring efficient use of female labour presupposes first

220

Table 14.4
Women students in various educational and vocational day schools in Hungary (1970–81)

	1970		1981	
	Number ('000)	Proportion (%) of total	Number ('000)	Proportion (%) of total
Students in tertiary education	24.0	44.7	31.8	50.1
Technical	3.1	21.4	31.1	18.5
Agricultural	1.4	20.2	1.5	28.3
Veterinary	0.1	15.7	0.1	15.8
Medical	3.4	52.8	3.8	54.4
Pharmaceutical	0.7	79.2	0.6	75.8
Public health	—	—	0.9	92.0
Economics	2.4	63.7	3.2	60.9
Law and administration	1.0	54.6	1.4	50.8
Pedagogy	10.0	77.9	15.6	76.5
Skilled worker trainees	55.0	24.6	50.5	32.1
Commerce	15.1	80.4	17.3	86.5
Clothing industry	8.4	92.4	11.5	96.4
Catering	4.4	51.1	4.2	47.9
Services	5.7	67.0	3.5	65.3
Leather industry	4.0	72.0	3.1	82.0
Textile industry	3.3	95.0	2.4	96.3
Students of secondary schools	82.3	66.9	120.3	57.5
Students of vocational secondary schools	53.7	49.6	59.6	51.3

Source: Central Statistical Office: *Data on the situation of women* (Budapest, 1982).

of all a continued improvement of women's vocational training and retraining to help relieve women further of the less creative and less responsible jobs, which are often physically strenuous. Secondly, in choosing their future occupations and careers, boys and girls continue to be influenced by traditional attitudes towards male and female work. For example, in Hungary there are pressures on women with skilled worker qualifications to leave their jobs in favour of semi-skilled jobs because of family responsibilities.

Occupational and career patterns

A closer look at the labour market reveals that women tend to have different occupations from men and fewer career opportunities. This inherent segregation of jobs based on sex manifests itself in many ways, two aspects of which may be singled out here. First, in many countries a large number of women are concentrated in a narrow range of traditional or "female" occupations. Secondly, within the same industry, occupation or profession, men tend to occupy the higher and women the lower ranks of the occupational hierarchy. There are of course exceptions to this rule but the general picture, even during the past decade, has been one of men in executive and supervisory positions and women in secondary or subordinate jobs, men as managers and women as assistants or secretaries.

It cannot be denied, however, that occupational and career patterns are changing. In many countries women are entering occupations that used to be male-dominated, such as architecture or engineering, while scientific and technological developments have eliminated much of the heavy physical work that formerly made many jobs (for example in the metal trades) inaccessible to women. Social perceptions that have attached an external "value" to a job are also changing, as may be seen from the fact that in France and the Federal Republic of Germany, for instance, women are now occupying jobs requiring intermediate skills, such as plumbers, that previously were regarded as "unsuitable" for them. Similarly, most women have access to such jobs in the centrally planned economies. The trend towards the elimination of the distinction between men's jobs and women's jobs is also observed in the Scandinavian countries. Elsewhere, however, it has not yet brought major changes in the occupational distribution of women workers, although it may influence the labour market in the years ahead.

The origins of occupational segregation are multifaceted; mention has already been made of inadequate education and vocational training, traditional social attitudes and tangible and intangible discrimination. Whatever the cause, segregation has serious consequences for women workers, for it affects their daily lives. It contributes to wage differentials between men and women, restricts women's occupational mobility in the labour market and increases their rate of unemployment.

There is also evidence that when an occupation or profession becomes preponderantly "female", its economic and social status diminishes. This happened towards the end of the last century and in the early years of this century when male clerks were replaced by women secretaries, and later on when women came to occupy the majority of teaching posts (in primary and secondary schools) in such countries as France, the Federal Republic of Germany and the United Kingdom. A similar shift is now apparent in the newly industrialised countries, such as in Brazil, India and Nigeria, where women are replacing men as secretaries and teachers.

Developing countries

Underlying occupational segregation in the developing countries is the fact that female literacy rates are low, that the educational and training infrastructure is inadequate and that the content of education and training is not adapted to the needs of women. Consequently, women working in industry continue to be employed in the textiles and clothing industries, in electronics and, in some countries, in construction, the shoe and leather industry and the hotel and tourism sector.[17] In the textiles industry they are mostly production workers and operators, and in the electronics industries they work on the assembly lines. In the garment industry they work as tailors, stitchers, sewing machine operators, clothes pressers and assistants – jobs requiring relatively low levels of skill and offering relatively little opportunity for

advancement. There are a few skilled jobs in this industry, such as fashion designing and computer designing or marketing of footwear, but often they are out of the reach of women.

There have been marked differences in some occupations during the past decade. A recent survey in Singapore showed that women account for 87 per cent of the total labour force in a typical electronics plant, but only 3 per cent of the supervisors, 5 per cent of the technicians and 5 per cent of the white-collar workers. Government policies there have encouraged the upgrading of women into higher-skilled, higher-productivity operations over the past decade so that these figures point to a major shift from traditional to non-traditional jobs.

Industrialised market economies

In the industrialised market economies, the proportion of women in the various occupations ranges from less than 1 per cent in some to nearly 100 per cent in others. In France,[18] for example, women account for 0.9 per cent of transport equipment operators, 1.8 per cent of skilled workers in the mechanical trades, 3.9 per cent of skilled painters and decorators, but 97.6 per cent of secretarial staff, 86.2 per cent of health staff (proficiency certificate level) and 68.6 per cent of unskilled non-manual workers.

Several reports from other countries, such as Sweden and Finland,[19] tend to confirm a growing tendency for job opportunities to be announced explicitly for both men and women. Partly as a result of such a policy many occupations in the United States were opened up to women: for example, in 1961, 9 per cent of insurance adjusters were women; two decades later, in 1981, women accounted for 58 per cent. Similarly, female bill collectors increased from 22 per cent in 1961 to 63 per cent in 1982. Women are beginning to outnumber men also among real-estate agents and brokers, photographic process workers, checkers, examiners and inspectors, and production-line assemblers. In 1971, 4 per cent of lawyers and judges were women; a decade later their share had increased to 14 per cent. In 1971, women made up 9 per cent of the country's physicians, in 1981, 22 per cent. The proportion of female engineers also increased from 1 per cent in 1971 to 4 per cent in 1981.

Centrally planned economies

In the USSR women are represented in almost all of the 290 major occupational groups covering the various types of industrial activity and account for upwards of 50 per cent of the labour force in 156 major occupational groups. There are a limited number of occupations involving heavy and arduous work, such as lorry driving, to which they are not admitted.

Women account for 51 per cent of industrial workers and office employees,[20] 47 per cent of research workers, 63 per cent of administrative workers, 73 per cent of workers in education and recreation, 82 per cent of workers in health, physical recreation and social security and 83 per cent of workers in commerce and public catering. Characteristically, women are moving into new areas of employment, acquiring in particular a growing share of employment in what are now known as "creative" occupations. A comparison of the data contained in the 1939 and 1979 national censuses gives a comprehensive picture of the substantial redistribution in women's share of physical and intellectual work. While women still accounted for 46-47 per cent of all manual workers at the end of this period as at the beginning, manual labour occupied only 65 per cent of all gainfully employed women in 1979 as against 88 per cent in 1939. Over the same period women increased their share of the intellectual workforce from 12 to 35 per cent and their share of office jobs from 26 to 60 per cent.[21]

Examples of occupational concentration can be found in other centrally planned economies. For instance, the Hungarian Statistical Office notes that in 1980 more than 91 per cent of statisticians, nearly 87 per cent of technical designers, 81 per cent of laboratory workers, more than 92 per cent of tailors and textile workers, nearly 84 per cent of hairdressers and more than 79 per cent of sales personnel were women.[22] In 1975, women in Czechoslovakia accounted for over 80 per cent of the personnel in the medical and social services and nearly 76 per cent of staff in commerce and restaurants.

An increasing number of women participate on an equal footing with men in the management and organisation of the economy. In the USSR, for example, more than half a million women are directors of industrial enterprises or hold executive posts on construction projects, in offices and in government departments. Over 26,000 women are heads of, or chief experts at, collective and state farms.[23] In the German Democratic Republic 50 per cent of judges and 50 per cent of jury members are women and every fifth school principal is a woman.[24] In Hungary, during the first half of the United Nations Decade for Women, i.e. 1975-80, the proportion of women in leading state and economic posts increased at the national level, and this trend continued throughout 1980-81. The proportion of women in high-level posts in the various economic sectors was estimated to be 27 per cent in 1981 and 29.6 per cent in 1982.[25]

Wage differentials

The principle that men and women should receive equal remuneration for work of equal value has been included in the ILO Constitution since 1919. In 1951, the International Labour Conference adopted a Convention (No. 100) and a Recommendation (No. 90) dealing specifically with this subject; the Convention has now been ratified by 104 member States (see Annex 3).

The Equal Remuneration Convention, 1951 (No. 100), lays down the general principle that each ratifying State shall promote and, in so far as is consistent with the methods in operation in its country for determining rates of remuneration, ensure the application to all workers of the principle of equal remuneration for men and women workers for work of equal value. Equality must be applied not only to the basic or minimum wage, but also to "any additional emoluments whatsoever, payable directly or indirectly, whether in cash or in kind, by the employer to the worker and arising out of the worker's employment". The notion of "work of equal value" which is used by the Convention has a wider meaning than that of "equal work". It applies to comparisons between different types of work and not only to similar or identical jobs. In practice, it can be difficult to determine whether certain types of work are of equal value, in particular when the work tends to be performed mainly or exclusively by one sex. For that reason the Convention and the Recommendation advocate measures to promote objective appraisal of the work to be performed.

The term "work of equal value" figured already – as noted above – among the general principles enunciated in Part XIII of the Treaty of Versailles (1919). Following the adoption of ILO Convention No. 100, it was also used by the European Social Charter and the 1966 International Covenant on Economic, Social and Cultural Rights, while the 1948 Universal Declaration of Human Rights referred to "equal work".

It is very difficult to measure the real extent of discrimination against women in this area. Data on average wage differentials between men and women (as shown in table 14.5) cannot serve this purpose, because the "average" man tends to work longer and has higher qualifications than the "average" woman, and tends to work in different occupations and sectors.

One also has to be careful in comparing wage differentials between countries. The definition of wages is of course not always the same and the

Table 14.5
Male-female wage differentials in manufacturing: Selected countries, 1975 and 1982

| Country | Female wage as % of male wage | |
	1975	1982
Australia [h]	78.5	78.2
Belgium [h]	71.3	73.5
Burma [m]	88.5	88.8 [1]
Cyprus [w]	45.9	56.3
Czechoslovakia [m]	67.4	67.9
Denmark [h]	84.3	85.1
El Salvador [h]	90.4	85.9
Finland [h]	72.6	77.2
France [h]	76.4	78.1 [1]
Germany, Fed. Rep. of [h]	72.1	73.0
Greece [h]	69.5	73.1
Ireland [h]	60.9	68.5
Japan [m]	47.9	43.1
Kenya [m]	66.1	75.8
Korea, Rep. of [m]	47.4	45.1
Luxembourg [h]	60.9	60.0 [1]
Netherlands [h]	74.7	74.0
New Zealand [h]	65.6	71.1
Norway [h]	78.0	83.2
Sweden [h]	85.2	90.3
Switzerland [h]	68.0	67.5
United Republic of Tanzania [m]	70.7	78.5 [2]
United Kingdom [h]	66.5	68.8

[1] 1981. [2] 1980.
h = hourly wages. w = weekly wages. m = monthly wages.
Source: ILO: *Year Book of Labour Statistics*, 1983, table 17 A.

information does not always cover the same group of workers. In addition, there are relatively few developing countries and centrally planned economies that provide data on wage differentials. None the less, the wage differentials in table 14.5 display marked variations among countries. In the Nordic countries average female earnings are more than 80 per cent of average male earnings, while they are less than 70 per cent in Japan, Luxembourg, Switzerland, Czechoslovakia, Ireland and the United Kingdom. Considerable variations also exist among the developing countries. Between 1975 and 1982 the trend seems to have been towards a narrowing of wage differentials.

International comparisons are also made difficult by the way the equal pay principle is implemented; some jurisdictions interpret the principle in a very restrictive way by requiring the "same work" or "substantially similar work", while others attempt to give full effect to the principle of "work of equal value". The latter interpretation aims at eliminating wage differentials between men and women by acknowledging that discrimination also arises from segregating workers into particular "sex-typed" occupations.

However, average wage differentials between men and women would still exist, even if the equal pay principle (either for "equal work" or for "work of equal value") were rigorously applied. Factors other than discrimination in wage fixing play a part here. The equal pay problem must be considered in the broader context of equality of opportunity and treatment as between the sexes, which is covered by Convention No. 111.

There are many factors that account for male-female wage differentials. First, women are often treated unequally, when they apply for a job – particularly after a period of absence from the labour force – as well as in their placement, in dismissal and in promotion. Secondly, women are concentrated in sectors and occupations where pay is relatively low. This is the case in industries such as textiles, clothing, leather and food and in services such as education, health, retail trade and tourism.

Female blue-collar workers are usually found in unskilled and semi-skilled occupations rather than in skilled and highly skilled ones, while protective legislation sometimes excludes them from certain arduous jobs where wages are relatively high.[26] In addition, managerial positions are still mostly in the hands of men. Such segregation creates problems in carrying out an objective appraisal of

jobs. Another cause of male-female wage differentials is the lower average qualifications of women. Even if girls spend the same number of years in school as boys, they tend to be concentrated in non-technical fields regarded as "female" spheres of activity. In addition, men often have better access to training than women. Yet another cause is the domestic duties of women. Even if women have a full-time job, they are still considered mainly responsible for housekeeping and feeding the family, and for bringing up the children and supervising their education. The time and energy spent by women on these domestic tasks can adversely affect their performance on the job, induce absenteeism, discourage them from raising their qualifications and make it difficult for them to pursue a career.

Industrialised market economies

In industrialised market economies the principle of equal remuneration for equal work has been widely recognised in constitutional or legislative provisions. While considerable progress has been made in reducing the gap between women's and men's earnings, discrepancies remain which may be accounted for to a large degree by the factors already mentioned. Some of the problems may also be attributed to the lack of proper job evaluation; for example, it is difficult to compare the value of work in industries or occupations largely dominated by women, with the result that these jobs tend to be accorded lower status and pay.[27] Moreover, one of the main difficulties derives from the manner in which wages are fixed in practice. Pay rates and pay differentials are normally the product of negotiation, the state of the labour market, the relative strength of the parties, or custom and usage.

More recently, some countries have moved towards the principle of equal pay for work of "comparable" value in an attempt to close the earnings gap and to remedy the present and future effects of past sex discrimination. The comparable worth theory is designed to apply especially to

225

those classes of jobs that have been traditionally undervalued and underpaid because they are held by women.

Recent French legislation – adopted in July 1983[28] – authorises trade unions to bring sex discrimination cases in the courts, unless the woman concerned is opposed to such action. In other countries, such as Norway and Sweden, the legislation is supplemented by collective agreements on equality policies introduced at the national level.

Developing countries

In the modern sectors of the developing countries the situation is similar to that in the industrialised market economies. Although there are marked differences between countries and occupations, in general women earn less than men in all sectors of the economy (see table 14.5). Owing to the general scarcity of employment opportunities and their lower levels of education and training, women have even less access to employment, particularly to skilled jobs with equal pay. Owing to structural factors and the extent of unemployment, women, in order to get or keep a job, must often accept lower wages than men, who are still paid a "family wage". Since it is mainly the supply of labour that determines the level of wages, any worker outside the purview of labour legislation can be easily dismissed and replaced by others from the long queue of unemployed and underemployed. Most women who work to ensure the survival of their families are reluctant to claim equal wages for fear of losing their jobs.

In the modern sectors most women are employed under the time-rate system which involves a given number of work-hours per day, week or month, but are often paid less than men for doing "similar work". Some countries interpret the concept of similar work as meaning work equal in quantity and quality (e.g. Thailand and Viet Nam) while others interpret it as meaning a job that

is of identical or similar nature. Wherever there is a provision for the "same job" or "equal work", it has been found necessary to put a narrower interpretation on the existing definitions. However, the present trend is towards a wider and more flexible meaning and it seems fairer to interpret the concept as meaning work of equal value.[29]

Of still greater concern, however, is the fact that the majority of women in Asia, Africa and Latin America remain outside the scope of the relevant legislation since they work mostly in agricultural undertakings, domestic service or family enterprises. For example, in Bangladesh, Nigeria and Peru agricultural workers are excluded, as are homeworkers in the Philippines. Nor are employees of small undertakings covered in Ghana. In Kuwait, civil servants are not covered by the provisions on equal pay. In Sri Lanka women are paid less than men by law, with the rates being fixed by official wage boards responsible for the industrial and plantation sectors.[30] Often, therefore, the scope of equal pay legislation is limited to the minority of women wage earners in the organised sector. In addition, discriminatory practices result from the lingering belief that women do not produce as much as men and should therefore be paid less.

Centrally planned economies

In the centrally planned economies the principle of equal pay for equal work is laid down in various constitutional provisions, as in the USSR (article 35), Poland (article 78 (2) (i)) and Bulgaria (article 41). As in many other countries, wages are determined not according to sex but according to the nature and complexity of work and other conditions; grades according to the quantity, nature and complexity of work and other conditions; grades are determined according to qualifications – the higher the qualifications, the higher the grade. In the USSR, for example, the wage rates of men and women are determined on the basis of the common manning table, common wage schedule and other regulations on supplementary remuneration for prolonged and uninterrupted work, particularly where working conditions are hard. Women are guaranteed equal pay for equal work by the centralised state system of regulating wages and salaries. This principle, already proclaimed in 1918, was reiterated in the Act to approve fundamental principles governing the labour legislation of the USSR and the Union Republics (1970); the chapter on "Remuneration, guarantees and compensation" prohibits any reduction in pay for reasons of sex, age, race or nationality. In 1977, a new USSR Constitution (article 40) confirmed the principle of equal pay for equal work irrespective of sex, by explicitly eliminating discrimination against women.

In addition to basic wages, there are in the centrally planned economies various bonus schemes for different occupations and skills that are drawn up jointly by management and trade unions. In agreement with the trade union committees, the factory management establishes "pay systems" for the different categories of workers and introduces output and service quotas – solely on the basis of the work performance of the individual, irrespective of sex.[31]

Working conditions and special protective legislation

A distinctive feature of women's work is that frequently they combine paid employment with their multiple household duties. This entails longer working hours for them and additional physical and mental stress. Working women therefore face specific problems at the workplace. The impact of work on family life is greater for women than for men since working women must reconcile the various demands of the job with their family responsibilities in order to strike a balance between the two. However, women who work outside the home tend to have fewer children, and therefore fewer household responsibilities.

While women workers have the same general problems and difficulties as their male counterparts in the production process, their reproductive function places them in a special situation at the workplace. They require a different type of protection but without being discriminated against on this ground, whether or not they have children. Some studies have raised the question whether special protection for women is compatible with the notion of equality at the workplace. Depending on the socio-economic and cultural context, the provisional answer of several studies is that special legal provisions to protect working women – for example maternity benefits – do not necessarily conflict with the principle of equality of treatment if it is interpreted in a broad sense and not in the narrow sense of identical treatment.

Other protection, such as protection with regard to night work, occupational health and safety and early retirement, is also often provided. However, there is a debate as to whether women need special protection in these areas.

Maternity benefits

Since maternity is considered to be a social function and is so defined by several ILO standards, in most countries laws, regulations and agreements have been adopted providing special benefits for women workers during or after pregnancy and safeguarding their jobs during their absence from work. These measures are intended primarily to protect the health of the future mother and child and to guarantee a continued source of income and security of employment.

It is perhaps under the influence of women's new attitudes to work and the resulting changes in ideas about the respective roles of men and women in society that maternity protection arrangements for women workers were considerably broadened or reinforced in a large number of countries during

227

the past decade.[32] Moreover, although their final purpose is still to protect the health of the woman and her unborn child, the measures taken in recent years appear to have been conceived in the broader context of national policies concerning the work of women. In fact, today these measures have a fairly explicit second purpose: to make sure that the period of pregnancy and the care required by very young children do not restrict women workers in exercising their right to work.

A recent ILO survey[33] has revealed a general trend towards increasing the normal duration of maternity leave. In fact, during the past decade, and especially since 1980, new legislation has been enacted in several countries to improve maternity benefits as regards both the amount payable during maternity leave and its duration (e.g. in France, Hungary and Sweden). Some countries have also adopted provisions for nursing breaks (e.g. Algeria, Colombia, Federal Republic of Germany, Israel, Spain and Sri Lanka). Other trends are towards extending such protection to new categories of women workers, providing more effective protection against dismissal during pregnancy or after confinement (as in Angola, Grenada and Sri Lanka) and ensuring better supervision of safety and health conditions during the periods of pregnancy and nursing.

The legislation of some countries, for example Hungary and Sweden, also grants additional leave to care for children. A number of countries provide that such leave may be taken by either parent.

An area in which centrally planned economies have made considerable progress is the provision of maternity benefits and social facilities. For example, in the USSR all women giving birth to a child receive leave on full pay during pre-natal and post-natal maternity leave, regardless of length of employment and of trade union membership. Since 1981, additional, partly paid leave for mothers has been introduced to enable them, at their request, to look after their child until the age of 1. In the USSR, as well as in other centrally planned economies, enterprises may not refuse to employ women, dismiss them or reduce their earnings on any grounds relating to pregnancy or maternity. When a woman is transferred to lighter work because of pregnancy or the birth of a child, she retains her previous average monthly earnings.[34]

In all the centrally planned economies, women are granted long maternity leaves, ranging from 112 to 182 days, paid by the social insurance system. The leave is counted in the length of service and resumption of the previous employment is guaranteed. In addition to maternity leave, mothers receive special allowances on childbirth to cover purchases for the new-born baby. Between 1970 and 1980 government expenditure on social aid to mothers and social facilities for children increased by 50 per cent in the USSR.

When women receive adequate maternity benefits and good child-care facilities are available, they are encouraged to seek jobs. While some governments are pursuing dynamic policies aimed at creating public child-care services and definite progress has been achieved, much still remains to be done.

Night work

In most countries women are allowed to work at night in some services sectors such as health, but night work is generally prohibited in industry.

This prohibition is embodied in three ILO Conventions (No. 1, 1919, No. 41, 1934, and No. 89, 1948).[35] A general survey of the application of these instruments carried out in 1975 showed support for their revision, but insufficient agreement on the purpose and scope of such a revision. However, the view that new standards should apply to both men and women workers seemed to be gaining ground. Meanwhile, a number of countries, such as Bulgaria, Burma, Hungary, Ireland, the Netherlands and Uruguay, have decided to denounce these standards.[36]

228

Far-reaching technical and social changes have taken place since the last ILO Convention on the night work of women was adopted. What was originally welcomed as a measure to protect working women from additional fatigue now raises a number of objections. First of all, it deprives women of employment opportunities and constitutes an obstacle to the achievement of equality of opportunity and treatment for men and women workers. Secondly, it is argued, such a prohibition is no longer in line with present-day conditions in industry, where in some sectors conditions of work have improved as a result of new technologies. Finally, there is no medical evidence that night work is more harmful to women than to men (except during the period of pregnancy and nursing).

An ILO study on the subject points out that the vast majority of workers engaged in night work get no more than four to six hours of sleep during the day. The lack of sleep affects the health of men and women alike, but the accumulated fatigue on night shifts has particularly detrimental effects on the health of pregnant women and nursing mothers.[37]

Occupational safety and health

In many countries, both developed and developing, industrial expansion has occurred without sufficient measures being adopted for the protection of workers. It has been found that many women are employed in jobs involving special risks,[38] and since the majority of these work in small-scale industries or enterprises falling outside the scope of labour legislation, they enjoy little occupational safety and health protection. In occupations such as carpet and rug making or construction, women appear to suffer more from low-back pains than men. In electronics factories, women have serious eye problems, especially when they dip the chips into toxic acids or coat them with silicon, which can cause fatal lung disease. In Japan semi-conductors are assembled in special "sterilised" rooms designed to protect them against dust, overheating and humidity. The women who work in these excessively dry and cool conditions complain of body fatigue, physical debilitation and deterioration, even though they may be still young (20-29 years of age).[39] Typing and office work, which often involves long hours, can cause eye strain, neck and back fatigue and more serious problems such as migraine and nausea.

Women's family and household responsibilities aggravate the harmful effects of occupational factors. Not only is the home an unsafe place (45 per cent of all injuries occur there) but the double workload of women who work both in and outside the home results in constant fatigue, stress and therefore higher susceptibility to certain types of diseases and accidents.[39]

Social security and other benefits

Apart from maternity legislation which establishes various benefits for women during pre-natal and post-natal leave, there are a number of areas in which women, as workers, receive unequal social security benefits. In developed countries various international standards have been adopted that require States to ensure equal statutory rights in social security; but the main problem is eligibility since some women may not be considered permanent workers. On entering and leaving the labour market, they are often underprotected and not entitled to social security and other benefits. Moreover, in many countries women workers with family responsibilities often have to give up their jobs in order to bring up their children and consequently are at a disadvantage because most social security schemes are wage-oriented and the benefits depend on length of service, the payment of contributions, etc.

229

[1] For a detailed analysis, see OECD, *Employment outlook*, op. cit., Ch. IV.

[2] On this point see analysis of income and expenditure of a large sample of households by the United Kingdom Government for the years 1968 and 1981, in *The Guardian* (London), 18 Jan. 1984.

[3] UNESCO: *Women, education, equality: A decade of experiment* (Paris, 1975).

[4] A WHO preliminary study on women as health providers shows that in several countries women are not participating in decision-making on health policy issues concerning them (in preparation).

[5] ILO: *Labour force estimates and projections, 1950-2000* (Geneva, ILO, 2nd ed., 1977), table 4, pp. 62-68.

[6] D. R. Sen Gupta and S. Akhtar: *Bangladesh country paper on participation of women in training programmes*, paper presented at the ILO/APSDEP Regional Meeting, Islamabad, November 1982, p. 5.

[7] K. Ijaz: *A report on participation of women in training programmes in Pakistan*, paper presented at the ILO/APSDEP Regional Meeting, Islamabad, November 1982.

[8] A. Sarvaria: *A report on the participation of women in training programmes in India*, paper presented at the ILO/APSDEP Regional Meeting, Islamabad, November 1982. The figure is calculated on the basis of table 2.4: "Number of students receiving vocational training: (1) craftsmen training scheme, (2) apprenticeship training scheme", p. 54, and table 2.4a: "Number of students receiving vocational/special and other education by sex and type of education", p. 57.

[9] A. G. Mitchell: *Training women for economic development: Some issues and areas of action*, paper presented at the South Asian Regional Conference on Skilled Manpower Development, Colombo, January 1984, pp. 4 and 5.

[10] M. Salami: *Contribution du Niger au séminaire sur la formation professionnelle féminine organisé par le CIADFOR*, Abidjan, December 1981, p. 3.

[11] Office national de formation professionnelle: *Emploi et formation professionnelle des femmes en Côte d'Ivoire*, Dossier statistique (Abidjan, 1981), p. 18.

[12] E. Knollmayer: *National report on women's education, training and employment in Austria*, paper prepared for the International Seminar on Women's Education, Training and Employment in Developed Countries, Tokyo, December 1980, p. 5.

[13] Commission of the European Communities (CEC): *Women in Portugal* (Brussels, 1980), Supplement No. 11 to *Women of Europe*, p. 27.

[14] Federal Republic of Germany, Federal Ministry of Labour and Social Affairs: *Politiques d'égalisation des chances des femmes – Rapport, analyse et effets*, Report presented to the OECD (Bonn, 1982), p. 53.

[15] L. Paukert: "Personal preference, social change or economic necessity? Why women work", in *Labour and Society* (Geneva, International Institute for Labour Studies), Oct.-Dec. 1982, pp. 317-318.

[16] *Convention on the Elimination of All Forms of Discrimination against Women, Consideration of reports submitted by States Parties under Article 18 of the Convention, Initial reports of States Parties: German Democratic Republic*, United Nations Committee on the Elimination of Discrimination against Women, Second Session, November 1982 (CEDAW/C/5.Add.1), p. 6.

[17] See, for example, UNIDO: *Women in the redeployment of manufacturing industry to developing countries*, UNIDO Working Papers on Structural Changes, No. 18 (Vienna, 1980).

[18] M. Huet, O. Marchand and R. Salais: *The concentration of female employment: The example of France* (Paris, OECD, 1982), pp. 7-8.

[19] Sweden, National Labour Market Board: *Equality in the labour market* (Stockholm, 1982); and M. L. Anttalainen: *Women's work – men's work* (Helsinki, Council for Equality, 1981).

[20] Central Statistical Office of the USSR: *Narodnoe Khozyaistvo SSSR 1922-1982* (Moscow, "Finansi i Statistika", 1982), p. 403.

[21] E. B. Gruzdeva and E. S. Chertikhina: *Trud i byt sovetskikh zhenshchin* (Moscow, Politizdat, 1983), pp. 19-20.

[22] Központi Statisztikai Hivatal: *Adatok a nők helyzetéröl*, op. cit., pp. 13 and 15.

[23] Biryukova, op. cit, p. 18.

[24] *The GDR presents itself* (Foreign Press Information Office, 1981).

[25] Based on data of the Central Statistical Office and the Secretariat of the Council of Ministers.

[26] E. Gömöri: "Hungary", in ILO: *Work and family life: The role of the social infrastructure in Eastern European countries* (Geneva, 1980).

[27] According to a recent ILO study, it appears that the use of job evaluation techniques for the enforcement of the equal pay principle has been very limited for various reasons, the chief of which is that "job evaluation" is essentially used as an instrument by the management and it may not aim at equity in economic rewards. The technique itself is not neutral and the selection of criteria is essential for the implementation of the equal pay principle. ILO: *L'évaluation des emplois* (Geneva, 1984).

[28] Act No. 83-635 to amend the Labour Code and the Penal Code in matters respecting equality between men and women.

[29] See editorial in *Women at work* (Geneva, ILO), No. 2/82.

[30] The reason for not according equal wages to women has been based on the view that equal pay in the plantation sector would have negative consequences for the industry when faced with outside competition.

[31] All state measures in the sphere of output quotas and pay rates are carried out with active trade union participation. In the period of the Tenth Five-Year Plan (1976-80) the AUCCTU and the central committees of sectoral unions were directly involved in introducing pay rises for 31 million people employed in education, the health services, the field of culture and other non-productive spheres, in which women comprise more than 70 per cent of the workforce.

[32] See *Maternity benefits in the eighties: World-wide legislative survey* (Geneva, ILO, 1984). See also M. C. Séguret: "Women and working conditions: Prospects for improvement?", in *International Labour Review*, May-June 1983, pp. 295-311.

[33] For information on maternity leave and benefits in 117 countries, see ILO: *Conditions of work: A cumulative digest* (Geneva), Vol. 1, Nos. 1 and 2, Summer 1982, "Fact sheets", pp. 2-20.

[34] Reply of the USSR Government to the United Nations questionnaire for the World Conference of the United Nations Decade for Women (Nairobi, 1985).

[35] With the aim of protecting women's health, the International Labour Conference adopted in 1919 and revised in 1934 and 1948 the Night Work (Women) Convention. See also the Night Work of Women (Agriculture) Recommendation, 1921 (No. 13).

[36] Between 1964 and 1982 the Conventions had received 18 denunciations and three partial denunciations.

[37] ILO: *Médecine du travail, protection de la maternité et santé de la famille* (Geneva, 1984), p. 21. See also J. Carpentier and P. Cazamian: *Night work: Its effects on the health and welfare of the worker* (Geneva, ILO, 1978).

[38] For a detailed analysis, see E. Zabolai-Csekme: *Women and disability* (development education kit) (Geneva, JUNIC/NGO, 2nd ed., 1981).

[39] *Women, health and development* (development education kit) (Geneva, JUNIC/NGO, 1982).

230

Conclusion

The day is still far off when working women will everywhere be equal partners with men in the efforts to achieve economic and social progress. None the less, there have been many signs of far-reaching change, pointing to new prospects for women's work, new insights into their work performance and new ways of evaluating their economic and social contribution. During the next decade new methods of promoting equal opportunities for women in employment and eliminating discrimination against them will be more clearly identified and more effectively carried out. What are the main obstacles on the long road to equality and the elimination of discrimination?

The global economic crisis and increasing unemployment have had serious consequences for both men and women workers in most countries. But in a number of countries the consequences for women have been worse since they do not have equal access to education and training, and to most occupations in the modern economy. They continue to be concentrated in occupations and in industries such as textiles, clothing and electronics where wages are low. In industrialised market economies, several surveys and studies have shown that new technologies are likely to reduce women's employment in office occupations.

In the rural sector of many economies, women's lack of access to land, credit and financial and technological resources continues to keep down their income-earning capacity and to limit their employment opportunities. This is particularly so in the rural labour markets of developing countries. Discrimination against women persists in various rural occupations, with the result that they have fewer employment opportunities, receive lower wages and are more likely to be dismissed. Moreover, too often local and national policies directed at rural areas make the household their target without considering the particular impact on different members of the household. This approach is also commonly found in developed countries, which do not take into account the input of women's labour in various tasks in agriculture.

There have been major achievements over the past decade that deserve special mention. First, the fact that women are an integral part of economic and social life and the development process has been formally recognised by most governments. Second, among the industrialised market economies a number of countries have made significant efforts to adopt anti-discrimination legislation and have set up institutional machinery to promote equality between women and men. Third, in developing countries the increase in literacy rates has produced a positive change in the skill profile of women entering the labour market. Fourth, as an awareness of women's problems gradually gains ground, more and more women are joining and taking an active part in trade unions, organisations, associations and groups, and encouraging them to focus on their special interests. Fifth, considerable progress has been achieved in centrally planned economies where equality of men and women workers is being ensured by a combination of social, economic and legislative measures.

Over the past decade countries have adopted many different approaches to the question of working women. In some, special programmes may have even increased occupational segregation by focusing on stereotyped roles of women. In others equal employment opportunity for men and women in certain sectors is a reality and job security is ensured. In still others different and new barriers to equality have been erected. As a result, policies and legislation to eliminate discrimination and promote equal sharing of rights and responsibilities between women and men have not yet become a reality in many countries.

There are some further encouraging trends that are likely to continue. More and more women will continue to seek jobs outside the household despite fiscal disincentives, social barriers and the economic crisis. By the end of the century, the majority of households in most countries will have two wage earners and the distinction between primary (male) and secondary (female) earners will become less clear-cut. More and more women will be members of national parliaments and grass-roots organisations, formal organisations and associations, and trade unions, which will give them more influence in decision-making. Finally, women's aspirations to redefine economic activities and reduce the area of unpaid work will inevitably affect assessments of the economic and social value of women's work, especially of unpaid family work, household work and activities in the informal sector.

There are three major priority areas for action in the future: (1) women's work should be perceived in even more countries as an essential component of the development process; (2) special measures should be taken to ratify and implement under national legislation ILO and United Nations standards, especially on equal employment opportunities, equal pay for equal work, working conditions, job security and maternity protection; and (3) there is a need to formulate national policies to accelerate the creation of productive and equal employment opportunities for women so as to enable them to participate more fully in economic growth and social progress.

Annexes

Selected bibliography

The chapters in this volume are based on information and studies originating both inside and outside the ILO. References to them can be found in the notes at the end of each chapter. Within the scope of this volume, it would be difficult to provide an extensive bibliography for each of the 14 chapters. The titles in this short bibliography are mainly ILO publications which generally have the advantage that they cover several countries or groups of countries. This bibliography is therefore reasonably representative of work undertaken by the ILO, but not of that undertaken outside the ILO.

Part 1 : Labour relations

Workers' organisations

Bain, G. S.; Price, R. *Profiles of union growth* (Oxford, Basil Blackwell, 1980).

Córdova, E.; Ozaki, M. "Union security arrangements: An international overview", in *International Labour Review* (Geneva, ILO), Jan.-Feb. 1980, pp. 19-38.

Jivkov, T. *New conceptions of labour and labour relations in socialist Bulgaria* (Sofia Press, 1983).

Prokhorov, V. I. "Influence of trade union organisation at national and enterprise levels on establishing productivity and remuneration standards in the USSR", in *Labour and Society* (Geneva, IILS), July-Sep. 1981, pp. 263-277.

United Nations, Department of International Economic and Social Affairs. *Report on the world social situation* (New York, 1982; Sales No.: E.82.IV.2).

Windmuller, J. "International trade union movement", Ch. 6 of Blanpain, R. (ed.): *Comparative labour law and industrial relations* (Deventer (Netherlands), Kluwer, 1982), pp. 98-116.

Employers' organisations

ILO. *Papel de las organizaciones de empleadores en el desarrollo económico-social en América latina*, Report of the Regional Seminar for the Employers' Organisations of Latin America, Buenos Aires, 21-25 April, 1981 (Geneva, 1983, doc. ACTEMPT/2; mimeographed).

–. *Trade union situation and labour relations in Hungary*, Report of an ILO mission (Geneva, 1984).

–. *Trade union situation and labour relations in Norway*, Report of an ILO mission (Geneva, 1984).

Oechslin, J.-J. "Employers' organisations", Ch. 11 of Blanpain, R. (ed.), op. cit., pp. 190-207.

–. "Employers' organisations: Current trends and social responsibilities", in *International Labour Review* (Geneva, ILO), Sep.-Oct. 1982, pp. 503-517.

Poliakov, V.; Silin, A. "Personnel management in Soviet undertakings under the economic reform", in *International Labour Review* (Geneva, ILO), Dec. 1972, pp. 527-542.

Schregle, J. *Negotiating development: Labour relations in southern Asia* (Geneva, ILO, 1982).

Windmuller, J. P.; Gladstone, A. (eds.). *Employers' associations and industrial relations: A comparative study* (Oxford, Clarendon Press, 1984).

Labour-management relations

Blanpain, R. (ed.). *International encyclopaedia for labour law and industrial relations* (Deventer (Netherlands), Kluwer, 1982).

Commission of the European Communities. *Problems and prospects of collective bargaining in the EEC Member States*, Social Policy Series, No. 40 (Brussels, July 1979).

Córdova, E. (ed.). *Industrial relations in Latin America* (New York, Praeger, 1984).

de Givry, J. "Prevention and settlement of labour disputes other than conflicts of rights", Vol. XV, Ch. 14 of International Association of Legal Science: *International encyclopaedia of comparative law* (Tuebingen, J. C. B. Mohr, 1978), pp. 1-84.

ILO. *Promotion of collective bargaining*, Report V (1), International Labour Conference, 66th Session, Geneva, 1980.

–. *Collective bargaining in industrialised countries: Recent trends and problems*, Labour-Management Relations Series, No. 56 (Geneva, 1978).

–. *Workers' participation in decisions within undertakings* (Geneva, 1981).

–. *Conciliation and arbitration procedures in labour disputes: A comparative study* (Geneva, 1980).

–. *Collective bargaining: A response to the recession in industrialised market economy countries* (Geneva, 1984).

OECD. *Collective bargaining and government policies* (Paris, 1979).

–. *Collective bargaining and government policies in ten OECD countries* (Paris, 1979).

Part 2: International labour standards

Freedom of association

Bartolomei de la Cruz, H. G. *Protection against anti-union discrimination* (Geneva, ILO, 1976).

Caire, G. *Freedom of association and economic development* (Geneva, ILO, 1977).

Erstling, J. A. *The right to organise* (Geneva, ILO, 1977).

Gernigon, B. *Tenure of trade union office* (Geneva, ILO, 1977).

ILO. *Freedom of association: Digest of decisions of the Freedom of Association Committee* (Geneva, 1976).

–. *Freedom of association and collective bargaining*, Report III (Part 4 B), International Labour Conference, 69th Session, Geneva, 1983.

Servais, J.-M. *Inviolability of trade union premises and communications* (Geneva, ILO, 1980).

Abolition of forced labour

ILO. *Abolition of forced labour*, Report III (Part 4 B), International Labour Conference, 65th Session, Geneva, 1979.

–. *Forced labour*, Extract from the report of the 38th (1968) Session of the Committee of Experts on the Application of Conventions and Recommendations (Geneva, 1968).

–. *Forced labour*, Part 3 of the report of the Committee of Experts on the Application of Conventions and Recommendations (Geneva, 1962).

–. "Report of the ILO Committee on Forced Labour", in *Official Bulletin* (Geneva, ILO), 1959, No. 6, pp. 236-257.

United Nations/ILO. *Report of the Ad Hoc Committee on Forced Labour* (Geneva, ILO, 1953).

Termination of employment

ILO. *Termination of employment at the initiative of the employer*, Report VIII (1), International Labour Conference, 67th Session, Geneva, 1981.

International Society for Labour Law and Social Security. *Employee termination*, Vol. II of Proceedings of the Tenth International Congress (Washington, DC, Bureau of National Affairs, 1984).

Yemin, E. (ed.). *Workforce reductions in undertakings: Policies and measures for the protection of redundant workers in seven industrialised market economy countries* (Geneva, ILO, 1982).

Part 3: Training

American Assembly of Collegiate Schools of Business/European Foundation for Management Development. *Management for the XXI century* (Boston, Kluwer, 1982).

Batyshev, S. Y. *Aktualnye problemy podgotovki rabochikh vysokoi kvalifikatsii* (Moscow, Pedagogika, 1979).

Briggs, V. M., Jr.; Foltman, F. F. (eds.). *Apprenticeship research, emerging findings and future trends* (Ithaca, Cornell University Press, 1981).

Canada, House of Commons. *Work for tomorrow: Employment opportunities for the '80s* (Ottawa, 1981).

CEDEFOP. *Legislative and regulatory structure of vocational training systems: Federal Republic of Germany, France, Italy, United Kingdom* (Berlin, 1980).

ILO. *Education for development*, Report III, Fifth African Regional Conference, Abidjan, 1977.

–. *In-depth review of the ILO's Vocational Training Programme*, ILO Governing Body, 224th Session, Geneva, Nov. 1983 (Geneva, doc. GB.224/PFA/10-1-4; mimeographed).

–. *Introduction to work study* (Geneva, 1979).

–/APSDEP. *A study of apprenticeship in Asia and the Pacific* (Islamabad, ILO, 1981).

–/CINTERFOR. *Pobreza, marginalidad y formación profesional*, Estudios y monografías, No. 57 (Montevideo, 1982).

Indian Institute of Management. *Professionalisation of management in developing countries* (Ahmedabad, 1978).

International Academy of Management. *Management education: A world view of experience and needs*, Report of a Committee (London, 1981).

Jain, S. K. *Management education to the end of the century: The Asian scene*, Paper for the Eighth Regional Conference of the Asian Association of Management Organisations, Penang (Malaysia), 1983 (Geneva, ILO, 1983, doc. MAN DEV/31; mimeographed).

Kanawaty, G. *Management development in the Asian Arab countries* (Geneva, ILO, 1983, doc. MAN DEV/23; mimeographed).

Kostin, L. "Vazhneishee uslovie uskoreniya sotsialnogo i ekonomicheskogo razvitia strany", in *Sotsialistichesky trud* (Moscow), Dec. 1981, pp. 15-25.

Kubr, M.; Wallace J. *Successes and failures in meeting the management challenge: Strategies and their implementation*, World Bank Staff Working Papers, No. 585 (Washington, DC, The World Bank, 1983; mimeographed).

Ozira, V. et al. *Soderzhanie i metody podgotovki kadrov upravleniya* (Moscow, Ekonomika, 1977).

Richter, H. et al. *Aus- und Weiterbildung sozialistischer Leiter* (Berlin, Verlag Die Wirtschaft, 1981).

Schwartz, B. *L'insertion professionnelle et sociale des jeunes: rapport au Premier Ministre* (Paris, La Documentation Française, 1981).

Shaw, P. "Manpower and educational shortages in the Arab World: An interim strategy", in *World Development* (Oxford), July 1981, pp. 637-655.

Umentani, S. *Vocational training in Japan*, Mitteilungen des Instituts für Asienkunde, No. 114 (Hamburg, 1980).

UNDP. *Programme implementation evaluation*, Report of the Administrator, UNDP Governing Council, 31st Session, June 1984 (Geneva, doc. DP/1984/18; mimeographed).

–. *Human resources in Africa: A continent in rapid change*, World Bank paper submitted to the Conference of African Governmental Experts on Technical Co-operation among African Countries on Human Resources Development and Utilisation, Libreville, August 1982 (Libreville, doc. TCDC/AF/4; mimeographed).

United States Department of Labor. *Employment and training report of the President* (Washington, DC, 1981).

Part 4: Conditions of work

Occupational safety and health

Brazil, Ministry of Labour. *Boletim Estatístico*, No. 06/80 (São Paulo, Fundacentro, 1980).

Council for Science and Society. *The acceptability of risks* (London, 1982).

Cronin, J. B. "Cause and effect? Investigations into aspects of industrial accidents in the United Kingdom", in *International Labour Review* (Geneva, ILO), Feb. 1971, pp. 99-115.

France, Caisse nationale de l'assurance maladie des travailleurs salariés. *Statistiques technologiques d'accidents du travail (année 1979)* (Paris, 1981).

Germany (Fed. Rep.), Ministry of Labour and Social Affairs. *Arbeitssicherheit '80: Unfallverhütungsbericht*, Report on the prevention of accidents and diseases in the Federal Republic of Germany (Bonn, 1980).

National Safety Council. *Accident facts* (Chicago, 1981).

Parmeggiani, L. "State of the art: Recent legislation on workers' health and safety", in *International Labour Review* (Geneva, ILO), May-June 1982, pp. 271-285.

Philippines, Ministry of Labour and Employment. *Work accidents '81* (Manila, 1981).

United Kingdom, Committee on Safety and Health at Work. *Safety and health at work: Report of the Committee 1970-72*, the "Robens Report" (London, HMSO, 1972).

–, Health and Safety Commission. *Report 1980-81* (London, HMSO, 1981).

Singapore, Ministry of Labour. *1979 Yearbook of Labour Statistics* (Singapore, 1980).

Working time

Cuvillier, R. *The reduction of working time: Scope and implications in industrialised market economies* (Geneva, ILO, 1984).

ILO. *Conditions of work: A cumulative digest*, Fact sheets 1982-84 (Geneva).

–. *Working time: Reduction of hours of work, weekly rest and holidays with pay*, Report III (Part 4 B), International Labour Conference, 70th Session, Geneva, 1984.

Marić, D. *La durée du travail dans les pays en voie de développement* (Geneva, ILO, 1981).

Labour inspection

Bequele, A. "The costs and benefits of protecting and saving lives: Some issues", in *International Labour Review* (Geneva, ILO), Jan.-Feb. 1984, pp. 1-16.

Council of Europe, Social Committee. *Labour inspection: Scope, organisation and administration* (Strasbourg, 1967).

ILO. *Labour inspection: A world survey of national law and practice* (Geneva, 1966).

–. *Labour inspection in agriculture*, Report IV (1) and (2), International Labour Conference, 53rd Session, Geneva, 1969.

–. *Labour inspection: Purposes and practice* (Geneva, 1973).

–. *Labour inspection: A brief survey of the scene in Asian and South Pacific countries*, ARPLA Series, No. 7 (Bangkok, 1979).

–/CIAT. *Organización y funcionamiento de los servicios de inspección del trabajo* (Lima, 1981).

–/CLAC. *Labour inspection in the Caribbean*, Report on the Seminar for Labour Inspectors, Castries (St. Lucia), 1983 (Barbados, 1983).

Liaisons Sociales (Paris), Special issue 8898: "L'inspecteur du travail", Dec. 1982.

Rakitin, G. "Labour inspection in the USSR", in *International Labour Review* (Geneva, ILO), Oct. 1971, pp. 289-305.

Quality of working life

Butera, F.; Thurman, J. E. *Automation and work design* (Amsterdam, Elsevier, 1984).

Delamotte, Y.; Takezawa, S. *Quality of working life in international perspective* (Geneva, ILO, 1984).

ILO. *Evaluation of the International Programme for the Improvement of Working Conditions and Environment (PIACT)*, Report VII, International Labour Conference, 70th Session, Geneva, 1984.

–. *Automation, work organisation and occupational stress* (Geneva, 1984).

–. *New forms of work organisation*, Vols. 1 and 2 (Geneva, 1979).

Kanawaty, G. (ed.). *Managing and developing new forms of work organisation* (Geneva, ILO, 1981).

237

Part 5: Women at work

1. General works

Biryukova, A. *Soviet women: Their role in society, the economy, the trade unions* (Moscow, Profizdat, 1981).

Boulet, J. A.; Lavallée, L. *Women and the labour market: An analytical framework* (Ottawa, Economic Council of Canada, 1981).

International Centre for Research on Women: *Keeping women out: A structural analysis of women's employment in developing countries* (Washington, DC, Agency for International Development, 1980).

Middle East Research and Information Project: *Arab women workers*, Merip Reports, No. 50 (Washington, DC, 1976).

Rzhanitsina, L. *Female labour under socialism: The socio-economic aspects* (Moscow, Progress Publishers, 1983).

Saito, H.; Williams, R. N.; Amoradhat, L. *Comparative study of women workers in the textile industry of Japan and Thailand: A socio-economic profile* (Tokyo, Japan Foundation, 1982).

United States National Commission for Employment Policy. *Increasing the earnings of disadvantaged women*, Report No. 11 (Washington, DC, 1981).

2. ILO publications

Equal remuneration, Report III (Part 2), International Labour Conference, 60th Session, Geneva, 1975.

Equality of opportunity and treatment for women workers, Report VIII, International Labour Conference, 60th Session, Geneva, 1975.

Equal opportunities and equal treatment for men and women workers: Workers with family responsibilities, Report V (1) and (2), International Labour Conference, 67th Session, Geneva, 1981.

Report and background papers, Subregional Seminar on Status and Role of Women in the Organised Sector, Dacca, 1977 (Bangkok, ILO Regional Office for Asia, 1978).

Night work, Paper submitted to the ILO Tripartite Advisory Meeting on Night Work, Geneva, 1978 (Geneva, doc. TAMNW/1978/1; mimeographed).

Women and trade unions in Asia, Paper submitted to the ILO Asian Seminar on Women Workers' Participation in Trade Union Activities, Kuala Lumpur, 1979 (Geneva, doc. ILO/W.11/1979; mimeographed).

Report on the Seminar on Equality of Treatment for Women Workers in Southern Africa (Arusha, Tanzania, 20-25 October 1980), (Geneva, doc. ILO/UNDP/NLM/79/001; mimeographed).

Women in the Indian labour force, Papers and proceedings of a workshop (Bangkok, ILO/ARTEP, 1981).

Rural development and women in Asia, Proceedings and conclusions of the ILO Tripartite Asian Regional Seminar, Mahabaleshwar (India), 1981 (Geneva, 1982).

Papers submitted to the ILO Regional Tripartite Seminar for Latin America on Rural Development and Women, Pátzcuaro (Mexico), 1981 (doc. WEP 10-4-04-24-1-86; mimeographed).

Promotion of employment and incomes for the rural poor, including rural women, through non-farm activities, Report ACRD X/1983/II, and *Rural labour markets and employment policies: Issues relating to labour utilisation, remuneration and the position of women*, Report ACRD X/1983/III, Advisory Committee on Rural Development, 10th Session, Geneva, 1983.

Women's participation in the economic and social activities in the USSR and European socialist countries, a statistical analysis, (Geneva, doc. ILO/W.4/1980; mimeographed).

Agricultural modernisation and Third World women: Pointers from the literature and an empirical analysis, by Bina Agarwal (Geneva, 1981; mimeographed World Employment Programme research working paper, doc. WEP 10/WP 21; restricted).

Impact on women of technical co-operation activities, Results of a survey conducted during the first half of 1982 (Geneva, doc. ILO/W.7/1983; mimeographed).

Micro-electronics and office jobs: The impact of the chip on women's employment, by D. Werneke (Geneva, 1983).

"Recent legislation and case law in the EEC on sex equality in employment", by C. E. Landau, in *International Labour Review*, Jan.-Feb. 1984, pp. 53-70.

Ratifications per member State
(1 June 1984)

Europe		Africa		Americas		Asia and the Pacific	
Austria	46	Algeria	51	Antigua and Barbuda	15	Afghanistan	15
Belgium	79	Angola	30	Argentina	60	Australia	43
Bulgaria	80	Benin	18	Bahamas	26	Bahrain	4
Byelorussian SSR	35	Botswana	0	Barbados	35	Bangladesh	31
Cyprus	34	Burkina Faso	30	Belize	27	Burma	21
Czechoslovakia	52	Burundi	23	Bolivia	39	China [a]	14
Denmark	56	Cameroon	43	Brazil	57	Democratic Yemen	13
Finland	72	Cape Verde	7	Canada	26	Fiji	17
France	104	Central African Rep.	35	Chile	40	India	34
German Dem. Rep.	24	Chad	19	Colombia	47	Indonesia	8
Germany, Fed. Rep. of	66	Comoros	29	Costa Rica	40	Iran, Islamic Rep. of	11
Greece	52	Congo	14	Cuba	86	Iraq	49
Hungary	45	Djibouti	62	Dominica	20	Israel	44
Iceland	14	Egypt	55	Dominican Rep.	26	Japan	37
Ireland	55	Equatorial Guinea	0	Ecuador	52	Jordan	17
Italy	97	Ethiopia	8	El Salvador	4	Kampuchea, Dem.	5
Luxembourg	55	Gabon	31	Grenada	25	Kuwait	14
Malta	27	Ghana	40	Guatemala	40	Lao Republic	4
Netherlands	85	Guinea	53	Guyana	40	Lebanon	28
Norway	90	Guinea-Bissau	30	Haiti	23	Malaysia	11
Poland	74	Ivory Coast	28	Honduras	20	Mongolia	8
Portugal	56	Kenya	42	Jamaica	23	Nepal	3
Romania	39	Lesotho	11	Mexico	65	New Zealand	55
San Marino	0	Liberia	20	Nicaragua	58	Pakistan	30
Spain	108	Libyan Arab Jam.	27	Panama	69	Papua New Guinea	19
Sweden	74	Madagascar	30	Paraguay	33	Philippines	21
Switzerland	43	Malawi	19	Peru	62	Qatar	2
Turkey	27	Mali	21	Saint Lucia	25	Saudi Arabia	13
Ukrainian SSR	43	Mauritania	37	Suriname	26	Singapore	21
USSR	43	Mauritius	31	Trinidad and Tobago	12	Sri Lanka	27

Annex 2   *(continued)*

Europe		Africa		Americas		Asia and the Pacific	
United Kingdom	77	Morocco	40	United States	7	Syrian Arab Rep.	45
Yugoslavia	70	Mozambique	11	Uruguay	83	Thailand	11
		Namibia	0	Venezuela	47	United Arab Emirates	4
		Niger	27			Viet Nam [b]	23
		Nigeria	28			Yemen	11
		Rwanda	20				
		São Tomé and Príncipe	7				
		Senegal	34				
		Seychelles	18				
		Sierra Leone	32				
		Somalia	12				
		Sudan	12				
		Swaziland	30				
		Tanzania, United Rep.	28				
		Togo	18				
		Tunisia	52				
		Uganda	21				
		Zaire	27				
		Zambia	35				
		Zimbabwe	7				

[a] Ratified before 1 October 1949.   [b] The ratifications of Conventions Nos. 4, 5, 6, 13, 27, 29, 45, 52 and 80 were registered in 1953. The remaining ratifications were registered after 1954 in respect of the territory of the former Republic of South Viet Nam.

Annex **3**

Ratifications of selected basic human rights Conventions by member States [a]
(1 June 1984)

	Freedom of association			Forced labour		Discrimination	
	No. 87	No. 98	No. 141	No. 29	No. 105	No. 100	No. 111
Europe (32 countries)							
Austria	×	×	×	×	×	×	×
Belgium	×	×	–	×	×	×	×
Bulgaria	×	×	–	×	–	×	×
Byelorussian SSR	×	×	–	×	–	×	×
Cyprus	×	×	×	×	×	–	×
Czechoslovakia	×	×	–	×	–	×	×
Denmark	×	×	×	×	×	×	×
Finland	×	×	×	×	×	×	×
France	×	×	–	×	×	×	×
German Dem. Rep.	×	×	–	–	–	×	×
Germany, Fed. Rep. of	×	×	×	×	×	×	×
Greece	×	×	–	×	×	×	×
Hungary	×	×	–	×	–	×	×
Iceland	×	×	–	×	×	×	×
Ireland	×	×	–	×	×	×	–
Italy	×	×	×	×	×	×	×
Luxembourg	×	×	–	×	×	×	–
Malta	×	×	–	×	×	–	×
Netherlands	×	–	×	×	×	×	×
Norway	×	×	×	×	×	×	×
Poland	×	×	–	×	×	×	×
Portugal	×	×	–	×	×	×	×
Romania	×	×	–	×	–	×	×
San Marino	–	–	–	–	–	–	–
Spain	×	×	×	×	×	×	×

241

Annex 3   *(continued)*

	Freedom of association			Forced labour		Discrimination	
	No. 87	No. 98	No. 141	No. 29	No. 105	No. 100	No. 111
Sweden	×	×	×	×	×	×	×
Switzerland	×	–	×	×	×	×	×
Turkey	–	×	–	–	×	×	×
Ukrainian SSR	×	×	–	×	–	×	×
USSR	×	×	–	×	–	×	×
United Kingdom	×	×	×	×	×	×	–
Yugoslavia	×	×	–	×	–	×	×
Total	30	29	12	29	22	29	28
Africa (50 countries)							
Algeria	×	×	–	×	×	×	×
Angola	–	×	–	×	×	×	×
Benin	×	×	–	×	×	×	×
Burkina Faso	×	×	–	×	–	×	×
Burundi	–	–	–	×	×	–	–
Botswana	–	–	–	–	–	–	–
Cameroon	×	×	–	×	×	×	–
Cape Verde	–	×	–	×	×	×	×
Central African Rep.	×	×	–	×	×	×	×
Chad	×	×	–	×	×	×	×
Comoros	×	×	–	×	×	×	–
Congo	×	–	–	×	–	–	–
Djibouti	×	×	–	×	×	×	–
Egypt	×	×	–	×	×	×	×
Equatorial Guinea	–	–	–	–	–	–	–
Ethiopia	×	×	–	–	–	–	×
Gabon	×	×	–	×	×	×	×
Ghana	×	×	–	×	×	×	×
Guinea	×	×	–	×	×	×	×
Guinea-Bissau	–	×	–	×	×	×	×
Ivory Coast	×	×	–	×	×	×	×
Kenya	–	×	×	×	×	–	–
Lesotho	×	×	–	×	–	–	–
Liberia	×	×	–	×	×	–	×
Libyan Arab Jam.	–	×	–	×	×	×	×
Madagascar	×	–	–	×	–	×	×
Malawi	–	×	–	–	–	×	×
Mali	×	×	–	×	×	×	×
Mauritania	×	–	–	×	–	–	×
Mauritius	–	×	–	×	×	–	–

Annex 3   *(continued)*

	Freedom of association			Forced labour		Discrimination	
	No. 87	No. 98	No. 141	No. 29	No. 105	No. 100	No. 111
Morocco	–	×	–	×	×	×	×
Mozambique	–	–	–	–	×	×	×
Namibia	–	–	–	–	–	–	–
Niger	×	×	–	×	×	×	×
Nigeria	×	×	–	×	×	×	–
Rwanda	–	–	–	–	×	×	×
São Tomé and Príncipe	–	–	–	–	–	×	×
Senegal	×	×	–	×	×	×	×
Seychelles	×	–	–	×	×	–	–
Sierra Leone	×	×	–	×	×	×	×
Somalia	–	–	–	×	×	–	×
Sudan	–	×	–	×	×	×	×
Swaziland	×	×	–	×	×	×	×
Tanzania, United Rep.	–	×	–	×	×	–	–
Togo	×	×	–	×	–	×	×
Tunisia	×	×	–	×	×	×	×
Uganda	–	–	–	–	×	–	–
Zaire	–	×	–	×	–	×	–
Zambia	–	–	×	×	×	×	×
Zimbabwe	–	–	–	×	×	–	–
Total	28	35	2	41	37	34	33
Americas (33 countries)							
Antigua and Barbuda	×	×	–	×	×	–	×
Argentina	×	×	–	×	×	×	×
Bahamas	–	×	–	×	×	–	–
Barbados	×	×	–	×	×	×	×
Belize	×	×	–	×	×	–	–
Bolivia	×	×	–	–	–	×	×
Brazil	–	×	–	×	×	×	×
Canada	×	–	–	–	×	×	×
Chile	–	–	–	×	–	×	×
Colombia	×	×	–	×	×	×	×
Costa Rica	×	×	–	×	×	×	×
Cuba	×	×	×	×	×	×	×
Dominica	×	×	–	×	×	×	×
Dominican Rep.	×	×	–	×	×	×	×
Ecuador	×	×	×	×	×	×	×

243

Annex 3   *(continued)*

	Freedom of association			Forced labour		Discrimination	
	No. 87	No. 98	No. 141	No. 29	No. 105	No. 100	No. 111
El Salvador	–	–	–	–	×	–	–
Grenada	–	×	–	×	×	–	–
Guatemala	×	×	–	–	×	×	×
Guyana	×	×	×	×	×	×	×
Haiti	×	×	–	×	×	×	×
Honduras	×	×	–	×	×	×	×
Jamaica	×	×	–	×	×	×	×
Mexico	×	–	×	×	×	×	×
Nicaragua	×	×	×	×	×	×	×
Panama	×	×	–	×	×	×	×
Paraguay	×	×	–	×	×	×	×
Peru	×	×	–	×	×	×	×
Saint Lucia	×	×	–	×	×	×	×
Suriname	×	–	–	×	×	–	–
Trinidad and Tobago	×	×	–	×	×	–	×
United States	–	–	–	–	–	–	–
Uruguay	×	×	–	–	×	–	–
Venezuela	×	×	×	×	×	×	×
Total	27	27	6	27	30	24	26

Asia and the Pacific (35 countries)

	No. 87	No. 98	No. 141	No. 29	No. 105	No. 100	No. 111
Afghanistan	–	–	×	–	×	×	×
Australia	×	×	–	×	×	×	×
Bahrain	–	–	–	×	–	–	–
Bangladesh	×	×	–	×	×	–	×
Burma	×	–	–	×	–	–	–
China	–	–	–	–	–	–	–
Democratic Yemen	–	×	–	×	–	–	–
Fiji	–	×	–	×	×	–	–
India	–	–	×	×	–	×	×
Indonesia	–	×	–	×	–	×	–
Iran, Islamic Rep. of	–	–	–	×	×	×	×
Iraq	–	×	–	×	×	×	×
Israel	×	×	×	×	×	×	×
Japan	×	×	–	×	–	×	–
Jordan	–	×	–	×	×	×	×
Kampuchea, Dem.	–	–	–	×	–	–	–
Kuwait	×	–	–	×	×	–	×
Lao Republic	–	–	–	×	–	–	–
Lebanon	–	×	–	×	×	×	×
Malaysia	–	×	–	×	×	–	–

Annex 3   *(continued)*

	Freedom of association			Forced labour		Discrimination	
	No. 87	No. 98	No. 141	No. 29	No. 105	No. 100	No. 111
Mongolia	×	×	–	–	–	×	×
Nepal	–	–	–	–	–	×	×
New Zealand	–	–	–	×	×	×	×
Pakistan	×	×	–	×	×	–	×
Papua New Guinea	–	×	–	×	×	–	–
Philippines	×	×	×	–	×	×	×
Qatar	–	–	–	–	–	–	×
Saudi Arabia	–	–	–	×	×	×	×
Singapore	–	×	–	×	×	–	–
Sri Lanka	–	×	–	×	–	–	–
Syrian Arab Rep.	×	×	–	×	×	×	×
Thailand	–	–	–	×	×	–	–
United Arab Emirates	–	–	–	×	–	–	–
Viet Nam	–	×	–	×	–	–	×
Yemen	×	×	–	×	–	×	×
Total	11	20	4	29	19	17	20

[a] No. 87 Freedom of Association and Protection of the Right to Organise Convention, 1948; No. 98 Right to Organise and Collective Bargaining Convention, 1949; No. 29 Forced Labour Convention, 1930; No. 105 Abolition of Forced Labour Convention, 1957; No. 100 Equal Remuneration Convention, 1951; No. 111 Discrimination (Employment and Occupation) Convention, 1958; No. 141 Rural Workers' Organisations Convention, 1975.